The
IMPACT *of*
THE SOCIAL SCIENCES

The

IMPACT *of*

THE SOCIAL SCIENCES

HOW ACADEMICS AND THEIR RESEARCH MAKE A DIFFERENCE

SIMON BASTOW · PATRICK DUNLEAVY · JANE TINKLER

with involvement from Raphaëlle Bisiaux, Leandro Carrera,
Sofia Goldchluk, Avery Hancock, Ellen Harries, Rebecca Mann,
Anne White, Sierra Williams and Joan Wilson

Los Angeles | London | New Delhi
Singapore | Washington DC

Los Angeles | London | New Delhi
Singapore | Washington DC

SAGE Publications Ltd
1 Oliver's Yard
55 City Road
London EC1Y 1SP

SAGE Publications Inc.
2455 Teller Road
Thousand Oaks, California 91320

SAGE Publications India Pvt Ltd
B 1/I 1 Mohan Cooperative Industrial Area
Mathura Road
New Delhi 110 044

SAGE Publications Asia-Pacific Pte Ltd
3 Church Street
#10-04 Samsung Hub
Singapore 049483

Editor: Natalie Aguilera
Assistant editor: James Piper
Production editor: Ian Antcliff
Proofreader: Kate Harrison
Indexer: Sheila Dunleavy
Marketing manager: Michael Ainsley
Cover design: Francis Kenney
Typeset by: C&M Digitals (P) Ltd, Chennai, India
Printed and bound in Great Britain by Ashford
Colour Press Ltd

MIX
Paper from
responsible sources
FSC
www.fsc.org   FSC® C011748

Library of Congress Control Number: 2013950175

British Library Cataloguing in Publication data

A catalogue record for this book is available from
the British Library

ISBN 978-1-4462-7509-2
ISBN 978-1-4462-7510-8 (pbk)

Contents

List of figures

No escape is possible from broader inter-disciplinary standards if the enterprise of social science is to prove useful to humanity.

John Gerring

Preface

There is an interesting asymmetry between the huge volume of literature on the mission and core practices of the individual social science disciplines and the very restricted amount of serious discussion of the social sciences taken as a whole. For each subject like economics, sociology, social psychology or political science, there are swathes of inward-looking books, papers, commentaries and reflections, setting out radically different views and disputing fiercely over future directions, subject priorities, methods issues and rival conceptions of the discipline. When we first began this research in 2009 we naively expected that what was true of the component disciplines must also be true of the discipline group. Yet our searches for any equivalent massing of views and approaches at this broader level yielded only a smattering of gold-dust (extensively referenced in the pages to follow), after which our searches quickly petered out in subject-specific discussions of little wider relevance or in silted-up backwaters of the history of academia or methods development.

So in the end we have written a far larger and more ambitious book than we originally anticipated. In some small part this has been to compensate for the missing contemporary literature on the broader role and mission of the discipline group and its place in the development of contemporary human societies. But far more extensively it reflects the extraordinary value of the 'impact' lens as a way of capturing and addressing some common problems and current changes across the social sciences as a whole. When we ask why social science research and insights have been scantily adopted in business, and have been less influential than one might expect in government and civil society; and why the public prestige and government funding of the social sciences lags so far behind that of the 'physical' sciences – these questions automatically point to and prompt a social science solidarity. They draw on a commonality of experience, and awaken awareness of some foundational affinities that the daily academic practice of each discipline tends to fragment and sublimate. There is a fundamental similarity in how social science disciplines are placed within the fabric of our modern, globalizing civilization, one that is thrown into sharp focus by questions about improving impact.

Every social science focuses on constantly shifting human behaviours; conscious that human beings have an innate and un-erodible capacity to change what we do in response to being told why we act as we do, or how we are expected to act in future. No social science produces immutable laws that once established last unchanged. And despite the apparatus of proofs and lemmas found in some mathematicized sub-disciplines, no social science propositions can be proven logically – without depending on a usually extensive and always contestable repertoire of assumptions and 'primitives' (such as the concept of what a 'rational actor' will or must do). All social science generalizations are inherently probabilistic, none are determinate, and all depend on large and baggy *ceteris paribus* clauses. Every social science must handle an inescapable tension between knowledge advanced by the reductionist research tactic of focusing down on simple processes while 'controlling' for more and more factors; and the recognition that all social processes operate in complex, multi-causal environments, where hundreds or thousands of influences flux and interact with each other to shape any given social or behavioural outcome, and where the same outcome can eventuate through multiple diverse causal pathways.

As a result of these features, every social science has a research process that is cumulative, largely missing the 'breakthrough' discoveries or 'lone genius' insights on which public images of the physical sciences and technological disciplines still focus. Only a tiny percentage of social science research results in patents (for which embedding in physical products remains essential), and the vast bulk of university social scientific achievements are solely new (or partly new) ideas. They cannot be copyrighted, protected by intellectual property rights nor used to build scaleable products or comparative advantage for firms in the way that physical technologies often may. And despite many social scientists lusting after the outward trappings of 'normal science' practices, all social science disciplines still operate in ways that are a long way off what Randal Collins (1994) calls the 'high consensus, rapid advance' model that has served the physical sciences so well since the mid-nineteenth century. Asking about the ways in which social science subjects resonate (or not) with business, government, civil society or the media, unfailingly throws these inherently shared features across the discipline group into a tightly focused spotlight.

Impact as a focus also addresses some critically important aspects of contemporary change in the social sciences. For any societal research to be successfully applied in public or organizational decisions it must be timely, produced speedily, capturing the salient features of a situation and behaviours that may shift quickly in response to new factors, or interaction with previously separate phenomena. All applied and impactful academic knowledge must also be 'translated' from single-discipline silos; 'bridged' and integrated with the insights of other disciplines in the social sciences or beyond in the applied and human-focused physical sciences; and assimilated into a joined-up picture so as to adequately encompass real world situations. Research advances and insights must also be communicated or transferred to non-academic people and organizations, and their lessons mediated, deliberated and drawn out in useable ways.

In the modern world the transformations of information systems and now scholarship itself via digital changes condense and accelerate many of these necessities, creating a vastly extended set of interfaces between academia and business, government and civil society; allowing the direct and open access publication and broadcasting of academic research and ideas without the intermediation of conventional publishing or media systems; and greatly speeding up the potential tempo of knowledge production and transfer. Again the impacts agenda speaks directly to these potentially common, civilization-wide changes that now occupy a central place in the evolution of modern academia.

For these reasons we make no apology for the resolutely 'broad-front' focus of this book on the social sciences as a whole, and our complete refusal to discuss in particular detail any component subject within the discipline group. We recognize that thinking at this scale is not familiar or easy for most social scientists. But we urge readers to make the intellectual leap involved, to scale up their frame of reference, and to look wider than has become customary in universities in our specialized age. The social sciences have a critical role to play in the development of human civilization, but it will not be achieved in fragments or by focusing down on bit-part roles or narrowly technical scraps of argumentation. The post-war wave of research specialization has yielded enormous benefits and advances, so that all the social sciences of today are almost unrecognizably further developed than they were in the 1930s. Yet the dialectic of intellectual development has now swung emphatically towards an open social science – one that is far more inter-disciplinary, far more integrated with many applied physical sciences, and far more democratically accessible to and directly interacting with citizens and organizations in civil society.

Of course, a necessary defect of working on a big canvass is that key details may be brushed over, and no small group of authors can have mastery of the whole field. So we warmly encourage readers to update us, and to contest, critique, extend or comment on the book's analysis in any form that seems best.

Simon Bastow
s.j.bastow@lse.ac.uk
@simonjbastow

Patrick Dunleavy
p.dunleavy@lse.ac.uk
@PJDunleavy

Jane Tinkler
j.tinkler@lse.ac.uk
@janetinkler

LSE Impact of Social Sciences blog
http://blogs.lse.ac.uk/impactofsocialsciences/

Acknowledgements

One of the key features of modern research is the growth of large team projects, and in a three year effort of this scope a far larger cast list was involved in generating data, evidence, ideas and arguments than could practicably be involved in the writing of a single, coherent book. All the members of LSE Public Policy Group (PPG) who are listed on the title page made important contributions to the *Impact of Social Sciences* project at various points in its lifetime. We are deeply grateful to them for their insights and endeavours. In alphabetical order: Raphaëlle Bisiaux worked on the civil society chapter (7), building up a picture of third sector organisations in the UK and undertaking interviews. Leandro Carrera (now at the Pensions Policy Institute) worked on the early stages of design and compilation of the dataset of 370 academics, and since leaving PPG has played an important advisory role in helping us to refine our understanding and analysis of the data. Sofia Goldchluk helped develop the guidance for our coders, to ensure that the information collected for the dataset was systematic and comparable. Avery Hancock in the early stages of the project pulled together the information needed to create the quota samples for the dataset and helped get the LSE *Impact of Social Sciences* blog started. Ellen Harries looked at how impact information is collected and deployed by universities, and undertook an in-depth analysis of the LSE's systems. Rebecca Mann helped us gain access to interviewees from the business community and contributed in many ways to the development of our thinking for this chapter (5). Anne White helped us early on in collecting and analysing publicly available information on government funding and investment into the social sciences and STEM disciplines. Joan Wilson took over a lead role in compiling and analysing our dataset from January 2011 and was an important member of the PPG research team until the end of the project in December 2012. Despite the importance of all these people's inputs, it goes without saying that only the three main authors hold any responsibility for the final interpretations offered in the text here. We are also most grateful to Richard Lewney and Chris Thoung from Cambridge Econometrics, and to Rachel Redman and Robin Brighton from SQW. Each of their firms undertook a targeted piece of research for us that generated important evidence described in the book.

In addition, we thank a large number of people who worked at PPG on particular aspects of the project or for shorter periods. Amy Mollett and Danielle Moran were the first Managing Editors of the *Impact of Social Sciences* blog, whose importance is described below, and Sierra Williams continued this role during 2013. Naomi Crowther, Sangeeta Goswami, Anthony McDonnell, Andreea Moise,

Dominic Muir, Matthew Oxenford, and Jennifer Winter all provided vital research assistance at various stages. We are also grateful to a team of LSE post-graduate students who undertook the time-consuming tasks involved in Google-searching for our dataset of 370 academics covered in Chapters 2 and 3.

During the project, the wider PPG team has played a leading role in the development and growth of academic blogging in the UK. In February 2010, we set up our first academic multi-author blog called *British Politics and Policy*, in the run-up to the May 2010 UK general election. This initial experiment went from strength to strength, and it led us to replace our earlier plan for a conventional website for the *Impact* Project (which would inherently have been visited by only very few determined folk) with a second multi-author blog covering the *Impact of Social Sciences*. This started in September 2011 and it quickly became a vital and integral research resource for the project, attracting a large audience from a very active community of contributors and commentators. We are most grateful to HEFCE again for funding the blog as part of the project, and later for renewing its support throughout 2013. There were 48,000 unique visitors to the site in the last four months of 2011, 176,000 in 2012 and 195,000 in the first eight months of 2013. By September 2013 weekly views of the blog were running at 9,000 visitors; the blog had almost 11,700 Twitter followers, not just from the UK but across the world; and nearly 2,500 Facebook likes. Some 350 academics, practitioners and experts contributed posts over this period, from which we learnt a huge amount. The success of the *Impacts* blog reflects not just the efforts of its editors Amy Mollett, Danielle Moran and Sierra Williams, but also the inputs of our PPG blog expert Chris Gilson; of the other PPG blog editors Paul Rainford, Mark Carrigan, Joel Suss, Stuart Brown; of Cheryl Brumley who creates the podcasts for all of our blogs; and of Stephen Emmott and LSE's over-worked web and IT support staff.

Above all the authors and readers of the *Impact* blog told us so much that was new and unexpected, so quickly and painlessly in real time, that we have no hesitation in saying that this book would have been immensely poorer without them. We are most grateful for the contributions of a huge variety of academics and experts who are collectively far too many to name. But they include Bjorn Brems, Dorothy Bishop, Melonie Fullick, Matt Lingard, Deborah Lupton, Paul Manners, Tim McCormick, Cameron Neylon, Ernesto Priego, Melissa Terras and Pat Thomson. Many other academics, vice-chancellors or pro-vice chancellors, university administrators and higher education experts also attended the two main Impacts conferences held in London, or shared with us very stimulating informal conversations at numerous other conferences, seminars, and dissemination events where we gave presentations.

This book comes out of a three year research project that was funded by the Higher Education Funding Council for England (HEFCE), to whose support we gratefully record our heaviest single debt. We would like to thank all those at HEFCE who have worked with us during the lifetime of the project, especially David Sweeney and Graeme Rosenburg who provided helpful insights into HEFCE's thinking on impact and the design and implementation of the Research Excellence Framework (REF). In addition, Ed Hughes, Gemma Cadogan, Nick Dibley, Rose Spicer and Rebecca Jackson helped us to set up and administer a complex project.

The wider *Impact of Social Sciences* project involved collaboration between three universities: the London School of Economics and Political Science (LSE), Imperial College London and the University of Leeds. LSE Public Policy Group provided the central team, with four other research 'labs' at LSE, Imperial and Leeds undertaking applied research on particular aspects of impact. We thank all these colleagues who worked with us in this wider effort and helped shape our understanding of how impact processes work in different sectors and subject areas: Ralph Martin and John Van Reenen from the LSE's Centre for Economic Performance; John Wright and Elias Mossialos from LSE Health; at Imperial, Sarah Lester, Neil Hirst and Simon Buckle at the Grantham Institute of Climate Change; and Anna Wesselink and Andy Gouldson from the Sustainability Research Institute at Leeds.

We would also like to thank staff at SAGE for backing this project and the idea of the book so enthusiastically from the beginning. The transition of the project from research to book writing was made easier by some thought-provoking discussions with SAGE's Global Publishing Director Ziyad Marar and Senior Commissioning Editor Natalie Aguilera. Natalie has overseen the whole process of production of the book, and has been continually patient, ever helpful, and basically a joy to work with. We also thank other staff at SAGE including David Mainwaring, Michael Ainsley, Katie Baker, Sally Hooker and Mithu Lucraft. We thank too Amy Ricketts, an independent designer who created the visualisations of some of our data.

Finally, of course, the study of academic impact outside universities inherently depends on talking and liaising with a huge range of people from other sectors, especially UK and US business corporations, central and local UK governments, NGOs and charities in civil society, and numerous think tankers, professionals, lobbyists, journalists, and media people (the professional 'intermediators') – as well as with senior academics who clearly have themselves achieved substantial external impact. We undertook formal interviews with 165 research users and some influential academics across the government, business, and civil society sectors, and we are deeply grateful to all those who spared time from their busy schedules to give us their experiences, insights and commentary. We also convened a range of elite focus groups where executives, officials and research users discussed their use of academic research and how barriers to improving relations with researchers might be overcome. We are grateful especially to the executives, officials and NGO leaders who spoke at the Impact conferences, or attended and participated in discussions, or generated contributions for the *Impact* blog. We have listed all the organizations interviewed or otherwise involved in our extended methods report that accompanies this book, at http://blogs.lse.ac.uk/impactofsocialsciences/book. Without the active help and committed involvement of all these people, and their willingness to go out of their way to help us think through difficult issues, this research would not have been feasible. They are the necessarily anonymized heroes of this narrative.

List of abbreviations

AHRC	Arts and Humanities Research Council (UK)
BBSRC	Biotechnology and Biological Sciences Research Council (UK)
BIS	Department for Business, Innovation and Skills (UK)
CAD	Creative Arts and Design
CRM	customer relationship management
Defra	Department for Environment, Food and Rural Areas (UK)
DfID	Department for International Development (UK)
DKI	dynamic knowledge inventory (see Section 9.1)
EBPM	evidence based policy making
ERA	Excellence in Research for Australia – government research audit/assessment exercise
EPSRC	Engineering and Physical Sciences Research Council (UK)
ESRC	Economics and Social Research Council (UK)
HEFCE	Higher Education Funding Council for England
HESA	Higher Education Statistics Agency (UK)
HPoP	Harzing's 'Publish or Perish' software programme
HSS	humanities and social sciences
IP	intellectual property
IPO	Initial Public Offering
IPR	intellectual property rights
JIF	journal impact factor
MOOCs	massive open online courses
MRC	Medical Research Council (UK)
NERC	Natural Environment Research Council (UK)
NGO	Non-governmental organisation
NICE	National Institute for Clinical Excellence (UK)
NPM	new public management
PBR	payment by results
PSI	professional social inquiry
QCA	qualitative comparative analysis
QR Funding	Quality Related funding (UK, key part of HEFCE support to universities)
R&D	research and development
RAE	Research Assessment Exercise (UK, earlier form of REF)
RCT	randomised control trial
REF	Research Excellence Framework – government research audit/assessment exercise
SMC	Small or medium charity
STEM	Science, technology, engineering, mathematics
STFC	Science and Technology Facilities Council (UK)
WoS	'Web of Science', a bibliometrics database run by Thomson Reuters

1

The social sciences in modern research

Thou shalt not sit With statisticians nor commit A social science.
  W.H. Auden[1]

[N]o public policy can be developed, no market interaction can occur, and no statement in the public sphere can be made, that does not refer explicitly or implicitly to the findings and concepts of the social and human sciences.
  Björn Wittrock[2]

We live now in a world without frontiers to the unknown, one intensively-investigated planet with a pooling civilization, converging cultures, a single mode of production, and a fragile but enduring peace between states (if one still marred by inherently temporary imperial adventures, civil wars, ethnic divisions, dictatorial excesses, and governance collapses). Human societies also operate within a single global ecosystem, from whose patterns of development there is (and can be) no escape. Perhaps the single best hope for the survival and flourishing of humanity lies in the development of our knowledge – about 'natural' systems; and about the complex systems that we have ourselves built and the ways in which we behave within them. The scope of systems on Earth that are 'human-dominated' or 'human-influenced' has continuously expanded, and the scope of systems that are 'purely' natural has shrunk – to such an extent that even the climate patterns and average temperatures across the planet are now responding (fast) to human interventions in burning fossil fuels.

This is the essential context within which the social sciences have moved to an increasingly central place in our understanding of how our societies develop and interact with each other. The external impact of university research about human-dominated and human-influenced systems – on business, government, civil society, media and culture – has grown enormously in the post-war period. It is entering a

[1] Quote from the poem Under Which Lyre: A Reactionary Tract for the Times (Auden, 1946).
[2] Wittrock (2010: 207).

new phase as digital scholarship produces knowledge that is 'shorter, better, faster, free'. The social sciences play a key and more integrated role in contemporary knowledge development. Yet the processes involved in social science research influencing wider decision-making have been relatively little studied in systematic ways, and consistently under-appreciated by observers outside academia. Within universities themselves scholars in other discipline groups have also been consistently and often vocally sceptical, especially physical scientists and technologists, whose central roles in knowledge development is already universally recognized and (mostly) lauded.

This book is an attempt to redress this past neglect and to re-explain the distinctive and yet more subtle ways in which the contemporary social sciences now shape and inform human development. It is based on a three-year research study of UK social science, which on most indices and for most disciplines is ranked either second in the world (to the US), and sometimes first (BIS, 2011). In objective world terms the UK is a small island of 60 million people – but in academic terms it can yet punch above its weight, and not least in the social sciences.

Britain is also a mature advanced industrial country, with a stable (perhaps inflexible) system of governance and political process, a services-dominated economy with a vibrant civic culture and media system. These generally favourable background conditions set up very neatly some of the key problems in the funding, organization and transfer of academic knowledge into other spheres of the economy and society. While the UK is in no sense 'typical' of anywhere else in the world, it is none the less a case study with many lessons for elsewhere. Britain as a medium-sized country is large enough not to face the 'group jeopardy in world markets' problem that sustains exceptional academic and societal cooperation in the small economies of Scandinavia. At the same time it does not have the 'imperial' reach of the US's or (now) China's political systems and corporations, a scale and exceptionalism that creates distinctive problems and opportunities in the interactions between universities and external actors. Finally, Britain inherently sits within a European civilization and society (much broader than the country's recurrently disputed membership of the European Union). In Europe the practices of higher education institutions have converged rapidly over the last two decades, partly on an Anglo-American model. So although our focus is primarily on UK social science, the impacts that we chart here play out on EU, wider European and international scales. The issues we discuss are far from being only domestically focused.

We begin by defining what we count as the social sciences, and scoping out how large this field of academic endeavour is in the UK, in terms of resources and the numbers of academics and students involved. The second part concludes our scene-setting by discussing in a preliminary way how the social sciences fit into the wider analysis of 'human-dominated' and 'human-influenced' systems, and the burgeoning inter-connection of knowledge that such complex systems encourage and necessitate. If we are to understand academic research contributions it is vital that we have schemas and concepts in mind that are attuned to contemporary realities, and not defined by the entrenched mental silos of disciplines, professions and universities.

1.1 The scale and diversity of the social sciences

For historical reasons, the social sciences are often defined
as the disciplines that are in between the humanities
and the natural sciences. As a result, the decision
on which disciplines are parts of social sciences and
which are not varies a great deal from one country to
another and over time.

Françoise Caillods and Laurent Jeanpierre[3]

Any discipline with science in its name, isn't

Ron Abrams

Most of the core social sciences with the strongest 'scientific' aspirations (such as sociology and economics) do not have science anywhere in their name. Even in political science there are scholars who insist on a broad 'political studies' label still, while other
analysts distinguish between a wider, eclectic mass of 'political scholarship' and its
vanguard area 'political science' (Dunleavy, 2010). The social science discipline group
also spans across a very wide range of subjects shown in Figure 1.1, some of which make
many, and others relatively few, claims to scientific practice. Many social sciences

Figure 1.1   The social sciences and how they relate to other disciplines

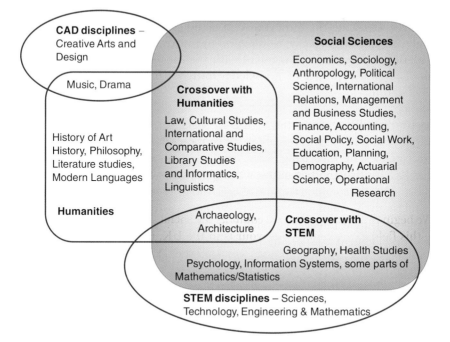

Source: LSE Public Policy Group.

---

[3] ISCC (2010: 3).

overlap extensively with the STEM (science, technology, engineering and mathematics) discipline group. Here, our focus includes strong 'social' sub-disciplines within wider disciplines such as psychology, geography, health studies, information systems and archaeology. The most qualitative modes of enquiry occur in large sub-fields that are centred and rooted in social science theories and analytic or quantitative methods, yet that also stretch into the humanities discipline group, including law, history, philosophy and modern media analysis.

What unites the disciplines grouped as social sciences in Figure 1.1? The key common features are:

- They focus on the study of contemporary human societies, economies, organizations and cultures, and their development.
- The intellectual spine of all these subjects is provided by formally set out theories, normally developing logically consistent 'models', often utilizing mathematical notation, but always with distinct rules and logics of theory development.
- They focus a great deal on systematically collecting data and information using well-worked out and rigorously tested methods, with most branches making significant use of quantitative data.
- All social sciences look for 'laws' of social development, for patterns of association and causation that make sense theoretically and can be evaluated by careful empirical investigation.
- Finally, the social sciences strongly share or seek to emulate standards of good science and of effective scholarship as developed in the physical sciences, stressing the importance of using carefully checked data, analysing data rigorously, replication of information, critical testing of evidence and critical engagement with theories and models, and a conditional acceptance of 'knowledge' only to the extent that it survives falsification.

Many sub-disciplines within the Figure 1.1 social science category harbour doubts about one or two of the features above, or contain scholars whose work stresses very informal modes of theorizing, very detailed qualitative work, or authors who emphasize narrative and persuasive writing in their scholarship. But such variation does not qualify the common features above. And wherever disciplines use quantitative data and analysis, 'digital scholarship' methods, formal theoretical statement, or social theory as their intellectual spine, their identity as social sciences seeking 'laws' of social development is especially apparent.

We shall use the core discipline group labels in Figure 1.1 repeatedly across the rest of the book:

- the STEM disciplines – the (physical) sciences (including medicine), technology, engineering and mathematics;
- the CAD disciplines – creative arts including design, art, film, drama, some forms of media, and creative writing;
- the humanities; and
- the social sciences.

These categories seem obvious, in some sense sanctified by recurrent usage and myriad variants of 'similar discipline' groupings enshrined in university organization across the world. Most universities and governments also denominate the physical sciences more carefully. In government's case this is because it is these disciplines that receive the lion's share of funding, so a boundary has to be drawn. The longer-established physical science professional organizations (like the Royal Society in the UK) have long played an important role in determining government policies and priorities. Yet still, a report by the Science and Technology Select Committee of the House of Commons (STSC, 2012) found considerable difficulties in defining what constituted STEM subjects. The MPs pointed out the need for concerted action by government and university groups to agree on a common definition of STEM subjects. To go further in firming up any of the four discipline groups above is still surprisingly difficult because of an absence of any well-developed official or government categorizations. Systematic statistics can only be produced when such typologies are fully and stably elaborated. So the problems that we tackle here for the social sciences are not unique to them.

To characterize UK-based social science research, we set out to determine the number of staff active in research across the discipline group, the numbers of postgraduate research students, and the financial resources flowing into the university sector both from government funding and from non-academic external sources. Because building up such a well-quantified picture in a reliable way is not a straightforward undertaking, the sketch of the scale and diversity of social science research as a discipline group that we provide here is littered with 'rule of thumb' approximations or assumptions that are eminently contestable. We offer it as a preliminary picture only.

Our key source is the Higher Education Statistics Agency (HESA), which has collected data for many years from British universities on numbers of university research staff and post-graduate research students, as well as other supplementary figures, such as the monies spent on research grants from external funders to universities. Collating standardized information of this kind is supposed to be the core competence of HESA, yet it is still not possible to reach what we might call a definitive set of figures on the number of academic research staff working in social science disciplines. Whereas HESA collects data on the numbers of students studying particular social science disciplines, they do not collect equivalent data on the areas in which staff do research (and teach). They record only the subject disciplines in which staff received their highest qualification. In this format, they ask universities to provide a primary subject discipline for their researchers, and then also give a subdiscipline or a secondary discipline where applicable, in order to narrow down their field of expertise. For example, a political scientist may specialize in public policy or a researcher may have qualified in computer science, but minored in sociology. These data give a reasonably layered picture of the qualification background and expertise of researchers. But they do not provide an accurate picture of the disciplines in which researchers are currently or primarily working. Some degree of estimation is therefore inherent in our numbers.

HESA also does not collate together in any standard way a discipline group for the social sciences, opting instead for a large number of highly specific subject or single

Figure 1.2   Our definition of the 'social sciences'

DISCIPLINES	SHARE OF SOCIAL SCIENCE				SHARE OF OTHER		
	100%	75%	50%	25%	25%	50%	75%
ACADEMIC STUDIES IN EDUCATION							
ACCOUNTING							
ANTHROPOLOGY							
BUSINESS STUDIES							
ECONOMICS							
HUMAN AND SOCIAL GEOGRAPHY							
HUMAN RESOURCE MANAGEMENT							
INFORMATION SERVICES							
MANAGEMENT STUDIES							
MARKETING							
MEDIA STUDIES							
PLANNING (URBAN, RURAL AND REGIONAL)							
POLITICS							
PUBLICITY STUDIES							
PUBLISHING							
SOCIAL POLICY							
SOCIAL WORK							
SOCIOLOGY							
TOURISM, TRANSPORT AND TRAVEL							
FINANCE							
OPERATIONAL RESEARCH							
STATISTICS							
JOURNALISM							
LAW BY AREA							
LAW BY TOPIC							
LINGUISTICS							
ARCHAEOLOGY							
ENVIRONMENTAL SCIENCES							
INFORMATION SYSTEMS							
PSYCHOLOGY							
ARCHITECTURE							
HISTORY BY PERIOD							
HISTORY BY AREA							
HISTORY BY TOPIC							
PHILOSOPHY							
THEOLOGY AND RELIGIOUS STUDIES							

KEY:

- SOCIAL SCIENCE
- STEM
- HUMANITIES
- CREATIVE

Sources: Our analysis of HESA data, 2010–11. Visualization by Amy Ricketts.

Figure 1.3a   The numbers of students in UK universities, by discipline groups for academic year 2010–11

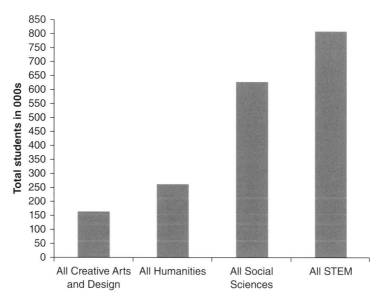

Figure 1.3b   The numbers of academic staff in UK universities, by discipline groups for academic year 2010–11

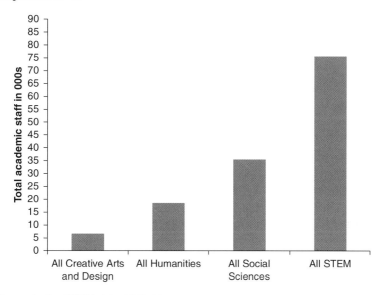

Source: Our analysis of HESA data, 2010–11.

discipline labels. So we have had to decide which HESA categories are inside or outside the social science grouping. Figure 1.2 shows the 'blueprint' classification that we ended up using, after making many different checks. We distinguish 'core' social science subjects, such as sociology, economics, or anthropology, where all the staff

Figure 1.4   The numbers of research students and research staff, by discipline groups for academic year 2010–11

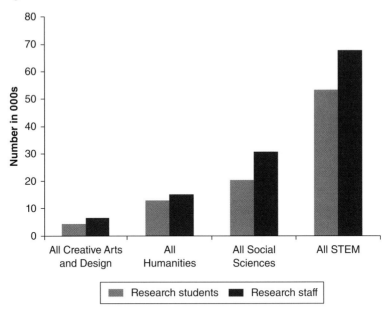

Source: Our analysis of HESA data, 2010–11.

Note: We exclude taught undergraduate and Master's level students from student numbers.

involved are social scientists, and 'crossover' subjects where varying proportions of staff are social scientists. We cannot measure this last number in any fine-grained way using HESA data, and have instead opted for assigning quartiles of staff as lying within overlapping areas. This is an important limitation, which should be carefully borne in mind when interpreting all the data below.

Using this template, Figure 1.3a shows that there were just under 630,000 social science students registered in UK universities at undergraduate and postgraduate levels in 2010–11. There were approximately 35,500 academic staff involved in social science teaching, research, or a combination of both (as shown in Figure 1.3b). For comparison there were just over 800,000 students and more than 75,000 staff in STEM disciplines in UK universities, while the humanities and CAD discipline groups were far smaller. Roughly speaking, the staff:student ratio in social science was one staff member for every 19 students. This is a lower level compared to the staff:student ratio of 1:11 in STEM subjects. Comparing ratios is somewhat misleading, however, because around 35 per cent of STEM scientists work in research-only jobs and therefore have little or no contact with students, whereas for the social sciences this proportion is only 11 per cent.

Some social science staff across the university sector hold 'teaching only' positions, but in Figure 1.4 we estimate that there are around 32,500 academics in UK universities engaged in research work in social science disciplines (the bulk of those in the field). This number is broadly compatible with previous detailed estimates carried

Figure 1.5a **Estimated number of social science academics doing research in UK universities, 2010–11**

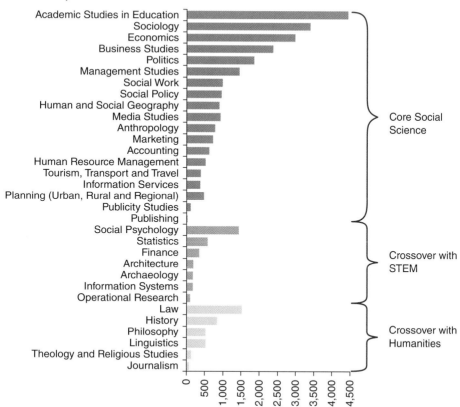

out in the last ten years by the Economic and Social Research Council (ESRC), the government funding agency for social science (ESRC, 2006).

Looking in more detail, Figure 1.5a shows the disciplinary backgrounds of research active staff, shedding light on how many researchers are working in core social sciences or the social science components of crossover social science disciplines (again using the allocations in Figure 1.2). The HESA category for 'academic studies in education', economics and sociology are top in terms of staff numbers. But there are several business-focused sub-disciplines included in the HESA categories (including business studies, management, marketing and accounting). If they were cumulated into a single 'business studies' heading they would be close to the top of the list with around 4,000 staff. In the crossover disciplines, social psychology and statistics are the largest STEM overlap disciplines, and law and history are the largest subjects in the overlap area with the humanities.

Turning to the profile of research students as shown in Figure 1.5b, both 'academic studies in education' and business studies/management studies clearly top the core disciplines table, while economics research students are less common than staff numbers might lead us to expect. In the humanities crossover area there are relatively few law research students and relatively numerous history ones. In the STEM crossover

Figure 1.5b   Estimated number of social science students doing research in UK universities, 2010–11

Source: Our analysis of HESA data, 2010–11.

Note: We include research Master's and doctoral studies students.

area social psychology students are relatively numerous, but numbers elsewhere are fairly low.

A final important dimension of assessing social science research concerns the funding of research efforts across the discipline group. Of course, in Britain much of the funding flows 'automatically' into research from government via two mechanisms:

- The support of high quality research (so-called QR funding) within universities across the country, which is distributed following a government-audit exercise previously operated under the label of Research Assessment Exercise (RAE) but from 2008 called the Research Excellence Framework (REF). In 2012–13 the QR sums amounted to £1.6 billion for all UK universities.

Figure 1.6   Estimated value of research grants and contracts to UK universities in 2010–11, by type of donor and discipline area

Source of funding (in £ millions)	Creative Arts and Design	Humanities	Social Sciences	Science, Technology, Engineering, and Maths	All Disciplines
Quality-related (QR) research funding from HEFCE	78	135	312	1,033	1,558
Government research councils	14	45	138	1,428	1,625
Total internal government	**92**	**180**	**450**	**2,461**	**3,183**
Total as percentage (%)	**3**	**6**	**14**	**77**	**100%**
UK civil society	2	19	53	838	912
UK government	6	4	144	622	776
Government outside the UK	4	6	90	293	393
UK industry	3	1	47	224	275
Other sources	2	4	37	111	154
Industry outside the UK	0	0	15	122	137
Civil society outside the UK	1	3	15	106	125
Total external funding	**18**	**37**	**401**	**2,316**	**2,772**
Total as percentage (%)	**1**	**1**	**14**	**84**	**100%**
Total for all internal and external sources	**110**	**217**	**851**	**4,777**	**5,955**
Percentage of total grants and contracts	**2**	**4**	**14**	**80**	**100%**

Source: HESA Statistics, 2010–11.

Note: Data for Quality-related (QR) research funding is for 2012–13. Data for is taken from the most recent available year, 2010-11, and includes all funding from MRC, EPSRC, BBSRC, ESRC, NERC, STFC, and AHRC, plus the Royal Society, British Academy and the Royal Society of Edinburgh. See List of abbreviations for further details.

- Finance for specific research projects from government research councils for medicine, various STEM sub-groupings, the social sciences and the arts and humanities, all of which distribute grants in response to project applications that pass stringent review procedures. In 2010–11 these totalled £1.6 billion (see Figure 1.6).

It might be argued that these inflows to the university sector do not reflect concrete 'demands', since they are basically administered by academic committees and reviewers on behalf of government and the research councils involved. However, all these inflows are highly responsive to the efforts made by academics and departments to attract funding through academic success.

We estimate the breakdown of these two flows in the first two lines of the table in Figure 1.6. In the STEM subjects the research councils accounted for over a third of all

Figure 1.7   Total expenditure across simplified discipline group categories in UK universities, 2010–11

	Humanities and CAD disciplines	Social Sciences	STEM Disciplines
Total higher education expenditure	£1.53 bn	£3.35 bn	£5.53 bn
Percentage of total expenditure	14.7%	32.3%	53.1%
Disciplines included in each grouping	Humanities and language-based studies. Archaeology. Design, creative arts and performing arts.	Administrative, business and social studies. Education. Architecture and planning.	Medicine, dentistry and health. Biological, mathematical and physical sciences. Engineering and technology. Agriculture, forestry and veterinary science.

Source: HESA Finance Statistics, Table K, 2010–11. Analysis by Cambridge Econometrics.

research income. And their proportion was almost half for the humanities and CAD disciplines (which receive few funds from elsewhere). However, these 'automatic' funds accounted for only just over a quarter of funding for social sciences research. The rest of Figure 1.6 shows that a big component of the remaining funding for the social sciences comes from research directly paid for by UK government departments and agencies. A further large component comes from overseas governments, including here European Union agencies and funding programmes. STEM disciplines receive large amounts from UK civil society (chiefly foundations or charities supporting medical research). Apart from this, the social sciences funding patterns is quite similar to that for STEM subjects, albeit on a much smaller scale (less than a fifth of the large grouping). By contrast the amounts received by the humanities and CAD disciplines from funding sources other than government are very small.

We show only the second of these two flows in the first line of the table in Figure 1.6 looking at the value of research grants. In the STEM subjects the research councils accounted for over a third of all research income. And their proportion was almost half for the humanities and CAD disciplines (which receive few funds from elsewhere). However, these 'automatic' funds accounted for only just over a quarter of funding for social sciences research. The rest of Figure 1.6 shows that a big component of the remaining funding for the social sciences comes from research directly paid for by UK government departments and agencies. A further large component comes from overseas governments, including here European Union agencies and funding programmes. STEM disciplines receive large amounts from UK civil society (chiefly foundations or charities supporting medical research). Apart from this, the social sciences funding pattern is quite similar to that for STEM subjects, albeit on a much smaller scale (less than a fifth of the large grouping). By contrast the amounts received by the humanities and CAD disciplines from funding sources other than government are very small.

Figure 1.8   How spending is allocated within the main discipline groups

% of total expenditures spent on:	Humanities	Social Sciences	STEM disciplines
Academic staff costs	63.9	60.9	57.1
Other staff costs	16.9	15.3	19.1
Other operating expenses	18.3	23.0	21.1
Depreciation	0.9	0.7	2.7
Totals	100.0%	100.0%	100.0%

Source: HESA Finance Statistics, Table K, 2010–11. Analysis by Cambridge Econometrics.

Figure 1.9   The economic impacts of the spending of UK social science departments, in 2010–11

	£ billions
Value added in social science departments (direct)	2.7
Value added elsewhere in the economy (indirect)	0.5
Value added that is stimulated by spending from wages for academics and other staff (induced)	1.6
Total value for the economy	**4.8**

Source: HESA Finance Statistics, Table K, 2010–11. Analysis by Cambridge Econometrics.

Overall, although social science disciplines account for just over 20 per cent of all research staff and research students in the UK, they receive around 14 per cent of the total research funding flowing to UK universities. By comparison, STEM subjects account for around 60 per cent of research staff, compared to 80 per cent of total research funding.

Finally in sketching the importance of the social sciences we asked Cambridge Econometrics to analyse the scale of economic activity undertaken across the discipline group. Because of the make-up of the financial statistics used by HESA, it was necessary in this analysis to use a more simplified and condensed version of the discipline groupings than that we deployed above. In particular, the consultants merged the humanities and CAD disciplines data from Figure 1.6 into one category. And the dividing line between the social sciences and STEM disciplines was necessarily somewhat cruder to fit with available statistics. The key conclusion shown in Figure 1.7 though is that the social sciences accounted for over £3,350 million of expenditure in 2010–11: approximately a third of all UK university spending from all sources. The STEM disciplines accounted for the largest slice (over half the total), and the humanities and CAD subjects for somewhat less than a sixth. Even on this cruder basis of division, the social sciences as an 'industry' are clearly more than twice as large as the humanities and CAD subjects.

Using the same groupings, Figure 1.8 shows that patterns of spending are relatively similar. All three spent around three fifths of expenditure on academic staff, somewhat more in humanities and less in STEM subjects where other staff costs are higher – for instance to operate laboratory equipment – which also boosted depreciation here. The social sciences showed the largest proportion of 'other operating expenses', for reasons that are not entirely clear.

By 2010–11 the UK government was no longer providing any grant support for students undertaking first degrees in social science, so most resources flowing into social science departments consisted of student fees for courses, plus support for research and some limited grants for students to do PhDs. It should be apparent that the UK social sciences are a large-scale activity, and it is worth mapping out their role in the wider economy in somewhat more detail.

These sources of income sustained the bulk of expenditure across the departments, which on the limited Cambridge Econometrics definition amounted to £2,700 million, as Figure 1.9 shows. In addition, however, this volume of extended economic activity had two extra effects:

- indirectly, the spending on social science work added to demand in the economy for other products and services, generating extra value added of £500 million; and
- the salaries paid to academic staff and other employees in social science departments created 'induced' demand in the rest of the UK economy, a multiplier effect that amounted to £1,600 million.

Adding these effects to direct spending, and remembering that the definition of social science used here is a restrictive one, we can conclude that by 2010–11 the social sciences were a substantial industry sub-sector, creating more than £5 billion annually in gross value added to the UK economy.

1.2 The social sciences and human-dominated systems

One foot on the concrete shore, One foot in the human sea.

Jackson Browne[4]

Disciplinary and subdisciplinary specialization, and the emphasis on internal academic communication, peaked in the late twentieth century. North American social science is increasingly oriented outward and focused on pressing public problems.

Craig Calhoun[5]

The concepts we use to organize our thinking are never neutral. Instead they tend to produce specific effects that are progressively lost to sight the more they become 'conventional' categories. The juxtaposition of the social sciences with the 'natural' or 'physical' sciences, deployed in the previous section, is a case in point. The contrast seems intuitive, has spread universally and is easily recognized by wide audiences. It

---

[4] From the song 'Walking Town' by Jackson Browne featured on the album 'The Naked Ride Home' (released 2001 on Elektra Records).

[5] Craig Calhoun, 'Social sciences in North America' (ISSC 2010: 58).

also lends itself readily to the propensity of western thought to revolve around antonyms and contrasts. For decades, almost from the moment that 'social science' came into use, a surprisingly wide range of scholars in STEM disciplines have revelled in the sense of superiority that the dichotomy creates for them. As late as 2009 Michael Kinsley could write without fear of contradiction that: 'Many "hard" scientists regard the term "social science" as an oxymoron. Science means hypotheses you can test, and prove or disprove. Social science is little more than observation putting on airs' (Kinsley, 2009).

Yet the invocation of an acronym, STEM, to group together science disciplines, and even more overtly the antonymic and ideological terminology of 'hard' and 'soft' disciplines, both speak to the decreasing usefulness of the idea of 'natural' or 'physical' sciences. In an increasingly human-made world, in what sense are the subject matters of engineering, medicine, dentistry, agricultural science or modern mathematics concerned only with 'natural' or even 'physical' systems? In what ways too are mathematical or quantitative social sciences such as econometrics or actuarial science any less 'hard' than biology or zoology? How is a randomized control trial carried out in social work or public management any less 'hard scientific' than one in medical pharmacology?

The mathematicization, quantification, formalization and theorization of the social sciences are still very partially advanced, but they are clearly the intellectually dominant trends in most disciplines – although the first three shifts are contested bitterly by a still predominant rear-guard of 'constructivists' opposed to any 'normal science' or 'positivist' model of the social sciences. But the impact of successive waves of scientific advances and fashions have made evident changes to the standards of what counts as 'evidence' in every social science discipline. In 1995 the biologist Edward O. Wilson could still lament in highly critical language the persistence of foundational disputes in social science: 'A great many [scholars] even enjoy the resulting overall atmosphere of chaos, mistaking it for creative ferment' (Wilson, 1995: 182). Yet constructivist critiques have shifted character in all the social sciences in the last decade, only infrequently now decrying the use of organized empirical evidence. Instead they emphasize the need for multiple sources of evidence, multiple methods of study, a focus on holistic phenomena, close attention to meanings as well as behaviours, and frequent triangulation of different kinds of evidential information.

From the early 1960s commentators began to note that the old C.P. Snow concept of 'two cultures' – one formal, mathematical and scientific versus the other informal or thematic, literary and qualitative, and mutually unable to understand each other – seems inadequate (Leavis, 1962). Recognizing the scale and salience of the intellectual effort charted in Section 1.1, some observers suggest 'three cultures', with social science in some sense bridging the previous divide, deploying mathematical and quantitative approaches in similar ways to STEM subjects, yet also in repeated dialogue with more foundational internal critics inside and across humanities disciplines. The 'third culture' is also adapted to the fact that law-like propositions are hard to formulate when applied to human behaviours, with their ever-changing capacity for reflexivity, where actors may change behaviours as they discover that their previous patterns of response have been analysed. Thus, most social scientists would probably now agree with John Gerring (2011: xxi) that: 'Social science is not simply an offshoot of the natural sciences or the humanities … It is, rather, a distinct realm of inquiry'.

It is also important to point out that both in their origins and in their current patterns of development, most social sciences do not form any kind of field opposed to STEM disciplines, or are in orthogonal conflict, contradiction or even competition with them. The social sciences were founded initially, and expanded (after 1945 especially), in a kind of lock-step with STEM subjects. Craig Calhoun (2008: 20) observed that in the latter half of the nineteenth century

> the social sciences came to the fore as part of a rebellion against exclusive study of the old disciplines [such as classics, law, philosophy, or rhetoric]. They grew along with science and technology because they were deemed forward-looking and important to 'progress', relevant to solving contemporary problems and furthering positive innovations.

In their book on the changing knowledge institutions and forms of academic work, Ian McNeeley and Lisa Wolverton (2009) credited 'the laboratory' together with the German model of a research university as the last two of the essential ingredients of the modern academic paradigm. Yet they also stressed that it is wrong to think of a closed laboratory as just a building, or an isolated physical environment where closely controlled conditions can be created for the reductionist testing of single causes in experiments. Instead, many sciences have fieldwork where lab-like conditions of control are replicated externally. For instance, in Pasteur's key investigations leading to the development of inoculations against anthrax, although closed lab work was vital, an equally important role was played by the development of an ability to undertake carefully specified field investigations in complex, multi-causal environments (Stokes, 1997). For many physical sciences, 'the lab' was not just something inside the university, but an ability to create an environment for close observation, measurements and manipulation in the wider natural or social world outside. This is overwhelmingly a matter of professional training, socialization and careful organizational specification.

The other key element of lab experiments and field investigations alike was the development of reliable statistical analysis to allow researchers to systematically anticipate probabilities, and to differentiate results from small samples that might apply within wider populations from those that could not. These techniques developed first in physical sciences to help researchers distinguish causal influences from multiple confuser variables in multi-causal field situations. Later the development of randomized control trials played a key role in medical and drug development, extending scientific methods into realms (like holistic human physiology) where lab controls were infeasible. But the same sequences of statistical developments also impacted and defined the social sciences, albeit often requiring long time lags for the successful specification and accumulation of controlled data and the development of theories to explain multi-causal processes.

> The growth of well-informed social reflexivity and understanding from the late nineteenth century drew extensively on the societal applications of statistics, but

also on key social science theories and expansions of understanding. Between the 1880s and the early 1950s the development of reasonable economic analysis of economic cycles, the development of reliable social surveys and opinion polls, and the extension of social psychology created radically changed self-knowledge capabilities in advanced industrial societies. Combined with rapidly evolving capabilities in organizational design and analysis they also made feasible huge increases in social control capabilities, changes that have been variously characterized as liberating or oppressive (Dunleavy and Tinkler, 2014, section 1.1).

It was during the explosive growth of the research university – first in late nineteenth century Germany, and then the United States, fed back later into the slower-changing university systems of Britain and France – that the social sciences emerged and grew, especially in sociology, psychology and anthropology, with Marshallian economics already beating a significantly differentiated and more Anglo-American path. This familiar story is regularly told in terms of 'great books' and classic authors, who at first like Marx or Comte often operated outside university systems as independent intellectuals. Yet the less familiar story is of the initially German and later American specialization of disciplines that first strongly created sociology, psychology, political science and anthropology as separate academic professions, each based around PhDs and professional journals following the science model. Figure 1.10 charts some later significant institutional milestones for the mainly Anglo-American and European development of these four core disciplines, in terms of the founding of key departments, professional bodies and journals.

The most extensive period of foundational activity stretched from the 1880s to the early 1950s, with many apparently 'obvious' developments often taking decades to achieve, and involving many detours, especially in political science. For instance, the first chair of 'political science' in England was founded in the 1890s in the history faculty at Cambridge, before later becoming part of an anti-social-science humanities bloc that stopped Cambridge creating a genuine politics department until the 2000s. Similarly, the London School of Economics and Political Science was founded in 1905, but chose to later create a Department of 'Government'. And it was nearly 50 years before a UK Political Studies Association was established, which to this day also eschews any scientific pretensions in its name.

Yet particularly since the late 1960s the concreting-in of highly siloed disciplines spread from STEM subjects across the social sciences, with

- the progressive elimination of polymath intellectual gurus like Marx or Weber (and, of course, their more disastrously ideological early counterparts such as Spengler or Sombart)
- the pushing out of strongly or overtly normatively or ideological driven theories (especially in the normalization after the Second World War), and
- the fuller acceptance and implementation of Weber's model of 'neutral' and objective professional practice within the bounds of academia.

As Debray (1981) noted for France, from around 1930 the universities progressively ceased to be the key habitat of public intellectuals, with this locale moving first to

Figure 1.10 Timeline of some key developments in US and European social sciences

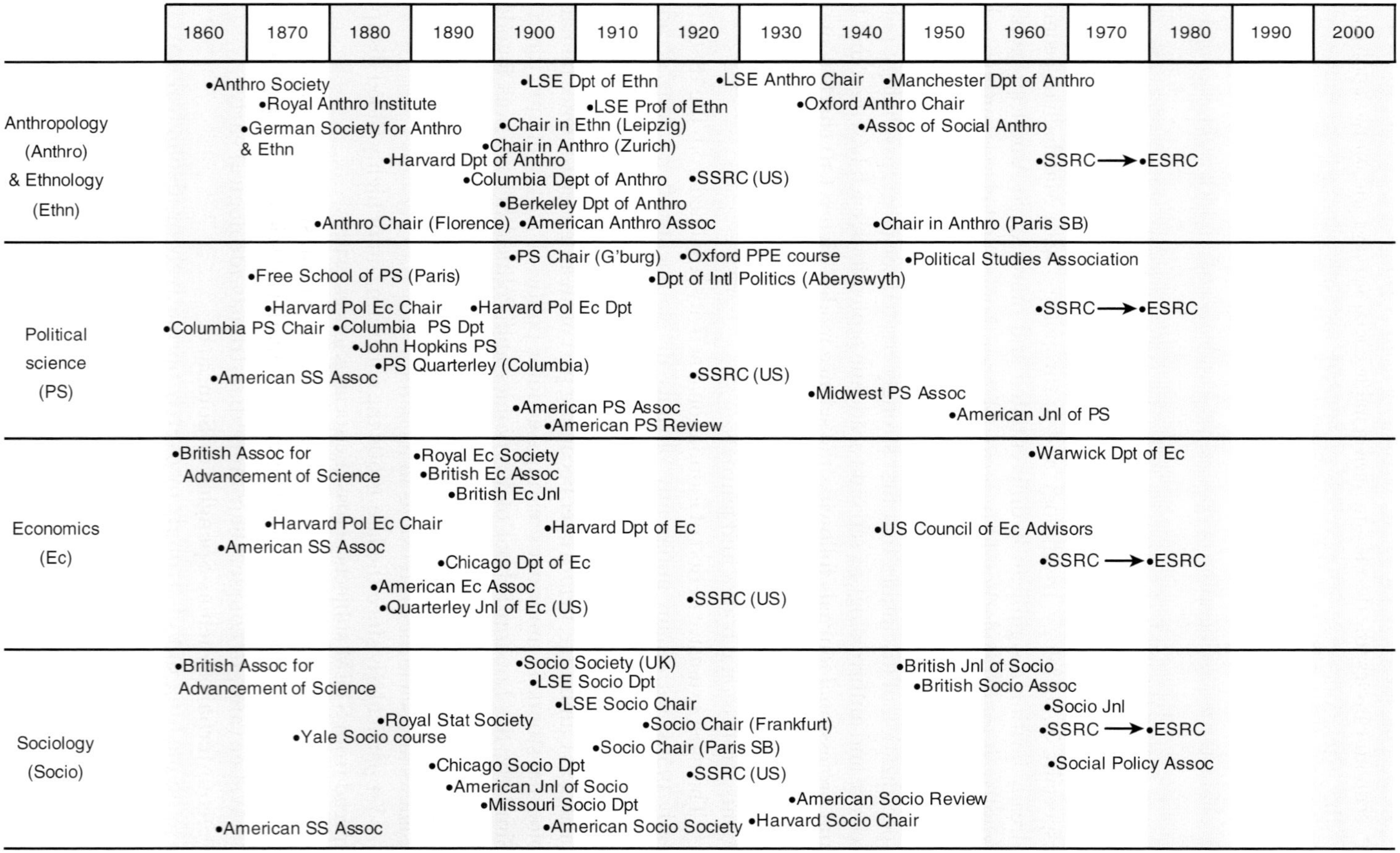

	1860	1870	1880	1890	1900	1910	1920	1930	1940	1950	1960	1970	1980	1990	2000
Anthropology (Anthro) & Ethnology (Ethn)	•Anthro Society	•Royal Anthro Institute •German Society for Anthro & Ethn	•Harvard Dpt of Anthro	•Chair in Anthro (Zurich)	•LSE Dpt of Ethn •Chair in Ethn (Leipzig) •Columbia Dept of Anthro •Berkeley Dpt of Anthro •American Anthro Assoc •Anthro Chair (Florence)	•LSE Prof of Ethn	•LSE Anthro Chair •SSRC (US)	•Oxford Anthro Chair		•Manchester Dpt of Anthro •Assoc of Social Anthro •Chair in Anthro (Paris SB)		•SSRC → •ESRC			
Political science (PS)		•American SS Assoc	•Free School of PS (Paris) •Columbia PS Chair	•Harvard Pol Ec Chair •Columbia PS Dpt •John Hopkins PS •PS Quarterley (Columbia)	•PS Chair (G'burg) •Harvard Pol Ec Dpt •American PS Assoc •American PS Review		•Oxford PPE course •Dpt of Intl Politics (Aberyswyth) •SSRC (US)		•Midwest PS Assoc	•Political Studies Association	•American Jnl of PS	•SSRC → •ESRC			
Economics (Ec)	•British Assoc for Advancement of Science	•Harvard Pol Ec Chair •American SS Assoc	•American Ec Assoc •Quarterley Jnl of Ec (US)	•Royal Ec Society •British Ec Assoc •British Ec Jnl •Chicago Dpt of Ec	•Harvard Dpt of Ec		•SSRC (US)			•US Council of Ec Advisors	•Warwick Dpt of Ec	•SSRC → •ESRC			
Sociology (Socio)	•British Assoc for Advancement of Science	•Yale Socio course •American SS Assoc	•Royal Stat Society	•Chicago Socio Dpt •American Jnl of Socio •Missouri Socio Dpt •American Socio Society	•Socio Society (UK) •LSE Socio Dpt •LSE Socio Chair •Socio Chair (Paris SB)	•Socio Chair (Frankfurt)	•SSRC (US)	•American Socio Review •Harvard Socio Chair		•British Jnl of Socio •British Socio Assoc		•Socio Jnl •SSRC → •ESRC	•Social Policy Assoc		

Figure 1.11 The changing balance of the UK's economy, 1970 to 2007

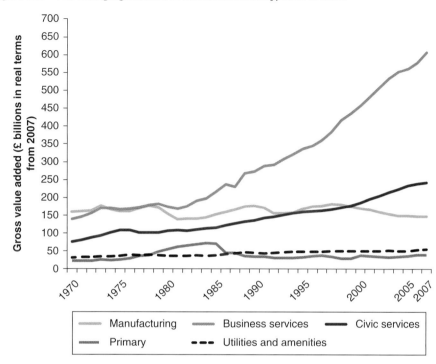

Source: Our analysis of EU Klems data, 2009.

literature or independent authors, and from the 1960s onwards towards media-intellectuals (see also Reul, 2003).

Only from the 1970s did formalized peer review really lock down across the social sciences, with the explosive growth of academic journals and sub-fields within disciplines made possible by staff expansions and more generous government research funding support. Here too was the heyday of 'physics envy', as western mainstream economists and psychologists especially, pursued a 'normal science' model of disciplinary endeavour, aspiring to the 'rapid advance, high consensus' model of early physical sciences (Collins, 1994). This period also saw the beginning of a wider sequence of intellectual 'fashions' in methods approaches across the social sciences inspired by STEM changes such as evolutionary theory development, systems theory, chaos theory, advances in genetics and most recently emulation of science and engineering 'big data' approaches. The differentiation of the social sciences from each other, and from the STEM subjects in particular, was matched by the wider and wider gulf opened at many points between the operating approaches of the core social sciences and the older, unformalized or thematic/literary humanities disciplines.

A fundamental post-1945 shift in advanced industrial economies also particularly affected the inter-relationships of the social and STEM sciences. Figure 1.11 shows that in the UK, business and civic services were far and away the most strongly growing economic sectors, and these were inherently sectors far closer to many social sciences. Services are not easily defined and most attempts made have limitations. For instance, the popular *Economist* definition, that services are 'anything sold in trade that cannot be dropped on your foot', fails to take account of public sector services. And by overstressing the intangible aspect of services it omits the strong modern trend for services to be 'productized' and 'commoditized' (Cusumano, 2010), especially using zero touch technologies where human interactions are minimized in favour of nearly complete digital transaction processes. Yet this trend also has a counterpart, for products to be servitized for instance, leasing fully operational aero engines to airlines instead of selling the physical product and later maintenance kits.

Many modern services (such as mobile or cell phones and data) equally centre on hard technology and specific products, pulling in complex technologies, and highly skilled engineers, IT and technical staff from many STEM disciplines. Yet these are the minority of private service sector employees, with greater numbers for marketing, administration, pricing and business organization specialists. The relevance of business schools and disciplines in modern business services is stronger than for older economic sectors. And in the public sector, the welfare state and state health care provision virtually created new social science disciplines across Europe, such as public administration and management, social policy, social work, housing and urban studies. State health services absorb many psychologists and health discipline researchers with a social science orientation. Government patronage of professional services like law, planning, or infrastructure remains huge, despite years of privatization waves in advanced industrial economies. We shall see below that an orientation towards government and public policy issues spread widely and deeply across the social sciences for this reason. Meanwhile Figure 1.11 shows that three other sectors traditionally linked in very integral ways to the STEM disciplines (manufacturing, utilities and primary industries) have at best oscillated or gradually declined as sources of gross value added over the last four decades in the UK.

So both current economic and technological trends essentially call into question the woefully inadequate contrasting of 'natural' or 'physical' or 'hard' sciences with human-focused or 'soft' social sciences inherited from earlier periods. Instead Figure 1.12 makes a three-fold distinction as follows:

- *Natural systems* are aspects of the physical environment that do not involve or are not significantly affected by human interventions and actions. We would argue that in this sense there are increasingly few systems that are completely 'natural' – and consequently that it is only in fields like astrophysics and pure maths that scientific disciplines exist with a genuinely or fully 'natural' focus.
- *Human-influenced systems* are basically erstwhile 'physical' systems on Earth that remain mostly or essentially autonomous in their mode of operation, but where there are nonetheless significant human interventions or efforts at control. The development of knowledge here is often focused on warning or prediction systems and on formulating human responses – as with climate and weather predictions, or efforts to monitor and anticipate earthquake pressures and to formulate engineering responses.
- *Human-dominated systems* encompass all the numerous artefacts of human civilization (cities, markets, organizations, firms, government

Figure 1.12   How the social sciences focus on human-dominated and human-influenced systems

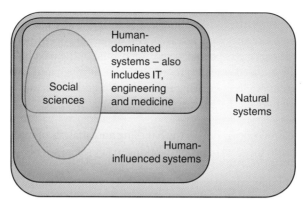

institutions, agriculture, transport and infrastructure systems, IT, communications and data systems); all aspects of the social and economic organizations and issues thus created; and the human physiology and medical/health sciences interventions.

In these terms, the social sciences are primarily centred in the study of human-dominated systems, but their coverage also spans extensively across into human-influenced systems. It follows that there is no sharp contrast between the social sciences and many STEM subjects – especially medicine and health sciences, IT and information analysis, and engineering and risk management in all their forms (Wittrock, 2010). As Kenneth Boulding (1966: 7) noted: 'The case for the social sciences is simply the case for specialized, organized knowledge-producing industries at the level of complex systems'.

Increasingly, a recognition of this argument underlies the ways in which social science approaches of many kinds interpenetrate and inform STEM disciplines, creating knowledge of organizational arrangements, organizational cultures, 'soft' technologies, citizen or consumer demands, social behaviour in complex systems, critical self-awareness of potential biases, collective action and co-ordination problems, behavioural science and 'nudge' insights, and so on.

Equally the social sciences themselves incorporate many toolkits and approaches inherited from or first developed in STEM disciplines, including a now distinct tradition of mathematical and formal theory expression, and the rigorous quantification and assessment of evidence, plus some version of the 'normal science' apparatus of critical evidence accumulation and peer review. Fifty years ago, at a point of great optimism for the social sciences, Boulding (1966: 22) observed that:

> Every great advance in science seems to have been associated with a twofold movement ... One is the development of a new theoretical insight or point of view, a restructuring of the image of the world, which creates, as it were, evolutionary potential for the increase of knowledge. The second condition is an improvement in instrumentation, that is, in the methods by which information coming from the outside world can be detected, sampled, and processed.

Today the onset of digital convergence in the social sciences is especially highlighted by shifts towards 'big data' approaches:

> In the last half-century, the information base of social science research has primarily come from three sources: survey research, end of period government statistics, and one-off studies of particular people, places, or events. In the next half-century, these sources will still be used and improved, but the number and diversity of other sources of information are increasing exponentially, and are already many orders of magnitude more informative than ever before. (King, 2013: 3)

As a result new areas of cooperation in the handling and analysis of massive data sets have already developed, and the kind of people working in key social sciences has begun to shift:

> A ... pattern [of knowledge transfer] is now beginning to emerge between several traditional social science disciplines and computer science. Graduate students in economics, political science, and sociology now regularly learn computer languages, and are starting to do formal training in computer science as part of their graduate degrees. Associated with this development is computer scientists doing research in what is effectively social science. Indeed, this activity is being formalized in some new departments at some universities, often under the banners 'computational social science' or 'applied computational science'. (King, 2013: 5)

Other developments pulling the social sciences towards their partner disciplines focusing on human-dominated systems include the spread of randomized control trials, systematic review and meta-studies from medicine and health sciences into many different social sciences; and the rapid generalization of 'public understanding of science' approaches into increasingly similar and increasingly digital knowledge exchange efforts in the social sciences also, on which we have much to say below.

1.3 Perceptions of 'impact' from the social sciences

> For better or for worse, individuals really do share their thoughts and they do to some extent harmonise their preferences, and they have no other way to make the big decisions except within the scope of the institutions they build.
>
> *Mary Douglas*[6]

> We did the thing that social science does best, right? Which is not to answer a particular question, but to change the way in which people think about what the questions are.
>
> *Research executive in a major US hi-tech firm*

Tracking the impacts of the STEM sciences and especially medicine has become a huge industry. Governments and philanthropic foundations pump billions of dollars or pounds annually into these disciplines, and are naturally keen to monitor closely what

---

[6] Douglas (1986: 128).

economic benefits they secure in return. Modern theories of economic development assign huge significance to scientific innovations, as measured by indices such as the numbers of scientific patents registered; the frequency of launching new products with a high university value-added embedded in them; or the numbers of 'spin out' companies for science, technology, bio-genetics, or medical research that are linked to the university sector.

   None of these measures work when applied to the social sciences, and so the impression has been created a long time ago, and consolidated by waves of superficial commentaries and 'evaluations' since, that the social sciences lack external impacts, especially in business and the private economy. Writing in 1963, Leeds and Smith commented:

> Industry consistently utilizes the findings from the physical scientists who work in universities and laboratories. Units and departments that specialise in determining the practical uses of the research of a physical scientist are established in industrial organizations. But there is no counterpart of this in the social sciences; there is virtually no similar machinery for developing and testing the application of social ideas. (p. 50)

Asked to explain their impacts, social scientists in earlier times themselves often took refuge either in very specific case studies of particular disciplines, mapped across long historical eras, or in 'hand-waving' generalities. A frequent theme was that social science ideas were imperceptibly changing how society operated, but on a very long time-scale analogous to that of the long historical lags involved in many scientific innovations really being industrialized and generalized for extensive use. Thus Kenneth Boulding argued:

> I suspect that the story of the impact of the social sciences will not be written for five hundred years. It will take at least that long for the implications of present knowledge to work themselves out. (1966: 19)

None of this elicited much confidence from treasuries, finance ministries or politicians, and unsurprisingly the social sciences repeatedly lost out in competitions for funding with STEM subjects, creating the historical patterns charted earlier in Section 1.1. In the digital era this disadvantage has only worsened, as the rate of adoption of new technologies speeded up, and the 'scalability' of tech changes meant that IT or genetics companies with breakthrough products could become major global players inside five to ten years. Set against this time scale, Boulding's extreme pessimism seems almost comical, and social scientists have increasingly struggled to come up with different and better answers. Yet even when trying to be more effective, serious scholars in elite universities can still be found convening conferences or publishing leaflets with a kind of zero-based assumption built into them, asking: 'What Use are the Social Sciences?'.[7]

   The problems and disadvantages for the social sciences in demonstrating impact are in fact multi-layered, and they cannot be explained in only one way, or in the same ways across different disciplines. This is terrain that we cover in depth over

---

[7] This was the title of a large public seminar convened at Kings College, London in May 2013.

the remainder of this book, but it is worthwhile taking a brief aerial look or advanced reconnaissance of some of the key factors:

1 *Social science research is generally 'collective' in character – it does not lend itself to the 'unique discovery' image of research closely associated (by outsiders) with STEM subjects.* Figure 1.13 shows Boyer's famous four-way categorization of scholarship with 'discovery' research – finding new and unknown empirical or theoretical phenomena – as only one of four types of scholarship (Boyer, 1997). The other three types of scholarship are: 'integration', sifting and making sense of new discoveries and creating systematic theories to accommodate them; 'application', using integrative theories and discoveries to tackle practically useful problems; and 'renewal' of the scholarly or scientific profession itself via teaching and socialization.

   Discovery research accounts for a relatively small part of overall scholarship activities, and only a tiny fraction of work genuinely uncovers new findings, but especially for STEM subjects this activity is often seen by disciplines themselves and the wider world as the core part of or even the 'be all and end all' of the scientific mission. Discovery work also lends itself well to the populist 'lone wolf' narrative of scientific genius, with its characteristic stress on mavericks and isolated nerds battling against the odds or a conventional wisdom to achieve breakthrough results.

   In fact, almost all scientific work is replicating or incremental, and cannot be patented. But the exceptions that can, and the industrial implications of the most successful patents, still dominate professional, government, and university thinking. By contrast, almost all social scientific work is either incremental or integrative, either extending, consolidating, refining or reinterpreting known phenomena, or seeking to integrate it within complex causal models and theoretical frameworks. The only exceptions focus on mapping genuinely new social behaviours (e.g., how people use brand new social media), or accounting for unexpected or unparalleled developments (e.g., perhaps an 'out of the blue' crisis of state or economic stability). All social science work clearly depends on and feeds into the collective knowledge of its disciplines and professions, rendering the non-applicability of the unrealistic 'discovery' archetype particularly visible.

2 *Social science research has also not been capital intensive, nor have its key results been patentable* (which essentially requires embodying innovations into physical products). Especially since the spread of PCs, the cheapening of computing power following Moore's Law, and the diffusion of cheap analytic software into firms and governments, social science departments cannot fence around their knowledge with the protective apparatus of equipment or unique skill sets found in STEM departments, nor embody it in a physical product. Their products are ideas and information that cannot even be copyrighted. So, taken together with the collective nature of research advances, the social sciences have received little or no support from the dominant intellectual property (IP) regimes of western countries in internalizing a flow of benefits from their work. The apparatus of patents and trademark protections has offered little or no opportunities for social scientists to create any IP returns beyond author fees for books and copying fees for articles or book chapters.

Figure 1.13   Visualizing the flow and potential impacts of social science research in the academic, mediating and wider societal domains

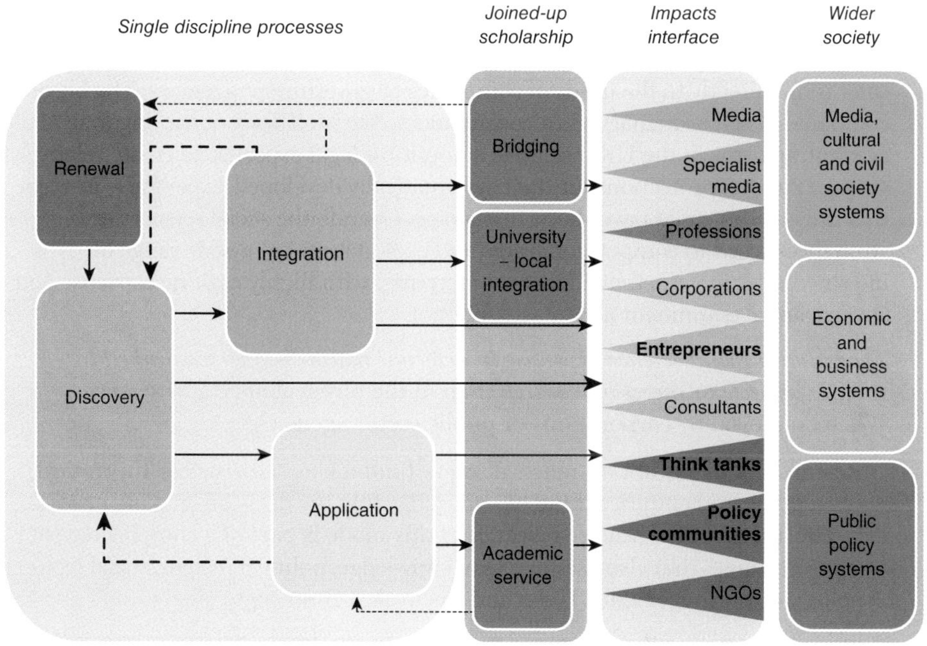

Source: Dunleavy and Tinkler (2014).

3   Consequently, *social science research rarely generates any strong or distinctive 'first mover advantages' for firms or governments that adopt its insights,* especially no quickly cashable comparative advantage of the kind that profit-maximizing businesses must seek. There are some exceptions. Some social science mathematicians and econometricians produce formulae that (if kept secret) can generate specific and calculable profitable margins over competitors for hedge-funds or finance market speculators. Similarly some forms of survey sampling, psychological testing, human relations approaches, talent management policies and organizational culture specialisms can generate cashable advantages for companies in more diffuse ways. But the more general picture is that social science advances are quickly apparent to or known by competitors, because of their collective character.

4   All the above features also mean that *the social sciences are more exposed to competition from the full range of intermediaries shown in Figure 1.13 than are their STEM counterparts.* Intermediary institutions include management consultants, think tanks, specialist consultants, survey companies, professions and media companies. These organisations can more easily keep up to date with social science scholarship, and re-express it cheaply without offering or needing to support the infrastructure costs of social science research than in STEM disciplines. They can often strip out ('cream off') the most commercially valuable or standardizable tasks to specialize in. And by focusing more directly on lobbying and tendering for contracts, and public relations marketing, these intermediary

bodies are also often able to commoditize the benefits of scholarly work essentially undertaken in universities, and claim credit for ideas and innovations conceived elsewhere. All the intermediary bodies shown also combine social science knowledge advances and ideas with their own proprietary procedures, 'ordinary knowledge', or applied modes of working so as to create amalgam products that cater more directly to the needs of companies or government agencies. The biggest companies, such as management consultancies like McKinsey or the 'big four' accounting firms in the UK, use huge amounts of legal expertise to create relatively strong IP rights protections for their systematically developed 'expertise' – in ways that universities could never hope to manage. Overall, the social sciences are strongly exposed to competition from (and exploitation by) a wide range of intermediaries in ways that STEM counterparts, with highly esoteric expertise and strong capital equipment advantages, are not.

5 *The value of social science expertise in external realms* is *also less linked to specific projects or pieces of research* than in the physical or STEM sciences. When employed by corporations or public sector agencies:

> Researchers bring not so much discrete findings as their whole theoretical, conceptual, and empirical fund of knowledge into the decision-making process ... The 'use' of social science research in this mode is part of a complicated set of interchanges that also uses practical knowledge, political insight, social technologies, and judgement. (Weiss and Bucuvalas, 1980: 12)

Critics of the Research Excellence Framework's (REF) way of assessing external impacts via case studies have pointed out that its focus on discrete research projects or publications having specific impacts is STEM-centric and misses the importance of the 'wise counsel' aspects of academic service by social scientists (Tinkler, 2012). Social scientists' work for government advisory committees or as consultants to companies often draws on their cumulative, lifetime experience of a research field, and not on any one single (and necessarily incremental) research output or discovery.

6 A great deal of external influence of the social sciences is concentrated in the public policy realm, as we show below. Yet here social scientists themselves have often suggested naïve or overstated views of what should count as 'impact', *creating an 'impossibilist' image or benchmark of what real influence would consist of,* implying a level or style of power that inherently cannot be attained.

This problem has several component parts, beginning with an over-claiming of what a fully developed social science could do. At the start of the 1980s, Weiss and Bucuvalas (1980: 14) noted that a:

> tendency to inflate the real contributions of the social sciences into eternal truths, good for all seasons, places a burden on them that they are not yet prepared to meet. And since each advance in research seems to uncover unsuspected complexities and new sources of variability, the quest for elegant and parsimonious laws of social behaviour, on the model of the laws of the physical sciences, may never be successful.

Charles Lindblom and David Cohen mounted a strong critique of a kind of 'hyper rationalist' approach to 'professional social inquiry' (PSI, a term they used to represent not just the social sciences but also the work of many social science educated professionals outside the higher education sector itself). They critiqued the tendency of professionals to over-claim authoritativeness, and under-estimate their dependence on the 'ordinary knowledge' with which we all navigate the social world. At any one point in time, Lindblom and Cohen argued, the contributions of PSI knowledge are inherently likely to always constitute isolated pinpricks of superior knowledge, located within a wider landscape of causation. The implications and salience of these islands of PSI knowledge can only be understood using ordinary knowledge and this situation will never change – there is never going to be a complete algorithm or a fully-PSI-tested body of knowledge to rival the STEM sciences.

> As a result of inattention to the limited contribution of [PSI] to social prob-
> lem solving so far, [practitioners of] PSI often succumb to the belief that,
> given enough PSI, all social problems can be significantly ameliorated by it.
> [...] Much of the world's work of problem solving is accomplished not through
> PSI but through ordinary knowledge, through social learning, and through
> interactive problem solving. (Lindblom and Cohen, 1979: 91)

Similarly Wagenaar (1982: 25) emphasized that:

> Research is only one of the various ways of human learning, but one which,
> amidst other forms of obtaining knowledge, occupies a special position because
> of its objectivity, its susceptibility of control, its dependence and reliability.

7   Finally applying social science and wider PSI knowledge that is limited in all the above ways within the public sector and government has created particular difficulties as bodies of knowledge seem to be 'politicized' or 'subjective'. The first problem here is the danger that we overlook the intrinsically political nature of public policy. 'Unless there is total consensus about the ends to be achieved, the knowledge component is only part of the solution. In fact, the knowledge itself is often mired in value and interest assumptions' (Weiss and Bucuvalas, 1980: 15).

Getting to a realistic conception of what is possible here has not been helped by the highly over-simplified (and automatically pessimism-inducing) ideas of what effective public policy influence should look like, stressing some kind of Platonic guardian role for social scientists advising public officials devoid of knowledge or competences:

> The implicit image is decision maker as fresh blotter: the decision maker is
> expected to soak up all the relevant research. An even better metaphor might
> be decision maker as fresh stencil. Social science research imprints its message,
> and the decision maker is expected to transfer it to the stack of blank pages
> awaiting his [or her] action. If pressed to examine their assumptions,
> presumably no social scientist would make such extravagant claims. Yet much
> of the [academic] chorus of disillusion about the state of research use seems
> to rest on premises almost this farfetched. (Weiss and Bucuvalas, 1980: 15)

Again Lindblom and Cohen took a far more robustly pluralist line, arguing that in any liberal democracy policy making will and must always be subject to 'adversary politics' influences, where decision-making responds to a contest of rival advocacy coalitions:

> [P]olicy is actually made not by a policy maker but by interaction among a plurality of partisans. Each participant in the interaction ... needs information specialised to his [or her] partisan role in it. ...
>
> It would not follow that a [practitioner of professional social inquiry] should bias his [or her] results to suit an audience, but it would seem to follow that in performing any given research he [or she] could usefully work for one of a variety of possible audiences and take [an] orientation not from an implicitly postulated 'the' public interest, as is common, but from one of the various explicitly recognized partisan interests each playing its role in the resolution of the policy conflict. (Lindblom and Cohen, 1979: 64–5)

At the same time, the authors clearly were not just arguing for the minimal impact of the social sciences, stressing instead the often key role of PSI compared with any other knowledge framework. PSI will normally succeed in displacing less adequate 'ordinary knowledge', without necessarily having the capacity to replace it in a way that rivals the prestige or frequent high levels of control-effectiveness achieved by many STEM disciplines:

> [E]ven if policy makers do not turn to PSI in many of the ordinarily expected ways – for specific data, hypotheses, evidence, or policy evaluation – they may take the whole organizing framework or perspective for their work from academic social science. It may be decisive though not authoritative. (Lindblom and Cohen, 1979: 79)

These realism views undoubtedly gained a lot of traction during the 1980s and '90s when neutralist social science research conceptions (emphasizing long-run, longitudinal studies and 'pilot before implementation' advice) were overwhelmed and displaced by a wave of 'best practice' research in liberal democracies swinging to the political right, with many authors promising not just to describe the world but to change it. The strongly ideological advance of Thatcherism, Reaganism and later the 'Washington consensus' in international development were all driven by eclectic collations of multiple possible prescriptions, all derived from first principles economics (or market-analogy or public choice thinking). They were then speedily applied in joined-up ways where solutions that worked in very different contexts were appropriated and pooled into complete handbooks for economic or public sector change. This contrasted with the long-time horizons and siloed nature of academic work, about which Ansoff (1986: 20–21) remarked:

> In today's world of 'big science', research is costly and no longer has a uniformly beneficial impact. The ethic of basic research for the sake of research is being challenged on the basis of both economic and social relevance. On the level of applied research there is the additional challenge of the utility of projects which consume large amounts of money but produce no visible benefits for society ... Perhaps the most dramatic example of the gap between researchers' choices and

society's needs is in the fact that most research is being done from the vantage point of single disciplines, whereas the key social problems are multi-disciplinary.

The characteristic form of 'best practice research' united a quasi-paradigm of top-level guiding themes and ideas, allied with swarms of flexibly developed, and constantly evolving detailed practices that could be quickly deployed in specific situations (Dunleavy and Margetts, 2013). For the new public management (NPM) credo that dominated western democracies' public administration for a quarter of a century, the top themes were disaggregation (splitting up large hierarchies into smaller organizations), competition (removing monopoly rights to production for in-house producers) and incentivization (creating specific pecuniary incentives for staff to meet public interest objectives) (Dunleavy et al., 2006a and 2006b). Dozens of different specific strategies (such as privatization, outsourcing, quasi-markets, purchaser–provider separation, introducing private finance and performance-related pay) were then linked to a rolling programme of change that jumped across national and even continental boundaries to achieve a cumulative, global impact.

In turn the failure and crises of these ambitious reformist programmes, especially new public management in the government sector (Dunleavy et al., 2006a and 2006b), cast a cloud over best practice research. Their vulnerability was in turn exploited by a new drive from social science 'imperialists' to push a strengthened model of professional social inquiry, now founded on randomized control trials (RCTs), using medical research templates and approaches. For instance, in 2013 the UK government solemnly established new 'What Works' centres in various aspects of welfare state policy, founded in part on the model of the National Institute for Health and Care Excellence (NICE).

It seems likely that for the foreseeable future there will be permanent oscillations in western liberal democracies around a three-pole dialectic of:

- conventional social science expansionism ('evidence-base everything, use universal RCTs, emulate STEM discipline claims') versus
- best practice research ('do quick and dirty research strongly influenced by theories/ideologies, implement fast, and learn by doing') versus
- pluralist 'realism' accounts of policy processes ('do limited partial research to help one advocacy coalition or another', and 'speak truth to power', remaining aware of the permanent and inherent limits of professional social inquiry).

Conclusions

Between a third and two fifths of all the university research (and much of the wider professional, government and business research) being undertaken in advanced industrial societies takes place in social science subjects. In addition to those working directly in the social sciences, many professional people are working in jobs where they either produce social science research themselves, or else 'translate' it back to business, government departments and public sector agencies, and a wide range of civil society organizations. (We look in more detail at the role of translation later on in Chapter 9.) The scale of this knowledge-intensive industry is substantial.

In this chapter we have established the boundaries of the social sciences as a discipline group and defined the subjects that are wholly included and the key overlap areas with the STEM and humanities subject groupings. We have also argued that the old oppositions or contrasts between the 'physical' or 'natural' sciences and the 'social' sciences have little or no contemporary relevance. The social sciences are concentrated in the fields of human-dominated and human-influenced systems, but so too are many of the most salient modern STEM disciplines, such as medicine, engineering, and information and computer sciences – in all of which it is crucial to understand in depth how human behaviour conditions the operations and risks of physical science interventions and strategies. A huge range of methods and approaches, ranging from randomized control trials, through systematic review, most core statistical methods, key types of algorithms, big data analytics, and systematic qualitative or text-based research are appropriately deployed across both STEM disciplines and the social sciences. Neither in terms of their subject matter, nor in terms of their methods, are the social sciences necessarily any less quantitative or 'scientific' than STEM counterparts. There have been many key historic limitations of the social sciences, especially the past paucity of data, restriction to survey-based methods, long time periods for research, highly siloed discipline structures and exceptionally poor communication to lay audiences. But as we explore later in the book many of these problems are now being rapidly addressed and eroded by shifts to a digital social science where research is 'shorter, better, faster, free' (Dunleavy and Tinkler, 2014).

Yet a negative or impoverished impression of the external impacts of the social sciences has been created over many decades by misleading efforts to read across what normal science looks like from STEM-specific archetypes, and by crudely formulated notions of what real influence would entail. Some of the worst false standards of influence have also been propagated by hyper rationalist social scientists themselves telling 'fairy tales of influence' to governments or funders in efforts to secure more research support. And some of the most pessimistic estimates of influence have been made by observers who seem to believe in 'imperialist' visions of a caste of Platonic social science guardians guiding 'blank slate' decision-makers in simplistic ways on what they ought to do.

The rest of this volume undertakes the difficult work of redressing this imbalanced and badly-awry view of the social sciences, seeking to replace it with an integrated but also detailed and articulated view of how the whole discipline grouping operates. We set out the role that university research already plays, and yet might play, in the co-operative guidance of complex multi-causal social systems. The role of academic scholarship and science will necessarily be only a small component in the way that economic, social and political developments evolve – but it has already been of immense significance, and can be more so for the future. We begin in Part I by etching a quick pen portrait of how the modern social sciences function as academic professions, and how the work of individual researchers and scholars gets to be known and picked up outside higher education itself.

PART I

How Academics Achieve External Impacts

> It is too common for those who have been bred to scholastic professions, and passed much of their time in academies where nothing but learning confers honours, to disregard every other qualification, and to imagine that they shall find mankind ready to pay homage to their knowledge, and to crowd about them for instruction.
>
> *Samuel Johnson*[1]

> The delicate thing about the university is that it has a mixed character, that it is suspended between its position in the eternal world, with all its corruption and evils and cruelties, and the splendid world of our imagination.
>
> *Richard Hofstadter*[2]

The science fiction novel, *Anathem*, by Neal Stephenson (2008), posits a future world where people who want to do intellectual or scientific work have to enter a completely closed but secular 'monastery' for fixed periods (of 10, 100 or 1,000 years), taking a vow of poverty so that their only personal possessions are a habit, a belt and a lamp, in exchange for access to life-lengthening secrets. Every ten years, the monasteries open to exchange information with the parent society, to allow inmates to leave and to let new entrants in. The back story explaining this system is a history of earlier scientists coming up with disruptive discoveries and technological changes, while other scholars undermined religions and cultures, and predicted too accurately the next turns in societal developments. These disruptions and interventions sparked violent populist backlashes, culminating in repeated sustained efforts by mobs or rebels to hunt down and kill all intellectuals and to burn down their universities. In Stephenson's brilliantly realized fable, the limited and set opening periods are key times when a negotiated set of innovations can reach society, with 'monastery' leaders carefully weighing up what information the local wealth and power holders can tolerate or accommodate.

Scholars and scientists will smile wryly at the apt elements of Stephenson's book; such as the reasons why poverty and powerlessness must be an inevitable concomitant to learning; the enormously long apprenticeship periods and arduous discipline involved in acquiring knowledge; the incestuous community life of the 'monasteries'; or the outsiders' irrational suspicions of and disdain for intellectuals. But most modern academics will jib at the idea that it is the dangerousness – the disruptive potential of new technologies and knowledge – that both constantly threatens a populist backlash to defend the status quo, and explains the extraordinary institutional set-up that Stephenson posits as essential to regulate intellectuals' impacts on society.

---

[1] Samuel Johnson, Rambler #137 (1751) quoted in Bate and Strauss (1968: 363).

[2] Quote from a public address made on 4 June 1968, in the Cathedral Church of St. John the Divine at Columbia University, where Mr. Hofstadter was De Witt Clinton Professor of American History.

The prevalent pessimism of academia instead laments the extent to which worthwhile knowledge goes unrecognized and ignored beyond the narrow boundaries of a particular discipline (or even sub-discipline). Yet track this pessimism back to its source and (as we noted in Section 1.3) it normally turns out to be rooted in a deeply improbable or idealistic conception of what a society run in an academically-influenced or evidence-based way would look like. Not for the first time, sometimes science fiction seems to do better than social scientists in accurately appreciating the long run dynamics of civilizational advance.

A key foundation for this over-pessimism has been a lack of knowledge about how academic and scientific disciplines actually work, a deficit that is far worse for social sciences than it is for the more intensively researched STEM subjects. We have important sub-disciplines now covering the history of STEM disciplines and of social science, and relatively well developed pictures of how major research figures and schools of thought link one to another. But we were surprised in undertaking this research, how little is known about the concrete activities of social science professions, and how fragmented is the existing evidence base about what social scientists actually do and how they are recognized beyond universities themselves.

Our task in this Part is to sketch out a more helpful and accurate picture, largely drawing on an extensive dataset comparison of several hundred social scientists, matched against a further set of academics and researchers in some core STEM disciplines. Chapter 2 sets the scene by establishing some key facts about first the academic impacts of social scientists and, second, their external recognition and 'occasions of influence'. It seems likely that there will be some connections between the academic influence of researchers and their external recognition, but there are rival hypotheses about how this linkage works. Our main focus is to show in detail the discipline group, but where feasible we seek to illuminate some of the variations between disciplines also. Multiple causal factors drive both the academic and external influence of social scientists, and in Chapter 3 we seek to unpick and weight them using a multi-variate regression approach. As might be expected, the story that emerges is not the simple 'difference that makes the difference' that perhaps government decision-makers or business executives might want to hear. Chapter 4 explores this inherent complexity in the relationship between factors that determine impact and the nature of impact itself. We deploy a qualitative comparative analysis (QCA) framework in order to look at this relationship more closely for 15 'high-impact' case-study academics. In doing so, we do push back a good deal the frontiers of what was previously known, creating a solid foundation for the more granular analysis of interactions between external 'clients' and university researchers in Parts II and III.

2

Social scientists' pathways to impact

Let no one say that I have said nothing new ... the arrangement of the subject is new. When we play tennis, we both play with the same ball, but one of us places it better.

Blaise Pascal[3]

A lot of learning can be a little thing.

Spike Milligan[4]

During this research, dozens of well-informed and experienced academics explained to us how they perceived the dynamics of external influence in their sub-field, and two broad narratives regularly emerged. The first perspective was that because it takes a lot of time and effort to 'translate' academic work for audiences outside higher education, and even more to get it noticed or accepted by significant decision-makers, this was increasingly a specialized academic role. The most successful social scientists in getting research taken up are thus those who already specialize in applied work, have established networks of contacts, and for whom securing external influence is more salient than for others. In this view there need be little correlation between the quality of an academic's work within higher education and their external reputation. Some of the most externally prominent researchers may only ever make incremental academic contributions, but they may be great networkers, fluent communicators, 'pop academics', effective grants entrepreneurs, or successful consultants. By contrast, the most research-committed academics will focus relentlessly on pushing back the frontiers of knowledge, tackling esoteric issues of theory or complex methods that cannot be easily explained to non-experts. Since this storyline clearly does not accommodate all prominent academics, its exponents have mostly added a coda, that a scattering of other researchers will regularly 'get lucky' when their work happens to strike a chord with the public, media or elites in the ever-shifting trajectory of societal development.

The second perspective was that in any discipline or institution the same sets of people tend to be more efficient and effective than their colleagues, across all aspects. Since the fundamental job of social scientists is to generate research,

---

[3] Pascal (1958).
[4] Milligan (2003).

excellent researchers tend to have high academic reputations. And as they become senior figures they also become most visible outside the confines of the discipline itself. Governments or businesses want experts as advisors, and journalists want guidance from authoritative sources who 'know their stuff', so they all naturally turn to the most academically prominent people for advice or inputs. A bit of a personality filter operates at this stage, since some academics are not interested in being helpful. Others are keen to get involved but turn out to be poor communicators or nervous advisors, without the personal confidence needed to adapt well in unfamiliar environments. These successful researchers never get into, or get filtered out of, external impact networks, but they are a minority. Most high-flying academics are talented and personable enough to overcome this threshold, and especially later in their careers they often have managerial experience within universities that helps them adapt well to external requests. In this view then there should be a strong overall correlation between the quality and frequency of researchers' publications, academic ranks and reputation and their external visibility and persuasiveness.

To evaluate these alternative hypotheses we need to look closely at the full range of things that social science academics and researchers do across different stages of their careers. Conventionally universities have summed these up under headings like research (measured essentially via publications and grants), teaching students (carefully equalized by departments as an aspect of collegiality), and administration (for their department or university). Increasingly now 'dissemination and impact' activities constitute an important pole of activity for senior academics as well, since in the UK research funders require formal reporting of external impacts achieved and efforts to communicate research to wider audiences. The main UK agency supporting general research, the Higher Education Funding Council for England (HEFCE) now measures impacts periodically (via the REF) and allocates a fifth of all research monies accordingly.

To help assess how these different activities fit together we created a dataset of 270 social scientists, spanning across 12 main disciplines, and selected in a quota sample manner. To provide a point of comparison we also added to the dataset information on 100 academics from five STEM disciplines. For all groups we sought to assemble and code comprehensive information on each researcher's academic record and their external visibility or activities outside the university sector itself. Specifically we collected information on *academic outputs*, covering all traditional academic publications such as peer-reviewed articles, books and book chapters, working papers, conference presentations, and so on; and on *external outputs*, covering all activities and publications carried out by the researcher for audiences or clients outside academia, such as government agencies, businesses, press and media, civil society organizations, and the public at large. For each researcher in the dataset, we then compiled a fine-grained picture of their *external visibility*, involving hundreds of hours of manual searching, consulting university and professional sources, and sifting and coding aspects of their electronic footprint in digital databases. Full details of the coding frameworks and of the information collected are given in a Research Design and Methods Report available via the *Impact of Social Sciences* blog[5], and we also outline

---

[5] Available to download from the LSE *Impact of Social Sciences* blog – http://blogs.lse.ac.uk/impactof-socialsciences/book. We also list this in the Bibliography at Bastow et al. (2014).

other aspects at different points in the rest of this chapter where they are relevant. Indeed the dataset plays a key foundational role throughout the book as a means of characterizing the scale and patterns of outputs and visibility of researchers, and we return to it for detailed insights and lines of inquiry in the later Parts of the book.

We begin by looking at our researchers' strictly academic profiles, the patterns of outputs and the academic-influence characteristics of social science as a disciplinary group.

2.1 The academic impacts of social science researchers

Q: What is the task of all higher education?
A: To turn men [or women] into machines.
Q: What are the means?
A: Man must learn to be bored.

    Friedrich Nietzsche[6]

It is perfectly obvious that in any decent occupation (such as bricklaying or writing books) there are only two ways (in any special sense) of succeeding. One is by doing very good work, the other is by cheating.

    G. K. Chesterton[7]

An impact created by an academic or researcher is 'an auditable or recordable occasion of influence'. Within academia itself, the central form of such influence is for author B to cite an earlier author A's work, which implies that B has read the work and found it valuable in some respect. Outsiders often object at this point that a citation might be critical or hostile, but in fact this is rare. Academics very seldom cite other work that does not meet high professional standards or seems incorrect – they just ignore it. Consequently, 'the life blood of most academic influence is producing publications that get picked up and cited by other researchers and scholars' (Dunleavy and Tinkler, 2014). They argue that citations have eight key functions including: formally acknowledging sources and assumptions; affirming the author's presence and competence in an 'advanced conversation'; showing that arguments are evidence-based and cumulative; demonstrating consistency with all empirical results; affirming collegiality and acknowledging precedence and previous work; and providing a sub-structure of links that allow readers to recreate and engage with the author's own knowledge-development (Dunleavy and Tinkler, 2014). Hence we focus chiefly here on publications and their citations by others as the key measure of researchers' influence on other academics.

To assess academic outputs we searched on Google Scholar for all the books, monographs, journal articles, chapters in edited books, research papers, working papers and conference papers written by the researchers and academics included in

---

[6] Kaufmann (1954: 532).

[7] Chesterton (1915).

our dataset, focusing attention on a fixed period of five calendar years from 2004 to 2009. (Unfortunately our study period pre-dated the widespread development of academic blogging in the UK. We also did not search explicitly for information on 'non-standard' outputs (such as videos, podcasts etc.), but any instances of all these type of works that left some form of electronic footprint would be included under 'other' outputs). We cross-checked this information against established databases such as the ISI Web of Science (WoS) (which covers only journal articles for this period), and against the web pages or personal CVs of the researchers involved (where these were available, which surprisingly often they were not). For each publication, we collected the number of times that it had been cited according to Google Scholar, which is by far the most inclusive and comprehensive database covering the social sciences. Essentially in this period WoS has an internal coverage rate for the social sciences of only 30 to 44 per cent. (This internal coverage figure measures the percentage of articles cited by WoS articles that are also included in the database.) This range is far too low to make it useful. Google Scholar's internal coverage rate, by contrast, is around 95 to 98 per cent for social science disciplines, making it a far better resource for all our disciplines (see Dunleavy and Tinkler, 2014).

Academic articles published in peer-reviewed journals are far and away the most numerous and the most important forms of publication across the social sciences. The core elements of promotion cases and REF submissions, social science articles are typically lengthy (8,000 to 10,000 words), exceptionally carefully written, and often laden with intensive formulae, quantitative data or difficult language and complex theories. Processes and timescales of peer review vary a lot across disciplines, and between the premier journals and more middle range or marginal outlets. The very best journals may take three months from submission to a decision about publication, but most take at least six months and many a good deal more than that. Often papers are not accepted outright but authors instead get a light 'revise and resubmit' verdict, and sometimes a 'heavy R and R' that is basically 'inclined to reject but we might look again if it was drastically improved' verdict. All this takes time, after which the paper goes into a queue for production that is rarely less than six months, and may stretch to a year or more. Even when published electronically and available online a paper may well queue for a further period of six months to a year before being included in a specific issue of a journal, a stage that is still very important in the least electronically-orientated disciplines (such as political science). In the most technical fields, such as economics, the timeline from submission to publication may well take three and a half years with one journal. But of course, many papers are rejected and then have to be extensively revised and submitted all over again to other journals before being eventually accepted and published, lengthening the process even more.

Journal articles have increased and become more salient in all social sciences over time for various reasons. They allow assessors in government audit exercises (like the REF in the UK and ERA (Excellence in Research for Australia)), and non-experts on university promotion or review committees, to rely on the proxy measure of journal reputation in order to assess the 'quality' of a complex piece of work that they could not otherwise understand. This approach was crystallized for decades by the now thoroughly discredited journal impact factor (JIF), which is

Figure 2.1   Estimated average number of peer-reviewed articles published per year by UK-based social scientists, by discipline

	Articles per year per academic	Extrapolated total articles published per year per subject
Geography	2.2	2,310
Economics	2.0	5,950
Psychology	1.6	3,020
Philosophy	1.6	1,000
Business and Management	1.2	6,000
Media studies	1.2	2,670
Anthropology	1.2	900
Political Science and IR	1.0	2,190
Social Policy	1.0	1,910
Law	1.0	1,230
History	1.0	950
Sociology	0.9	2,960
Total Social Sciences	*1.7*	*31,090*

Source: LSE PPG dataset. Extrapolation from our analysis of HESA data, 2010–11.

still universally publicized by journal publishers despite being criticized over many years (Brembs, 2011; Brembs et al., 2013), and being rejected in 2012 by the San Francisco Declaration (DORA, 2012). Although relying on JIFs has now been formally banned in the UK and Australian audit exercises, the underlying pressures for this kind of shorthand judgement are still strong (Huang, 2012). Finally, we should note that the conventional JIF method of assessing citations inherited from STEM subjects focuses on how often papers have been cited in the last two years; but outside of perhaps economics, geography and psychology such a timeline is way too short for assessing the reception of social science outputs. We instead look across five years wherever possible to track those outputs that elicit greater or less response from other members of the discipline or neighbouring disciplines.

Looking across the 270 social science researchers included in our dataset, the highest number of articles published by any single author in our five-year period was 49 (just under 10 per year) by a highly prolific professor of anthropology. The second rank was taken by a professor of economics with a still very exceptional 32 articles. The mean number of papers for our researchers as a whole was 8.5 over five years, however. Figure 2.1 shows the average number of articles published per year by these academics across disciplines. Geographers and economists were the most prolific, followed by psychologists and philosophers. The most qualitative (but also the more book-orientated) social sciences come at the bottom of the table with half the top rates. Extrapolating these rates across all our disciplines, and scaling up for the appropriate number of academics in each (discussed in section 1.2 above), suggests that over 31,000 publications a year are generated by the UK social sciences, of which over a third are in the two top subjects, business and management, and economics, each on around 6,000 outputs. The second echelon disciplines on 2,000 to 3,000 outputs each include sociology, media studies, geography, political science and then social policy, with the remaining subjects around half their sizes.

Books remain important forms of publications in the more qualitative social sciences. They are typically around eight times as long as articles (say, 70,000 words as opposed to 9,000 word articles), and so normally take a much longer time to produce. Figure 2.2 shows that researchers in media studies and philosophy on average published a book in less than five years, and in six years in sociology, social policy and history. In many of these disciplines an expectation is still prevalent that a book is needed for promotion to full professor or Reader (Associate Professor) rank. In our dataset the most prolific academic in terms of book publishing was a professor of philosophy with ten books during the five-year period. By contrast, academics in our dataset in the bottom disciplines published books only every ten years. Books here may often be limited to textbooks, 'popular social science', the occasional summation of a research career by a distinguished researcher, and rare monographs with more extensive appeal. In terms of the extrapolated numbers of authored books published, sociology and media studies lead the ranking, followed by business studies and social policy.

The status and efficacy of book publishing has increasingly been challenged in the digital era because Google Scholar and other systems measure indices only from bibliographies, and identify by titles only. So the multiple chapters in a complete book count as only one citation when referenced by another author, whereas they would count as several different source cites if spread across multiple articles or chapters. Similarly the REF audit process still counts a book as only one output of the four that British academics must submit for this assessment every five years. Assessing books is also more difficult for rushed or inexpert audit panels or university committees, since they are more *sui generis* in character. For books the only proxy quality index (also probably widely if illegitimately used by members of audit panels and university committees) is the prestige of the publisher, with the Oxbridge or Harvard university presses at the top, followed by other university presses, then established commercial publishers, and last newer publishers.

Paper books also quickly became uncompetitive in the digital era up to 2013, because it was difficult to use them for teaching in a period when students expected to find all the readings needed for a course easily available to them via electronic course learning systems (like Moodle or Blackboard) – which makes digital access feasible for all journals now but not paper books (Dunleavy, 2012). Since then the increase in digital titles (and less restrictive publisher formats for digital books) have perhaps begun to redress this problem. After lengthy legal problems, Google Books also offers far greater possibilities for finding out about books, and viewing many of them either in full text or in 'snippet' or sample chapter mode, which has certainly helped professional academics' search processes.

Figure 2.2   Estimated average number of books and book chapters published per year by UK-based social scientists, by discipline

Books	Books per year per academic	Extrapolated annual books published per subject	Edited books and chapters	Edited books or chapters per year per academic	Extrapolated annual chapter/ edited books published per subject
Media Studies	0.23	510	Philosophy	0.9	540
Philosophy	0.23	150	Geography	0.5	480
Sociology	0.17	520	Sociology	0.3	1,010
Social Policy	0.17	320	Media studies	0.3	750
History	0.16	150	Social policy	0.3	470
Law	0.12	150	Law	0.3	410
Economics	0.1	310	History	0.3	320
Geography	0.1	110	Business and management	0.2	940
Business and Management	0.09	450	Political science and IR	0.2	330
Political Science and International Relations	0.09	200	Anthropology	0.2	170
Psychology	0.08	140	Economics	0.1	380
Anthropology	0.04	40	Psychology	0.1	200
Total Social Sciences		*3,050*	*Total Social Sciences*		*6,000*

Source: LSE PPG dataset. Extrapolation from our analysis of HESA data, 2010–11.

Book chapters and edited books to some extent follow the books pattern, playing an important role in sociology, media studies and social policy. But Figure 2.2 shows that there are individual discipline effects as well. Philosophers like books, but they love chapters in books or edited collections, publishing one of these outputs almost once a year. Geographers are also five times more likely to use these formats than they are to publish books, and historians and academic lawyers also are active in these ways. By contrast, in economics and psychology, chapter outputs are relatively rare. In terms of the extrapolated numbers of chapters and edited books, sociology leads our listing, followed by business and management and media studies, and then the remaining higher book use disciplines noted above.

The value of chapters in books, and of edited collections, has been questioned intensively in recent years. Chapters were so numerous and so untagged that they were for many years exceptionally hard to find or track. They had very low initial audiences compared to journal articles circulated in print form to many professional academics and publicized through email alerts. Unless a researcher could physically skim and handle an edited paper book in a bookshop or at an academic conference, they had practically no way of knowing that a chapter was there, or what its argument was. Even publishers' catalogues now rarely give complete titles and authors for chapters in edited books. Where Google Books allows some degree of access to contents, it is especially useful for edited books in finding out what different contributions cover. But Google Books indexes only book titles and authors, not chapter titles and authors – so you have to reach the volume itself first to access information on its component parts. Google Scholar does index chapters as separate elements, however, and so it has progressively remedied the neglect of book chapters in the older databases. With more authors now depositing green open access versions of their chapters in university repositories, more Scholar links now also lead to free full-text versions of chapters.

Chapters in edited books count individually in government audits of academic outputs, and are typically no longer than a journal article. But they are also especially hard for audit panels or non-experts on university committees to assess. The reputation of the publisher counts, as for books, and the academic credibility of the book's editor(s) and perhaps of other authors. Yet the quality of most collections cannot take proper account of these assessments, targeting (as they do) only one author and one chapter. So some academics (even in the most qualitative subjects) argue that edited collections are rarely as valuable as authored books, with some collections being uneven or too loosely edited or focused. There are some suggestions that they are also less commonly reviewed by journals.

Yet it is the accumulation of all these difficulties that really counts for their critics. As citation metrics began to become more important in academia, so the lesson for any remotely ambitious academic seemed to become plain – don't write chapters in books. After explaining how she valued the relative freedom of chapter writing, outside of the straight jacket of journal formats, psychologist Dorothy Bishop (2012) nonetheless concluded that in her own case they are clearly much less cited than empirical articles or review articles in journals. She concluded:

> [I]f you write a chapter for an edited book, you might as well write the paper and then bury it in a hole in the ground. Accessibility is the problem. However good your chapter is, if readers don't have access to the book, they won't find it. In the past, there was at least a faint hope that they may happen upon the book in a library, but these days, most of us don't bother with any articles that we can't download from the Internet.

The mixes of publication forms cited across disciplines gives another interesting perspective, different from the outputs data reviewed above. We look here at the extent to which different forms of publication by authors in our dataset were cited. Figure 2.3 shows clearly the predominance of journal articles being cited: across the discipline group they generally made up between half and two-thirds of all citations to our authors (and over four-fifths in psychology). We have arranged the disciplines in the declining importance of all kinds of book outputs (authored books, edited books and chapters). They accounted for nearly two-fifths of cites in philosophy, and over a quarter of cites in sociology, history and media studies, but

Figure 2.3 The relative importance of book outputs and journal articles in citations within each social science discipline

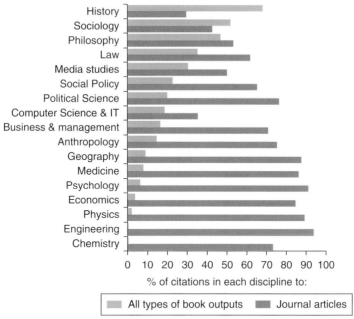

Source: LSE PPG dataset.

dropped to a tenth of cites or less in economics and psychology. In economics and psychology there were eight times as many citations of journal articles as there were of books, but in sociology and media studies the ratio was more like two to one. Disaggregating the books element here, Figure 2.4 arranges the disciplines in terms of the decreasing importance of citations of books, a ranking that does not differ all that radically for edited books, which are cited in a fairly standard way across most disciplines but are absent in economics and psychology. Edited collections are also more referenced where many cites are to chapters in books, along with history, law and anthropology – all mostly discursive subjects with relatively little presentation of quantitative information. However, the Figure clearly shows that chapters in books fluctuate sharply in their importance. They account for a quarter of all citations in philosophy, followed by sociology, media studies, history, law and geography. Book chapters are almost completely uncited in psychology and economics, and very little in business studies.

Patterns of citations can be assessed across all the social scientists in our dataset looking not just at the three main publication forms above but also including research papers, working papers, conference papers and other often important 'grey literature' sources included in Google Scholar's reach. Since 2009 the accuracy of this database has begun to increase as Google Scholar Citations allows academics to organize and keep a close watch on their citation profiles and counts. Tools such as Harzing's Perish or Publish software also allow academics to take an instant snapshot of all their career publications, and citation counts per output. So for each of our academics'

Figure 2.4   The relative importance of books, edited books and book chapters in citations in each social science discipline

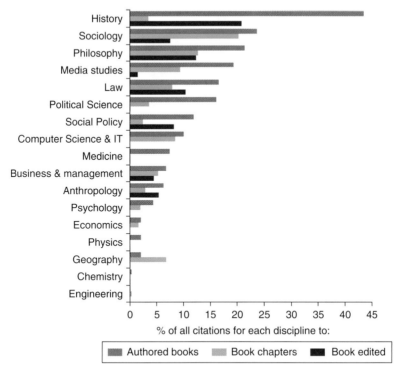

Source: LSE PPG dataset.

publications in the 2005–09 period, we were able to record and check a Google Scholar citation score. Given that our data was recorded in 2009–10, some publications had the advantage of having been published earlier in this period and therefore had more time to accumulate citations, but this is always the case and so the picture we draw is generally applicable.

Figure 2.5 shows separately the overall distribution of citations for academic articles, single or co-authored books, and edited books and book chapters. The vertical axis shows the logged citation level attained, and the horizontal axis shows how frequently that level of citation occurs, also logged. We use a log graph format in order to better see the patterns occurring at low numbers; without this transformation the 'floor' effect would render the key patterns invisible. The width of the dots graphically shows how many articles are included at each point on the chart. We found 560 journal articles with no citations at all (not shown in the graph), and 140 articles with only one citation. In our dataset, by the time we reach 20 citations, there are already only around 7 or 8 articles in total at this level. However, it is also apparent that there are a large bunch of individual papers on the vertical axis with between 50 and 140 cites each.

The pattern for *books* is broadly similar at a lower level of citations. We found 51 books without any citations in our publications dataset, either reflecting newness and

Figure 2.5   The logged citations per output charted against the frequency of occurrence for three kinds of social science outputs

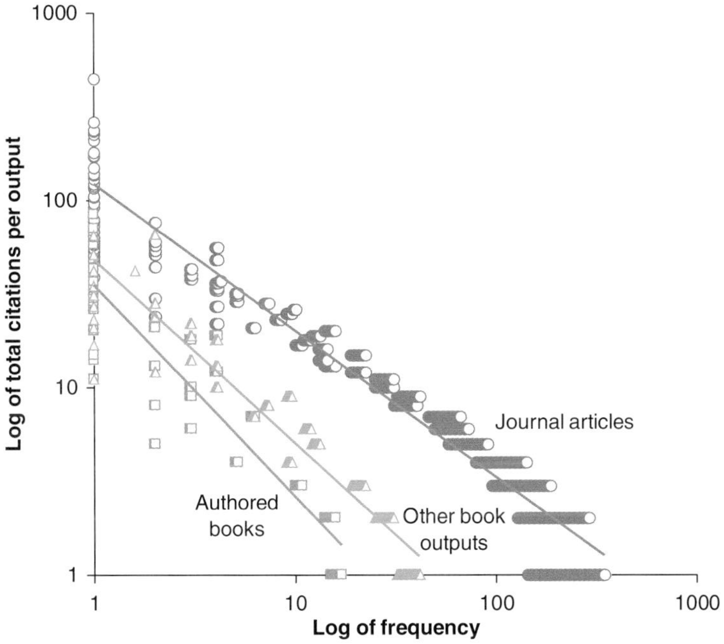

Source: LSE PPG dataset.

slow recognition, or failure to elicit a market. Perhaps surprisingly, given the criticisms of edited books reviewed above, we found that citations of edited books were somewhat greater than for authored books, perhaps because each of the component authors has an incentive to cite the book, or has different networks of contacts that somewhat expand the book's citation.

The distributions shown in Figure 2.5 seem consistent with that previously reported for citations of physics articles by Redner (1998 and 2005). His earlier study encompassed 15,000 papers, and he looked back on a long period from a safe distance (by which time they were sure to have been cited if they were ever going to be). Almost a quarter of physics papers were not cited by anyone (even the authors themselves) in the 20 years after publication. The pattern of physics article citations fitted a 'power law' expectation – with very few highly cited pieces and then many more low-cited articles.[8] In log charts the hallmark of a power law distribution is that it approximates a negatively sloping straight line. Figure 2.5 shows that this power law pattern applies in an approximate fashion to the three kinds of outputs here. Books and edited books have similar steep slopes, while the slope for articles is a somewhat gentler one.

---

[8] The power law occurs frequently in natural and human phenomena – for instance, there are very few high-power earthquakes, and a great many tiny ones. Similarly, there are few mega-cities but many more human settlements as the scale of settlement falls.

Across our dataset, eight articles and one book by social scientists gained more than 160 citations each. An article by a professor of geography achieved top position with 455 cites, and the other seven articles above 160 citations were spread across economics, geography, and psychology. Comparing top citations with the smaller number of STEM scientists included in our dataset (but not shown in Figure 2.5) the top cited piece achieved 413 citations and nine other articles amassed over 160 citations individually. For books, there are far fewer stellar-cited publications, the top social sciences book achieving 160 cites. It is perhaps surprising that fewer books rivalled the citation counts for top articles, but it is possible that the timescale for book cites may be longer, and their 'staying power' longer than for journal articles, an effect that our maximum five year period might not pick up.

The impact of co-authorship on citations is an important methodological question. In general social scientists tend to either single-author articles still (especially in the more qualitative disciplines) or to co-author with one, two or three colleagues. The pattern for the STEM disciplines is that almost all work is co-authored in teams from three to many authors, with some publications including 50+ authors. In the humanities, by contrast, 'lone wolf' publishing is the norm, and co-authoring is relatively rare. The essential problem is that current counting methods *may* tend to auto-increase the number of citations that co-authored pieces receive, and hence deform some of the data reviewed so far in artefactual ways (Lee and Bozeman, 2005; Wuchty et al., 2007). But should a single-author article receiving 10 citations in total be evaluated as more impactful or less impactful than a paper published by five authors and receiving 50 citations? If we attribute 50 citations to each co-author on the second piece, as most citation analysis systems now do (including Google Scholar Citations), are we rewarding multi-author work disproportionately? Because if we were just to take the average cites across all authors, both these papers rank equally. How far does this effect explain the greater citation rates for STEM disciplines and for the more quantitative social sciences (such as economics and psychology) recorded above?

A range of problems have been raised around how to interpret apparent co-authorship effects. For example, Wuchty et al. (2007) have shown that researchers who work in teams tend to produce more frequently cited research than lone authors and that this trend is visible across both STEM and social science disciplines. Perhaps the most straightforward explanation here might be that different co-authors will have varying networks of contacts or 'followers' likely to cite their work – for example spread across different universities and different countries. When they collaborate and the joint work is cited by these differing networks of colleagues there is a multiplier effect compared with that for single authored pieces, even after we allow for a lot of overlaps amongst co-author networks. It is also tricky to interpret findings showing that single authors are cited more than co-authored works, as Corley and Sabharwal (2010) found for top-cited publications in public administration in recent years. They attribute this finding to a possible transition period towards more collaborative working in this rather traditionalist sub-discipline. Senior academics have tended to work alone and their articles dominate the most-cited positions, whereas a younger generation of researchers are more collaborative but less well known at this stage.

We can try to get a first fix on this problem by comparing the citation rates of single-author publications only across disciplines in our dataset. Figure 2.6 shows that the

Figure 2.6   Average numbers of citations per single-author article, by discipline

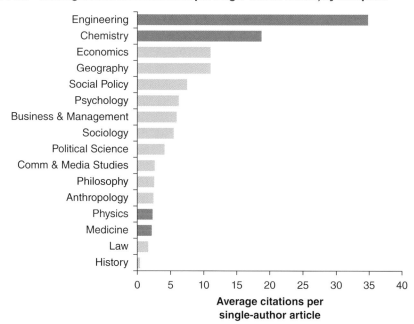

Source: LSE PPG dataset.

ranking of disciplines within the social sciences is pretty much the same as that reviewed earlier with economics and geography still top, but with psychology dropping down below social policy and at the same level as business. Comparing with our engineering or chemistry academics, the social sciences are clearly less cited, but not so with physics and medicine. However, it could be argued that single-authored pieces in both disciplines are unusual and not as mainstream as co-authored work (also perhaps true in psychology), so that not much can be read into these patterns.

A second step is to plot average citation rates against the average number of co-authors per publication in our dataset, controlling for disciplines. Figure 2.7 shows how STEM subjects cluster at comparatively high levels of co-authorship and average citation counts, fitting well with the view that they are more naturally collaborative subjects (Lariviere et al., 2006). Within the social science disciplines there seems to be a close relationship between co-authorship and citations. Adding more co-authors clearly seems to be associated with garnering more citations. However, economics outputs fit least well with this pattern, attracting far 'more' citations than they should do, given that their average number of co-authors is fairly low.

Looking at the equivalent graph for books and book chapters, Figure 2.8 shows a much less clear-cut relationship. For STEM subjects books and chapters are not well-referenced – with both chemistry and engineering near the bottom here – which may be a result of relatively few books being authored in these disciplines, apart from student textbooks that are rarely cited. By contrast, computer science/ IT books do well. For the social sciences, there are relatively low levels of co-authorship, as with academic articles, and there is only a gentle tendency for co-authored

Figure 2.7   Relationship between co-authorship on academic articles and the extent to which these articles are cited, by discipline

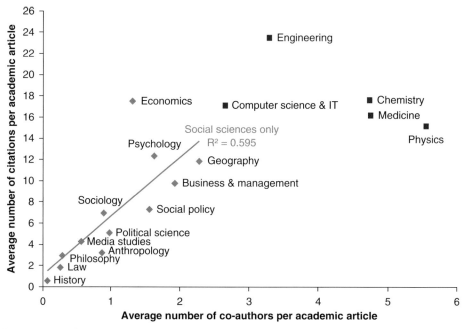

Source: LSE PPG dataset.

Figure 2.8   Relationship between co-authorship on books and book chapters and the extent to which these books or chapters are cited, by discipline

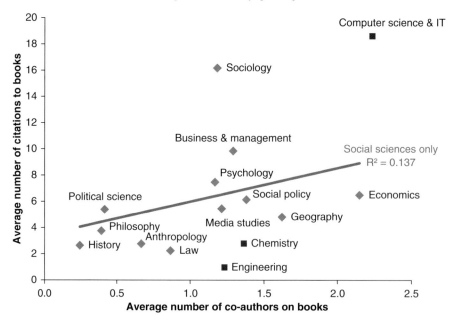

Source: LSE PPG dataset.

Figure 2.9   How the h-index is calculated

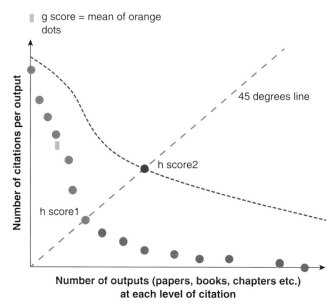

books to fare better in terms of citations. Sociology books and chapters are the main exception here, attracting high levels of cites while the average number of co-authors is only just over 1.2. Social science books in general receive low levels of average cites, rarely passing 20.

If more social scientists were to co-author articles and books, would this enhance the chances that their work will be cited? From the evidence we have reviewed, it is clear that co-authoring in the social sciences does seem to have positive effects that are not just due to citation counting systems. Yet it is also clear that there is more to co-authoring, teamwork levels and citations levels than just the co-author effect on its own. These aspects of behaviour are grounded in the nature of the discipline, to which both the ways in which researchers work together and the citation behaviours are related. None the less, it does seem clear that in cross-over areas with the human-ities, such as law and history, and more qualitative social sciences (such as political science or social policy) more co-authoring and team working are likely to lead to significant academic improvements (such as tackling more important or bigger-scale projects), as well as tending to improve citation rates.

'Inward' references and h-indexes provide a much longer-term perspective on how social science researchers get to be cited, and how their citations profiles develop over time. Here we move away from focusing only on our academics' publications during the 2005–09 period, and instead look at some key statistics for their citations across their whole careers. The h-index is the most widely used measure and Figure 2.9 shows how it is calculated. Essentially for each author we graph all their publications, with the vertical axis measuring the citations achieved by each article, book, chapter etc., and the horizontal axis showing the number of outputs achieving that level of cites. The orange and pink blobs show this profile for one author, and where the line of blobs cuts the 45 degree line is that person's h-index, as shown by h1 here.

Figure 2.10   The relation between h-index and 'inward' references to authors' work

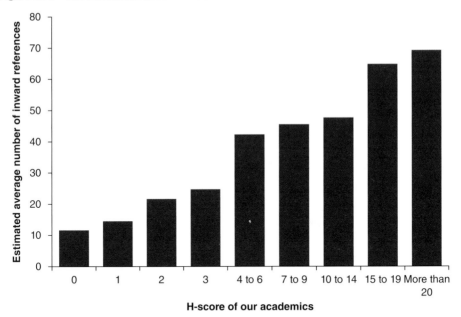

Source: LSE PPG dataset.

So an h-index of 10 shows that an author has ten pieces that have been cited at least ten times, an h-index of 30 shows that they have 30 items cited at least 30 times, and so on. Over an author's lifetime their cites will accumulate and hence this curve will move further out, for example to the blue dotted line shown here, and the h-index will expand to the h2 level shown. The average h-index across all our researchers and academics was 4. The highest h-index in our complete dataset was 33, achieved by a professor of chemistry. The highest social science h-index was 17, attained by an economist.

The g-index is the mean number of cites for all the author's outputs included in the h-index, that is, the average of all the orange blobs in Figure 2.10. Some analysts argue that this is a better measure than the h-index alone, because many authors have a few very highly cited outputs, which the h-index alone takes no account of, and hence under-values. Our source for the h-index and g-index was Harzing's 'Publish or Perish' software, which uses Google Scholar, the most inclusive database for social science.

To calculate inward references (from other authors) we entered the author's name in the advanced Google Scholar search function, but filtered out all self-citations. We looked at the first 100 relevant results only, and recorded who was referencing our authors and in what capacity. Well-established authors tended to reach the maximum 100 results, whereas references to other less well-established authors often ran out well before 100. Figure 2.10 shows that (as one would expect) there is a close relationship between author h-index and inward references.

Comparing citation rates in UK social science with other disciplines and countries helps set the academics and the research captured in our dataset in a wider context. The citation rates recorded here seem comparable with those found in other studies. According to Harzing (2010: 6): 'The average article in the social sciences and humanities is cited less than once a year'. And Figure 2.11 shows a comparison of citation rates across discipline groups (CSTS, 2007), computed by dividing the total citations for the group by the number of publications within it. Social science is clearly in an intermediate position, with citation rates half those of most STEM disciplines (and a lot less than this for medicine), but up to three times more than rates in the humanities.

Figure 2.11 Overall citation rates for the social sciences and other discipline groups, 2007

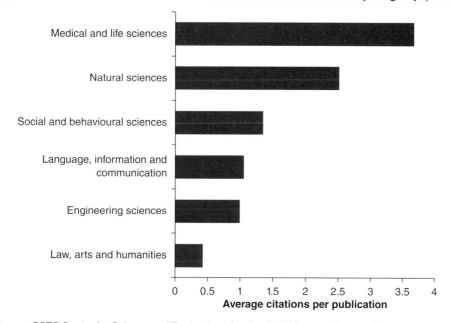

Source: CSTS Centre for Science and Technology Studies (2007), page 81 onwards.

Note: Data is calculated as an average of the 2003–06 values for citations per publication (excluding self-citations) for each sub-category in these six main disciplines groupings.

A recent analysis commissioned by the UK Department for Business, Innovation and Skills also compared the citation rates of social science publications across eight developed countries (RIN, 2009; BIS, 2011). Drawing solely on results in the Elsevier proprietary database (called Scopus), Figure 2.12 shows that on a crude measure of citation rates British research leads the pack, even edging slightly ahead of American work. The second column here uses a more sophisticated 'field-weighted' approach (which controls for the different mix of component disciplines across the countries compared). This change compresses the scores (with China the main beneficiary), but does not change the ranking. (The main caveat here must be that although Scopus includes some books, and hence is better for social sciences than the Thomson Reuters Web of Science, it remains highly orientated towards journal articles and has a far lower internal coverage rate than Google Scholar.)

In the period that we have completed this research there has been a rapid growth of interest in alternative ways of measuring the scale of the academic influence

Figure 2.12   Estimated citation impact of articles in the social sciences, by country

	Citations per article	Field-weighted citation impact
UK	2.42	1.15
US	2.25	1.05
Canada	2.20	1.05
Italy	1.64	0.98
Germany	1.68	0.93
Japan	1.12	0.73
France	1.10	0.66
China	0.75	0.58

Source: BIS (2011).

Note: Field-weighted citations account for the inherent differences in citation practices between fields and are preferable to citation counts or citations per article indicators for assessing research performance across countries of different size or research field focus.

achieved by researchers and by publications, so called 'altmetrics'. For instance, instead of just counting citations (which take a long time to appear and represent a heavy process of filtering) we might look at: views of a blog; the circulation of pre-publication document forms; downloads of a PDF; the extent to which outputs are 'liked' on Facebook or retweeted on Twitter; how many comments were left on blogs; and how the users of social media or open access journal sites directly evaluated an output, using the feedback mechanisms built into the new 'post-publication peer review' systems, notably developed by the Plos One journal. However, in our study period (2004–09), altmetrics were not in use in the social sciences, and social media were only just developing. So these elements were not included in our methods, which is an important limitation. However, using Google Scholar extensively meant that we could comprehensively track publications like working, research and conference papers, and the early academically-recognized blogs.

2.2 The external impacts of researchers

> Every man [or woman], from the highest to the lowest station, ought to warm [their] heart and animate [their] endeavours with the hopes of being useful to the world, by advancing the art which it is [their] lot to exercise; and for that end he [or she] must necessarily consider the whole extent of its application, and the whole weight of its importance.
>
> *Samuel Johnson* [9]

When academics and researchers influence actors beyond the higher education sector itself, charting their influence becomes undeniably more difficult. None the less, we

---

[9] Samuel Johnson, Rambler #9 (1750) quoted in Bate and Strauss (1968).

continue to approach this external impact as 'an auditable or recordable occasion of influence', meaning that we have to establish that a *potential* for influence from research on external audiences occurred, in a way for which evidence exists. This is a deliberately minimalist or first-stage approach. An occasion of influence arises when we can show that an outside decision-maker or actor was in contact with and aware of academic work or of research. But we go no further than that up the causal chain. The analogy is with showing that someone has viewed a TV programme or read an item in a newspaper. In these cases, as for academic work, we cannot go further in construing (for instance) whether the reader or viewer agreed with what they saw, let alone acted upon it, let alone acted solely or decisively upon it. We are concerned only with the first step on this causal path. To do more is methodologically infeasible in the inherently complex, multi-causal environments of action in Johnson's 'wide world' (Dunleavy and Tinkler, 2014).

In thinking about how social science disciplines achieve first-stage visibility with external audiences in business, government, public policy and civil society (including organizations located overseas) it is useful to compare social scientists and STEM scientists. We look here at how each group of researchers is visible in the world outside of academia, and the channels through which their expertise and research filters into wider use. Our methods stressed looking for a 'digital footprint' first, and then following up in detail on each academic or researcher studied.

Using full Google (i.e., *not* Scholar), we systematically searched for each researcher and built up a picture of external references made to them. We typed in each person's full name (using exact text restrictions), and worked through the first 200 relevant results, coding each result according to the type of reference and where we found it. We distinguished between different types of domain, excluding the researcher's own home institution, but encompassing the website domains of other traditional academic or university organizations, more intermediate or 'mediating' organizations, and external or non-academic organizations. For common names (for example, 'Joan Smith') we supplemented this with the name of the academic's institution or their discipline. In addition to this, we strengthened our picture of external visibility of each academic by carrying out supplementary searches. These included: using the Nexis and Factiva databases to search visibility in UK and overseas press and media; using limited-domain Google search to assess the visibility of researchers in specific domains such as 'gov.uk'; and making an assessment of whether our academics were active in social media (e.g., had they used Facebook, Twitter or LinkedIn by the end of the study period). For the more 'visible' academics, we would quickly reach our limit of 200 relevant results, and then stop the search. For less visible academics, we recorded total external references short of the 200 limit (often a long way short).

Inherently Google arranges its search results in line with its page-algorithm, grouping the most used or popular references at the start of the search, auto-eliminating duplicate pages (and we eliminated a few more in coding), and arranging references in a rank order. We were interested to see what proportion of the 200 or fewer wider web references were found on websites traditionally forming part of the academic or university realm. What proportion were we finding on the websites of media or other organizations operating at the impacts interface or in mediating roles with wider society? And what proportion were we finding on the websites of 'end user' organizations, such as government bodies, civil society and charity organisations, and in the private sector.

Figure 2.13 shows the comparative footprint of academics' visibility in the social sciences and in the four STEM disciplines included in our dataset (chemistry, physics, medicine and computer science/IT). At the bottom of the display, three fifths of all references to social scientists occur on websites in the 'traditional academic' realm including other university websites, academic publishers' websites, and those of institutional and online libraries. It would be a mistake to conclude that all these references have no relevance for assessing external impacts, however. Many activities in academic-focused organizations involve disseminating and marketing academic research. So some well-accessed references in university domains have some impact potential in the wider world.

The references linked to 'mediating' bodies in Figure 2.13 cover professional bodies, think tanks, general media and press, specialist media that are close to government, or trade journals in commercial sectors, learned societies and more focused academic networks, and independent research institutes and overt consultancies. (Less recognizable consultancies are included in business references below.) All of these organizations play key intermediary roles in translating and cumulating new work produced by social science researchers in forms helpful for potential end user organizations elsewhere in society. A further one fifth of references to academics are found on these organizations' web domains.

Finally, the top of the stack in Figure 2.13 records all references to our academics that we found on the websites of organizations in the government, civil society, and commercial sectors, with frequency declining in that order. One in five references to social science researchers, on average, can be found in these external sectors. Of course, as we show in section 2.3, there are some strong variations away from this 'average' footprint, depending on the circumstances and the field of research of the individual academic. For example, one social science researcher received 70 per cent of his references from end-users.

Comparing the average social science footprint with that for our five STEM disciplines, the key difference is that far more linkages to STEM academics run through intermediary organizations. Their pattern shows fewer references from 'traditional academic' web domains than in social science (half of references), but also fewer 'external society' direct references (one in six of the total). At first sight this may appear potentially contradictory. But given both the more heavily technical and often mathematical or data-heavy nature of STEM research findings, and the consequent superior development of science journalism and communication and public understanding of science' around STEM disciplines, it makes sense that intermediation is more important here. Professional and learned societies (ranging downwards from the Royal Society) play an important role in mediating and transferring knowledge from technical laboratories into more applied societal usage. We found only minimal similar activity by social science learned societies and professional bodies. Without this extended 'mediating middle', social scientists, by implication, must go more directly to potential users.

Figure 2.13   Average 'footprint' of social science and STEM academics, in terms of visibility of references to academics' work on websites

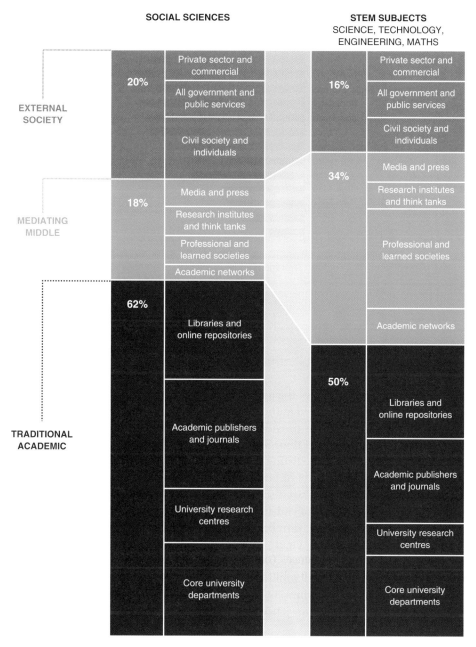

Source: LSE PPG dataset. Visualization by Amy Ricketts.

An interesting issue concerns how the patterns of social science (and STEM subjects) visibility varies at the level of individual disciplines. Our findings need to be treated cautiously here, since the number of individuals per discipline in our dataset

Figure 2.14   Average number of 'external society' mentions per researcher, by discipline

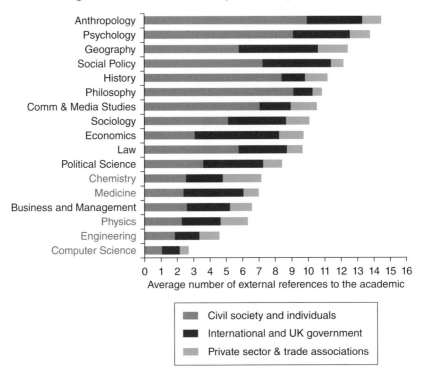

is restricted. Figure 2.14 shows the aggregate number of 'external society' mentions, with the social sciences grouped at the top of the pile, while the STEM subjects are at the bottom of the listing. This provides a more accentuated picture of social science being more externally focused than STEM. Psychology, social policy and anthropology feature near the top of the listing, but history and philosophy are also externally visible. Below the average level of law mentions, political science and business and management are the bottom two disciplines in the social sciences, despite their specialization on different types of end-user behaviour.

We now turn to the average number of references to academics in our dataset from intermediating organizations. Figure 2.15 shows that the order of the social science disciplines changes a little, with geography and philosophy both improving their ranking. But for our four STEM disciplines the shift here is more dramatic – chemistry jumps into the top four disciplines covered, and physics and medicine also come much further up the list. Computer sciences and engineering stayed close to the bottom however.

Even with the increased scale and power of Google's search algorithms, looking for linkages between researchers and organizations outside the university sector at the level of individual academics has some fairly clear limitations. No one method is going to give us a comprehensive picture of research impacts, and so we sought to triangulate this key aspect of our findings by using other data sources and methods. In 2012, we commissioned research from the consultancy firm SQW to

Figure 2.15   Average number of 'external society' and 'mediating middle' mentions per academic, by discipline

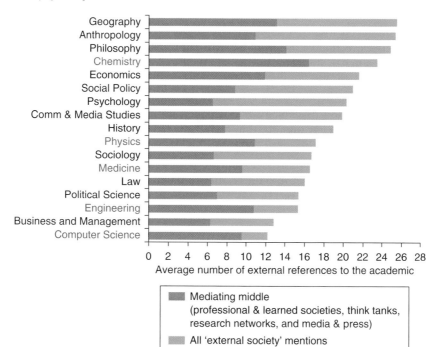

Average number of external references to the academic

Mediating middle
(professional & learned societies, think tanks, research networks, and media & press)

All 'external society' mentions

Source: LSE PPG dataset.

look at university department websites in fine-grained detail, recording any evidence of links between social science departments and 'external society' organizations. In essence this involved carefully trained coders spending a maximum of one hour on the websites of all the university departments with members included in our dataset. Coders recorded all references and links to external organizations found there. These were coded and weighted based on how major or substantial we judged the references and links to be. For example, we weighted mention of a large research programme funded by external bodies much more highly than, say, mention of external bodies attending a conference organized by the researchers in the department.

Starting from this whole-organization level then, Figure 2.16 shows the average number of website links from university departments to different types of external sector organizations, broken down by discipline. In this more institutional or corporate-focused picture two of the STEM disciplines we covered jumped to the top of the table and the other two were in the top half, reflecting the importance of direct business support both in cash terms and in terms of lab equipment, staff secondments and access to relevant data. Similarly, business and management departments are near the top, along with the more applicable social science disciplines of social policy, law and economics. Geography, psychology and anthropology drop to the middle of this listing, suggesting that their corporate applicability is less than suggested by the researcher-level data considered so far. Political science leads a group of more qualitative subjects at the bottom of this listing.

Across the social science disciplines as a whole, Figure 2.16 also shows that there were nearly twice as many links from department websites to government and public sector bodies as to private sector business or civil society organizations.

Only business and management departments showed strong linkages to the private sector, and only three other types of department showed moderate linkages – law, media studies and psychology. Social policy, anthropology and history showed strong links to civil society organizations, while medicine was the only STEM subject from our four with significant links here also. Social policy, economics, law and business showed higher than average links to public policy making organizations or government. We delve deeper into the relationship between social science and each of these three sectors in Chapters 5 to 7.

Figure 2.16   How university department websites referenced different types of 'external society' organizations, by discipline

	Government or public sector	Third sector or civil society	Private sector and commercial	Total external links
Engineering	10.1	4.6	14.1	28.9
Medicine	15.7	9.0	2.2	26.8
Social Policy	14.7	9.8	1.2	25.7
Business and Management	11.7	3.7	10.2	25.6
Law	12.3	5.5	5.1	22.9
Chemistry	7.0	2.3	13.3	22.7
Economics	14.5	4.4	2.1	21.1
Computer Science	7.5	1.7	5.3	14.5
Physics	4.8	0.0	9.2	14.0
Geography	8.9	2.2	2.5	13.5
Psychology	6.1	4.3	3.1	13.5
Anthropology	3.8	8.4	0.6	12.8
History	2.3	8.7	0.9	11.9
Political Science and International Relations	5.6	5.5	0.3	11.5
Sociology	7.3	2.5	0.6	10.4
Media Studies	4.2	1.5	4.1	9.7
Philosophy	2.3	2.9	0.7	5.8
Average for social science	**8.2**	**4.5**	**4.4**	**17.1**

Source: LSE PPG analysis of SQW research.

2.3 Profiling different types of academic and their impacts

> The naturalist has no desire to know the opinions or conjectures of the philosopher; the botanist looks upon the astronomer as a being unworthy of his regard; the lawyer scarcely hears the name of a physician without contempt; and he that is growing great and happy by electrifying a bottle, wonders how the world can be engaged by trifling prattle about war or peace.
>
> *Samuel Johnson*[10]

> A lot of science is unintelligible beyond its own specialist discipline and the evidential data that underpins scientific communications is not consistently made accessible, even to other scientists.
>
> *Royal Society*[11]

Academic researchers generate publications and achieve academic influence, and secure outside recognition and impacts in varied ways, depending on many factors, such as their discipline and sub-discipline areas of expertise, and their outlook, age, university position and career timeline. We noted in the introduction to this chapter two views of external impacts:

- The first view expects that external impacts are developed most by applied social scientists. There is only so much time in the day to excel in both academic and external arenas, and so researchers must choose to specialize either in traditional academic work, or in research that is more audience-focused. Those who focus proactively on doing more applied research and generating the most useable outputs (in the shape of consultancy or research reports for external clients) will be more recognized externally.
- The alternative account expects that the most academically prominent researchers will generally have more influence. The 'ecology of influence' amongst academics and university experts and mediating organizations means that government or business generally seek advice from top researchers rather than from less well-known figures. And the implied trade-off above may not apply – for instance, because applied work helps stimulate academic innovations, so academic and external influence can grow in tandem.

To round out the chapter we offer a preliminary assessment of both views – including the possibility that both have substance.

There are several possible approaches for tackling this question, and in Chapter 3 we take the road most travelled by social scientists, using a multi-variate regression approach to try and unpick the relative importance of many different possible explanatory variables for academic and external academics. Yet though such reductionist approaches are valuable, it is often helpful to consider them alongside

---

[10] Samuel Johnson, Rambler ≠118 (1751) quoted in Bate and Strauss (1968).
[11] Royal Society (2011: 16).

alternative impressions and more holistic descriptive views. In Chapter 4, we also use a 'qualitative comparative analysis' (QCA) framework to help us tackle some of the underlying causal dynamics determining impacts across different types of actors. Chapters 5 to 8 also offer more in-depth qualitative views of the complex processes involved. Our job here then is just to offer a first aerial map of the contours of academic and external influence.

Like any map our account seeks to compress a great deal of information into a particular format. A key step here was to construct two aggregate indices that each captured many of the most important components of academic influence on the one hand, and of external visibility for researchers on the other. We used six underlying variables for each aspect, as shown in this box.

Academic influence elements	External visibility elements
1. Average articles published per year	7. Total number of Google references
2. Average books and book chapters published per year	8. Proportion of references in the external domain
3. Total number of citations of these publications	9. Number of research reports found
4. Top cited publication	10. Proportion of references in civil society domain
5. Number of academic citations	11. Visibility in the gov.uk domain
6. h-index	12. Visibility in UK and international press

We have already described the sources for variables 1 to 10. For variable 11 we used Google advanced search for each of the 370 academics in our dataset on the UK government domain (gov.uk) using the Google advanced search. For variable 12 we used the international press database Nexis to search for references to our academics in UK and international press media. In both cases, the results of these searches were recorded in aggregated terms, and fed into the overall dataset. Both processes involved a fine-grained review of the results to ensure that we were not counting references to individuals with the same name. To aid aggregation we also recoded each variable in the box above into five categories from zero (the very lowest scores) to one (the very highest scores). Intermediate values were recoded into three mid-range categories (of 0.25, 0.5 and 0.75)[12]. Thus the scores any academic could attain on the dimensions for either academic influence or external visibility ran from zero to a maximum average of 6. Each component of the score is weighted the same, since after investigation we could not define an alternative well-evidenced basis for weighting.

We chart the resulting patterns of combined scores in Figure 2.17, which condenses data points for 370 academics into an overall map. We have additionally sketched onto the chart a grouping of the different clusters or groupings of academics as follows:

---

[12] The full list of coded categories is available in the Research Design and Methods Report available via the *Impact of Social Sciences* blog (http://blogs.lse.ac.uk/impactofsocialsciences/book). See also Bastow et al. (2014).

- *Invisibles* are researchers with low average scores (below 1) on both our dimensions of influence. Most of this group are young researchers who are still establishing their academic profiles and seeking permanent career posts or tenure, which leaves little spare time for impacts work, and means that their external visibility is inherently limited. Some older researchers or academics are also included here, perhaps because their work is esoteric academically, or perhaps of lesser quality, or not successful in being recognized.
- *Publishers* are academics who focus on creating articles or chapters that secure varying degrees of academic notice (scoring at least 1), without eliciting much by way of external visibility. Almost all academic influence scores here lie below 3.

Figure 2.17   Using external visibility and academic output scores to chart impact groupings

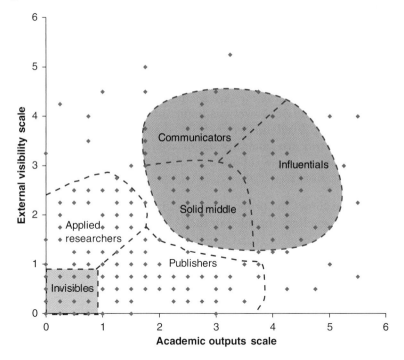

- *Applied researchers* by contrast are academics with relatively high external visibility (scoring above 1), but with academic influence scores that are lower. Again this group shows only a few isolated researchers with scores above 3.
- A *solid middle* group is the first of three higher achieving groups that we identify. They combine medium-strong academic influence scores (of 2 to 3.5) with reasonable external visibility scores (of 1.5 to 3). This group approximate the demanding image of an 'all round academic' that most UK universities still seem to expect from their staff.

Figure 2.18 The distribution of researchers across profile categories in social science and STEM disciplines

	% of academics in each profile category	
	Social sciences	STEM sciences
Publishers	27	32
Invisibles	25	33
Applied researchers	17	9
Solid middle	16	15
Influentials	9	9
Communicators	7	1
Total	**100%**	**100%**
Total *N*	270	100

Source: LSE PPG dataset.

Note: a small number of high performing individuals (just over 5 per cent of the overall sample) not allocated in profile areas in Figure 2.17 are counted with their nearest profile category here.

- A scattering of *communicators* are academics with high external visibility scores of 3 to 5, but with lower academic influence scores. They may fit best with the 'pop' academic or specialized applied researcher profiles.
- Finally *influentials* are generally senior academics who combine strong academic influence scores (above 3.5) with significant external visibility (scoring 1.5 or more).

Figure 2.18 above shows the proportions of our dataset researchers in social science and STEM disciplines included in each of these categories. A third of STEM researchers and a quarter of social scientists fell into the invisibles category. In both discipline groupings at least a quarter of researchers fell into the publisher category (but more in STEM subjects), and in both around one in six researchers were placed in the solid middle. The remaining third of social scientists and fifth of STEM researchers split across the other three categories, which were thus smaller groupings. Applied researchers and communicators are more common in social science.

Looking at the fit between the profile categories and the age ranges for academics was surprisingly problematic, since for almost three in ten academics in our dataset we could not find a clear birth year or age range. However, using the data that we could assemble, Figure 2.19 overleaf shows that only isolated individuals from the youngest academic group made the influential or communicator categories, and nearly two fifths were invisibles, a proportion that dropped by half for the next age category. At the other end of spectrum, half of the small influentials group were aged 55 or more, although this to some extent reflects automatic processes of h-indexes cumulating and network connections increasing with seniority. Communicators are more spread across our three age groups from 35 upwards.

Figure 2.19   The distribution of researchers by profile categories and age ranges

	Age: 34 or under	35 to 44	45 to 54	55 and older	*All ages*
Publishers	4	13	7	4	**28**
Invisibles	7	7	4	4	**22**
Strong middle	3	8	4	4	**19**
Applied researchers	4	6	3	3	**16**
Influentials	0	3	2	4	**9**
Communicators	0	2	2	2	**6**
All profiles	**18**	**39**	**22**	**21**	**100%**

Source: LSE PPG dataset.

Note: N = 251 because we could not assess age for some respondents. A small number of high per-forming individuals (just over 5 per cent of the overall sample) not allocated in profile areas in Figure 2.18 are counted with their nearest profile category here.

Conclusions

Both of the two popular (or conventional) views of how social scientists acquire external visibility are partially right and partially wrong. There is clearly a substantial group of academics who fall into the publisher category of fairly single-mindedly pursuing academic influence alone, with low external visibility. But there is no equivalently large group of applied social scientists who specialize in a kind of 'close to customer' academic work, and the smallish group here are also not especially visible externally. So at best, half of the specialization view finds support. On the other hand, the view that elite social scientists predominate in terms of external visibility clearly is also limited. In our dataset there were relatively few strong joint academic/external performers, falling into the communicators and influentials categories, and they were outnumbered by the solid middle group whose achievements on both dimensions are more mid-range.

Academics have often been reluctant to consider metrics relating to their performance. And perhaps social scientists have been more reluctant about looking at numbers than most, because of a sense that their disciplines lagged behind the STEM disciplines in terms of their external visibility, or in terms of citations. As elsewhere, facing facts can be unpleasant for internal morale. Yet we have also demonstrated that UK social science is a very consistently active field, with most researchers generating regular streams of publications that also attract extensive citations. Both more quantitative and solely journal-oriented subjects (like economics, geography and psychology) and more qualitative and book-orientated fields have creditable records and different patterns of publication and citation. Nor is there any yawning gulf between social scientists and STEM researchers in our dataset in terms of citations or publication, once we allow for field-specific differences. Their similarities are more striking than what sets them apart in academic influence terms.

In terms of external visibility the picture at the level of individuals is also broadly comparable, although STEM scientists' work is more intermediated than for social science. At the departmental or institutional level the evidence for applied work resonating more with government and business audiences is stronger.

Of course, looking at numbers as we have done so far tells us only part of a complex story and in Chapters 5 to 8 below we use in-depth interviews and other methods to understand in more detail how academics gain external impacts and visibility. But the basic lineaments of social science influence inside and beyond the university sector sketched here are a useful first stage in developing understanding. In the next chapter we put in place a second stage by attempting to assess causal influences more precisely.

3
Modelling the determinants of social science impacts

A few social scientists with vested interests, and meddlesome politicians who need to be seen to do something, can make some sort of argument for almost anything ...

     iConservatives e-bulletin[1]

Modern social systems embody relatively sophisticated methods for screening, transforming and aggregating information in ways that serve the purposes of businesses, governments, civil society organizations, the media and citizens at large – making 'information theory' of various kinds a burgeoning area of scientific and scholarly innovation (Gleick, 2012). Yet what we know about how academic knowledge first circulates within the university world, and then acquires a wider influence on actors outside, remains relatively restricted, partly because of academic resistance to assessment, and partly reflecting a lack of useful systematic data.

However, as we have seen, the increasing comprehensiveness and spread of online databases for academic publications are allowing studies to begin studying the patterning of citation counts across disciplines, rates of collaboration amongst authors, and other easily discoverable factors, creating the expanding fields of bibliometric and scientometric analysis. From the mid-2000s, some researchers questioned how far the proprietary bibliometric databases could help us to develop standardized measures of impact for academic publications (Archambault and Vignola-Gagne, 2004; Harnad, 2007; Norris and Oppenheim, 2007). They highlighted the comparative strengths and weaknesses of different databases, and showed how in particular the social sciences were less systematically covered than STEM disciplines, with the humanities in an even worse position. In 2008 the UK research funding body HEFCE decided against using any bibliometrics in the evaluation of publications by social sciences and humanities academics in favour of continuing with peer review by panels of academics.

Since then, however, the usefulness of citations-based analysis has been demonstrated by many studies. The growing availability of scientometric data on academic publications suggests that well-crafted metric-based indicators can perform relatively

---

[1] Quoted in Pawson (2006: 174).

well in terms of predicting decisions of peer review (Harnad, 2007 and 2008). Bibliometric citations predicted well the earlier Research Assessment Exercise (RAE) peer review outcomes (Butler and McAllister, 2007 and 2011). These authors argued that development of quantitative, metric-based indicators can provide a low-cost alternative to qualitative review, although they need to be modified to suit the specific characteristics of social science and STEM disciplines. Subsequent studies found that bibliometric evaluation is more reliable, cost-effective, and more standardized than peer review across large numbers of academics (Abramo and D'Angelo, 2010). Academic bodies have also begun to explore the potential for more systematic biblio-metric evaluation of academics and their institutions (British Academy, 2007; CSTS, 2007, 2008; HEFCE, 2009). The arrival of Google Scholar has broadened the cover-age of all academic disciplines and particularly removed many of the earlier problems about the under-coverage of the social sciences and humanities (Dunleavy and Tinkler, 2014). A huge advantage of all bibliometrics databases is that they update frequently and are designed for use by the whole academic community at a basic level, although accessing large volumes of data for research purposes still requires data-handling skills. However, other critics have offered more sceptical or cautious views about the potential for scientometrics to totally replace peer review in order to obtain a rounded picture of research quality (Richards et al., 2009; Burrows, 2011).

Citations of one author by other scholars have been the focus of most of this work, but they tell us about only one particular information flow within the aca-demic community. There are no current databases that bear very usefully on the external impacts of academic work in society, although the rise of 'altmetrics' has developed a range of broader metrics (such as the numbers of views, downloads, or 'likes') that are very useful for considering academic impacts on larger audiences (Bar-Ilan et al., 2012). Anne-Wil Harzing, the originator of the innovative 'Publish or Perish' software, writing with Nancy Adler, called for the social sciences to develop better ways of assessing scholarly impact (Adler and Harzing, 2009). They argued that prevailing systems for measuring academic impact are 'nonsense', in danger of doing more harm than good as academics are pushed towards a regime of publishing academic work that is judged on narrow citation (or 'peer review') terms within a solely academic realm, while the difference this work makes in wider society is unknown.

Of course, external impact issues are now given a lot of importance in the UK, thanks to pressure from the Research Councils and government. Yet so far the only not-very-innovative data strategy pursued for tapping the external influence of aca-demic work has been HEFCE's collection of an estimated 5,000 impact 'case studies' as part of its 2014 REF audit exercise. Their idea is that along with an enormous pile of perhaps 200,000 research outputs, the 20,000 pages of case studies will be assessed by peer review panels for each discipline, now including some research user members as well as academics. What useful insights this will generate seems moot. However, when digitized and re-analysed by inventive researchers, these new data sources might yet generate some strong insights in the future.

In this chapter we are able to go beyond the 'first impressions' analysis given above and to use multi-variate analyses of the information about academics in our dataset to shed light on two key problems:

- the factors shaping academic influence, as measured by citations; and
- the factors shaping the external influence of academic work, as measured by web references, the 'digital footprint' that research makes in the wider community.

The first section describes how we collected information about our academics and constructed variables, and some of the problems encountered in achieving full information, which in the end only proved feasible for a large sub-set of the individuals we sought to cover. The second section uses the resulting dataset to analyse the determinants of academic influence, sifting out the main variables that are involved. The final section extends the approach to cover external impacts.

3.1 Multi-variate modelling of impacts

> In variable-oriented work, multiple cases of 'the same thing' are highly valued, because they create the possibility of quantitative analysis and statistical inference.
>
> *Charles Ragin*[2]

One way of trying to grip complex processes is to code multiple different variables for all units in a dataset and then to use regression techniques (or other modes of statistical analysis) to try and sort out which explanatory or independent variables are genuinely causing the behaviour or dependent variable to be explained. Wherever there is a reasonably complex causal process, some independent variables will be correlated with each other, and in building alternative models it is important to try and discover which of these are the ones most strongly associated with differences in the dependent variable. In Chapter 2 we created indexed scores for two groups of variables in order to plot the relationship between academic impacts and external impacts in a preliminary way. However, in such a simplifying approach the effects of individual explanatory factors are easily lost within the overall picture. Some independent variables in the mix may play more important roles than others in explaining impacts, or there may be important inter-relationships between variables that together help us to refine the way in which we understand the origins of impacts. Multi-variate analysis helps to disentangle these relationships in a more systematic way using statistical inference, and it can allow us to compare the relative importance of possible causal variables and the performance of alternative overall models.

The basic variable list for our analysis is based on the individual variables used to construct the indices in Chapter 2 along with six characteristics of the individual academics, shown in Figure 3.1.

We are interested to see if there are specific traits or characteristics that lead their research to attract more citation. We might expect, for example, that high status academics at elite universities, or those in professorial roles would have more impressive academic publications, and hence higher citations. But then conversely, we might also hypothesize that younger academics feel greater pressure to get their work in highly

---

[2] Ragin (2000: 43).

Figure 3.1 Three groups of variables used in our impact modelling analysis

Individual characteristics variables

A. Age, gender, and nationality
B. Highest academic qualification
C. Status of the current and former institution
D. Years in academic role
E. Academic position held
F. Visibility online of the academic

Academic output variables	External visibility variables
13. Average articles published per year	18. Total number of Google references
14. Average books and book chapters published per year	19. Proportion of references in the 'external' domain
15. Total number of citations of these publications	20. Number of research reports found
16. Top cited publication	21. Proportion of references in civil society domain
17. Number of academic citations as a measure of career credibility	22. Visibility in the gov.uk domain
	23. Visibility in UK and international press

ranked peer-reviewed journals, and to build their smaller citation counts with excellent publications, and hence they may publish in more citation-attracting ways, whereas senior academics tend to eschew the rough and tumble of journals reviews. Perhaps both these effects may operate at the same time, and our analysis must find a way to weight them. Turning to external impacts, we can ask the same questions about how the characteristics of individual academics condition their being referenced or linked to by business, government, civil society organizations or the media, thereby creating an electronic footprint that we can access and measure.

To implement these questions we rely on the dataset of academics described in Chapter 2. However, because regression techniques rely strongly on the assumption that a dataset is a random sample, it is worth reiterating and enlarging on some key points concerning the selection of academics for inclusion in the whole dataset, and in the sub-set of fully recorded individuals that we will focus attention on here. We constructed our dataset in three consecutive waves, encompassing a total of 370 academics from seven core social science disciplines (wave 1, used to pilot and refine our data-recording and variables); some other and more crossover social science disciplines (wave 2); and STEM disciplines (wave 3) – details in Figure 3.2. Beginning in February 2010, we randomly selected five universities for each discipline from a full list of UK universities, and then compiled a full list of all academic staff working in each of the chosen departments. From this list of academic staff, we then randomly selected 20 staff from each discipline list for our sample. The same procedure was used for each of the discipline lists. For business and management, we boosted the number to 30 academic staff in order to encompass the broader range of disciplines incorporated in this general subject heading. Wave 2 expanded our dataset to cover five 'crossover' subject areas, using the same sampling procedure. We supplemented our dataset for waves 1 and 2 by adding 20 academics selected randomly from respective departments at the London School of Economics. Finally, we repeated the same process for five STEM disciplines (as discussed in Chapter 2), to provide some comparative dimension with the social science disciplines. All data collection and coding was carried out over 18 months, using the same time frames (and recording when each data-point was added). All our data then underwent a very detailed process of scrutiny, cleaning and checking. We analysed the final dataset using the statistical package STATA.

Figure 3.2   Number of academics in our original sample and attrition due to inadequate biographical information

	Number in original sample	Attrition due to insufficient biographical details found	Number of cases in final regression analysis
Core social science subjects (Wave 1)			
Business and Management	30	12	18
Economics	24	1	23
Political Science	24	6	18
Sociology	24	6*	18
Anthropology	20	5	15
Communication and Media Studies	20	6	14
Social Policy	20	6	14
Total for Wave 1	**162**	**42**	**120**
Crossover social science subjects (Wave 2)			
Geography	24	1	23
Law	24	6	18
Philosophy	20	6	14
History	20	8	12
Psychology	20	12	8
Total for Wave 2	**108**	**33**	**75**
Selected STEM subjects (Wave 3)			
Chemistry	20	5	15
Medicine	20	8	12
Physics	20	8	12
Engineering	20	9	11
Computer Science and IT	20	14	6
Total for Wave 3	**100**	**44**	**56**
All disciplines	**370**	**119**	**251**

Source: LSE PPG dataset.

Note: (*) includes one academic in our sample who died during the period of our analysis.

One of the most unexpected things for us was the difficulty of establishing the basic biographical and career details (listed in the top box of Figure 3.1) for a large proportion of academics and researchers. Our information collection was done unobtrusively (Webb et al., 1999), and based on online information in the public domain. For each academic, we searched all available CV material, all personal and university web pages, all available social media, plus other reputable sources of online biographical information such as the US Library of Congress, British Library, the LSE's British Library of Political and Economic Science, amongst others. The biographical search work proved far more difficult than anticipated, and was carried out painstakingly by PPG staff in the first half of 2012. By the end of this period, we had only found sufficient biographical information for 251 academics out of 370, just over two thirds of our original sample. Figure 3.2 shows the scale of these problems across different disciplines, which reduced the size of the dataset for our regression analysis to 251 academics, because of the centrality of information like individual's ages and career time in higher education. The highest attrition rates were for academics in psychology, computer science, and engineering, while the fullest information by far was available for those in economics and geography.

Although we found a great deal of biographical information for our included academics in specific and exact form, we were also forced to use interpolation extensively to achieve a full complement of data so that the maximum number of academics could be retained in our regression sub-sample. Establishing the age of our academics was highly problematic. As Figure 3.3 shows, we were only able to find exact published ages for around 35 per cent of the eventual dataset.

The remaining 65 per cent was found through extrapolating from a 'known year' in an academic's career – usually an undergraduate degree or a doctorate. Working backwards from these known years, we applied simple 'rule of thumb' estimates for the number of years back to year of birth. In the case of undergraduate degrees, we subtracted 22 years to estimate birth date. In the case of doctoral theses, we subtracted 28 years. Other information was used in a further one third of cases to estimate the age group of the academic.

We were not able to find even basic biographical information on one third of our academics, and closer to half in the sample of STEM academics. Putting this another way, around a third of our sample of academics and researchers choose to provide no

Figure 3.3   Establishing year of birth for academics in our regression dataset

	Wave 1		Wave 2		STEM		ALL Subjects	
	N	*%*	*N*	*%*	*N*	*%*	*N*	*%*
Exact year of birth found	49	41	32	43	7	13	88	35
Year of birth estimated from undergraduate or PhD year	32	27	18	24	32	57	82	33
Year of birth estimated from other online sources	39	32	25	33	17	30	81	32
Total	120	100	75	100	56	100	251	100

basic information about themselves or their professional career in the public sphere. There are some good reasons why academics (and others) might withhold information about their age: for instance, mature students and those taking career breaks may not want to draw attention to these aspects in their CV. However, to reveal little or no information about qualifications, education, career trajectory, and so on, seems a more fundamental and indeed puzzling omission. The reduction by one third of our original sample size had some implications for the overall profile of the 251 academics included in our regression analyses, changing the disciplinary base a little as shown in Figure 3.3, and potentially leaving out more older researchers (although we could not be sure of

Figure 3.4   The basic demographic characteristics of academics included in our dataset

	Core social science subjects		Crossover social science subjects		STEM subjects		ALL subjects	
	Total	%	Total	%	Total	%	Total	%
Number of academics in sub-sample	120	48	75	30	56	22	251	100
Male	88	35	53	21	38	15	179	71
Female	32	13	22	9	18	7	72	29
Lecturer/Sr. Lecturer/Other	87	35	49	20	43	17	179	71
Reader/Professor/Em. Prof.	33	13	26	10	13	5	72	29
Age below 47	69	28	43	17	34	14	146	58
Age above 47	51	20	32	13	22	9	105	42
British	69	28	44	18	36	14	149	59
Non-British	51	20	31	12	20	8	102	41
PhD or higher	108	43	70	28	53	21	231	92
Masters or lower	12	5	5	2	3	1	20	8
Employed at Russell Group institution								
No	73	29	33	13	42	17	148	59
Yes	47	19	42	17	14	6	103	41
Highest qualification Russell Group/Ivy League								
No	64	26	42	17	26	10	132	53
Yes	56	22	33	13	30	12	119	47
Region								
London	28	11	25	9	12	5	65	26
North	19	8	22	10	10	4	51	20
Rest of UK	30	12	6	2	15	6	51	20
Midlands	26	10	12	5	9	4	47	19
South of England	17	7	10	4	10	4	37	15

Note: n = 251. Source: LSE PPG dataset.

this). Perhaps the most obvious effect of the attrition was a worsening ratio of men to women, with male academics forming 71 per cent of those analysed below, compared to 65 per cent in the original full sample. Figure 3.4 gives a breakdown of demographic characteristics of these 251 researchers included in this multivariate analysis.

In our regressions below, the dependent variables consist respectively of proxy measures for academic and external impacts. For academic impact we define three different possible proxy measures, each of which give a slightly different aspect to our evaluation of academic impact and its potential determinants. For external impacts the dependent variable is the number of external references we found made to the academic or their research in our full Google web search. We explain this in more detail later in the chapter. First, however, it is necessary to set out the range of possible independent variables that may help us to explain why some academics have impacts and some do not, either considered individually or in the way these variables interact with others. The independent variables included in the regressions are as follows:

1 *Basic biographical data* – This is a set of basic indicators relating to six background characteristics of individual academics:

   o their *age* in 2012, and
   o a quadratic term, *age²*, allowing for non-linearity in the age-impact relationship;
   o a *gender* dummy variable, coded 1 for males and 0 for females;
   o a dummy variable for the academic's *nationality*, coded 1 if the academic is from the UK and 0 otherwise;
   o a dummy indicator for the *region* comparing academics working at institutions in London (coded 1) with academics working in all other regions of the UK (coded 0). We use the geographical location of the institution employing the academic at the time when we collected our data;
   o a dummy variable coded 1 for academics working in the *wholly social science disciplines* of anthropology, business and management, media studies and communications, economics, political science, social policy, and sociology. These academics are compared to those in the core STEM disciplines of chemistry, computer science and IT, engineering, medicine, and physics (core STEM-based academics are coded as 0);
   o a dummy variable coded 1 for academics in *social science disciplines overlapping other discipline groups* (STEM or humanities subjects), compared to academics in our five STEM disciplines (coded 0);
   o an indicator for collaboration in academic work measured by the average number of co-authors involved in the publications produced.

2 Career progression:

   o a dummy variable for *academic position* coded 1 for full Professors and 0 otherwise (i.e., lecturers, senior lecturers, readers, and other academic titles);
   o a dummy variable for the *academic's highest qualification*, coded 1 if this is a PhD level or higher, and 0 for a Masters degree or below;
   o a dummy variable for *highest qualification from a Russell Group* or *Ivy League University* (coded 1 for yes and 0 for no); and
   o a variable that counts the *years between the academic's highest qualification and the data collection year*, our best available proxy for time spent in academia.

3 *University status* controls for the social science status of the institutions where each academic works. This has a possible maximum score of 4 depending on if they work for a Russell Group (RG) institution (at the time of our data collection); and if there are any British Academy Fellows at the academic's employing institution (an indication of esteem).

4 *Biographical visibility* codes the visibility of the academic and whether it is easy to find basic biographical information about them and their research. This records whether each academic:

   o has a full CV online;
   o has a profile on their university's or department's website;
   o has a personal webpage;
   o has a presence on LinkedIn (all the above coded 1 for Yes and 0 for No), and
   o the extent to which the academic's background data had to be estimated.

5 *External impacts visibility* captures the extent to which an academic's external impacts score influences their 'academic impacts' dependent variable. This includes the total number of external mentions to the work of academics in our sub-sample.

3.2 The factors shaping academic impacts

Serious academics want to publish in the best journals; they want to have major influence that they get through leverage. If you have the right journal articles, you'll find your way into text books; you'll find people being taught your stuff. So there is big leverage from being years ahead of the curve with cutting edge research.

Business school professor in interview

Academics, quite honestly, are so removed from what the realities are. Some of the stuff you read, you think, 'which planet are you living on?'

University professor in interview

Academic impact or influence (their professional credibility and influence on other academics in their field) is a complex thing in 'real life', composed of many strands of professional assessment and personal reputation. Yet in regression analysis we must simplify this down to something specific, a proxy variable that can stand in for the complex and less tangible thing we mean. No one measure captures academic impact very effectively so we use three different forms of the dependent variable:

● *The average number of citations to all the outputs published by an academic between 2004 and 2009.* This is based on our Google Scholar coding work (described in Chapter 2). It shows the across-the-board citations impact of the academic in recent years;

● *The top-cited output produced by the academic between 2004 and 2009:* that is, cites for the academic article, book or book chapter, research report or working paper most referenced by peers. An academic's top score may often be very different from their average;

- *Career references to the academic.* We used Google Scholar to count the number of times other academics have referenced each person in our dataset, during the recent period, from 2004 to 2009. This shows how far each individual has accumulated current credibility with their peers from a whole body of work across their career.

We present the results for three regression analyses focusing on these three alternative measures of academic impact in Figure 3.5, shown in the right-most three columns. The rows in the first column show the independent variables discussed above.

Before we present the results from the regression, it is worth saying something about our choice of regression model and how it fits the particular type of dependent variables that we have here. In all our regressions the dependent variables are 'count' values, in other words, they are discrete, bounded at zero, and are generally countable. Continuous variables, on the other hand, can take values that are fractions of full integers (i.e., rather than 1 or 2, a continuous variable can hold any value between 1 or 2, say, for example, 1.753) and can potentially be negative. For regressions using continuous dependent variables, it is usually standard practice to use 'ordinary least square' (OLS) regression models. However, for regressions in which the dependent variables are countable values, it is generally the case that statisticians will use either Poisson or Negative Binomial Regression models (NBR). (Using OLS regression models with countable variables runs the risk of under-estimating regression coefficients).

Choosing between Poisson and NBR however depends on the extent of dispersion of the dependent variable data. For data that tends to be strongly 'over-dispersed' (from the mean), it is more appropriate to use NBR instead of Poisson. Our Chi-squared tests for each model showed our data to be over-dispersed, and hence we opted for NBR. In the regression tables below, we report two measures of overall goodness of fit with NBR models – 'pseudo log likelihood' and an 'alpha value'. These show the extent to which the distribution of our data fits the NBR model, and demonstrate that the over-dispersed distribution of our data is such that it is more appropriate to use NBR rather than Poisson.[3]

NBR coefficients cannot be directly interpreted, as they only tell us whether there is a positive or a negative relationship between any of the independent and dependent variables. Therefore, we present and interpret the coefficients in terms of a rate ratio, known as the Incidence Rate Ratio (IRR). The IRR is framed in terms of a probability that a unit increase in the independent variable will result in a unit increase (or decrease) in the dependent variable. The direction of the change is signified by the

---

[3] Poisson and Negative Binomial Regression (NBR) are therefore more commonly used to analyse count data. These two techniques differ in their assumptions. Whereas Poisson regression requires the conditional mean and variance to be equal, NBR corrects for 'over-dispersion' of data with regards to the mean. If the conditional distribution of the outcome variable is over-dispersed, the confidence intervals for the NBR are likely to be narrower as compared to those from a Poisson regression model. This means that we are more likely to fail to reject the null hypothesis of a statistically significant effect of the independent variable. We used the Pearson Chi-Square goodness-of-fit test to measure the distribution of the data before choosing between Poisson and NBR. Each set of regressions for the four dependent variables; average citations, top citations and career references, and external references, yield a p-value of 0.000 ("Prob>Chi²") which falls below the conventional threshold of 0.05. This indicates that NBR is more appropriate for this dataset.

amount that the IRR is either above or below 1. Say, for example, that we are interested to know what the effect is on total average citations of an increase in the number of co-authors with whom an academic publishes. In other words, what is the expected probability of change in total average citations if we raise the average number of authors by one? As we find below, the IRR in this case has a value of 1.30. This would indicate that increasing the number of co-authors by 1 would result in a 30 per cent increased probability of a unit increase in the total average number of citations, holding all else equal. Similarly, an IRR of 0.70 is a 30 per cent probability of a unit decrease in the dependent variable with every unit increase in the independent variable. It is important to underline here that the 30 per cent (either up or down) denotes a probability of an increase (or decrease) in the dependent variable, rather than the scale of the increase (or decrease) itself.

In Figure 3.5, each of the results cells in the body of the table shows a first number that records the IRR as described above. The second number (in brackets) in each cell is the standard error for the IRR. The size of the error number (relative to the IRR) conditions for each ratio whether it is significant or not, that is, how far it is likely to have arisen by chance. We report standard error here solely for regression aficionados, because we can also directly show the significance level for each coefficient. Other readers should thus pay attention chiefly to cells with back-shaded numbers, where the coefficient passes one of these three levels of significance:

- **Bold and dark orange shading** = significant at 1% level (the strongest relationship). This variable has to be included in the model tested.
- **Bold and grey shading** = significant at 5% level. This variable should also be included.
- *Italics and light orange shading* = significant at 10% level. This variable probably should be excluded from the model but is interesting.

Numbers in plain text and not in back-shaded cells are not significant and cannot be included in the model, although experts may find points of interest even so. For each cluster of independent variables, we can read across the three columns to understand the strength and direction of the relationships. Although these three proxy dependent variables are separate and emphasize different aspects of potential impact, together they provide confirmation on the relative strength and importance of these independent variables.

Focusing first on the basic demographic variables (at the bottom of Figure 3.5), once we include the other variables tested here, the personal characteristics show little or no causal influence on any of the three measures of academic impact. There is no significant relationship involving gender or the nationality of our academics. We might expect to see a strong, positive relationship between age and citations – but once we have controlled for an academic being a professor or not, having a PhD or not, and for the time since items were published (because citations take time to grow), the age effect is not significant, even for cumulative citations in the period. However, a person's length of time in academia does matter for top citation levels (at weak significance) and total career references (at strong significance). However, this is still only a relatively small effect (despite having strong significance). An additional

Figure 3.5   Exploring the factors associated with academic impact

Independent variables	Dependent variable: Academic impact		
	Average Citations [Model 1]	Top Citations [Model 2]	Career References [Model 3]
Academic position (Professor = 1)	**1.45** **(0.19)**	**1.74** **(0.28)**	**1.70** **(0.30)**
Region (London = 1)	**1.54** **(0.22)**	**1.82** **(0.29)**	**1.41** **(0.20)**
Academic's highest qualification (PhD or higher = 1)	*1.73* *(0.54)*	**3.49** **(1.12)**	*1.71* *(0.55)*
Years since academic's highest qualification	1.01 (0.01)	*1.03* *(0.01)*	**1.04** **(0.01)**
Status of academic current institution (RG = 1)	1.31 (0.23)	1.30 (0.22)	*1.35* *(0.23)*
Average number of co-authors (outputs 2004–09)	**1.30** **(0.11)**	**1.37** **(0.15)**	– 0.96 (0.07)
Total external mentions from outside academia	1.00 (0.004)	**1.01** **(0.004)**	**1.02** **(0.01)**
Average time since publication	**1.37** **(0.16)**	**1.40** **(0.22)**	1.05 (0.07)
Status of highest qualification institution (RG = 1)	1.14 (0.14)	1.16 (0.17)	**1.55** **(0.28)**
Visibility of the academic	1.08 (0.08)	1.07 (0.07)	1.10 (0.06)
LinkedIn profile (Yes = 1)	1.20 (0.17)	1.11 (0.21)	1.02 (0.14)
Core social sciences (relative to STEM subjects)	1.01 (0.23)	.10 (0.34)	1.01 (0.28)
Crossover disciplines (relative to STEM subjects)	−0.74 (0.26)	−0.81 (0.31)	−0.93 (0.28)
Age	−0.97 (0.05)	1.06 (0.08)	1.05 (0.06)
Age^2	1.00 (0.001)	−1.00 (0.001)	−1.00 (0.001)
Gender (Male = 1)	1.07 (0.16)	1.21 (0.21)	1.24 (0.20)
Nationality (British = 1)	1.00 (0.17)	−0.93 (0.16)	1.16 (0.19)
Pseudo log likelihood [i]	−628.5	−959.8	−1026.0
Alpha (dispersion indicator) [ii]	0.76	1.25	1.30

[i] Statistical models for 'count' variables (e.g. Logit, Poisson, NBR) use the 'logarithm of the likelihood' (log likelihood) to estimate overall goodness of it. The closer the log likelihood value is to zero, the better the overall fit of the model. In all the models that we use here, the log likelihood is closer to zero than in an equivalent test using Poisson distribution.

[ii] The *Alpha* test is an estimate of the dispersion parameter. We show it here to demonstrate that using Negative Binomial Regression (NBR) is a more appropriate option than Poisson. If the dispersion parameter equals zero, the model can be reduced to the simpler Poisson model. If the dispersion parameter, alpha, is significantly greater than zero, then this means that the data are over-dispersed and are better estimated using NBR rather than Poisson.

Note: The first number in each column shows Incidence Rate Ratio (IRR). This is the probability that a unit increase in the independent variable will result in a unit increase (or decrease) in the dependent variable. Values > 1 show increase, and < 1 show decrease. Standard errors are shown (in parentheses). Statistically significant results are shown as: dark shading and bold text at the 1% level (the strongest relationship); grey shading and bold text at the 5% level; and light shading and italic text at the 10% level.

year of academic tenure is associated with a 4 per cent improved probability of a unit increase in career references. Although a relatively small effect year-on-year, the cumulative accretion of this over a career of, say, 30 years may seem more impressive. To square this with the apparent lack of relationship with age, we must remember that regressions are a kind of tournament where two associated variables contest to achieve more significance. If variable B itself depends on A (as here time in tenure is linked to age) B may mop up some of A's effect.

Academic seniority is an important predictor of academic impact (shown in the top row of Figure 3.5). Professors are more likely to have higher average citation counts and highly-cited publications, compared to academics of lower rank. This relationship stands across all three dependent variables. In contrast to the previous example, the probability ratio suggests a much larger effect at somewhere around 1.70. This relatively high coefficient is largely the result of the binary independent variable in which the academic concerned is either a professor or not (i.e., 1 or zero). The shift to professorship here is potentially a much larger 'input signal' than, say, a unit increase in the average number of co-authors. If an academic moves to professor, the probability that this will lead to a unit increase in their top citations is around 70 per cent. This is a strong effect, and in our model, it demonstrates high significance. The interpretation here is that with professorial seniority comes improvement in academic reputation and impacts. Yet of course, there is a two-way relationship here, because highly cited academics are more likely to be promoted to professor. So we would need to decompose this linkage to find the true worth of professor status in gaining more citations.

Academics who have achieved PhD-level qualification are likely to have a higher probability of getting cited or being referenced. For cases where academics have a PhD, there is a nearly 250 per cent increase in the probability that they will have a unit increase in their top citation score. However, since 92 per cent of our sub-sample is qualified to PhD level, it is really our academics without a doctorate who seem to be a small and exceptional minority in academia. This effect is less visible in the relationship with total average citations and career references, possibly because some highly cited authors were appointed in an earlier period when not having a PhD was more usual.

Academics working at institutions within the Greater London area are more likely to have higher average citations than those located outside, especially affecting top citations, but strong across the piece. This may reflect the attraction of more dynamic academics to London institutions, or greater competition for such posts. Being in London can increase the probability of getting a higher top citation by 82 per cent. This is comparatively much higher than the effect of being in London on total average citations and career references, suggesting that 'stellar' academics, who succeed in publishing heavily-cited articles or books, may gravitate towards London (or by implication, other major universities in key cities).

Different universities have differing levels of status in society, reflected in rankings and university league tables. We use a composite variable for this status, based on a coding of whether the academic is currently employed at Russell Group University (which claims to be academia's Premier League) and on the number of British Academy Fellows that the university has. This measure of status seems only to shape career references positively – albeit at relatively weak significance. Again, however, there is probably a dual causation effect here, with higher status universities over time recruiting more reputable researchers, and their high university status incentivizing other academics to cite them a little more.

In measuring disciplinary effects our excluded category are academics in STEM subjects – in other words, we compare core social science and crossover social science disciplines to STEM. There is however very little sign of any significant relationships in this case. We also looked at each of our academic's 'average number of co-authors' (likely to be highest in STEM disciplines), and find that the more an academic publishes with co-authors, the greater their average citations. But this relationship is less significant for top citations, and not at all significant for career references.

Some other research has suggested that academics who are active in publicising their work on Twitter or other social media, can dramatically increase the rate at which their work is cited (Puustinen and Edwards, 2012). We cannot measure directly how actively academics promote their work or are outgoing people who go to conferences etc., rather than being hermits locked in their study and not communicating with others. However, having a LinkedIn account, for example, does not seem to be associated with any of our dependent variables.

Finally, we entered the level of 'external mentions' of an academic on the wider web as an explanatory variable here. It is positively and significantly associated with both top citations and career citations, but not with average recent citations. With every reference made from an external domain to an academic, we find an increase in probability that these academics will increase their top citation and career references rates. This makes intuitive sense. The effects of the relationships still appear only very small, however, no more than an increase in probability of 2 per cent. But again, this reflects the fine-grained nature of the comparison. With every increase of 1 in external references, we have a similarly marginal probability increase of 1 or 2 per cent. Over the long term, of course, the cumulative effect of this effect can be large, as 'grains' of impact build up. But seen at the level of the single grain, the impact is still rather minimal. This may suggest a relatively weak 'celebrity' factor feeding back into the university realm. When people hear about an academic through external channels, it seems to incentivize them to then cite the person more.

3.3 The factors shaping external impacts

'Where does policy come from?' is interesting but misleading. There is generally a surfeit of policy ideas in society.

Frank Baumgartner and Bryan Jones[4]

We realised that it was quite interesting to have these conversations between people at [corporation B] and those outside. Because we started talking about the literatures that were developed in social science that did not have immediate application to B's research engineers, but could be translated by someone.

Sociologist in interview

---

[4] Baumgartner and Jones (2009: 11).

When we shift towards trying to explain how much the world outside universities takes notice of researchers, our dependent variable is a single proxy measure. We typed the full names of our academics into Google and recorded in a fine-grained way all the references to them and their work found on the web domains of non-academic organizations. We limited our search to the first 100 relevant search results. The searches were unrestricted in terms of time coverage (because it takes time to build up external visibility). So they show the cumulative accretion of references to our academics as a result of their work over the years.

Most of the explanatory variables included in this set of regressions are identical to those included in the previous modelling of academic impact. The new element here is the dependent variables, which is featured at the top of Figure 3.6. This is the total number of external references found in our full Google search. The dependent variables from the previous regression in Figure 3.5 are now included in this next regression (Figure 3.5) as independent variables potentially influencing external impact. These are:

- total number of publications per academic (2004–09);
- average recent citations (2004–09);
- number of citations achieved by the top-cited piece of work of the academic (2004–09);
- total career references, defined as the total number of cites or inward references to the academic that are not self-citations i.e., are from other academics (in outputs by these peer academics published during the 2004–09 period).

Figure 3.5 shows the results from three separate regressions explaining external impact. Again, we use the NBR model, as explained above. Rather than having three different dependent variables, we use the same dependent variable and progressively expand the range of independent variables used from left to right, so as to build more sophisticated models. One immediate overall impression is that fewer variables seem to have strong significant relationships as we move rightwards across the three models. Three variables are present in all three models, and show fairly stable probabilities. There is a positive association between being in a core social science (wave 1) discipline and external mentions (again comparing here with our academics in STEM subjects). These disciplines may handle subjects that are more accessible and relevant subjects for policy makers, civil society organizations and the media (as we show in Part II), while economic and business school research has general interest for companies. The results suggest that researchers have an approximately 40 per cent improved chance that they will increase their external references if they are social scientists (as opposed to working in our STEM disciplines). It is interesting also that the age^2 independent variable appears to have a negative association with external references. However, the significance of this relationship dwindles as we increase the sophistication of the model, and the probability showed no change either way (at 1.00). This is perhaps an anomaly as age^2 is usually included in linear OLS models in order to compensate for potential non-linearity in the relationships. As we are using NBR here, it is likely that the age^2 variable is redundant. The 'age' variable however suggests that with an increase in age, there is a marginally greater likelihood that external references will increase (somewhere between 10 and 15 per cent).

Figure 3.6   Exploring the factors associated with external impact

Independent variables	Dependent variable: External references					
	[Model 4]		[Model 5]		[Model 6]	
Total publications (2004 to 2009)			**1.03**	**(0.01)**	**1.03**	**(0.01)**
Total average citations (2004 to 2009)			**−0.99**	**(0.003)**	**−0.99**	**(0.001)**
Top citation (2004 to 2009)			1.00	(0.02)	1.00	(0.003)
Total career references (i.e. inward references)			**1.01**	**(0.02)**	*1.01*	*(0.003)*
Core social sciences (relative to core STEM subjects)	**1.41**	**(0.22)**	**1.42**	**(0.24)**	*1.41*	*(0.28)*
Age	**1.15**	**(0.05)**	**1.10**	**(0.04)**	1.10	(0.07)
Age^2	**−1.00**	**(0.01)**	**−1.00**	**(0.004)**	*−1.00*	*(0.001)*
Highest qualification (PhD or higher = 1)	**4.66**	**(3.31)**	*1.69*	*(0.54)*	*1.74*	*(0.52)*
Region (London = 1)	**1.54**	**(0.29)**	1.40	(0.34)	*1.41*	*(0.26)*
Academic position (Professor = 1)	**1.55**	**(0.28)**	1.40	(0.31)	1.36	(0.26)
Visibility of the academic			**1.09**	**(0.50)**	1.08	(0.08)
Multi-authored publications					*−0.74*	*(0.12)*
Highest qualification (from RG institution = 1)			1.31	(0.28)	*1.33*	*(0.21)*
Gender (Male = 1)	1.01	(1.49)	−0.88	(0.13)	0.89	(0.15)
Nationality (British = 1)	−0.94	(0.15)	−0.95	(0.15)	0.93	(1.68)
Crossover disciplines (relative to core STEM subjects)	1.22	(0.22)	1.33	(0.27)	1.38	(0.31)
Years since highest qualification	−0.99	(0.01)	1.00	(0.01)	1.00	(0.01)
Status of academic current institution (RG institution = 1)			−0.91	(1.20)	0.87	(0.15)
LinkedIn profile (Yes = 1)			−0.81	(1.34)	0.84	(0.13)
Pseudo log likelihood	*−856.1*		*−856.1*		*−854.6*	
Alpha (dispersion indicator)	*1.33*		*1.16*		*1.15*	

Note: The first number in each column shows Incidence Rate Ratio (IRR). This is the probability that a unit increase in the independent variable will result in a unit increase (or decrease) in the dependent variable. Values > 1 show increase, and < 1 show decrease. Standard errors are shown in parentheses. Statistically significant results are shown as: dark shading and bold text at the 1% level (the strongest relationship); grey shading and bold text at the 5% level; and light shading and italic text at the 10% level.

We can work through the three models from left to right. Model 4 is a simple one that seeks to find out how far mainly individual characteristics shape external visibility. Here we find relatively strong significance across six variables. In addition to the positive effect of working in a core social science, a positive increase in visibility with age, and a negative falling-off of external visibility with *age²* (perhaps as older people wind down activity) were clearly significant; although as we have said, *age²* shows no clear direction either upwards or downwards. We also find strong significance from the effects of working in London (which is more accessible for predominantly London-based media, corporation and government headquarters) and being a professor (a status that builds external credibility). Not surprisingly, we also find strong significance and a strong positive relationship between external impacts and having a PhD.

In Models 5 and 6 we included measures of academic impacts. In Model 5, we find that all of them – total publications, total average citations, top citation, and career references – have either strong or medium significance, but the probabilities show only very marginal change around 1. These are only very small effects. For example, with an increase of one publication, there is a 3 per cent likelihood that this will translate into increased external references. Again, the cumulative effect of say 10 or 20 additional publications will likely have a much larger effect on the probability that external references will increase. Similarly, with each one unit increase in cumulative inward references, an academic can expect a 0.01 unit increase in external mentions. The probabilities appear small here because of the relatively smaller increments of change in the independent variable. Again, the cumulative effect of say 10 or 20 additional mentions is likely to boost the probability of external references. It seems clear then that being well-cited within academia is a strong predictor of external impacts.

Interestingly, however, there is a significant negative relationship between total citations and external impacts – with every unit increase in total citations, the probability of an external mention drops, albeit marginally. In effect, this is saying that with every unit increase in average citations, the probability of a unit increase in external references drops by 1 per cent. Keeping in mind the grains of sand effect, the cumulative impact may be fairly important. It seems to show that (in a five year period) if an academic focuses more on producing outputs that are highly cited by their peers, less of their work is picked up by external actors.

In Model 5 we add in a variable for the external visibility of each academic, in terms of the availability of information about them online and via social media. This is significant and positive in this model. As the academic moves up the scale in terms of being visible online, there is a good chance that this will translate into increased numbers of external references. (This strongly significant relationship however dissipates in Model 6.) Indeed, the inclusion of these new variables (on academic output, visibility, and others such as status of the institution) has a combined effect of weakening the significance of some of the demographic variables. Age and being in a core social science appear to retain their relevance, but being in London and being a professor both lose their significance.

However, in Model 6 we add an additional variable for the level of multi-authoring that an academic does (likely to be associated with STEM subjects, plus overlap disciplines and perhaps people doing large-team work in core social sciences). This variable has a significant negative effect (albeit relatively weak) on external visibility. The negative direction on this probability is quite stark. With every unit increase in the number of authors with whom an academic works, the probability of an increase in external visibility drops by around 30 per cent. The addition of this variable also has a kind of muting effect on the other significant relationships established in Model 5. Although most of them keep their direction and general probability magnitude, the significance levels drop. One major effect of controlling for multi-authorship is that the significance of the 'core social science' independent variable decreases somewhat. The core social sciences are still more likely than STEM to engender external visibility, but when seen in real terms, this relationship is slightly less strong.

Conclusions

Regression analyses have many limitations. The mix of variables available to the analysts can make a difference to the coefficients found, especially if important variables are omitted, if variables are not well-specified, and if there are dual causation processes between explanatory and dependent variables. Especially when handling a small and expansive dataset of the kind assembled here, the lack of larger Ns can be restrictive. Some analysts doubt the wider value of running regressions as a kind of tournament between explanatory variables, or investing much weight in significance levels or variables that are present in some models but not in others. None the less, regressions can take us a long way further in assessing the relative weight to be assigned to multiple variables in relatively complex causal processes. They help us to sift out some core variables to which we need to accord close attention, and to separate them from other variables that may seem relevant at first sight but may be correlated with other factors. The messages here about the factors shaping academic impacts and those shaping external impacts are relatively simple but important, and the models that we have presented here are the topmost tip of a much larger set of models tested against our data.

We have seen something of the possibilities and limitations inherent in large-scale regression work. The relationships are apparent but we are not left with nailed down models of academic or external impact, and there is still much uncertainty about the actual mix of determining factors and how they interact dynamically. However, there are some important strands or hints that we can follow. In our first regression, factors such as seniority, experience in academia, co-authorship, regional location, and external visibility are all strong predictors of academic impact. Looking at the determining factors of external impact, the picture becomes much hazier. It is clear that the extent to which academics are able to build their own academic outputs (and impacts) can have a marginal effect on their external visibility and potential impact outside of academia. Academic impact and external impacts may be constituent of each other – in other words, those who do the former well will generally do well at the latter (but this is still only a weak relationship, and far from a sure thing). In general, therefore, the picture for determining factors of external visibility is still unclear. We have some reasonable clues to what does not matter, and the relative weights of what does. But we need a deeper understanding of some of the qualitative variations in the impact dynamics. We can supplement these insights by using other methods, specifically designed to generate this understanding of multi-causal processes, to which we turn in the next chapter.

4
Comparing individuals' impacts

Researchers bring not so much discrete findings as their whole theoretical, conceptual, and empirical fund of knowledge into the decision-making process. The 'use' of social science research in this mode is part of a complicated set of interchanges that also uses practical knowledge, political insight, social technologies, and judgement.

Carol Weiss[1]

The intermittent nature of high-level attention to a given problem builds into our system of government the possibility not only of incrementalism, but also of periodic punctuations to these temporary periods of equilibrium.

Frank Baumgartner and Bryan Jones[2]

Traditionally researchers looking at complex causal processes have faced a choice between using a case study approach, looking at rich qualitative data assembled for a very small number of cases (the approach used in much of Part II); or a 'large N' approach, where stripped-down information is defined as 'variables' for a substantial sample of cases and statistical tests and inference are used for analysis (as in the previous chapter). A trend to 'mixed methods' has been one important way of trying to overcome or transcend this dichotomy and to seek more 'triangulation' of information assembled using different methods (Gerring, 2011).

The approach adopted in this chapter is somewhat different. Called 'fuzzy set' social science, or qualitative comparative analysis (QCA), it starts by developing information on quite a number of cases in a lot of detail, but then seeks to collate and summarize this rich evidence in a set of judgements that can facilitate a systematic comparison across the cases. Specifically we focus on a set of 15 relatively closely matched social scientists, each of whom has achieved significant external impacts. We then seek to follow through and condense their very different stories by comparing them in a standardized way, posing common questions with limited

---

[1] Weiss and Bucuvalas (1980: 12).
[2] Baumgartner and Jones (2009: 10).

answers that summarize a lot of complex information in a series of judgements. We begin by briefly setting out the rationale for using a fuzzy set/QCA approach. We also explain how the cases were selected; how we obtained the large volumes of information needed to operationalize this approach effectively; and how judgements were coded. The second section focuses on four sets of four key categorization questions that encompass the main information, each summarized in visual terms showing the diverse ways in which high impact academics operate. The last section pulls together these codings to draw an overall picture of the diverse ways in which social scientists achieve high external impacts.

4.1 Using case studies of high impact academics

> Everyday experience and qualitative research both indicate that [complex] causation, where the same outcome may follow from several different combinations, is common.
>
> *Charles Ragin*[3]

The central rationale for fuzzy set or QCA methods is to allow a different kind of analysis of complex causation, where many different factors interact to shape social outcomes in variable configurations. Many combinations of conditions may lead to the same outcome, which are not 'caused' in any simple pattern that can be accessed easily through regression 'tournaments' attempting to assign causality (or association) between possible explanatory variables. The problem may be that a condition is a necessary one for something to happen in some routes or combinations, but not in others. And on its own an individual condition may not 'do' anything unless it is switched on by the presence of others. In the case of social scientists achieving external impacts we might find that a combination of conditions [A, B, C] sometimes works, but so too does a [B, D] combination or an [A, C, E] mix. In principle, variable-orientated regression analyses can address some of these issues by analysing variable interactions, and there are sophisticated techniques for doing so. However, the problem may be that only pretty major variables are included in datasets, and not what might be termed 'micro-variables' that may often do the 'switching on or off' functions for major variables. Similarly in large N studies variable lists tend to be those factors occurring at least across a sub-set of cases, omitting factors very unique to one case. Depending on the size of datasets, regression methods may also not get very far in surfacing complex interaction effects, even if all relevant variables are covered.

Fuzzy set or QCA methods do not start from a variable-orientation, but instead from a whole case orientation. The concept of 'casing' involves a form of holistic deliberation about what are the essential links between the ideas that a researcher wants to test, and the evidence in front of him or her (Ragin 1992 and 2000). For Ragin: 'Casing is an essential part of the process of producing theoretical structured descriptions of social life, and of using the empirical world to articulate theories' (1992: 225). For the rest of this chapter the cases we discuss are 15 selected social

---

[3] Ragin (2000).

Figure 4.1   The anonymized individual cases used in this chapter

Academic status		Discipline	Form of external influence
Professor	A	Social psychology	Research with central/local government and public services on social integration of minority groups
Professor	B	Political science and government	Research and consultancy on public management and administrative reform in devolved governments
Reader	C	Health economics	Consultancy and research for UK Department of Health and other related regulatory bodies on health equality
Professor	D	Public policy and government	Consultancy and research for government departments responsible for social security and welfare reform
Professor	E	Social policy and housing	Commissioned research for large charity on issues relating to housing, homelessness, and social exclusion
Professor	F	Planning and urban studies	Advising government and private sector on urban planning, design and logistics for international cultural events
MBA	G	Finance and management	Specific research and data consultancy for large multinational financial and business services firms
Emeritus Professor	H	Finance and business	Specific research and data consultancy for large banks and financial institutions, particularly design of indexes
Reader	I	Sociology and technology	Research and consultancy for international tech firms on social experiences of domestic technology
Professor	J	Social psychology and technology	Commissioned research for large technology firms on user experience and innovations around hi-tech products
Professor	K	Sociology	Consultancy and research for product and manufacturing companies, and government on consumer behaviour
Senior Lecturer	L	Social work and psychology	Research and consultancy for government and charities involved in policy and delivery of post-adoption services
Senior Lecturer	M	Political economy and development	Commissioned research for food manufacturers on sustainable sourcing from developing countries
Senior Research Fellow	N	Anthropology and development	Commissioned research for charities and international governments on mobility/transport in developing countries
Professor	O	Law and religion	Research that influences civil society organisations working on issues of legal and constitutional theory and religion

scientists whose anonymized details are briefly covered in Figure 4.1. We decided to focus on a set of academics who have all in one way or another achieved important external impacts or a strong level of engagement in the non-academic realm. We looked to see if we could categorize and work out the combinations of conditions important within this selection.

Our 15 cases cover a fairly broad range across social science disciplines, the types of research undertaken, and the external sector where impact or engagement was achieved. We make no claim that these cases are the 'best' or the most 'typical' cases; nor do they make up a formally representative sample of all cases of impact. They are instead just a strong selection that evolved over the course of 18 months in the latter phases of the research project. They are also cases where we have been able to create knowledge in depth. As we interviewed social scientists about impact, and talked to people in government, business and civil society organizations about their experiences of working with university researchers, we got dozens of perspectives on what counts as high impact for academics. We asked our external interviewees to nominate academics who in their view had been influential in changing something that their organization did, or in shifting how wider public policy was made. In turn, we interviewed many of these nominated academics.

Amongst this latter population we selected a small sub-set to pursue in as much detail as we could muster. We followed up on each of these individuals through unobtrusive analysis, establishing a full CV and record of research. We then spoke directly to the academics about how their links to outside organizations had evolved over time, how they worked best, what barriers or problems they encountered, how they perceived their own impacts, and about other organizations for which they had done work or with which they had strong links. We also interviewed people who could give demand-side or client-side views of each social scientist's contribution. Broadly speaking, for each selected case, we conducted between three and six interviews with the academics concerned and selected users (with interviews usually lasting around 40 minutes each). We also reviewed key literature and documentation recommended by our interviewees. Each case therefore contains rich qualitative information and a fair degree of detail. Finally, the judgements made in the next two sections are all based on a deliberative, team review of the data, evidence, and interview transcripts.

In QCA, researchers have to have a fairly good idea *ex ante* about what the potential causal relations are likely to be, in order to be able to design a framework to show the difference that those key causal relations make. Our logic for focusing on social scientists with well-established high levels of external impacts was to illuminate further the issue of how far and in what ways there is a tension between academics focusing on the one hand on peer-reviewed academic publications that could become highly cited by other academics and researchers in their field; or on the other hand, focusing on growing their engagement with external stakeholders usually in one or two sectors, such as business and commerce, or public policy, or civil society. Depending on which combination of these two strategies social scientists pick, Figure 4.2 sums up the earlier discussion in Chapter 2, and shows that four possible outcomes are feasible.

Given the selection process for our chosen academics, we know that none of them fall into the bottom right category in Figure 4.2, that is, academics who are 'otherwise engaged' without either a strong academic record or external engagements. We also know that some of our selection at least will sit within the top left-hand cell of 'stellar academics', for whom a strong level of academic publications and successfully achieving

Figure 4.2   Relationship between academic outputs and external engagement

Academic outputs	External engagement	
	Emphasized	*De-emphasized*
Emphasized	Academic outputs and external engagement reinforce each other. These researchers are *stellar academics,* able to integrate both roles.	Researchers stress their academic work. They are *passive producers* who have little proactive engagement with the external domain.
De-emphasized	*Practitioner-orientated academics* assign most time to external engagement, and have less time for peer-reviewed work. This group includes contract researchers and academics with 'celebrity' or 'pop scholar' profiles.	Neither role is dominant – academics here are *otherwise engaged,* perhaps in teaching or in departmental and university administrative duties.

external impacts are closely associated, combining together to help ensure that their work is well-respected and influential. Yet an alternative route to high impacts is also feasible in the bottom left-hand cell of Figure 4.2, where 'practitioner-orientated' academics assign a lot of time and effort to keeping up a network of contacts and research engagements with external sectors, in the process assigning a lower priority to traditional academic research and publishing. Finally, our selection includes at least some cases where social scientists have focused chiefly on producing peer-reviewed publications and research of interest primarily to academics. But some of these passive producers in impacts terms included in our selection have none the less been successful in achieving high external influence, despite assigning it relatively little time or focus, for instance, perhaps due to serendipity, or perhaps because of personal contacts.

In the analysis below we seek to condense the very varied set of practices across our 15 social scientists by asking a set of qualitative questions, which allow us to make use of the rich information gathered about each academic and about how their individual pathway to impact operated. Our focus is especially on two issues:

- Both stellar and practitioner-orientated academics are interested in doing research that 'makes a difference' in the world, and achieve external impacts – but the orientations vary in each case. Practitioner-orientated academics more explicitly focus on doing applied research that is directly usable by external stakeholders and that maintains their position in external networks and communities of practice.
- Do academics who emphasize and prioritize external engagement with external stakeholders in fact have more external impacts? Is the passive producer style of academic also less impactful than the proactive and externally-oriented model?

In the analysis, we look at four main dimensions of how social scientists work and achieve influence. The first two components here are the same as those already used in

Figure 4.2, the extent to which individuals are orientated towards producing academic outputs and publications, and whether an academic has an external influence orientation. These form the focus of the next section. Section 4.3 then looks in more detail at two different aspects of impacts and public engagement, distinguishing between 'concentrated' impacts in one specialist area, and a more 'diffuse' impacts pattern.

4.2 Explaining high impacts at the individual level

> To be honest, if you are going to do academic research which is based on what is happening, rather than some pre-ordained theory you have picked off the shelf, you've got to go in. The world out there is changing so fast.
>
> *University professor in interview*

Our first line of inquiry for each of our case academics is to establish where they sit on an overall dimension of being orientated towards (traditional) academic work. At this point we also need to introduce an essential element of the QCA approach, which is the formation of clear judgement-based questions that are resolved to produce specific codings from qualitative information, codings that can be compared across individuals. However, these codings are relatively 'fuzzy' and deliberately not precise. They are not 'values' for specific 'variables', but instead vehicles for systematizing complex judgements about rich qualitative information just enough to facilitate comparison.

The way in which coding is undertaken depends in large part on the nature of the underlying information. We are essentially trying to sort the 15 academics on whom we focus into sets, asking through groups of conditions how far each of the cases can be said to exhibit the characteristics of belonging to a given set. For example, in trying to determine whether an academic is influential amongst their peers we can define a set criterion of being 'highly cited by academics in the academic domain'. Note that in considering this issue we can use judgement and contextual information to control for the discipline that an academic works in, their sub-field and type of research, and their demographic characteristics – so that we are asking whether someone with these Y citations in this field W and sub-field W1, and these personal characteristics (like age), can be seen as highly cited amongst their fellow academics.

The 'fuzzy' coding that we use for this first question (and then throughout the rest of this chapter) are these:

1	= the individual is clearly included in the set (here, highly cited academics)
0.75	= probably the individual is within the set, but this is not clear cut
0.5	= the individual might be in or outside the set, it is too hard to judge in this case
0.25	= probably the academic lies outside the set, but this is not clear cut
0	= the individual clearly lies outside the set (here, 'not at all' highly cited).

Figure 4.3 shows how these criteria can be applied to judging whether an academic is a prolific publisher of highly-cited peer-reviewed journal articles

(shown in Column 1) and of highly-cited books or book chapters (Column 2). To determine these allocations, we used Harzing's 'Publish or Perish' software to create datasets of all publications for each academic, including the number of Google Scholar citations recorded for each one.[4] We looked at their h-index and g-index scores for journal articles and books items, and made a judgement based on some standardised (but discipline-specific) parameters about the extent of set membership in both cases.

The third element of judging our researchers' orientation towards academic work looks at whether they are highly cited by their peers (Column 3). Here we based our judgements on the Google Scholar number of citations to our academics made by other academics (during the period 2004 to 2009), again set against the academic's field. The final question asked in Figure 4.3 is whether our case academics attracted research council or other academic funding. We looked at whether they won ESRC grants, and checked other relevant funding council and foundation websites, and the academics' own CVs, to find any reference to grants for research projects. Again our judgements controlled for the kind of work that each social scientist does (some inherently involving big budgets, and others not) in deciding where they sat on this criterion.

Looking along the rows in Figure 4.3, there are some important differences in the detail of the patterns for our group of academics. At the top of the table, Prof K in sociology and Prof A in social psychology are both full members of all four sets – they clearly count as prolific academics in the established sense. As we move down the rows there are still many incidences of full set membership, as we would expect given our criteria for selecting cases. But gradually the numbers begin to drop to reveal signs of some distinct profiles. Academics further down the listing have been comparatively less successful in securing funds from UK research councils, for instance. As later Figures show, this often reflects these academics undertaking more applied work and securing funds more easily or quickly from other sources. However, there were only weak signals amongst our cases to suggest that more applied academics are less likely to produce large numbers of peer-reviewed articles, and perhaps publish more books or book chapters. For instance, five of our academics are rated higher on publishing books than research articles (after our judgements controlled somewhat for discipline context).

At the right side of Figure 4.3, Column 5 shows the *intersection* set {A ∩ B} for the four criteria used in Columns 1 to 4. The idea here is simply that to join the set of 'tall, blond people' a person needs to be both tall and blond. We cannot admit short blonds or tall brunettes without the meaning of the set collapsing; and nor can blondness 'compensate' for shortness (as a variable-based approach might assume). So our interaction set in Figure 4.3 delimits the set of people who fully qualify for the set of academically influential researchers by requiring that they do well on all the relevant

---

[4] The superiority of Google Scholar for any citations-related work in the social sciences is set out in detail in Dunleavy and Tinkler (2014) and LSE Public Policy Group (2011: Ch. 2). Essentially the internal inclusiveness of other widely used proprietary databases, such as the Web of Science or Scopus, are just lamentably too small to be of any reliable use outside core physical science disciplines. See also Harzing (2010).

Figure 4.3   Evaluation of case study academics and their academic outputs, citations, and inward references

			1 Academic is a prolific publisher of highly cited journal articles	2 Academic is a prolific publisher of highly cited books or book chapters	3 Academic has built a strong reputation specifically amongst academic community	4 Academic has been successful in winning RCUK funding over the years	5 Inter (min)	6 Union (max)
Prof	K	Sociology	1	1	1	1	1	1
Prof	A	Social psychology	1	1	1	1	1	1
EProf	H	Finance and business	1	1	1	0.5	0.5	1
Rdr	C	Health economics	1	0.75	0.5	0.5	0.5	1
Rdr	I	Sociology and technology	0.5	1	1	0.5	0.5	1
Prof	J	Social psychology and technology	0.5	0.75	1	1	0.5	1
Prof	E	Social policy and housing	0.5	0.5	1	0.75	0.5	1
SRF	N	Anthropology and development	0.75	0.5	1	0.75	0.5	1
SL	M	Political economy and development	0.5	1	1	0.25	0.25	1
Prof	O	Law and religion	0.5	1	1	0	0	1
Prof	F	Planning and urban studies	0	0.75	0.25	0	0	0.75
MBA	G	Finance and management	0.75	0.5	0.25	0	0	0.75
SL	L	Social work and psychology	0.5	0.5	0.25	0.5	0.25	0.5
Prof	B	Political science and government	0.5	0.5	0.25	0.5	0.25	0.5
Prof	D	Public policy and government	0.5	0.5	0.5	0	0	0.5

criteria. We code here by taking the minimum score achieved across Columns 1 to 4. As we move to the bottom of the table, the scores suggest more tenuous or varying degrees of membership. Finally, Column 6 in the Figure shows the *union* set {A U B} of all four values, given by the highest value achieved across Columns 1 to 4. Ragin (2000) argues that we can productively compare performance on the interaction and union sets to characterize the differences between cases, here giving an indicative picture of how conclusively each academic can be said to be a member of the overall set. Looking just at Columns 5 and 6 gives a very good feel for the variety amongst our selected academics in their approach to traditional academic work.

We turn next to look at how far our case academics were orientated towards external impacts or engagement. Again Figure 4.4 presents four possible criteria that could count here. Making judgements is clearly much more of a qualitative process than it was earlier, and we combined many different pieces of information in order to determine whether our case academics fell into each of the four sets shown in Columns 7 to 10 here. We drew on a range of unobtrusive measures based on analysis of academics' CVs, supplemented by information gained from interviews with the academics themselves and with the government officials, business executives or NGO personnel with whom they worked.

Column 7 assesses the extent to which our academics were proactive in building their media profile, through making links with traditional press and media (where we also looked at their coverage level, relative to the norm in their discipline) and their level of activity with social media. Next we assessed how integrated our academics seemed to be in relevant practitioner networks (Column 8). We looked at whether they had spent any time as a practitioner prior to entering a university career, and if so had they brought into academia a ready-made familiarity with their relevant fields of research? Additionally, we assessed to what extent each academic's own research expertise relied upon having good links to outside organizations, perhaps firms, government agencies, or charities.

The next two columns (9 and 10) relied even more on judgemental factors and different pieces of evidence. To see whether an academic was proactive in seeking external impacts we looked in part at their behaviour. But we also ran some basic textual analysis of our interview transcripts to see whether people voluntarily stated (without prompting) that they were strongly in favour of academics trying to create external impacts. We also coded these transcripts for signs that academics were thinking proactively about impacts of their research in external contexts. For instance, one academic commented about getting outside funding:

> I'm very aware that you have to tell a good story in industry. ... Having a [corporation S] grant is ten times the work of having an ESRC [research council] grant. Because you have people who actually want to use the knowledge. They ring you up and say: 'Have you done anything on this?' ESRC never rings you up and asks you anything about that. The amount of hand-holding, interactions, people passing through town who want dinner. It is really a lot of work.

Similarly in Column 10 we coded our case academics on whether they said they networked with practitioners in relevant sectors, and how practitioners also saw their

Figure 4.4 Evaluating academics' orientation to having external impacts

			7	8	9	10	11a	11b	12
			Academic is highly proactive in building their media profile (including use of social media)	Academic is strongly integrated into relevant practitioner networks	Academic is highly proactive in prioritizing potential impacts of their research	Academic is highly proactive in maintaining links with relevant practitioners	Inter (min) [7.8.9.10]	Inter (min) [8.9.10]	Union (max)
EProf	H	Finance and business	1	1	1	1	1	1	1
Prof	J	Social psychology and technology	1	1	1	1	1	1	1
Prof	F	Planning and urban studies	1	1	1	0.75	0.75	0.75	1
MBA	G	Finance and management	1	1	0.75	0.75	0.75	0.75	1
Rdr	I	Sociology and technology	0.75	0.75	1	1	0.75	0.75	1
Prof	B	Political science and government	1	0.75	0.75	0.75	0.75	0.75	1*
Prof	K	Sociology	0.5	0.5	1	0.75	0.5	0.5	1
SL	L	Social work and psychology	0.5	1	0.75	1	0.5	0.75	1
SL	M	Political economy and development	0.25	1	0.75	1	0.25	0.75	1
Prof	E	Social policy and housing	0.25	1	1	1	0.25	1	1
Rdr	C	Health economics	0.25	0.75	0.5	0.5	0.25	0.5	1
Prof	D	Public policy and government	0.75	0.75	0.5	0.5	0.5	0.5	0.75
Prof	A	Social psychology	0.25	0.75	0.75	0.75	0.25	0.75	0.75
SRF	N	Anthropology and development	0.25	0.75	0.75	0.75	0.25	0.75	0.75
Prof	O	Law and religion	0.25	0	0	0.5	0	0	0.5

Note: (*) The union score for this academic shifts to 0.75 if we exclude sub-set 7.

behaviour and attitudes, as well as checking for other supporting evidence (such as talks or conference presentations to practitioner audiences).

The last three columns again present the summary codings for this area. In looking at the intersection set there is a judgement to be made about including the media codes (Column 7) or not. We show both options in Columns 11a and 11b and the choice makes a difference for five people, a third of the cases covered. Leaving out media scores raises all these academics' intersection score, suggesting that they are 'behind the scenes' operators who would rather avoid the public eye. For the other two thirds of our cases this choice makes no difference. Given the selection basis for our 15 academics it is not surprising that the scores for the union set in Figure 4.4 are generally high. Academics at the top of this listing have a particularly impressive record in all aspects, not least the way they have talked about the importance of external impacts and their proactive efforts in this area.

The next stage of our analysis is to stand back from the greater level of detail considered so far and instead compare the relationship between academic impacts and external orientation for each of our 15 cases using only the interaction and union set codings from Figures 4.3 and 4.4. The charts in Figure 4.5 show the results (using Column 11b as the interaction set for external impacts and hence excluding the media effect). The main variation shown is between social scientists who show both substantial academic impacts and a strong external orientation, basically the nine academics in the top line of charts here, and the rest. There are five cases of academics who seem to be less academically and more practitioner-orientated, shown in the right of the middle row and two bottom row charts of Figure 4.5. One of our case academics is unusual because they have been externally influential (which is why they are included) but clearly have had this influence somewhat thrust upon them. This person showed very little inclination to be externally oriented in their work – instead conforming closely to the 'passive producer' type mentioned above.

We turn attention next to estimating in a more granulated way the precise form of external impacts achieved by our academics. Again we base our codings here on a wide range of data sources, including unobtrusive data-collection and telephone interviewing with the academics and a small number of research users. All codings were then reviewed by our team, and in cases of difficulty we sought more information.

We also made a distinction between concentrated impacts and diffuse impacts. 'Concentrated' impacts are those that are unmediated, they are achieved primarily through direct and evolving relationships between one of the case academics and particular organizations in government, business or civil society. Here we are looking for signs that the academic has built up a degree of continuity and commitment with the same or similar organizations, and that these relationships were seen as valuable by the 'clients' involved, usually because they produced strong or clear benefits. Almost all our interviewees (and many practitioners also) stressed to us that academics achieve impact because of the cumulative effect of building these relationships over time, and using them as a basis for the development of useful and relevant research.

For concentrated impacts, Figure 4.6 shows four specific questions that we used to help us to categorize cases. Column 13 covers one of the most obvious possible signs of concentrated impact, namely the willingness of the organizations to part with hard cash for research or for access to research expertise. For each academic, we compiled a list of funding or grants they have received from external clients (excluding

Figure 4.5   Relationships between academic impacts and external orientation, for our 15 academics

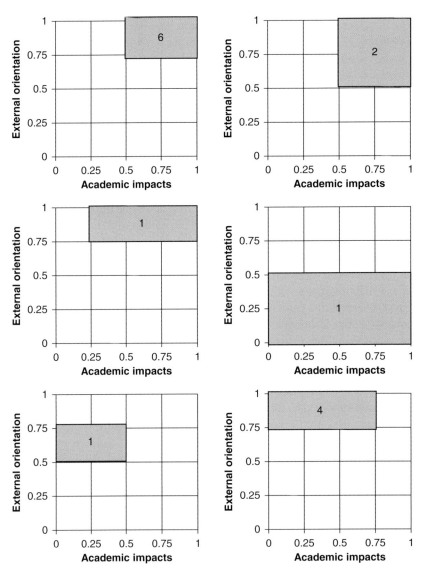

Note: The number of academics in each set grouping is denoted by the figure inside the box. These numbers total 15.

government research councils), and checked these, both through interviews and unobtrusive analysis of CVs. To help our codings we averaged the grant sums involved over the estimated length of that academic's career. Academics coded 1 here had received anything up to £10 million over their careers from external funders. For others, the amounts were less or much less, and these varied all the way down to no funding.

For many private sector clients, the very fact that substantial amounts of funding were changing hands for research activities was evidence enough that they felt the

Figure 4.6 How our case academics scored in achieving concentrated impacts

			13	14	15	16	17	18
			Academic has accumulated money from same organizations over a period of years	Academic has built strong relationships with specific individuals in external organizations over a period of years	Academic's external impact profile is strongly concentrated in a particular sector or organization	Academic has achieved considerable impacts with their work on specific organizations	Inter (min)	Union (max)
E	Prof	Social policy and housing	1	1	1	1	1	1
I	Rdr	Sociology and technology	1	1	0.75	1	0.75	1
H	EProf	Finance and business	1	0.75	0.75	1	0.75	1
J	Prof	Social psychology and technology	1	0.75	0.75	1	0.75	1
M	SL	Political economy and development	1	1	0.75	1	0.75	1
F	Prof	Planning and urban studies	0.5	0.75	0.5	1	0.5	1
N	SRF	Anthropology and development	0.75	0.75	1	0.75	0.75	1
D	Prof	Public policy and government	1	0.5	0.5	0.5	0.5	1
G	MBA	Finance and management	1	0.5	1	0.75	0.5	1
C	Rdr	Health economics	0.75	0.75	0.75	0.75	0.75	0.75
B	Prof	Political science and government	0.75	0.75	0.75	0.5	0.5	0.75
L	SL	Social work and psychology	0.5	0.75	0.5	0.5	0.5	0.75
K	Prof	Sociology	0.25	0.5	0.25	0.25	0.25	0.5
A	Prof	Social psychology	0.25	0.5	0.25	0.5	0.25	0.5
O	Prof	Law and religion	0	0.25	0.5	0	0	0.5

research was having some kind of impact inside their organization. One academic near the top of Figure 4.6 recalled how she asked an executive in her client organization for documentary proof of the impact of her research activities. This was met with puzzlement. 'When I say "Write me a letter"', explains this academic, 'she [i.e., the client] says: "Of course. But this makes no sense? I wouldn't have funded you if you didn't have impact"'. Yet we also found a certain frustration amongst other academics that money is often not forthcoming from public sector agencies or business, despite strong academic impacts and external engagement. One leading academic commented:

> What I would have loved was for our research to have triggered interest from [the clearly relevant government department] and for them to have come up with some money. Even some of the money to match the ESRC funding or something like that. They've always said: 'We've got no money'.

Column 14 in Figure 4.6 focuses on the extent to which academics and their clients are able to point towards well-established relationships that have involved repeat or recurring research links. For example, academic researchers may produce annual digests or analyses for government or private sector clients. These are often published as joint research outputs, branded with the client logos as well as the academic's university or institution. Many interviewees stressed the importance of these trusted and reliable inter-connections, both formal and informal, as a key contributing factor for sustaining impacts.

In Column 15 we sought to judge how far an academic's impact is focused in a particular policy sub-field, business topic or sector of society. Our codings drew on unobtrusive data. We searched each academic's full name in the main Google search engine, and working through the results in a systematic way to record all references to that academic in external domains – i.e., government, business, civil society, think tanks, and so on. We looked at the total number of external references found, and the extent to which these references were concentrated in particular sectors. The higher the significant concentration, the more definitely that person could be assigned sub-set membership.

The last substantive codings here, in Column 16, show our judgements of the extent to which the academic's involvement with their client organization(s) created specific and substantial impacts. To inform these codings we assessed as systematically as possible the statements that our interviewees made about impacts, and the extent to which these were corroborated by clients. Clients and academics both stressed to us that it is mostly not possible to say with any certainty or precision exactly what the specific impacts of the links with academics were, only that there was a clear sense that the research and interaction had helped in significant ways. As one academic commented:

> I don't think we'll ever be able to point to a change in policy and say that was because of [our research]. It more helps to inform and shape the context of the debate.

A repetition or cumulation of involvements was often a useful indication here. For instance, research based on an ESRC-sponsored programme, led to the principal investigator being invited into Parliament to brief a ministerial working group on issues relating to current policy. Departmental officials confirmed that work by this

Figure 4.7 How our case academics scored in achieving diffuse impacts

			19	20	21	22	23	24
			Academic has developed a high profile in the media and press	Academic has strong visibility across a wide range of sectors	Academic publishes a broad range of research reports for different external organizations	Academic can show research or advisory links to a wide range of external organizations	Interaction (min)	Union (max)
H	EProf	Finance and business	1	1	1	1	1	1
M	SL	Political economy and development	0.5	0.5	1	1	0.5	1
F	Prof	Planning and urban studies	1	1	0.5	0.75	0.5	1
E	Prof	Social policy and housing	0.5	0.75	1	0.5	0.5	1
G	MBA	Finance and management	1	0	0.5	0.75	0	1
J	Prof	Social psychology and technology	0.5	0.75	0.75	0.5	0.5	0.75
N	SRF	Anthropology and development	0	0.75	0.75	0.5	0.5	0.75
K	Prof	Sociology	0.5	0.75	0.75	0.75	0.5	0.75
A	Prof	Social psychology	0.75	0.25	0.75	0.75	0.25	0.75
I	Rdr	Sociology and technology	0.5	0.75	0.25	0.5	0.25	0.75
C	Rdr	Health economics	0.75	0.5	0.25	0.5	0.25	0.75
D	Prof	Public policy and government	0.25	0.5	0.75	0.25	0.25	0.75
B	Prof	Political science and government	0.5	0.75	0.25	0.25	0.25	0.75
L	SL	Social work and psychology	0.25	0.25	0.25	0.75	0.25	0.75
O	Prof	Law and religion	0.25	0.75	0	0	0	0.75

academic formed the basis for the specific development of policy on an aspect of UK social provision. Similarly, along with colleagues, another of our case academics had developed a number of widely-used market indices for the comparative assessment of business performance in the UK and internationally. Over many years, these indices had been sponsored and proactively marketed by large financial institutions. Or again, a senior executive at a large manufacturer described the work of another case academic as 'seminal' in influencing the firm's strategy on the sustainable sourcing of its core materials from developing countries. The work created a basis for the firm to invest hundreds of millions of pounds in achieving sustainable sourcing, with strong benefits for its marketing profile in a publicly visible consumer sector.

To assess the *diffuse impacts* of our case academics, Figure 4.7 focuses on criteria about their wider public profiles and the spread of the academic's, links across different organizations and across the public sphere. Our judgements for Column 19 draw on an extensive search for mentions of each academic between 2004 and 2009 in all national and international press and media using the Factiva and Nexis databases. We also recorded the number of mentions by press and media in our Google search. From this, we were able to estimate the extent to which references to our academics were visible across a wide range of different organizations, coded in Column 20. Next the codings in Column 21 draw on the number and range of research reports by each case academic, which we found by searching the Google Scholar database directly and using the Harzing 'Publish or Perish' software. This showed the number of organizations with which our academics had significant research or advisory links over the years, and our judgements took account of the career time involved, the academic's age and discipline, and so on. Finally, in Figure 4.7, not all research finds its way into publication. Academics with strong external impacts often undertake consultancy or small pieces of work that form components of a wider programme of work by their client organization. Column 22 shows codings for this kind of work, based on information collected from interviews and unobtrusive measures, such as a fine-grained coding of CV information and Google search results. Together these four questions gave us a useful picture of the overall breadth of the academics' external links over the years.

4.3 Pulling together the analysis

For my kind of research, where I am interested in changing the way people do things, and because I have an empirical leaning, the two [academic publication and external influence] go hand in hand.

Business school professor in interview

You can't just go in and give them [practitioners] boring [discipline A] facts. They bore most [A] students, let alone people who aren't committed to the discipline. So something different had to happen.

University professor in interview

Key to the QCA approach is the overall relationship between the independent or explanatory factors, in this case the orientations and activities of researchers discerned from multiple information sources (including the case academics themselves) and the phenomenon to be explained, that is the kind of impacts they have in wider society. Here we ask to what extent the relationships between the codings of our high impact academics' orientations and behaviours can help to illuminate the existence of multiple, differentiated pathways to impact.

We look first in Figure 4.8 at the relationship between academic impacts (shown on the horizontal axes) and achieving *concentrated* external impacts in a particular sector or policy field (on the vertical axes), plotting the range between the minimum (intersection set) and maximum (union set) values. For each academic this visual depicts the extent to which their behaviour on each dimension is coherent or spread out, and how the two dimensions are related. The smaller the two-dimensional area covered, the more compact the shaded area, the more tightly focused and linked the two are. The numbers within the blue shaded areas in Figure 4.8 count how many academics fit into this pattern, so the total across the six areas shown in the charts totals 15.

The largest cluster of academics are those who achieve both high academic impacts and high concentrated impacts (the top-left chart in the Figure) in a reasonably focused way, scoring between 0.5 and 1 on both dimensions. This group includes six of our case academics. This pattern counts against any argument that in order to have high impacts externally, academics must de-prioritize their academic work and focus more on practical applied work. The evidence for this largest cluster of cases suggests quite the opposite, that academic impacts and external impacts are likely to be constituent of each other in many cases. Time and again academics told us in interviews that their academic work and applied work are necessarily integrated, suggesting strongly that impact in one area begets impact in the other. Another academic scores high on concentrated impact, but has an academic score ranging down to 0.25 (shown in the top right-hand chart). This person seems to broadly hang with the group of six.

Also in the top right chart of Figure 4.8 there are two cases of professors with impeccable academic impacts scores, but who appear lower down (between 0.25 and 0.5) in terms of their concentrated impacts. Both these academics have received extensive funding from research councils and other funding bodies, and their research over the years has been very applied and empirical. But it has involved a great many different external organizations, so that their concentrated impact is restricted. They are not failing to have external impacts, just choosing not to concentrate their focus in a single area. Indeed, both academics told us of the difficulties they had experienced over many years in getting funding from public authorities apart from research councils, even though both have been consistently active in areas relating to government and public policy. In Chapter 6 we explore whether it is characteristic of the government sector that impacts on policy making are much harder to identify, and that because of a high turnover of officials and strict procurement rules perhaps longer-lasting relationships are harder to forge. Continuity and relationship-building in policy making can also be harder to sustain across changes of government, as several of our case academics stressed to us.

Looking at the middle row of charts in Figure 4.8, the three cases shown are again between 0.5 and 1 on concentrated impacts, but with lower academic scores from 0

Figure 4.8   Relationships between academic impacts and concentrated impacts

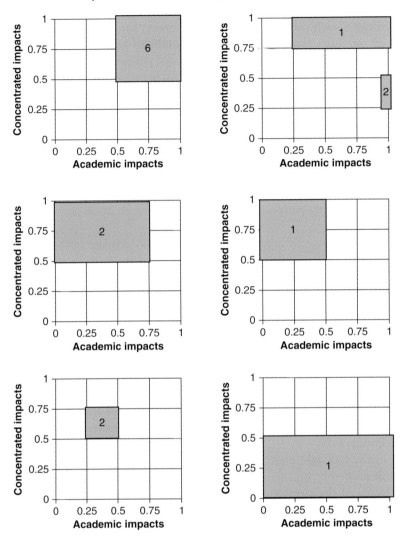

Note: The number of academics in each set grouping is denoted by the figure inside the box. These numbers total 15.

to either 0.75 in two cases and 0.5 in the other one. We might see these academics as located more towards the practitioner-orientated pattern. We could also include the two academics in the left-hand bottom-row chart, where the academic scores are compact and lowish (0.25 to 0.5) and the concentrated external impact score is compact and medium (0.5 to 0.75). Thus one in three of our case academics seem more strongly oriented towards achieving concentrated external impacts over academic impacts. This group includes academics who have tended to focus predominantly on growing their relationships with external stakeholders, and de-prioritising the amount of time spent generating traditional academic outputs.

Some of these academics have worked in other sectors previously, and have brought into academia with them their strong external orientations. Furthermore, they have tended to stick to the applied mode of working within the university. For instance, one such person was a finance and management academic who worked for many years in private sector finance before making the transition to a university career; he is explicit that his main role now lies in making bridges back to the sector he left. Not surprisingly, he scores very highly in terms of external orientation.

Figure 4.9 Relationships between concentrated impacts and diffuse impacts, for 8 cases ranking highly in terms of academic outputs

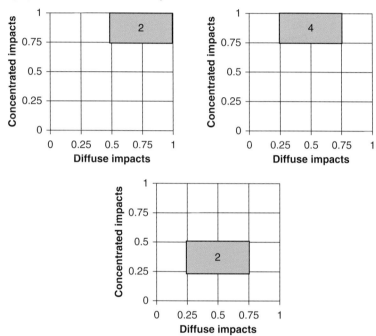

We turn next to consider in Figure 4.9 the relationship between concentrated external impacts and diffuse impacts, first examining how this link works amongst the eight case academics with the strongest academic profiles and influence in our set. Again we plot *minimum* and *maximum* values for diffuse impacts shown on the horizontal axes, and for concentrated impacts, shown on the vertical axes. For this high performing group of researchers concentrated impacts are greater and more focused than diffuse impacts for six academics (shown in the top two charts of Figure 4.8).

Two academics (one in finance and business, and the other in social policy and housing) out of 15 are able to sustain very high scores across all three areas – academic impacts (not shown here), concentrated external impacts and diffuse external impacts (which are shown). Four cases show high scores in academic impacts and concentrated impacts, but fall off slightly, although not by much, in terms of their wider diffuse impacts. Two academically influential researchers had somewhat middling diffuse impacts, but lower concentrated impacts.

Figure 4.10 Relationships between concentrated impacts and diffuse impacts, for 7 cases showing characteristics of 'practitioner-oriented' approach

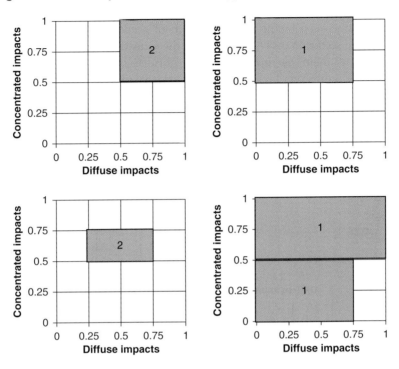

Finally we look at how concentrated and diffuse impacts were related amongst academics closer to the practitioner-oriented model, shown in Figure 4.10. These academics have lower scores in academic impacts, but are just as strong as the rest of our cases in terms of their overall external orientation and engagement. Two of these more practitioner-orientated academics (in the top left chart) scored highly in terms of both concentrated and diffuse impacts. One person here worked in planning and urban studies, and the other in political economy and development – the latter something of a stellar academic, although not having been very successful in getting research council funding over the years. In this case money was raised from the external world of policy making and practice, in the process de-emphasizing more traditional academic grant-seeking.

Finally it is worth mentioning one of our case academics shown lowest down in the bottom right chart of Figure 4.10, with a concentrated impacts score of less than 0.5, and those of diffuse impacts slightly up at less than 0.75. This academic was selected as one of the high impact cases because they received a relatively large number of external references in our full Google search. While relatively strong in terms of overall academic outputs, he has not received any funding from research councils or funding bodies. In interviews he also rejected fairly strongly ideas of external engagement and impact, and preferred to emphasize the production of academic outputs.

Conclusions

To what extent have we shed additional light on the pathways to achieving external impacts here? First, it seems clear that for an academic to achieve much influence (of either a concentrated or a diffuse kind) outside the university sector itself, they personally have to be externally focused or oriented. As one academic commented: 'In terms of interacting with people in the field you are researching, unless you do interact with them, and do what you can to keep in touch, then there aren't going to be any good luck stories, because you are outside of that social circle'. None the less, even in our case selection we found one academic with a good deal of external influence who achieved it while sticking to a traditional academic model and believing in a 'passive-producer' (they'll come to you) approach for academics.

There is only light evidence that achieving impact sometimes requires foreswearing academic influence in favour of a practitioner focus. Most of our case academics instead conformed pretty well to the 'do it all' model of stellar academics, with high academic impacts, a strong external orientation, concentrated external impacts and diffuse external impacts. They are consistently effective in external impact terms. But in the practitioner-oriented group, smaller though it is, the relationships are less clear-cut, with wider variations in how people were coded. Some practitioner-leaning academics were able to show strong concentrated and diffuse impacts, but there seems more variation amongst them.

One fundamental reason for the fuzziness that our analysis picks up about what makes high impact academics is very relevant for the 'specific publication' focus of the REF process, or the incessant search by funding bodies for evidence that individual pieces of funded research had some specific impact. Almost all academics stressed to us that this is not how the world works, and that when they did have impact it was often a reflection of the work of many different people, for which they happened to be the immediate agent of change. As one person commented:

> There was a technical cadre who do the analysis. So that is an example of impact. But it is the cumulative work of a lot of social scientists over time. It is not one. There are particular individuals who pushed it forward [...], for example, I would cite G and H, who is the founding vice-chair of [agency W]. So there are certain influential figures who interact with policy makers. But I think it is a more complicated team effort rather than one individual.

Overall the chapter shows a distinct link between scholars generating excellent academic research and publications and having concentrated external impacts. For academics able to do both these aspects well, each must become constituent of the other, so that the processes involved in researching, engagement with external organisations or sectors, and publishing, all enhance both aspects. A different group of practitioner-orientated academics focus more strongly on applied academic work, and achieving high external impacts is still possible via this specialization approach. However, these effects appear to be much less consistently visible – in this route there may be a higher degree of uncertainty about whether actual impact will follow, in whatever form. And there may sometimes be a penalty to pay in reduced academic influence. A further central message of the whole analysis has been the amount of variation amongst even high-performing academics, and the very many different ways of achieving external impact that there are. We move on next in Part II to flesh out the 'demand' side of external impacts, looking in detail at four different sectors and drawing on a wide programme of qualitative research into variations across business, government, civil society organizations and the conventional and social media worlds.

PART II

The Demand for
Social Science Research

> We all know that our science ... [indeed] every science treating the institutions and events of human culture, first arose in connection with practical considerations.
>
> *Max Weber*[1]

> Knowledge is not for knowing: knowledge is for cutting.
>
> *Michel Foucault*[2]

Modern life is specialized. The hypothesis of 'autopoeisis' associated with the German theorist Niklas Luhman (1986) sees the differentiation of societal sub-systems as the key engine of technological and social development. Over time each sphere of social life becomes more distinct from its environment (other aspects of social life governed by other sub-systems), and more autonomous (governed by its own internal logic, dynamics and imperatives). This is a picture of a 'social universe' in which galaxies are pulling further apart – for instance, by making it less and less feasible for the state to act (effectively) as the key (or single, master) co-ordinator of different societal systems. In this perspective the prospect for bridging more between higher education and other parts of society may look bleak at first sight. The engine of modernization that has separated out universities more and more as distinct spheres of social life is not likely to be reversible. Yet in Luhman's approach the key driver for continued differentiation is the growth of knowledge (including technology and organizational expertise) and associated complexity, for which society must constantly evolve ways of organizing in order to control and process. For instance, digital changes have created strong pressures for disintermediation, or 'cutting out the middle man', with far-reaching consequences for areas such as the retail, travel, publishing, music and entertainment industries. Just as some previously numerous occupations, such as typists, have greatly declined with the development of IT as all of us now do our own typing, so some separations can be reversed and re-modelled.

Correctly interpreted then, increased complexity, specialization and autopoiesis imply only that new and well-developed systems will be needed to re-simplify and reconnect what might otherwise become detached or out of sync. Arguments that higher education and university research have become overly siloed and inaccessible to external organizations have mixed levels of evidence behind them (Dunleavy and Tinkler, 2014), despite UK government policy and surrounding debate mostly assuming them as clear cut. Yet, even if we accept this premise for a moment, there is nothing inevitable or immutable about such a situation. Tackling or reversing it may require new forms of specialization of expertise and organizations to effectively counteract the source of problems – for instance, this may lead to the development of new expertise in fields like impact and knowledge exchange, public understanding of science, or public engagement.

---

[1] Quote from 'Objectivity in Social Science and Social Policy' (Weber, 1904: 3).
[2] Foucault (1984: 88).

In considering the demand for social science research in this Part we look at four very different sectors – business, government and public policy making, civil society, and the media and broader networks that constitute the public. The factors involved in achieving impacts vary considerably across these fields, and are changing in different ways. Yet there are also certain important continuities across the sectors in the issues faced by social science academics in growing their external visibility and influence.

For instance, researchers and academics clearly face an 'ecology' of demands on them. Universities and their staffs already feel themselves under pressure in multiple ways and insist in surveys and consultation processes that there are only so many hours in the day. A pessimistic view holds that the time dedicated to administration (such as that created by government research or teaching audits) or to creating and meeting more demand for external impacts has to come out of the time for the core academic activities of research or teaching. A more optimistic perspective holds out some hope that previously time-consuming tasks might be done more efficiently, and that the apparent tensions or contradictions between (say) achieving impact and advancing core research may be partially alleviated by changes in how scholarship and science operate – for instance, by shifting to digital scholarship processes that are 'shorter, better, faster, free'.

None the less, all social science departments face some significant issues in developing linkages with organizations outside higher education, issues that apply in pretty similar fashion in all of the next four chapters. Figure II.1 shows six stages in developing sustained links with outside organizations. The first stage is for researchers to have information about organizations that might be interested in their work. Sometimes in public policy settings or with some non-governmental organizations (NGOs) operating in civil society the potential application of research to a government body or NGO may seem straightforward at a rather macro-scale. But almost always in business settings this is not true, because corporations are interested in highly specific research issues and keep confidential new products or services that are in development. Similarly, the need for detailed work involved in implementing new policies in government (or arguing or lobbying against detailed changes) often becomes manifest quite suddenly, creating difficulties for researchers who cannot 'run up' relevant surveys, experiments or fieldwork overnight.

The second stage in Figure II.1 recognizes that at some point, academics and potential client organizations must make the connection with each other, either through inter-personal relationships, considered search by the organizations or marketing on the part of the academic, serendipitous meetings, or the academic's reputation or research catching the eye of interested executives or officials. Typical intermediating factors here often involve links created through the personal commitment or knowledge of senior executives or officials, or through staff knowing their alumni institution well, or researchers being proactive in bringing their work to the attention of relevant institutions or organizations. Even if these barriers are overcome, stage 3 here involves researchers and demand-side organizations being able to identify a clear 'quid pro quo' from the collaboration. Especially in relations with business or government, where researchers are unlikely

Figure II.1   Six stages in researchers and academics developing linkages with external stakeholders

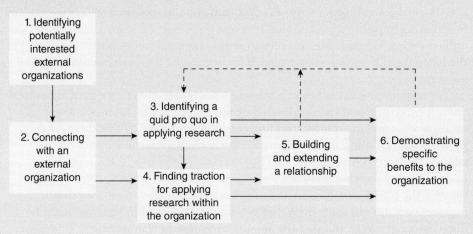

to see a pro bono case, if they are to commit large amounts of time there will have to be a flowback of benefits that makes co-operation worthwhile. But equally businesses (and government bodies partially) take a robust approach to the time of executives or officials and the amounts of funding that may be involved in developing research linkages. Unless a very specific benefit can be identified at the outset, attempts at partnership working will not progress far.

The fourth stage in Figure II.1 involves going beyond a possible reciprocity to deepen the relationship by finding real traction, genuine on-going utility from research or consultancy with universities for at least some aspect of the organization's key mission and purposes.

Sometimes a quid pro quo exists but remains undeveloped, so that the relationship between a university department and the external organization remains fragile and episodic, prone to disruption, disappointment with the research pay off, or distraction as other priorities and pressures impinge on the external organization. Getting to more sustained or deep links between researchers and client organizations involves academics gaining enough knowledge of their partner's problems and methods of working to be able to re-orientate or pivot research so that it directly addresses an on-going organizational need. Inherently this will require close contact, because tacit or implicit knowledge plays such a large role in how any organization works (Collins, 2001). In the same way that one team of researchers may have difficulties replicating experiments conducted at another lab (Collins and Evans, 2008), so outsiders can know a lot about an organization at an explicit knowledge level, and yet still not really understand its organizational culture, mission or operating procedures (Hood, 1998).

When traction is achieved, it provides the most secure basis for a sustained relationship between researchers and client organizations, the fifth stage in Figure II.1. However, it is important to recognize that other elements often play key roles here. For instance, in case studies of successful linkages we have often noted the importance of personal relationships between lead researchers (providing 'wise counsel' that is not necessarily linked to specific research projects) and executives or officials in the outside body.

Finally, the sixth stage in the Figure involves being able to demonstrate a specific impact from research. Firms especially often need to 'cash out' a benefit for a research contract to be maintained, and government officials must continuously demonstrate that public money is being spent in ways that are justified in public interest or resource-saving terms. In particular, if a relationship is to extend beyond a one-off contact, developing measures of success achieved is key – in terms of projects realized in government; or production, sales or marketing gains made in firms; or of savings made on alternative sources of information, research or consultancy across all organizations.

'Aculturation' and 'socialization' processes are those that allow people to understand how organizations in a different sector understand their work and see the world, and they apply both to researchers and to the demands of potential clients in business, government or civil society. Historically the processes that drive depth-knowledge of other organizations are time-consuming, revolving around in-person networking and linking contacts, which make up the base of conventional influence processes (shown in blue on the left side of Figure II.2). Historically, university departments' most fundamental way of achieving contact with client organizations has been via students taking jobs in different industrial sectors (creating significant first job placement links) and then progressing in their career paths (creating on-going alumni links). Job placement influences are especially high in technological fields and at postgraduate level where new graduates may understand the latest developments in theory or techniques, creating an important form of explicit knowledge transfer. Alumni connections operate much more in terms of graduates of a university department having a deep knowledge of its operating processes and personnel (in their day), and thus a great deal of tacit knowledge that is useful in the linking processes covered in Figure II.1.

The strength and relevance of these effects vary a good deal between:

- some STEM departments, with historically more concentrated links to relevant manufacturing or technological industries;
- industry-focused social science departments, such as business schools, and accounting, social policy or law departments; and
- social science and humanities departments whose students are 'generalist' educated and enter a wider range of occupations and industry sectors.

These differences across departments may perhaps have diminished in modern labour markets. While some 54 per cent of US university students now pursue vocational degrees (in hopes of a well-defined career pathway), only a quarter of US graduates actually work in jobs for which their major discipline is relevant, a proportion that increases a good deal in large conurbations and cities, and is lowest in smaller cities and towns.

Figure II.2   Some conventional and digital mechanisms involved in flows of influence

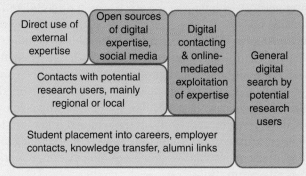

Note: Blue cells are conventional channels for linking. Orange are digital channel linkages.

The second conventional tier of influence in Figure II.2 involves direct contacts between universities and researchers and potential client users of their research, usually in terms of business executives, government officials or NGO staff attending conferences, seminars, talks or other events, or researchers and academics giving talks at outside events and attending professional or business conferences. Again personal contacts are key here because of their high 'bandwidth', flexibility and ability to convey tacit knowledge. A key aspect of these effects is that they are easier to set up and to sustain at low spatial scale, so that they are predominantly links in the same city or the same region as the university itself, an association often also embodied in the way that local or regional university departments have developed historically. The third tier of conventional influence represents more formalized and sustained knowledge transfer, which occur less commonly, creating the last of the blue-shaded boxes.

The expansion of digital information search capacities, essentially since the mid-1990s, has strongly and broadly supplemented the ways in which corporations, smaller businesses, governments and NGOs can monitor relevant academic fields (shown in the orange-shaded boxes on the right-hand side of Figure II.2). In the past only large corporations and major government departments could afford the luxury of Research Directors or Chief Scientists, part of whose jobs involve monitoring relevant university departments and fields of research for interesting developments. Two waves of digital changes have somewhat sapped the simpler functionalities of such roles, the advent of the internet in the 1990s, and the major improvement in search engines in the 2000s, making feasible the free, online intermediation of specialized knowledge. Using search to discover and utilize relevant information at short notice has become far easier for large organizations, summed up in the 'government by Google' notion of civil servants searching for expertise to back up this week's political priorities (shown in the rightmost orange-shaded box in Figure II.2).

Going beyond simple search is digital contacting and online-mediated exploitation of expertise. In business 'just in time' utilization of expertise is more feasible and small and medium enterprises (especially those with digitally well-educated staff) have been able to expand their search and adoption capabilities at low costs. To some extent though, easier direct access to expertise online may have undermined the importance of personal contact processes covered above, with offsetting implications for conventional contacts between university departments and potential clients. However, better digital search also has disintermediation effects, potentially reducing the role of consultants, think tanks and other intermediaries who acted as mediators in this process.

Finally the smallest orange-shaded box in Figure II.2 represents the role of the newest digital-drive changes, especially the shift away from closed access to open access publishing of scientific and scholarly work, which is furthest advanced in the US and UK but is a track also being followed across the European Union and Australasia. A powerful amplifier here is the growth of social media, especially shorter form and more timely communication via blogs, Twitter, data-sharing and replication networks, which may radically cut the costs of sustaining linkages and allow online equivalents of regular contact-making in person. Businesses or public agencies with focused expertise in a given area (so that they can decode or assess academic work directly) already have considerably wider access to research findings and literatures, and social media can help build or increase cross-sector liaison networks involving researchers and academics with external contacts. Yet the scale and influence of open access and social media remain new and mostly unassessed in formal terms, especially in relationships with the business sector, to which we now turn.

5

Business and the corporate sector

We are interested in people coming and sitting in on meetings with us. We are less interested in people going away and coming up with a really thick report. If you thought of academics more in the way of consultants, that is how we want them to be. We want them to help us solve problems and give us guidance about what would run our business better.

UK corporate executive in interview

I know there are British academics that have found engaging with industry incredibly stressful. It was too fast-moving, weird questions – they couldn't work out what was going on. And I respect that. Not everyone needs to be in the conversation.

US IT executive in interview

In 2001 Intel Corporation was the world's leading manufacturer of hi-tech silicon technology, and its mission statement read 'to do a great job for our customers, employees, and stockholders by being the pre-eminent building block supplier to the worldwide Internet economy'. Intel was then netting around $27 billion in revenue annually, and spending nearly $4 billion per year on research and development (R&D). By 2012 the corporation was still a pre-eminent supplier of advanced silicon technology, with net revenues of more than $50 billion, and R&D spending over $10 billion. Its new mission statement read: 'This decade we will create and extend computing technology to connect and enrich the lives of every person on earth'. Insiders argued that although the firm's emphasis was still on technology, the focus had shifted more towards the people for whom chips are being produced. As one business insider put it, the firm's vision 'shifted from being solely about silicon to understanding that there was no point in producing world class silicon if you weren't doing it for Something. And that something actually turned out to be "Some*one*"' [our italics].

This evolution from one mission statement to another crystallizes the idea that many large and dynamic firms are now as much social as they are technological, commercial, or legal entities. The contours of risk and opportunity are increasingly defined by economic, social, political, legal, regulatory and environmental considerations, which all matter a lot in market terms. So enhancing any large firm's ability to understand and perhaps anticipate or forecast how these factors will evolve has tended to increase as a priority. With this change has come an increase in the number of business staff whose job involves translating social science knowledge for in-house consumption. More social science trained staff in senior and management positions across large corporations especially has led to firms seeking social science professionals as in-house sources of expertise, and drawing more on social science inputs from intermediaries (like consultants) but also directly from researchers and academics.

We assess this changing picture in four main ways. We first outline a typology of ways in which businesses and academic researchers are linked, and consider the reduced extent to which social science departments participate in such links compared with STEM departments. We look next at the empirical evidence about current linkages between corporations and businesses and university social science (again comparing where feasible with STEM disciplines). The final section considers qualitative evidence from business interviewees about the continuing problems to greater involvement of social scientists in industry, and some positive changes that are being made that overcome barriers to wider use of social science work, especially in high-tech and service industries.

5.1 The range of university links with business

Social science research covers such a multitude of things. Yes, there are some things that are relevant, but there are some things that are completely irrelevant.

Business executive in interview

Good academics, the ones we work with in [University J and University K] – we have great relationships, where we all understand and share what our needs are. And make space for ourselves, so that we can all continue to do what is at the heart of our activities, which is research.

Business research director in interview

Corporations and smaller firms can link to university departments in a wide variety of ways, summarized diagrammatically in Figure 5.1.

The first three situations tend to assume that the firm is the dominant partner (for example with significant funding), while the university department or lab is likely to be the supplicant competing for resources or attention.

(a) With *episodic contracting* a firm encounters a problem where research could be helpful, does a quick search and 'spot' contracts with a university department for help urgently to solve that issue. The department undertakes a piece of ad hoc applied research or consultancy to meet the commission. The industrial funding received has little effect, because it was unexpected and is a one-off, while for researchers the work is often a bit difficult or inconvenient to do for the same reasons. In the UK, engineering researchers especially complain that small and medium firms are prone to behave in this way, expecting capabilities to be there when they need them, but without helping to fund their longer-term development.

(b) *Strategic commissioning* goes one stage further because the firm plans its research or consultancy needs in advance, undertaking a more considered search, and committing somewhat more resources over a longer term (perhaps two or three years). Pursuing a mix of in-house research and outsourcing helps firms to balance their R&D portfolios, spread the associated risks of doing research in-house, and access innovation and new knowledge from outside (Bower, 1992). On the university department or lab side of the exchange there is more foresight of potential client needs, and hence a greater ability to fit them constructively into an overall plan of research.

(c) *Continuous partnership* exists where the firm has a close and long-term relationship with researchers, providing a regular stream of funding that can translate into discrete projects, studentships and new equipment, and getting to know the department's or lab's staff and research capabilities in detail. The second part of the double bond here is that the researchers also come to understand the firm's procedures, priorities and capabilities in detail, and perhaps establish trust relations with particular executives (understanding the firm's 'politics' more). As a result, joint approaches to problems and issues can emerge and flourish, and researchers can suggest initiatives and relevant new work.

Figure 5.1   Ten main forms of business to university linkages

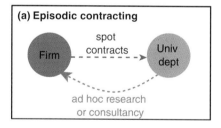

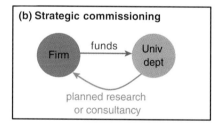

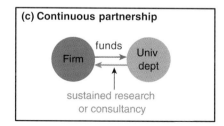

(Continued)

(d) University licenses research

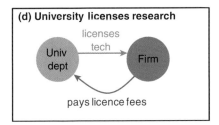

(e) Technology transfer

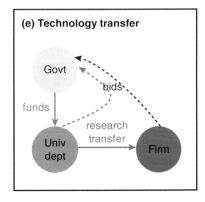

(f) Upward development spiral

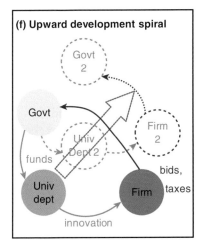

(g) Tech start up

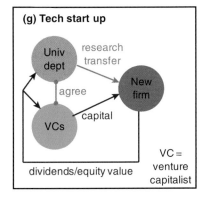

(h) Exit plus tech start up

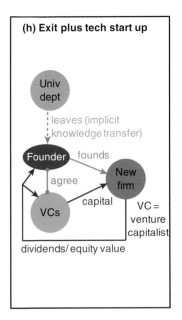

(i) Specific marketing

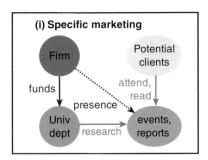

(j) Marketing and corporate social responsibility

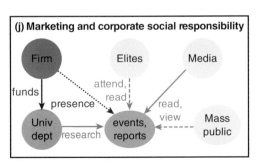

The next three situations are more balanced, with the university side possessing scarce resources that firms have need of:

(d) When a *university licenses research* then the department or lab controls a valuable resource (such as a patented or otherwise protected piece of intellectual property) created by previous research, which the firm pays to be able to use. Sometimes this kind of relationship is remote and purely commercial. At other times the lab and wider university may be involved with the client in seeking to develop new variants of the licensed intellectual property.

(e) *Technology transfer* occurs when government funding agencies provide resources to the university side (such as state-of-the-art capital equipment or funding for post-doctoral researchers) on condition that the department or lab then collaborates with industrial partners, so as to transfer knowledge of new techniques or subjects to relevant companies (Klingstrom, 1986; Bower, 1992). Normally the researchers and prospective partners have to bid jointly for funding, and to point to a past record of successful joint working. Secondments involving STEM researchers and science or technical firms are often a potent way of achieving on-going transmission of 'tacit knowledge' in using equipment, lab procedures or analytic techniques.

(f) An *upward development spiral* is something of a Holy Grail of technological development at regional scales. Here government supports university innovations that feed into industrial development (usually to firms located in the same region or city), in the expectation that employment and tax revenues will increase, with positive multiplier effects. The canvass here is often broader than tech transfer narrowly conceived, and the firms' involvement is key to unlocking government (or European Commission) funding. Etzkowitz (2008) envisages these links between business, universities, and governments as 'triple helix' configurations that involve semi-regularized and close-knit interaction between these actors.

The most lauded means of facilitating economic growth comes via the launching of new start-up companies linked to universities, especially in hi-tech industries, which can occur in two key ways:

(g) An organized *tech start-up* from the university viewpoint involves a department or lab developing research with potential commercial application. The university then does a deal with a venture capital firm, which may involve either private finance or in time an Initial Public Offering (IPO), so as to create a spin-out or 'starburst' company. The university has an equity stake and often key actors in the new company are university staff, sometimes retaining their involvement with the department. Spin-outs are especially successful where a university has created a science park to house new firms close by, for example in industrial regions like Cambridge in the UK or Silicon Valley in the US where close local synergies between universities and hi-tech industries can be maintained. The university benefits partly from dividends that the company pays out (which may not occur for a considerable time), but mainly from the increase in equity value of the company, which may be rapid and dramatic if it proves successful in exploiting a market niche.

(h) A *start-up via exit* is much more of a blow to the university side. Here a researcher who spots an industrial opportunity leaves the department or lab and negotiates individually with a venture capital firm to create the start-up company, presumably not using any IPR protected materials from their university employment. All dividends or equity gains flow back to the founder and investors here, with no formal return to the university unless the founder makes later donations. In the last decade, UK universities have greatly tightened up their ability to identify potentially commercial IPRs in work that their researchers are doing, and to ensure that they are able to share in the benefits. Sometimes in exit cases the university may secure a small equity stake in return for not raising IPR issues that could cloud a start-up.

The final set of linkages occur when the firm does not directly use the products of research in its own production work, but instead seeks a link for marketing or public relations reasons (see Figure 5.1):

(i) *Specific marketing* occurs where the firm sees an opportunity to fund research which will then lead to publications or events that attract the attention of potential clients or 'gatekeepers' determining the demand for its products or expertise. The firm here funds the research for charitable or corporate social responsibility reasons. But it has a strong expectation that there will be specific marketing opportunities created by the research to bring its executives into conversation with potential clients, to demonstrate corporate social purpose in ways that attract custom, and to enhance the firm's brand or reputation for foresightedness, acumen or competence in the field that the research relates to. Hence it is important to the firm that the resulting research is innovative, cutting edge and high quality and closely related to its activities, so as to attract the right audience to seminars or conferences, and the right readers for publications with the firm's logo on. This approach is most important where corporations deal with public sector agencies, or with professional groups (like doctors or architects) who place a high value on their independence from commercial interests.

(j) In more general *marketing and corporate social responsibility* the incentives for firms are far more diffused, simply incrementally building a brand with elite or general audiences that associate the firm with attractive or socially worthwhile research. Here the projects or activities supported by the firm may well have no direct relevance for its operations – indeed what gets done may lie a long way from its industry sector, much as if the company was supporting a symphony orchestra, an art exhibition, a medical charity, or an effort to alleviate world poverty. There is also scope for marketing-related research support that is intermediate between the general and specific types, where the corporation offering funding has some interest in the research topic, but rather remotely. Intermediate types sometimes form part of large corporations' talent management strategies. Here the company's support for general research in their overall area is used to help attract top graduates or PhDs. Sometimes too, support for conferences, seminars, sabbaticals and even higher degrees funding are a component of the firm's talent retention strategies for elite or promising staff.

Figure 5.2 Comparing the business linkages found across STEM and social science departments

Type of linkage	STEM departments and labs	Social science departments
Common	Strategic commissioning, Continuous partnership, University licensed research, Technology transfer, Tech start-ups, Exit start ups (with some equity for the university), Specific marketing, Marketing, Corporate social responsibility	Episodic contracting, General marketing
Sometimes found	Episodic contracting (with small and medium enterprises)	Strategic commissioning, Specific marketing, Exit start-ups (with no equity for the university)
Rarely found	Upward development spiral	Continuous partnership, Technology transfer, Tech start-ups
Almost never found	–	University licensed research, Upward development spiral

So, in summary, how do we expect company linkages with social science researchers to compare with those to STEM departments and labs? Using the typology set above and the existing literature, Figure 5.2 shows our expectations of the kinds of activities that commonly occur, sometimes occur, and rarely or almost never occur across the two discipline groups.

Some kinds of linkages in Figure 5.1 will rarely or almost never happen in social science – such as the licensing of IPRs, technology transfers and social science-only start-ups. We expect that social science departments generally have far greater difficulties than STEM subjects with three aspects: identifying a quid pro quo to sustain their continued involvement with large corporations; securing traction for specific company benefits; and demonstrating a measurable contribution to a corporate bottom-line. The only exception here concerns secondments, which some of our business interviewees saw as helpful and delivering good value for firms (considered in the last two sections below). We also found some cases where highly mathematized work in economics, finance or social science was directly incorporated in the work of hedge funds, with a flowback of benefits to the university department where the work originated. But these are clearly exceptional within the discipline group. Hence in social science we expect to see more episodic contracting with firms, fewer cases of strategic commissioning, and much rarer examples of continuous partnerships sustained over many years. However, in Section 5.3 below we identify a considerable number of cases where some characteristic underpinnings or foundations for more extensive and longer-term relationships have been identified by our corporate sector interviewees.

Given this pattern it is little wonder that the social sciences have for a long time lived somewhat awkwardly with models of impact that have been shaped by the discourse and practice of the STEM sciences. So an immediate caveat to Figure 5.2 is that existing

Figure 5.3 Percentage of social science academics reporting links with business in the last three years, by type of link

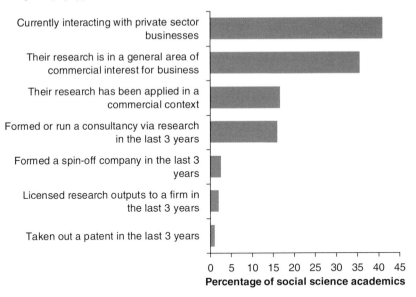

Source: Abreu et al. (2008).

research has approached the social sciences with partly ill-fitting models, set up in sub-optimal ways, or simply ignoring some important forms of linkage (such as points *i* and *j* in Figure 5.1) altogether. There may be better models to be found that will more comprehensively capture the specific relationships and dynamics that exist between social scientists and a wide range of business, especially in the services. We draw out some hopeful pointers in Section 5.3 below. On the other hand, however, established students of STEM-business interactions might argue that they should be directly applicable to the social sciences and that it has been a weakness of social science departments that they have not recognized and capitalized on the wider opportunities available. Perhaps if social scientists became more entrepreneurial in their research and faster in its application the current situation could change significantly?

5.2 The scale of social science involvement with business

What businesses do is partner with people who they think can help them. That's what open innovation is about.

UK business executive in interview

Financial incentives encourage researchers to shift rapidly from one topic to another, a practice which increases the atomization of knowledge.

International Social Science Council[3]

---

[3] International Social Science Council (2010: 112).

Figure 5.4 Percentage of social science academics reporting interactions with private firms, by sector, compared to five STEM disciplines

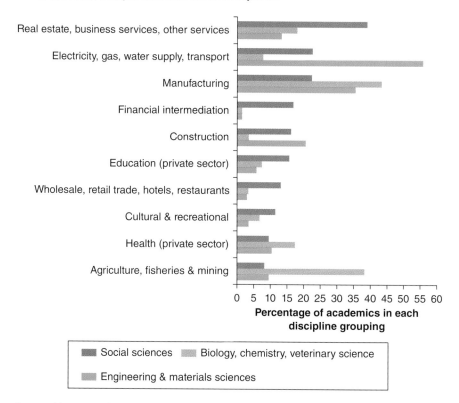

Source: Abreu et al. (2008).

There are no comprehensive or authoritative data sources that allow us to analyse social science departments' links with UK or international business. An inherent implication of the past STEM-dominated approaches to assessing universities' external impacts is that relatively little quantitative information or metrics have been gathered for social sciences. We instead consider three different data-streams, each of which has some considerable limitations and inadequacies: the reactive responses of social science researchers; the patterns of links with business visible in social science department websites; and the scale of financial support from business for social science research. By triangulating across these sources a reasonable quantitative picture of links with business can be obtained and some useful comparisons made with STEM disciplines.

We begin by considering the research by Abreu et al. (2008) on the links with business reported by UK academics. Figure 5.3 shows that two fifths of social science researchers reported some contacts with business firms and over a third believed that their work has some bearing for the private sector, although only half of this sub-set of respondents reported an actual commercial application of their work. One in six social science academics also undertook consultancy activity. By contrast, the last three bars in Figure 5.3 confirm that spin-offs, licensing and patents were rare at this time in social science.

This survey also allows us to compare how academics report their links with business across the main discipline groups. Figure 5.4 shows that social scientists reported most links with business services, utilities and manufacturing, and least with agriculture, health, cultural industries and retail. Compared with STEM disciplines, however, social science links were fairly evenly distributed. By contrast, engineering and materials science researchers focused on links with utilities, manufacturing and construction; and biology and chemistry researchers mainly linked with businesses in manufacturing, agriculture, health and business services. Outside their areas of strength, the two types of STEM discipline researchers reported few business links. As with all surveys, the key problem of the Abreu et al. (2008) data is that it is reactive, and we cannot be sure that researchers responding had the same ranges of activities in mind. It is possible that STEM researchers applied more stringent criteria on what counted as business links than social scientists, reflecting the differences in background levels of activity and contracting across the two discipline groups. We must to some extent hope that any differences here 'wash out', and that it is acceptable to treat all links as roughly equivalent in scale or meaning.

Turning to more objective, non-reactive measures, we can also analyse the evidence of linkages with business being reported on university department and laboratory web pages. For this project, we commissioned consultant firm SQW to do a fine-grained trawl of the websites of the same social science and STEM university departments' websites used in constructing our dataset of academics and researchers (discussed in Chapters 2 and 3 above). The SQW coders looked for all reported links to business, government or civil society organizations, either from the academic department corporately, or from its component centres and the webpages and research reports from individual academics within the department. This unobtrusive analysis involved coders spending up to an hour on each university department's website, and the individual pages of their prominent academics. They categorized every single reported link to businesses, and key qualitative characteristics such as the type of organization liked to, the nature of the link itself, and other supporting evidence of its depth, such as amount of funding involved or scale of programmes.[4] In interpreting the data presented it is important to bear in mind that our coders covered more social science departments at more universities than we did STEM subjects, in line with our individual dataset's construction. So for STEM subjects we only gather enough information for comparison purposes in five disciplines (medicine, computer science, engineering, chemistry and physics). Finally, we have also post-analysed the SQW dataset using the relatively full substantive information recorded by coders, but there are (of course) limits on the depth of re-analysis feasible.

Figure 5.5 shows how social science departments have set up linkages across different types of commercial and private sectors, and compares this to the apparently narrower focus of STEM disciplines.

Linkages entail any reference or mention of commercial organizations, and not just actual web hyperlinks to those organizations or their websites. For the social

---

[4] We set out the methods used for this work in more detail in the Research Design and Methods Report available via the *Impact of Social Sciences* blog (http://blogs.lse.ac.uk/impactofsocialsciences/book). See also Bastow et al. (2014).

Figure 5.5 The percentages of links from STEM and social science departments to different industrial and commercial sectors

	STEM Sciences		Social Sciences	
	Manufacturing and primary sector	Services	Services	Manufacturing and primary Sector
ICT and technology	25	20	12	5
Industrial, engineering and utilities	17	6	4	8
Bioscience	10	0	0	1
Consulting and business services	5	6	12	3
Financial services and insurance	0	1	9	2
Retail and products	6	2	10	2
Media, marketing, and creative	0	2	14	1
Law and legal services	0	0	8	0
Other (including professional associations)	0	0	9	0
% Sub-totals for sectors	**63**	**37**	**78**	**22**
Total for each discipline group	*100%*		*100%*	
N of links for totals	*281*		*417*	

Source: LSE PPG analysis of SQW data.

Figure 5.6 The percentages of links from STEM and social science departments to businesses operating in human-dominated and other systems

	STEM Sciences		Social Sciences	
	Manufacturing and primary sector	Services	Services	Manufacturing and primary Sector
Human-dominated systems (HDS): services	11	11	62	8
HDS: ICT, technology, bioscience	35	20	12	6
Industrial, engineering, utilities	17	6	4	8
% Sub-totals for sectors	**63**	**37**	**78**	**22**
Total for each discipline group	*100%*		*100%*	

Source: As for Figure 5.5.

sciences, the top foci for linkages were media and creative services (including the press and broadcasters), then business services in general and ICT services, and next retail services. By contrast, three quarters of STEM department linkages included in our unobtrusive measures dataset were in four areas – ICT and hi-tech manufacturing, ICT services, industrial and engineering manufacturing, and biosciences manufacturing. Figure 5.6 reframes this same data in terms of

Figure 5.7 Review of university department websites for links to private sector firms or associated representative bodies

Discipline	Small or medium enterprises	Domestic large firms	International scale corporations	Peak association	All types of firms
Engineering	2.3	2.4	9.5	0	**14.1**
Chemistry	3.2	1.5	8.7	0	**13.3**
Business and Management	1.6	1.5	6.2	0.9	**10.2**
Physics	1.4	2.2	5.6	0	**9.2**
Computer Science	1.0	0.2	4.2	0	**5.3**
Law	1.0	0.5	3.1	0.5	**5.1**
Media	1.1	1.1	1.8	0.1	**4.1**
Psychology	1.0	0.3	1.8	0	**3.1**
Geography	0.5	0.1	1.1	0.3	**2.5**
Medicine	0.8	0.5	0.8	0	**2.2**
Economics	0.5	0.5	1.0	0.1	**2.1**
Social Policy	0.5	0.1	0.6	0	**1.2**
History	0.4	0.2	0.3	0	**0.9**
Philosophy	0.1	0	0.6	0	**0.7**
Anthropology	0.2	0.1	0.3	0	**0.6**
Sociology	0.4	0.0	0.2	0	**0.6**
Political Science, IR	0.1	0.0	0.2	0	**0.3**

Source: LSE PPG analysis of SQW data.

human-dominated systems. Nearly four-fifths of the linkages from the social science department websites in 2012 were to service sector business, with only a minority in manufacturing or primary sector firms, reflecting well the economic and labour market importance of these sectors in the economy.

By contrast, three-fifths of STEM department linkages were with manufacturing or primary sector firms. Going a little deeper, the social science departments linkages were primarily with services firms in human-dominated systems, at least ten times more so than in STEM disciplines – where the main linkages were to firms operating again in human-dominated systems, but chiefly in IT, the hi-tech sectors and bioscience.

We next look (in Figure 5.7) at linkages at a single discipline level. Clearly the number of cases is far smaller here, so not too much weight should be placed on the numbers found. One clear pattern is that four out of the top five rows here are the STEM subjects we covered, with only business and management studies achieving similar levels of relations to firms. Medicine ranked with the medium-level social sciences such as law, media, psychology, geography and economics. At the bottom of the table, classic social science disciplines such as political science, sociology, and anthropology

Figure 5.8 Comparing the business links found across STEM and social science departments

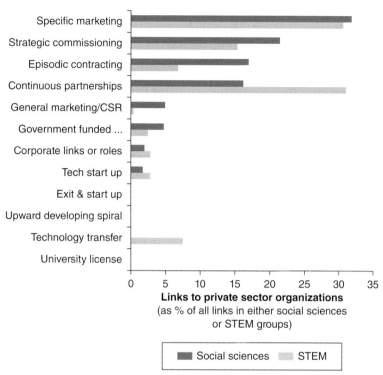

Links to private sector organizations
(as % of all links in either social sciences
or STEM groups)

■ Social sciences ▨ STEM

Source: LSE PPG analysis of SQW data.

have very low visibility rates of interaction and linkages with companies, along with overlap areas with humanities such as history and philosophy. In terms of the scale of companies involved, in all the STEM subjects, the bulk of relationships are clearly with international scale corporations, with those to small and medium enterprises (SMEs) and large UK firms fairly evenly represented at a lower level. In the social sciences, large company linkages are important in business and management, and in law, media and psychology in the middle of Figure 5.7, but they are not prominent in other disciplines.

Finally on the website analysis Figure 5.8 shows a breakdown of linkages in the social science and STEM departments we covered in terms of the cross-disciplinary categories of systems used in our typology in Figure 5.1. It is apparent that for STEM disciplines specific marketing and continuous research relationships linked to R&D were the most commonly occurring activities by a long way. In our interviews we found frequent reiteration of the reputational and branding advantages that come from linking to high-quality and independent academic research. Two quotes from executives encapsulate this:

> We wanted to differentiate ourselves, acknowledge that we didn't have a monopoly on the good ideas; and hence drawing external inputs – whether it's a constant consultative manner that doesn't actually get published, or whether it is actually to commission specific work as we have done with academic partners.

> There is a veneer of independence that we could get from a piece of academic research, which I think is very important. If it's got our name on it, then people are always going to want to question it. We do try to keep that independence and that's where the quantitative evidence helps. It's good to push [our firm] towards being a trusted stakeholder. If [we] are seen to push messages that grow [our own] business, they will soon be turned away.

For social science departments, specific marketing links were clearly most prominent, followed by strategic commissioning, episodic contracting and continuous relationships – giving a more mixed picture. General marketing was rare in social science and technology transfer entirely absent from the discipline group. Most other types of linkages could not really be detected in the website analysis, either for STEM or social science departments. Indeed, on patents one of our interviewees, who had made the move from a technology research role in the private sector to an academic research post in a UK university, commented on the lack of awareness and support in universities for exploiting intellectual property.

> The patenting game in universities is quite different. [The firm] would patent something as soon as you'd had the idea, as time is of the essence if it was remotely likely to be useful to the business. And they had a big budget to be able to do that. Coming to the university there is almost no budget in the enterprise services to be able to do this.

In summarizing the picture from this data it is important to bear in mind some potential limitations with this method of unobtrusive data gathering. In any web census of organizational sites some ('stealth') linkages may be hidden from public view, although this problem should not be large-scale for public universities and the academic sphere (Dunleavy, 2010: 242–44). Not disclosing corporate linkages could be reputationally far more damaging for departments or professional researchers than making them explicit. By focusing on departments we may also have missed some relevant links to the private sector in more multi-disciplinary research units or centres based in the university (King, 2013) in areas such as environmental sciences, public health, and aspects of development studies. None the less, the patterns here agree well with those found in reactive survey research.

Turning to a second source of non-reactive data, we look at the flows of funding into UK university departments and laboratories for insights on the comparative performance of the social sciences. Figure 5.9 shows estimates based on our definition of the social sciences disciplines (from Chapter 1). In 2010–11 just over a seventh of business-related funding went to social science departments, a ratio that is slightly higher for publicly supported business-related funding (a sixth) (HEFCE, 2010). Large corporations made especially little use of university social science departments for consultancy, preferring to use other firms for these roles. But university departments attracted a larger share of the small amount of consultancy in the SME sector. The two largest business-to-university flows in social science departments were for continuous professional development (accounting for a quarter of all value here from both large and small businesses), and contract research, mainly for larger firms. Around £90 million of direct funding from business flowed to social science departments, plus one and a half times as much public funding supporting collaboration with corporations and entrepreneurs.

Figure 5.9   The estimated gross revenue flowing to university social science departments from links with business, 2010–11

Income stream	Annual value from university-business interactions (£ million)	Estimated annual value for social sciences (£ million)	Estimated percentage of total value going to social sciences	Approximate share (%) of income stream going to social sciences
Publicly funded collaborative research with business	872	150	8.2	17.2
With large business				
Contract research	343	51	2.7	14.9
Consultancy	343	13	0.7	3.8
Continuing professional development (CPD)	116	29	1.6	25.0
With small & medium sized firms (SME)				
Contract research	39	5	0.3	12.8
Consultancy	39	8	0.4	20.5
Continuing professional development (CPD)	28	7	0.4	25.0
Revenue from intellectual property	59	*tiny*	*tiny*	*tiny*
Total gross value of interactions	**1,839**	**263**	*14.3%*	

Source: Our analysis of HEFCE Higher Education Business Community Interaction survey, 2010–11.

Note: HEFCE do not publish disaggregated data for the social sciences, so we have extrapolated figures based on the breakdown of funding allocations shown in Figure 1.6.

5.3 Barriers to greater use of social science research in firms

There is a bit of a 'valley of death' that exists between universities and business, that needs to be broken down. And part of that is about experience.

> *UK business executive in interview*

I was chatting to a social science academic from the States three or four months ago. He ventured the opinion that one of the issues we have here is that, in the United States academics tend to do research with business. In the UK, they do research about business. And that is quite an important distinction.

> *Business executive in interview*

The picture so far provides some quantitative foundation for understanding the relationship between UK social sciences and the business community. However, such data only tell us so much about the actual dynamics of this relationship, the barriers that constrain impact, and the various reasons (if any) to be optimistic about the future of impact in the business and commercial world. For this book, we also interviewed a wide range of stakeholders from the business community across diverse sectors, and a set of academics with established linkages to corporations. We collected numerous examples of impactful relationships, as well as insights into how impact can fail initially, or falter, fade or break down later on. In this final section, we build some qualitative colour onto the picture drawn above.

Looking across the six aspects covered in Figure II.1 (page 108), we can identify what seem to be common syndromes of impact across our different sectors. In the business sector, problems have been readily associated with the left-hand side of Figure II.1; relating to themes around making connections with business, establishing satisfactory 'quid pro quo' arrangements, and finding traction for research in a commercial setting. Indeed, for many British business executives interviewed for this study, it seems far-fetched that UK social science departments would be a regular (let alone the first) port of call in looking for answers to business problems. UK business culture has never been close to universities, unlike (say) Germany. One leading business figure commented in interview: 'I think if you look at the UK, our businesses seem to relate less to universities than in other countries'. Another commented: 'There is a long tail of [UK] businesses made up of people who have never been to university, don't care about university'. In such companies universities are seen as a world far removed from the commercial and operational imperatives of large firms, and such attitudes occur more widely too, for a range of reasons. Getting over this initial disconnect is one of the major barriers, it seems, to boosting impacts on business.

This may be a cultural characteristic across UK business (and universities) as a whole, not isolated to one particular set of disciplines, but its impacts on social sciences are perhaps especially severe. Business and management academics were one group of social science researchers in our dataset who had stronger relationships with business. Yet even here there are signs that UK academics are somehow not as well integrated into business communities as (say) their US counterparts. One senior executive at a global management consultancy reflected:

> I don't know of any British academics that are flying all over the world doing talks on this kind of stuff. It doesn't mean to say that there aren't any. But we are the second largest firm globally in this field. And none of them have ever contacted me to sell to me. And I have been the marketing director in the second and the third largest firms for the last eight years. No-one has ever contacted me other than [university R]. Either I'm not the right buyer, or they just don't enter the market.

This kind of ambivalence or uncertainty about the university social science world, and how it related to the work of professionals in large and small firms, was fairly common. In large and important commercial sectors such as finance and banking, and technology, asking questions about how firms linked with university social science would reveal rather sketchy awareness of any systematic use of social science. At best there were only fragmented or ad hoc patterns of collaboration with universities. Professionals from large and well-known firms commented on this general 'patchiness' and low awareness about university social science:

[Firm X], as you can imagine, is a very technology-led company. They understand engineering, science. Social science is a mystery to them, actually. They know about doing user surveys and doing user feedback, but it's always in the form of: 'Show technology to a user, get a reaction'. That's the way it went.

The problem of knowing how and where to connect with university social science was frequently mentioned by business professionals. As one senior research director told us:

The reason you don't have much impact on businesses is that they are in a hurry. They need to be able to find it [relevant research] easily. They need a place to go to say: 'If I needed stuff on this who should I talk to?' Or 'What have you got?' That doesn't happen in academia.

Another banking executive explained how he made the move to academia, and realised there was a world of untapped knowledge in academic research.

I was 24 years, basically working in investment banking. I wished that I had known [then] what I now know is out there, in journals that never get read by anybody in the practitioner community. And should, in terms of them being truly state-of-the-art, or even ahead of state-of-the-art.

Of course in sectors like banking and consultancy, there is a strong demand for social science knowledge amongst professionals and analysts, even if that knowledge gap may not necessarily be filled by academic research. Here the conventional and digital mechanisms sketched out in Figure II.2 come into play. Executives rely a lot on their own DIY research capabilities, and on the wealth of data and information available online. In some service sector companies, where large financial outcomes may hang on getting trends right, executives did recognize that their in-house teams or consultants were tapping social science literatures albeit indirectly and in apparently ad-hoc ways:

We've done an energy report recently and had half a dozen people working on that. One of the guys was doing a literature search, so when we do get into a topic, we do have people who get into [social science research]. We do try to find out what is being said by the academic world, as well as the business world, in that indirect way, when necessary.

In smaller and less wealthy firms, the capability for drawing on specifically academic social science research clearly diminished also. Small companies were seen as particularly remote from understanding what social science departments could contribute to their work.

We very rarely, in fact I don't recall that we have ever, sourced academic research. Over the last two to three years, we have started to think about whether we are missing a trick here. I guess there is a certain minimum size below which it is unlikely that a consultancy would want to engage in academic research?

If you are small company like a start-up, unless you come out of a culture where the team who conceived of what you are doing is a team that had social sciences as part of it, I think people would really struggle. I started a technology start-up in 1996. And if you asked me to hire social scientists, I probably would have said something rather rude to you, because I was hiring engineers and programmers. It's a matter of scale and what's going on in the company.

And again in line with Figure II.1, making an initial connection between business stakeholders and university social scientists is no guarantee of any lasting impact. Even if connections can be made, both parties usually need to recognize some clear quid pro quo in the benefits or incentives flowing both ways. There may also be a need for the research application to find some degree of traction, be it through human or financial investment, in the company. Finding, articulating, and sustaining this kind of quid pro quo is often tricky in business, as one technology executive noted:

There's always a danger that you bring people together and they have a conversation and that's it. It's right you have to get together, but I use the metaphor of lighting a fire. The conversations are the fire-lighters, and the money can act as kindling. And you hope that's enough to get things going, for there to be combustion and energy to be created out of the mutual desire to do something. That's difficult to execute. As soon as you tell an academic they have to cooperate with someone they will run a mile in the other direction.

From the perspective of the firms, a pretty fundamental requirement of this quid pro quo is the application of the research in a specifically commercial environment. One finance executive commented on a particular relationship that had worked well: 'We are a commercial organization. We want commercial output, and [academic H] helps us with that. And that is why we like him'. Often, though, the substantial aspects of this quid pro quo appear to run much deeper than this kind of direct, hard-edged 'bottom-line' evaluation. For many executives, there are also critical issues around the translation and the conversation that takes place in bringing academic research effectively into the commercial environment. One argued: 'It tends to be the difference between people looking at things just to reach a conclusion, and people looking at things with a sense of the goals the business needs to achieve, and how do you relate to those'. A sympathetic research director explained:

If you said to me 'What is the biggest challenge that you've got?', it is trying to bridge this huge gulf between business and academia. Businesses are still focused on 'What is my annual plan?', or 'What is my seasonal plan on sustainability?', and universities who actually want to say: 'Hold on. You are asking the wrong question, on the wrong timescale, in the wrong way'. It is really hard to bridge that.

He reflected:

It is just bloody hard to do to be honest. A lot is about skills that don't really sit easily here. So how do you translate? ... When the sociologist says: 'It's really, really complicated. It's all about the social, spatial, and cultural context'... then you are talking to somebody who is saying 'Yep, that's all fine. But I've still got to write my bloody [business] plan ... So where's my plan?'

As part of this bridging process, executives frequently mentioned the importance of academics being able to step outside of their narrow academic disciplines and be able to articulate the relevance of their work in a 'discipline-free' way. Useful academic research must be transitioned to a type of knowledge that can be integrated into the context of real-life business. A research director at a large technology multinational commented: 'Part of the challenge we have had in collaborating with academics is finding people who are good at talking beyond their discipline'. Another executive commented:

> If you want to make an impact, you need to have an inter-disciplinary approach. I find the traditional divisions between departments in universities to be a hindrance to the type of things I'm interested in doing.

An important aspect of this 'de-magnetizing' of research away from discipline-specific poles is the process through which these conversations and translations take place. Establishing and sustaining quid pro quo does not usually happen in one shot. Executives felt that it is often contingent on close and regular bouts of working together, getting round a table and talking through the options, rolling sleeves up, and so on. Often this kind of 'messier' collaboration is hard to get right, and interviewees frequently appeared dissatisfied with the results of commissioning work from academics, especially if they 'disappeared' for six months or a year, and delivered a non-useful 'product' at the end.

   Executives often pointed to a tendency for academics to focus excessively on the specifically academic significance of any applied research, rather than on the potential 'real-world' significance to the private sector client. One research director from a supplier to government told us:

> We are saying 'What does your work mean for actually delivering public services and public policies?' But they don't think like that. They don't think how it translates. They think about what it means for moving academic debates about social networks or whatever forward, and not how it relates to how you design policy round a network approach.

The rhythm of innovation processes in the private sector can also be at odds with academic research processes. Corporate managers perceive academic cycles to be much longer and, for better or for worse, more comprehensive. In contrast, the model of innovation in successful private sector firms often relies on very short time spans for research, particularly in product design and manufacturing. Company researchers are under more acute commercial pressures to demonstrate their innovations, and feed them into more mainstream business and strategy development:

> [Businesses] don't sit down and say: 'Let's gather all the knowledge there is on the planet about a topic, say environmental sustainability, and get 60 people thinking

about it for three years'. It's the open innovation approach which works for business, not the Foresight Reports [by UK government][5] that take years to produce.

In many of our conversations with business executives we also found surprisingly frequent negative assessments of the ability of academic researchers to deliver against expectations – even when a quid pro quo seems to have been established, and commitments made. Often the outcome or the products of collaboration were seen as weak or insufficient to keep the initial relationship going and interviewees argued that academics could not or would not take on board the applied perspective needed. A research director at a major consultancy said:

> The reason that I rarely use them is that they don't deliver. What I mean by that is that I normally have a very specific mandate. I say: 'Please can you write about something'. And what happens is that … they don't write what I ask them to write. They think that it is useful to be discursive, or write about what they are interested in. And from a business point of view that's no use to me.

Other interviewees made blunt complaints about the standard, usability and motivation of academic work they had encountered:

> [Academics] regularly don't deliver. They don't deliver anything. Or what they've done is a cack-handed review, which has been done negligently. They turn up to do presentations without any preparation. You'd be shocked how badly behaved some academics are. Now this doesn't mean we don't have good relationships with academics. But we are constantly, year in year out, shocked by the poverty of effort that academics put into working with non-academics. And that seems to be because of the disdain in which they hold non-academics. It's got nothing to do with us. Economists, sociologists, psychologists, philosophers [it's across the board].

Many large firms, particularly those in manufacturing, technology, and finance and consultancy, often have considerable in-house capacity to do social science research. For those who are able to access and control 'big data' resources, there is a sense that they are able to advance their own business-specific knowledge without drawing on university social science expertise. This self-sufficiency tends to marginalize academic social science in the process. As one sympathetic management consultant put it:

> I know I sound horrible, but because we speak with hundreds of firms and hundreds of clients, our research programs are much bigger than most academics could manage in many years.

Savage and Burrows (2007) foresaw a 'coming crisis of empirical sociology' because corporate resources (often analysed with non-social science techniques and

---

[5] Foresight Reports in the UK are joint academic, private sector and government look-ahead studies co-ordinated by a Whitehall department. They normally take two or three years to do, and produce large reports and many working papers.

algorithms) might outstrip the kinds of data sources painstakingly assembled by social science professionals. There were some clear signs in our interviews that academic social science research may quickly begin to look chronically outdated and surplus to requirement in a fast-moving commercial world. One executive commented:

> It's been routine in ethnography or sociology to study fifty people in great detail, understand everything about their lives over two or three years and then write a book or a thesis (this is a caricature, just to make the point). On the other hand, if you're at Facebook or Yahoo or Google (increasingly with academic colleagues), you instantly have data on hundreds of millions of people. It's just not at the level of depth and granularity that a social scientist is used to.

Another interviewee pointed out the same predicament for academics in responding to availability of large-scale transactional data in UK public services firms:

> I don't know if we are getting ahead of universities. But we are getting ahead of the government, that's for sure. I was at a Treasury thing yesterday with another colleague, and we were talking about datasets and so on, and this guy from the Treasury was saying 'That's all very well, but we survey 1000 people every week, and we feel pretty confident with that. How robust is your data?' And we were just like, 'Well this graph here is based on 207,000 people from yesterday'. So we are getting ahead there.

Although academic research in the social sciences is not generally expensive (compared with research consultancies), academics may not appreciate that similar sums to ESRC grants are extremely hard to stand up in the commercial world. At the heart of firms' investment decisions is usually a hard-edged judgement about the commercial returns on choosing to spend money on research or commit institutional resources to it. Generally speaking, firms do not make these decisions lightly, especially in a sector like retail where one executive described the interaction he could expect in proposing spending money on research:

> If I go to the board and ask for a million pounds, they ask: 'How is that million going to make me more [return] than spending a million pounds on a new shop? And that [the shop] gives me a return in 12 months. And you want me to give you a million for less return, that won't come for four years?' Hmm, that's an interesting question ... What do you think the answer is?

Many research directors interviewed spoke of the pressure on them to demonstrate value for money from their research programmes. So the challenge of finding traction for research in private sector organizations is more frequently subject to these hard-edged kinds of decisions, often made by research directors or executives or boards higher up the management chain.

In some cases, research funding decisions may be related to more fundamental strategic challenges in the firm, questions about how new research can help to open up new markets or reshape existing ones. One manufacturing executive summed up the fundamental question as:

> Can you turn research into commercial value? Some of the time, you can, but there isn't a 'burning platform', so you don't invest in it. Some of the time, there is a burning platform. The debate is how much of a burning platform? That then dictates how much you are prepared to invest in something.

However, it is important that we do not paint an excessively pessimistic picture of impacts in business. In many conversations and interviews we also found signs of executives reappraising their positions on how social science research might prove valuable. Indeed, we found a good range of examples of firms that have been working with social science academics for years, and being able to demonstrate strong impacts from these collaborations. In the rest of this chapter, we discuss some of these more positive signs.

Many large and well-established firms are now at a scale, or at a stage in the management of growing or mature markets, where they are increasingly seeing the benefits of utilizing far more social science expertise and knowledge. Often international in reach, these companies are directly recruiting social science professionals onto their staff (where once they would have used only scientists), and using research programmes to integrate social science insights throughout their strategy-forming and business operations. For some firms, this has been standard practice for many years now, and the prioritization of social science is backed up with equally sizeable research budgets and facilities. One research director in the technology sector told us:

> You don't have to make the business case anymore [for hiring social scientists]. We've advertised for people with social science PhDs both internally (within R&D) and externally. That's going on and has happened quite recently. Many people know academics and can put out the call to encourage them to apply. You don't have to justify or make the case in that way as you might expect.

Although this increasing focus on the perceived importance of social science seems quite a broad-based shift over the last 15 years, the rate at which it has happened varies across different sectors. In manufacturing, for example, the role of social science seems more widespread in areas such as product design. As one executive told us: 'It's right to say that social science has been kind of normalised. The experiment at the end of the nineties, the value of bringing in such people with such skills was proven. And so now it's quite routine to employ social science PhDs'.

In IT firms we found strong signs of social science core expertise (such as economics, anthropology, and sociology) being integrated into the way that innovation takes place, although as one research director pointed out:

> In the technology sector, the influence of the social science is still nascent. No doubt it will continue to grow. It's important to recognise that it is early days. If you want billions of dollars of impact, in multiple instances, you're not going to find that many.

Innovating with specific products and services mostly involves looking at how user behaviours can be modelled or influenced by design, using customer insights and feedback, and strongly feeding this learning into future developments and strategy. As one senior research director explained:

> Big corporations, they all have social scientists somewhere in the research or corporate strategy divisions. Each company does the take-up a little differently. But usually research and corporate strategy work together. Both are at the frontiers, trying to understand the new technology, and how the community will respond to it.

Some technology and manufacturing firms have created multi-disciplinary business and academic teams that included qualitative researchers, such as anthropologists, ethnographers, sociologists and social psychologists. The value of these disparate perspectives outweighed the (sometime) disciplinary language difficulties, especially in helping change how firms previously thought about the products that they designed and built. One executive commented:

> My model of an ethnographer is that they sit in the corner of a room quietly and watch what's going on. And then after a few days they come back and give you a completely different interpretation of what's happening compared to what you as an engineer saw … Some of that stuff fed into product development and was seen to be valued by the mainstream engineering part of the company.

Social scientists are increasingly involved in helping technology businesses understand social-cum-technological opportunities in order to create maximum benefit from them. The integration of computer science and economics has developed relatively easily, particularly around the analysis of 'big data'. Assumptions about consumer behaviour can be analysed on a massive scale, and modelled with much greater efficiency and accuracy, without the response bias and sampling problems of some other reactive survey methodologies. And while first generation big data analysis could be done in an engineering mode alone, more sophisticated uses require more inputs. Issues such as privacy around the linking and sharing of big data could potentially limit its use and transformational potential, and lend themselves to social scientific treatment.

University research can also be used in formulating medium and longer-term strategy and development processes, looking at both organizational problems, and potential market changes where insights into future trends are key. Two research directors commented on this broader and longer-term emphasis was where social science insights really bring value:

> I think it's probably more to do with changing the innovation process than being able to point to specific products. I think you possibly can. But I think what social science has done has really changed the way the company innovates and thinks about what its role is.

> Fundamentally, I think the better proof of the presence of social science inside [the firm] is that it changed the way it thought about who it was and how it described itself to itself and others. We profoundly changed the way in which we thought about ourselves and what we were doing.

Even during medium-term periods of financial pressure or the presence of a growing long-term risk, some firms can respond by taking a far-sighted stance. Rapid shifts of conditions can increase pressure for some kind of medium to long-term strategic response to the kind of 'burning platform' problem described above. Research can often help in deciding how to move from a status-quo stance. For example, a research director in manufacturing explained how increasing raw material prices posed a risk that the firm might not be able to meet growing product demands. The senior management of the company reacted by deciding to invest in extensive research into the sustainability and management of its supply chains.

The quid pro quo benefits for social scientists have also improved in several respects. They gain supplemental income or resources for their research teams, and insights into decisions and processes that they would not necessarily be able to access otherwise. In addition, they often get hold of company data and information that would not be publicly available. The REF impacts process also offers academic departments a concrete incentive to seek and acquire external influence, which may attract financial support from HEFCE and thus become somewhat more financially sustainable or justifiable inside universities. Many academics have been working for many years with business in particular areas, and some of those we interviewed reported that previously an external focus was often 'frowned upon' by their heads of department. Yet now in the era of REF and impact case studies, they observe that they are suddenly 'flavour of the month'.

Increasingly too, there are also researchers who 'fit the bill' for business because of the socialization that 'academic entrepreneurship' gives in packaging research projects to secure grant or external funding. A senior management academic remarked:

> I would say you don't have to work in business, but you have to work with business, to understand where it is. A lot of academics are hugely entrepreneurial because they have to be – pulling together teams, and funding and building their own little mini-business empire within a larger academic institution. And there is precious little help to do that [in universities], so they have had to do it themselves.

Business interviewees reported finding researchers keen to understand their particular business problems. An IT executive commended the economists and finance academics his team worked with: 'They've really rolled up their sleeves and said "What do you want to get out of it?" We've done some nice joint things where the models are collaborative efforts.'

This may in part reflect growing commonalities in professional outlooks between university and corporate researchers, where both parties understand each other's pressures more completely. A research director commented:

> One of the problems we find distressing is that we do understand that they are under ... pressures they might not have been under a few years ago, such as the impact factor. We say to them: 'We've been academics. I've run departments and supervise PhDs. We know the name of the game ... We can work together, and together in such a fashion that we can deliver for you on that. But you have to deliver for us on this'.

Academics and officials involved in 'new style' relationships have both emphasized the trust that results from greater understanding, and its circular beneficial impact. A research director commented on maintaining a long-run link to one professor:

> Yes we have a formal business relationship that is contractual where [academic T] does specific research pieces for us. But we have an informal knowledge-sharing relationship, where she tells me what she is picking up from the research data, and I tell her what is motivating industry. And that helps her to think about how the research might develop in the future. So it is a symbiotic conversation.

Or as one senior official in a large technology firm explained:

> The way I get answers to questions that I barely know how to frame is that I now have a network of academics that I've built up over many years, that I would go to and approach one of those who I thought was best-placed.

Many of our business interviewees most sympathetic to social sciences did not think it was appropriate to think of 'cashing out' the value of either social science research (or indeed most STEM research) in terms of particular projects. This may seem surprising. Surely, we might expect a large private firm to be able to calculate (or at least estimate) the commercial value of its links with academia? Doesn't a concern for a 'commercial edge' necessitate a more considered and analytical approach to estimating value from such links? As one research director observed, his peers constantly feel the anxiety of demonstrating impacts for both in-house work and outsourced projects: 'They will lie awake at night worrying about how much influence they have over policy in the business'. Yet corporate research directors' responses to such questions only confirmed how difficult and potentially complex such evaluation can be.

One partial aspect that executives frequently mentioned was the value of press coverage resulting from research jointly published with universities, a key part of the specific and general marketing strategies outlined earlier in the chapter. A research director summed up the benefits:

> What's the metric? One of my arguments is that 'column inches' is actually worth a tremendous amount to companies. If you look at the equivalent advertising cost, what it would cost you to do an advertising feature in a newspaper, it's expensive stuff. If you can get the newspapers come to you and say, 'Wow this is interesting stuff', there is real value associated with that. Brand enhancement, real money and your credibility and brand go up. So there's real impact but you measure the impact in different ways.

More generally, competing for funding in a hard-edged commercial context undoubtedly raised the bar on how academics package and make their work applicable. Bringing out the relevance and commercial value of research to firms can be time-consuming and hard work, and clearly does not attract all academics. However, where it is done then securing funding or commitment from the private sector for research might be seen as a clear demonstration that the research involved is being useful for or impacting on the firm itself. Large or sustained investment is likely to be enough to signal that the research process is having an impact on the business. As one experienced observer put it: 'When Tesco spent their £25 million or whatever on their Institute of Sustainable Consumption, they must see a business benefit out of it, mustn't they? Or it's not their money?' Similarly, when a large manufacturer decides to sink millions into researching the sustainability of its supply chains, we can assume that the underpinning research is having a significant impact. And one research director (of a mixed STEM and social science unit) commented:

> When I started there were eight people, and there are probably now 150. There was no research investment in anything. Now there is a fully-funded research centre with a three to five year investment to the tune of $10 million. If you were a company, would you 'Ten-x' your investment in something for which you did not think you were getting a reasonable rate of return? Probably not.

As another interviewee explained: 'If academic work is not being taken up by business, it may be because it's of little value to business. I tend to think of businesses as being fairly efficient at seizing opportunities. If academics were doing things that the businesses wanted, I think they would take them'. The corollary to this is that if firms are taking up academic research (particularly in a serial way), we may realistically assume that the research has some degree of impact. For academics who are able to build these relationships, and then renew and sustain them over time, the actual demonstration of impacts, in many ways, becomes contingent.

Conclusions

Pulling together the picture of social scientists' relationships with business above, Figure 5.10 suggests that the key difficulties arise in the first four phases of Figure II.1 – that is in researchers and firms finding each other, making initial connections, establishing an ongoing basis for co-operating and finding some 'traction' for research with the company. Once these difficulties are surmounted, extending relationships and demonstrating impacts tend to be easier to tackle. In particular, firms have relatively less difficulty in renewing linkages with researchers whose work proves valuable and growing relationships over time. We shall see in later chapters that this pattern is largely confined to business, and does not apply in the government or civil society sectors.

Overall, the links from social science departments to UK and international businesses are undoubtedly still far less developed than are the same academics' equivalent relationships with government and public sector organizations (discussed in Chapter 6). Social science departments also still lag some way behind the STEM sciences in terms of developing systematic or sustainable institutional links with business. In many ways this reflects the lowish applicability of models of impact based on a particular narrative around commercialisation, IP, technology transfer and discovery research leading to a competitive advantage for specific companies. These models do not connect with the more collective character of social science research and applied work, the lack of patentable IP, and the tendency for

Figure 5.10   Trajectory of difficulties in achieving impacts in private sector and business

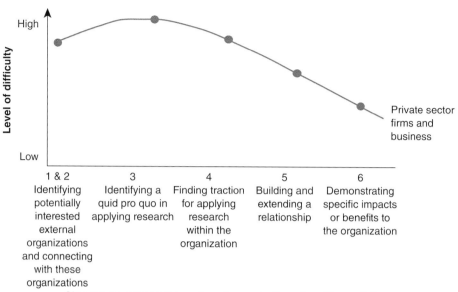

Six aspects of impact in external organizations (see Figure II.1)

knowledge exchange between businesses and social scientists to be far more subtle, interpretative and (where most successful) long term. These features depend more on integration forms of research, and they have their key impacts in a wide range of knowledge-intensive service industries, and only some specific areas of aspects of manufacturing.

Links to business corporations are not relevant for all disciplines or all academics. Many researchers may choose, for diverse reasons, to avoid the 'conversation', or to play as little part in it as possible. A challenge for business has been in finding the right kind of researcher, someone who is able to talk more widely about the potential applications of their work outside their disciplinary silo, and who appreciates that firms must always solve joined-up problems in getting products to market or pushing through hidden innovations of the kind common in service industries. Equally, inside companies, research directors and other executives need to find a role or an organizational advantage for their firm from sustaining links to academia, almost always involving enhancing their 'look-ahead' or 'look-deeper' capabilities in commercially relevant ways.

Yet we have also seen evidence that many large firms have developed substantial social science research capabilities in-house, recruiting bright graduates and PhDs when they can. And some large companies maintain collaborative networks with university departments, in a few cases supporting extensive research programmes. Service sector firms already suck in a great deal of the insights and expertise that the social sciences can bring. A wide range of social science disciplines were mentioned to us in interviews as integral to the development of strategy, products, services, and operations in a variety of different firms across different sectors – including business and management studies, economics, anthropology, philosophy, social psychology, sociology, and even international development, public management and political science in some cases. So although starting from a lower base, the business and private sector impacts of social science look likely to increase further.

6

Government and public policy making

What experience and history teach us is this – that people and governments have never learned anything from history, or acted on principles deduced from it.

George Friedrich Hegel[1]

The truth of an idea is not a stagnant property inherent in it. Truth happens to an idea. It becomes true, is made by events.

William James[2]

Since the later nineteenth century, the growth of the social sciences and the expansion of the state have been very closely linked. Both observers sympathetic to this trend, and those critical of it, acknowledge the intimate links between ambitions to reform or improve society using government intervention and 'seeing like a state' (Scott, 1998). This is a top-down gaze that constitutes the field of intervention in terms of synoptic (often statistical) data (and the constructed concept categories that alone make data feasible). Taken in the aggregate, the shifts involved here are never politically or socially neutral. Foucault famously, if controversially, observed: 'There is no power relation without the correlative constitution of a field of knowledge, nor any knowledge that does not presuppose and constitute at the same time power relations' (1975: 27).

Amongst social science researchers this long and close association with public policy making continues to generate tensions, misgivings and self-criticisms about the ethics of knowledge development with social and political consequences. Academics have frequently deplored the capacity of politicians and policy makers for self-deception, and their ceaseless incentives to mould both external advice and social situations themselves so as to accord with their previously held convictions and previously made commitments – pithily summed up in Nietzsche's dictum that

---

[1]Hegel (1892).
[2]James (1909).

'Power makes stupid'. So the linkages have never been devoid of problems, and governments in liberal democracies have responded by creating a large repertoire of intermediating professional and institutional arrangements for handling social science data and research in ways that respect the ethical and intellectual concerns of social scientists.

Despite the major issues still resonant here, social science links to policy makers are far stronger, more densely and more co-operatively developed than with business. Many social science academics have robust links with central government departments, regional and local governments, regulators, public sector health care agencies, public corporations or the huge range of quasi-government bodies. These relationships typically focus on the particular policy sectors for which a given discipline is most apt.

To examine the use made of research in depth, we first consider an overview narrative of how governments and public bodies have used social science in the UK (and other major western countries) in recent decades. We also consider a typology of government university linkages, again briefly comparing social science and STEM disciplines. The second section looks at the empirical evidence on the scale of these relationships, triangulating a range of different information sources. Finally we review evidence from our qualitative interviews about the barriers to and opportunities for further developing the role of social science research in informing policy making.

6.1 Social science and the policy arena

[The university's] failure as a community in which rational discourses about social worlds is possible ... is partly because rational discourse as such ceased to be its dominant value and was superseded by a quest for knowledge products and information products that could be sold for funding, prestige, and power – rewards bestowed by the state and larger society that is most bent on subverting rational discourse about itself.

Alvin Gouldner[3]

All government is an ugly necessity.

G. K. Chesterton[4]

The state still plays a critical role in public policy development, confounding both globalists who energetically predicted its imminent demise or marginalization before the great crash of 2008, and over-enthusiastic pluralists who saw modernized government as dissolving away into myriad networks (Dryzek and Dunleavy, 2009). Government may no longer be the pre-eminent 'controller' of all other societal systems that perhaps it seemed from the late nineteenth century to the early Cold War period (Luhman, 1986). But in liberal democracies a very wide swathe of public policies is still pervasively shaped by the electoral competition of parties and

---

[3]Gouldner (1973: 79).
[4]Chesterton (1917).

politicians, and the competing political pressures of interest groups, at national, regional and local levels. A complex and ever-changing mosaic of 'political' influence operates; a difference from the private sector that persists even when policy delivery functions are devolved to independent institutions, quasi-autonomous and ostensibly non-political agencies, 'non-partisan' city governments or contractors.

Of course the nation state (and in a lesser way sub-national governments down to community level) also embody many hopes, fears and ideologies – condensing and expressing the idea of a 'public interest' (or sometimes a 'national interest') that is key in attracting the loyalties and consent of citizens. There is a close fit here with the professional culture of the social sciences (and academia in general), which sees impartial service to knowledge and fostering the 'public interest' as the twin prime rationales for researchers' relative autonomy and independence from societal pressures (Johnson, 1972). There is consequently a strong attraction for academics in helping improve policy making.

It is offset, however, by the countervailing difficulties and complexities for professionals of operating in a pervasively 'politicized' environment. These conflicting pressures – to serve the public interest but not to let social science become politicized – are a key foundation for the typical 'dialectical' processes surrounding social scientists' involvement with policy making. We discuss three ways in which the influence of research on government policy making is reasonably distinctive – the meta-political level of party politics versus disinterested research; the mezzo level, where waves of public management 'fashions' help shape official attitudes to research; and the micro-level of how researchers link to government agencies.

At the macro-level the horizontal axis in Figure 6.1 shows a left–right political dimension, with the core of social science firmly placed in the centre, but with pulls from either side for research or evidence to fit with the political alignments of power-holders. Far more so than with STEM disciplines, politicians have tended to take substantively committed positions on the kind of social science they welcome or find credible. Politicians and parties on the left of centre (or liberal in US terms) have distinctive sets of supportive or aligned stakeholders – especially including trade unions and the labour movement (integrally linked to one main party in the UK), greens and the environmental movement, often urban ethnic minority groups, and groups representing the less well off in society. They consequently tend to look relatively favourably on the social science of inequality, social mobility, multiculturalism, urban or environmental impact analyses, human or civil rights law, Keynesian economics, and extended cost-benefit analyses that take full account of a wide range of social and environmental values, as well as economic or financial factors. Left or liberal politicians are often sceptical of 'raw' economics that assign priority to austerity or productivity without paying attention to the human costs of the changes implied.

By contrast, conservative or right wing politicians have aligned stakeholders mainly in particular business sectors, especially outsourcing, consultancy, the finance sector and other industries that fare well from privatization, and the self-employed. They also often draw support differentially from social interests placing a priority on low inflation (such as private sector pensioners), and sometimes from law and order and national security stakeholders (like the police and army). So conservative politicians, or others on the centre-right, strongly prefer economics, financial, accounting, business-orientated and legal/regulatory forms of social science.

Figure 6.1   Factors shaping the 'dialectic' of changing uses of social sciences research in public policy making and public sector organizations

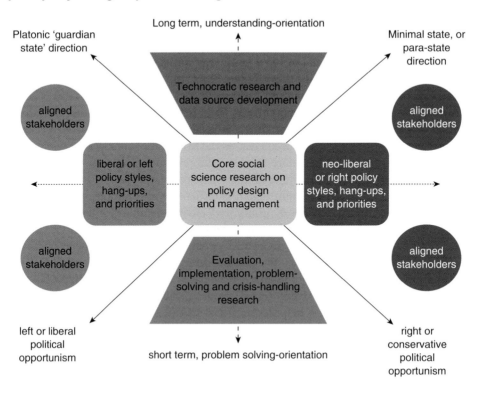

They tend to disparage much qualitative social science; particularly suspect sociology, cultural studies and environmental sciences; and may be hostile to political science not directed towards 'national security' interests (as in the US where Congressional Republicans in 2013 denied it government funding via the National Science Foundation). Right wing politicians particularly tend to be suspicious of university research (fearing most academics are 'liberals' or 'socialists'), and often in office tilt research more towards consultancy firms whose work seems more immediately relevant for their agenda and whose values are more overtly business-friendly or technocratic.

Of course, these are only recurring tendencies and many individual politicians of left and right, especially those who hold positions of power, acknowledge the need for a broad involvement with social science research, for three main reasons. First, of course, is the welfare-maximizing rationale of devising policies that work well, accomplish their intended aims and are properly evaluated – where social science knowledge and evidence is integral at each stage. Making carefully 'evidence-based' policy tends to improve policy effectiveness, whatever the values that politicians hold. The public sector is a zone of 'immortal' bureaucracies (Kaufman, 1976) and some UK departments can trace their lineage back to the thirteenth century. So there are also strong arguments for the 'energizing' effects of party politics. 'Without contraries, there is no progress' said William Blake.[5] And most UK policy makers would agree with Joseph Schumpeter: 'Though we proceed slowly because of our ideologies, we might not proceed at all without them' (1949: 345).

Second, maximizing policy effectiveness tends to produce political success for governments, via a large-scale and often imperceptible process well analysed by Gary Becker (a Chicago-school economist who takes a benign view of liberal democracy). He argues that at its simplest, government can be seen as an arena of competition between coalitions of subsidy-seekers on one side and taxpayers on the other (although each of us may be members of different coalitions depending on the context). Neither side likes or has an interest in maintaining ineffective policies. For instance, when a welfare scheme that aims to get monies to needy groups is a 'leaky bucket' (Becker, 1983), subsidy-seekers lose out because funding that should go to them leaks away or is wasted, reducing their support for such policies. Taxpayers oppose subsidies because they have to pay for them, but they fiercely oppose ineffective policies that add to costs, detract from economic growth and also deliver fewer subsidies to target groups than they should. Since the political process is a constant struggle of subsidy-seekers versus taxpayers, policy inefficiencies will automatically mobilize taxpayers to push down spending, while demobilizing the subsidy-seekers defending them. Becker concludes optimistically that welfare-maximizing, high effectiveness policies will always be selected by left or right politicians or parties to create a permanently optimal policy mix over time.

Third, many policy decisions are not shaped in detail by politicians or parties, but are extensively devolved to professions who deliver services using a degree of discretion – for instance, in schools systems, public health care systems, or planning and regulatory systems. Politicians delegate for very strong political reasons – essentially because: (i) the decisions involved are too complex and time-consuming for them to make directly; (ii) the rule of law means that they must set up impartial administrative systems for delivering policy; (iii) their constituents and stakeholders like policy settlements to be insulated from change by a new political majority, and this is best done by delegating to bureaucracies; and (iv) because where risks exist it is best for them to be allocated to the interests in society most able to insure themselves cheaply against them (Horn, 1995). Thus there are strong theory/empirical (as well as moral, public interest) reasons to expect that most power-holders, most of the time, will be open to adopting social science research that looks to be useful in improving policy outcomes.

However, the second, vertical dimension in Figure 6.1 highlights a second key consequence of the politicization of government sector decision-making, namely strongly contradictory pushes either to the long-run maximization of knowledge and understanding in 'technocratic' mode, or to a short-termist focus on solving specific, immediate problems (especially policy crises of many kinds). The upper wedge shape box indicates the involvement of significant numbers of social scientists in building, improving, interpreting and analysing large-scale and multi-use research databases, archives or research investments funded by government. These are key social science resources, but they also directly bear on policy information and setting. Major

---

[5]Blake (1908/Quote from *The Marriage of Heaven and Hell*).

examples in the UK have been longitudinal surveys of the labour market, family incomes, educational attainment, social mobility and experiences of crime, as well as the vast apparatus of work done in universities to support the national statistics systems and to contribute to the analysis of economic trends and decision-making. The links created here are overwhelmingly at the 'official' level between academics and government research directorates and social science professionals in central departments, with relatively long-distance involvement of ministers and elected politicians. It often involves the quasi-government agencies handling research funding.

On the other hand, the lower wedge box in Figure 6.1 shows a quite different style of short-run (often urgent) application of academic and social science work to government issues. The focus here is on evaluating policies, especially surfacing options at the early policy design stage and examining how implementation is progressing, coping with immediate problems, and especially handling short-run crises and events where indicators go worryingly off-trend. This is sometimes a much more political domain, where ministers and elected politicians set immediate priorities and make yes/no decisions that directly shape what their officials can do, but relatively rarely liaise directly with external academic researchers. In the UK's vigorous political party system, in which many academics are involved, ministers and politicians sometimes have direct contact or links with researchers, especially at the options development stage, bringing them in to chew over how key manifesto commitments or ministerial ideas might best be implemented.

Political pick-up of new ideas or research most often happens in fast-moving policy sectors where new social developments often outpace existing regulatory structures, and where 'established' social science seems out of date or out of touch. All government problems are inherently joined-up ones – involving ethical, political, social, cultural, economic and financial aspects at a minimum. So here the less siloed and more open thinking at the overlap fringes of disciplines often attracts politicians and administrators' attention.

The motor of constant change in the short-term area is the restless, unpredictable and constantly high-pressure dynamic of government terms typically no more than four or five years, and of ministerial or political reshuffles where the UK was the most volatile western government system (until the 2010 coalition government stabilized things) (Political and Constitutional Reform Committee, 2013). Administrative reorganizations of Whitehall and sub-national machinery have also been exceptionally frequent and large-scale in the UK (White and Dunleavy, 2010; NAO, 2010). Academics who become enmeshed one way or another in short-term policy work frequently complain of the 'chaotic' timetables, with urgent requests for studies and advice that then get dropped or passed over when delivered, as the focus of attention again shifts. Yet in a detailed study of policy analysts working directly to decision-makers in the US Department of Energy, Feldman (1989: 93) found that much the same process applied to their work:

> Bureaucratic analysts work in a situation characterized most of the time by a lack of attention by decision makers or policy makers. Many reports they write are not read; many contracts they set up are not used; much expertise they acquire is not called upon. Decisions about policies seem to be made on the basis of politics and

personal loyalties rather than the information and expertise that the analysts have to offer.

The chief consequence of these tensions – between left, welfare-maximizing and right wing pressures on how research is used on the one hand; and between long-run understanding and short-term problem-solving on the other – is a fairly consistent 'dialectic' of change in which the current direction of policy can swing radically between the four political poles or directions of development shown by the solid diagonal arrows in Figure 6.1. The bottom two arrows indicate either liberal/left or right/conservative political opportunism, where politicians ransack social science for supportive evidence or ideas to justify what they are resolutely set on doing anyway. The top left arrow indicates a kind of liberal or social democratic version of Plato's rule by 'guardians', where the emphasis is on evidence-based policy making (EBPM) and government by highly informed politicians, drawing systematically on research and academic information to pick only well-tested and effective policies. This 'rule by experts' may seem utopian (and even ambivalently-democratic in its impulse) but it sits very well with the philosophy of delegation of decision making to professionals in large fields like health care, managing crime or educating children. Concern to extend the sphere of well-directed policy in the economic development and public service fields is a recurrent theme.

The potential for constant changes shown in Figure 6.1, taken together with the large scale of social science involvement with public policy making, helps to explain the stress in the existing literature on diverse processes. In the mid-1970s, Caplan et al. saw social science involvement as 'a bit of legitimation here, some ammunition for political wars there, but a hearty dose of conceptual use to clarify the complexities of life' (1975: 17). American critics saw social science as offering policy makers different standpoints and new perspectives on age-old problems of government (Wagenaar, 1982; Weiss, 1982). Searching for direct impacts or influence from research was seen as infeasible given the strong involvement of so many other forces and factors in public policy decision-making. Carole Weiss (1977: 11) wrote:

> In such amorphous and diffuse decision processes, the use of social research is equally imperceptible. Concepts, generalisations, data, perspectives are absorbed from an array of sources, un-referenced and un-catalogued, and they make their way wraithlike, but sometimes with surprising power, into the emerging decision.

Most researchers concluded then that more work was needed to understand the inherent complexity of academic influence within what Wagenaar (1982) poetically referred to as 'a cloud of unknowing'.

At the meso– or intermediate level a further, important dimension of change has been over time alterations in the dominant ideas about how government social science research linkages should operate. Since most linkages, most of the time, run through officials and public sector managers, there have been three main phases in the development of these prevailing models of the role of social science, which broadly correspond with three phases in the development of dominant thinking (or 'conventional wisdom') in public management and public administration, as shown in Figure 6.2.

Figure 6.2 Overview of governance eras and implications for government research

	Governance and public management characteristics	Implications for government research
1960s – 1970s *Scientific rationality and government science*	• Traditional Weberian bureaucracy • 'Expansive' government • Hierarchical civil service • Scientific rationality	• Strong analytical professions • Scientific expertise in-house • Randomized control trials • Holistic planning & budgeting
1980s – 1990s *Managerialism and New Public Management*	• 'Core competence' government • Outsourcing and contracting • Marketization • Instrumental intervention and linear concepts of affecting change	• Outsourcing of science and technology • Commissioning expertise and research • Evidence-based policy making (EBPM)
2000s *Digital era governance and legacy-NPM* *Second and third waves of DEG*	• Reintegration of machinery of government • Digital change and radical disintermediation • Holistic focus on outcomes and needs of service users • Austerity and post-austerity • Web 2.0 and 'big data' • Continued marketization • Social enterprise and radical forms of collaboration	• More joined-up research infrastructure • Interdisciplinarity • New channels of research impact • Renewal of analytical professions • Hyper-quantitative approaches • Radical real-time impacts • Renaissance of integrative qualitative sciences • Randomized control trials

Throughout the post-war period up to the early 1980s, a modernized Weberian model of government bureaucracy prevailed, sometimes called 'progressive public administration' (PPA). This mixed the Weberian theory of bureaucracy with liberal democratic principles set out in detail by US and British pluralist thinkers. It stressed the development of large-scale, well managed agencies to handle the increased volume of government interventions in the heyday of welfare state development and a mixed economy. Traditional Weberian models focused on large 'machine bureaucracies' (Mintzberg, 1983) run in a tightly controlled hierarchical manner, focusing on delivering public services in a highly stable, routinized and predictable manner. Yet the Anglo-American model was more professionally orientated, and less state-orientated, than (say) France or Japan (Silberman, 1993). PPA stressed the need for welfare bureaucracies especially to be professionally run, more decentralized, and more client-orientated, but within an overall environment of strong and comprehensive planning, systemic thinking and input budgeting.

From the mid-1960s onwards PPA also began to draw more on social sciences. It encouraged the development of output measures, beginning with planning, programming and budgeting systems, and early manifestation of 'big data'. However, the main PPA view of academic inputs stressed applying scientific and professional knowledge in massive ways (like the US space program, or Great Society initiative). In the UK well-developed science professions developed in the civil service and these and quasi-government agencies acted as the main conduits for external advice and academic influences. In the UK government statistics, operational research, economist and legal professions were influential in social science areas. In local government, professional modernization was strongly associated with rational comprehensive planning (Carley, 1980), and merging councils to form larger authorities capable of offering full-spectrum services. This first wave of enthusiasm for evidence-based policy making (EBPM) was strongly associated with:

- investments in long term social science research assets, and
- early enthusiasm for policy experiments and piloting of proposed policy changes, mostly early and lengthy forms of randomized control trials – first mandated by the US Food and Drugs Administration in their modern form in 1980.

The main line of criticism was from pluralists (like Charles Lindblom) who stressed that 'professional social inquiry' could inherently only provide a small percentage of decision-relevant information and could not be scientifically authoritative; and neo-liberal critics who voiced Hayekian pessimism about any form of guidance except markets, and urged a minimal state as the solution to state incapacity to do rational planning.

In 1979–80 in the UK and US the new ascendancy of conservative administrations decisively set back this early social science and academic expansionism. The new governments were intolerant of the scepticism, time-consuming nature and studiedly neutral character of previous policy analysis and research professionalization within government. Instead the 'new public management' (NPM) orthodoxy developed by the mid-1980s stressed 'best practice research' (the speedy compilation of diverse 'lessons' and best practice from many different settings), and its marriage with deductive economic theories of rational actors' behaviour. The interpretation of NPM remains disputed, but an account by Dunleavy et al. (2006a and b) sees it as a two-level 'quasi-paradigm' movement dominated by three top-level, cross-government themes of:

- disaggregation, chunking up large, Weberian hierarchies into smaller, more focused agencies, e.g., dividing 'purchasers' from 'providers';
- competition, making providers compete with each other, typically by outsourcing functions to private contractors; and
- incentivization, scrapping previous public service ethos and professional systems in favour of contracts with pecuniary incentives linked to attaining targets, such as performance-related pay and Private Finance Initiative contracts.

These top-level themes were then linked to 'swarms' of smaller, supporting ideas that could be brigaded under each theme, mostly developed by right wing think tanks or consultancy businesses, and forced through against prevailing academic scepticism and resistance by professions in government.

NPM stressed strong corporate management, a cult of activist managerialism over professions and especially state sector trade unions. At first this emphasis generated masses more inputs and outputs data, allegedly on business lines, and NPM theorists genuflected briefly in terms of valuing outcomes and 'customer' views – values that were applied in more 'humanist NPM' such as the US National Performance Review, some 1980s Australian policies and some early Blair government changes in the UK. This aspect was most evidenced in the development of league tables for customers to compare the performance of schools, hospitals and local authorities, a key aspect of disaggregation, competition and incentivization.

As time went on, NPM's rituals of service modernization went unexamined and it placed more and more unevidenced stress on 'leaderism' (O'Reilly and Reed, 2010), a cult of leadership entrepreneurialism and activism. Many scientific activities in government were privatized and the previous government scientific professions became fragmented and ineffective. Politicians and their special advisors, consultancies and think tanks drove most policy change directly, with a focus on selecting favourable research information fitting within the quasi-paradigm. This created some greater use of accounting, economics and business management research, but downgraded evaluation research and was thoroughly hostile to EBPM. For at least a decade, the apparent self-sustaining momentum of the NPM paradigm appeared to support the Pierce dictum that is the epigraph to this chapter, that ideas 'become true' in the right climate.

By the early to mid-2000s, NPM policies began to be associated with administrative failures and policy crises. Evidence accumulated suggesting that reforms had many dysfunctional aspects, such as high costs, corporate dominance over outsourced services, flat levels of labour productivity over long periods, and the erosion of the public service ethos and its replacement by inadequately incentivized 'customer care' (Dunleavy and Carrera, 2013; Hood and Dixon, 2013).

Consistent with this paradigm has been a strong shift in ideas of how research can be applied in government, away from best practice activism. In the UK government professionalism began to be painfully reconstructed in the civil service (despite increased austerity pressures after 2010). Agencies were reintegrated into departments, limits were imposed on private finance capital schemes, and better outputs and outcomes data began to be generated. A second round of academic and professional pressure for EBPM focused on pervasively using randomized control trials; behavioural public policy experiments to develop 'nudge' methods quickly and at low cost, especially digitally; and exploiting government's huge piles of administrative big data. In the UK four new What Works Centres (or Evidence Centres) similar to the National Institute for Health and Care Excellence (NICE) were announced in 2013 looking at local economic growth, ageing, crime reduction and early intervention. The government rationale said:

> It is a fundamental principle of good public services that decisions are made on the basis of strong evidence and what we know works. Yet all too often evidence is not presented in a simple, relevant format that enables it to be used to its maximum potential by service providers, commissioners and policy makers (HM Government, 2013).

New EBPM approaches were also more inter-disciplinary, with academics often championing co-production with citizens and service users.

Figure 6.3   Five main forms of government to university linkages

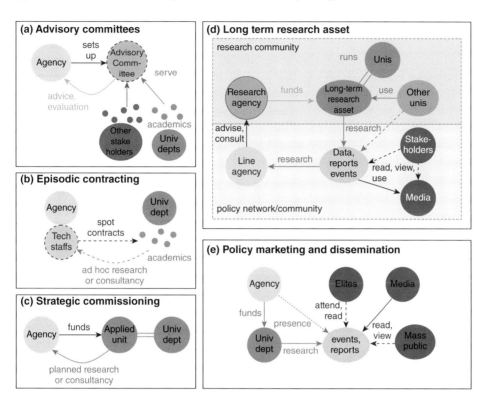

Finally, *at the micro level* of detailed institutional and organizational arrangements, discussions of social science influence on policy making have also suffered from an apparent eclecticism that lead many of our academic interviewees to argue that it is too often done on a 'case by case' basis, where 'whatever suits, works'. However, in practice civil service and public sector rules on procurement around research or consultation mean that the typology of government academic linkages is less diverse than for business, shown in Figure 6.3. All public sector research contracts over £20,000 in value have to be advertised, and officials also have to document when outside interests are consulted.

The most well-developed and widely used way of incorporating academics into government work is through service on advisory committees and bodies, of which there are a large range across UK government – situation (a) in Figure 6.3. Griffiths (2010: 734) looked at the 3,004 non-executive directorships of government departments, agencies and quangos. He found 214 of these posts were held by academics, of which a third or more are social scientists. Academics are more commonly used to head and advise Parliamentary inquiries and very extensively as witnesses to Parliamentary committees. Members are typically appointed for their individual merit and are not formally representatives of their home universities, and academics are usually diluted amongst representatives of business and occasionally other stakeholders. Some disagreements on points of policy aside, generally advisory committees are highly effective at co-opting senior academics into the administration of more technical areas of policy.

The next most common type of linkage with policy makers is 'episodic contracting' – situation (b) in the Figure 6.3. Here officials spot contract with individual academics to secure advice or analysis on a specific issue. These contracts often involve a literature or options-review, special analysis of academic datasets, or alternatively administrative datasets made available to researchers for that specific task. Contract sizes are often very small, to avoid delays due to advertizing rules and ministerial approvals needed for larger contracts, and experts are grabbed at short notice – especially when responding to urgent ministerial requests. Most of these contracts, meetings and linkages are one-offs and never develop into more sustained relationships.

Strategic commissioning (c) involves a government department directly linking with a department or centre within a university, often an applied unit that has been constituted to focus specifically on public sector work. Alternatively the government body links to the consultancy 'arm' of the university which pulls together research teams to undertake regular commissioned research across multi-disciplinary lines. Due to compulsory competitive tendering processes, in the 2000s government bodies began responding to the delays and costs of tendering by creating 'strategic partnerships' within which registered partners could tender more flexibly for smaller blocks of work. Individual academics cannot run large contracts with government because they need indemnity insurance and an ability to interface with complex procurement rules and machinery – little changed by allegedly easier online applications.

Government investments in creating long-term research assets (situation d) creates the most complex set of relationships. Here a government research council (for example the ESRC for the UK social sciences) contracts with a university fielding a dedicated and experienced team to run a long-term survey or database. The research council consults extensively with the most relevant government department(s) about meeting policy needs and priorities for information and evidence at the same time as the academic needs or interests in this area. A client department may joint-fund the initiative. The winning research team must then generate the flow of data, reports and evidence expected and often develops relatively close links to departmental research directorates and senior officials. Other universities can also analyse the data and the centre's research is extensively disseminated to stakeholders and the media, with the client department also sometimes 'piggy-backing' on these activities to maintain its consultation links with academia and societal interests.

Finally, situation (e) in Figure 6.3, public policy agencies may use academic research with a specific department to promote its policies (policy marketing), attract media and stakeholder attention and even influence or inform voters or citizens more widely. The agency funds the production of a report and often the holding of an event that attracts media reporting and elite attendance. This pattern is well-developed at the local and regional level where governments can draw on local academic expertise. For academics this work is often unproblematic, promoting public interest concerns in a locality. Hence it raises far fewer concerns over research being used for corporate purposes and publicity than are considerations in university relations with the businesses.

6.2 The scale of social science links to policy

The lower intelligentsia wants the state because it lives by the state ... and the higher intelligentsia wants freedom because it makes its living from the free market.

Régis Debray[6]

Whenever the cause of the people is entrusted to professors, it is lost.

Vladimir Ilyich Lenin

Turning from even well-informed theoretical considerations to empirical analysis is always difficult, normally entailing a coarsening of categories for which data are available, and almost always requiring triangulating across different sets of partially unsatisfactory data sources. Given that social science impacts have been more discussed than studied, the available quantitative evidence on social science impacts on policy making is no exception. We look at six main types of data – the relationships with government bodies reported by social science academics; links to social science research on central government department websites; citations and links to social science research across the wider government web domains; the evidence from our dataset of academics having linkages with government bodies; estimated expenditures on social science research across government departments and agencies; and estimates of the size of the professional staffs working in the public sector whose work mainly involves 'translating' social science research for public sector agencies and departments.

As with business relationships, the large-scale survey by Abreu et al. (2008) provides a first take on how social science researchers see their work as used by government bodies, and how their responses compares with other disciplines. Figure 6.4 shows that academics in the health sciences (some of whom are social scientists in our definition) reported undertaking the most activities with public sector agencies. But social scientists in the Abreu et al. definition came a close second, with strong links to all four kinds of public sector body: UK government departments; overseas governments and international organizations; quasi-governmental bodies; and regional development agencies. The levels of working with government bodies are greater than for STEM disciplines (outside health sciences) and those reported by arts and humanities academics (which are boosted here by Abreu et al. including law in this category, instead of social sciences). These data also accord well with other information gathered by reactive measures. An online self-submission survey for the British Academy in 2008 showed that social scientists rated their influence and impact in the government and public policy sphere as much more developed than for business linkages, and also as closer to realizing their disciplines' full potential for influence (LSE Public Policy Group, 2008). Humanities respondents in this survey were more pessimistic than in the Abreu et al. data.

Turning to non-reactive measures of linkages between government and academia, we look next at the analysis of social science (and some STEM) departments' websites carried out for our project by SQW. Just as for business linkages, expert coders recorded the number and the diversity of links between university departments and

---

[6]Debray (1981: 224).

Figure 6.4   The proportions of academics and researchers across discipline groups who reported links to different types of public sector agencies

	Government departments/ NHS	Overseas government, international organizations	Quasi-government agencies or quangos	Regional development agencies	Overseas, quasi-government bodies	**Any work with public sector**
Health	52.3	12.9	12.9	4.9	0.7	**66.0**
Social Sciences	36.9	19.3	14.3	14.7	1.6	**60.4**
Arts and Humanities	24.7	9.8	14.7	9.4	0.9	**46.1**
STEM (not health)	24.8	16.1	10.2	8.6	1.2	**43.9**
All discipline groups	*32.4*	*14.9*	*12.7*	*9.8*	*1.1*	**52.3**

Source: Computed from Abreu et al. (2008), Exhibit A8, p. 68.

Figure 6.5   Review of university department websites for linkages to government or public sector organizations, by discipline

	Local and regional UK government and NHS	**Central UK government**	**EU, overseas governments, international bodies**	**All public sector**
Medicine	7.5	5.2	3.0	**15.7**
Social Policy	5.2	6.4	3.1	**14.7**
Economics	3.9	6.5	4.1	**14.5**
Law	1.2	7.1	4.0	**12.3**
Business and Management	4.9	5.2	1.6	**11.7**
Engineering	1.3	4.6	4.3	**10.1**
Geography	1.9	4.7	2.3	**8.9**
Computer Science	0.2	2.0	5.3	**7.5**
Sociology	0.8	3.8	2.8	**7.3**
Chemistry	0.7	3.7	2.7	**7.0**
Psychology	2.4	2.8	0.8	**6.1**
Political Science	0.4	2.2	3.1	**5.6**
Physics	1.2	2.0	1.6	**4.8**
Media Studies and Communications	0.6	1.9	1.6	**4.2**
Anthropology	0.4	2.7	0.6	**3.8**
History	0.8	1.0	0.5	**2.3**
Philosophy	0.5	0.8	1.0	**2.3**

Source: LSE PPG analysis of SQW consultancy data.

Figure 6.6   The visibility of academic research on UK central government department websites (February 2007)

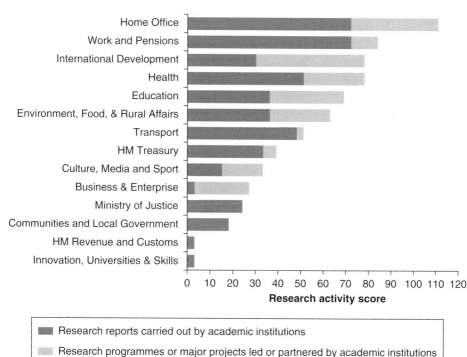

Source: LSE Public Policy group (2008).

Note: These data are based on a study that we carried out for the British Academy in 2008 on impacts of humanities and social science research.

government sector organizations in the UK, spending at least one hour on each department site, and encompassing all relevant satellite units and research centres, and at individual academics' CVs etc. Figure 6.5 shows the average number of references per university department website to different types of government organizations, looking across social science and selected STEM disciplines. Medicine departments show the strongest linkages, but four social science disciplines also show strong linkages (social policy, economics, law and business and management). There are four more social science disciplines that are generally comparable with STEM subjects in their government linkages, and then at the bottom of the Figure two disciplines (media studies and anthropology) are closer to the lower level of linkages found in some humanities departments (philosophy and history).

Looking at the extent of linkages from the government end of the telescope, Figure 6.6 gives a snapshot picture of which departments in UK central government showed most linkages or references to universities, academic research centres and labs in early 2007. There are limits on this data because government organizations have an overall culture of not making explicit the research that underpins policy decisions or administrative practices. They also had a policy of strictly limiting web links to non-governmental bodies. None the less, Figure 6.6 shows high visibility of

Figure 6.7   The extent to which different disciplines are represented in government and public policy domains, UK domestic and international

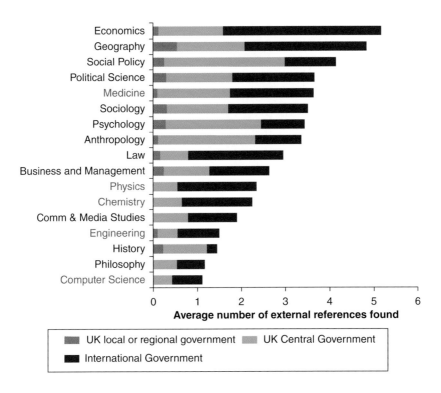

academic work in departments with very strong links to the social sciences, especially the Home Office (with law and criminology), the Department for Work and Pensions (with social policy) and the Department for International Development (DfID) (with economics and development studies).

The three departments of Health, Environment, Food and Rural Affairs (Defra), and Transport are more mixed users of both STEM and social science research. The smaller linkage departments are again mostly referencing social science research.

Our fourth source of data on social scientists links with public sector bodies comes from our dataset of 370 academics. We noted in Chapter 1 that our Google web searches found around 850 references in government and public sector domains in the UK and abroad to academics included in our dataset, amounting to 3.5 per cent of all references to them. Figure 6.7 shows the overall breakdown of this small minority with different disciplines appearing stronger at each level. Economics and geography are most strongly represented at the international governance level, whereas for national government, social policy, psychology and anthropology are most referred to. Local government references were significantly less.

In this area, the results for social science disciplines are particularly interesting when seen in comparison to STEM. We conducted a fine-grained analysis of references to each of our 370 academics in the UK's gov.uk web domain, coding all results and where we found them. Figure 6.8 shows that the comparator STEM scientists

Figure 6.8 Average numbers of references per academic in the gov.uk domain, UK domestic only

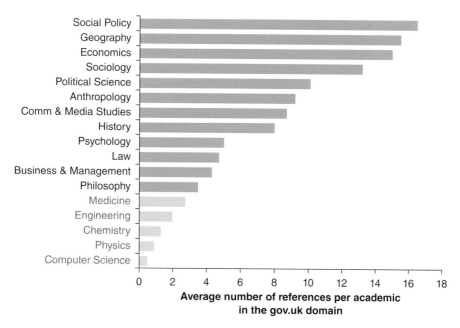

Average number of references per academic
in the gov.uk domain

in our dataset came towards the bottom of the ranking. Social policy, geography, economics and sociology were the top social science disciplines with an average of more than 10 gov.uk domain references per academic, with all the remaining social science disciplines grouped in the top and middle of the table. The fluctuation in individual disciplines' position here strongly reflects the exclusion of the nhs.uk domain, so that only central and local government links are included. Nevertheless, this limited picture still shows social science academic research being more extensively used in government.

No one ranking measure on its own can give a full picture of how different subject disciplines perform in terms of their visibility to and use by government bodies. To help get a more synoptic impression Figure 6.9 pools rankings of different disciplines from the three web domain analyses. The 'usual suspect' disciplines (social policy, economics, and geography) clearly are at the top with medicine; followed by a solid middle of other core social science disciplines (including law here); and again with anthropology and media studies at the bottom with the other STEM disciplines (included as comparators) and history and philosophy.

We turn next from the direct estimation of relative linkage levels to look at how central government departments allocate spending to university research, and the proportion flowing to social science departments. Our sources here are the detailed budgets of central departments and major spending ministries. Patterns vary a good deal over time. So we focus first on one individual department's spending pattern, the Department of Food, Environment and Rural Affairs (Defra). Figure 6.10 shows mixed fortunes for research spending with the onset of austerity clearly having an

Figure 6.9   A combined ranking of results for government, UK domestic and international

	From our survey of university departments (see Figure 6.5)	From our Google search of academics (see Figure 6.7)	From our Google search in the gov.uk domain (see Figure 6.8)	TOTAL indicative ranking (sum of all columns)
Social Policy	2	2	1	**5**
Economics	3	6	3	**12**
Geography	7	5	2	**14**
Medicine	1	1	13	**15**
Sociology	9	4	4	**17**
Business and Management	5	7	11	**23**
Law	4	9	10	**23**
Psychology	11	3	9	**23**
Political Science	12	8	5	**25**
Engineering	6	12	14	**32**
Anthropology	15	11	6	**32**
Media Studies	14	15	7	**36**
Computer Science	8	13	17	**38**
Physics	13	10	16	**39**
Chemistry	10	14	15	**39**
History	16	16	8	**40**
Philosophy	17	17	12	**46**

Note: The column on the right-hand side shows the cumulative ranking of each discipline based on three previous charts. It is an indicative overview of how visible each discipline is in the government sector. The lower rankings denote higher visibility.

impact after 2010 especially. The social science share of Defra research spending at first rose strongly from very low levels to peak at over a quarter of the total in 2007, but subsequently dropped back to around a seventh under the coalition government. (The establishment of a separate Department for Energy and Climate Change in 2007 may have somewhat affected this pattern, with the economics and social science of climate change moving to a separate department.)

Estimating how far central government research can be attributed across discipline groups is difficult from the very limited information contained in budget and resourcing documents. However, Figure 6.11 shows our estimates of five central ministries' research spending over the 1990s and 2000s. The strong spending by the Department for International Development (DfID) is clearly exceptional, and other departments show a strong downward movement since the peak of the Labour government's managerialist period in the later 2000s. The squeeze on all domestic department budgets

Figure 6.10   Social science research expenditure estimated as a proportion of total research expenditure paid to universities by Defra

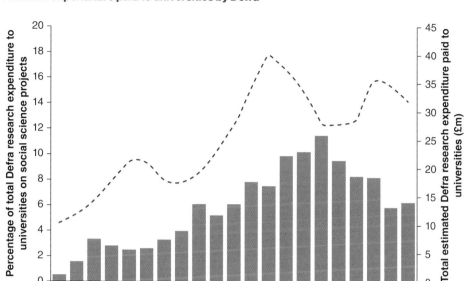

required by austerity cutbacks was accentuated in some ministries by Conservative ministers' traditional suspicions of social sciences.

We can gain a further insight into the evolution of recent expenditure patterns across UK central departments by considering them alongside some of the data already presented that used unobtrusive search techniques. During 2007 we trawled in a fine-grained way through the results in Google, coding two features: (a) the number of social science research reports that were available on departmental websites that had been carried out by university academics; and (b) the number of social science research programmes or major projects sponsored by departments but led or partnered by universities. Using a simple index, we created a 'research intensity score' for departments' use of science research shown on the horizontal axis of Figure 6.12. The strongest users of social science work were the Home Office, the Department for Work and Pensions, Department for International Development, Department of Health, and Department for Education as noted above. Against this measure, on the vertical axis of Figure 6.12 we chart the 2010 levels of research expenditure on social science, giving the fairly strong positive relationship shown. Somewhat over a third of variance in financial spend on social science might be explained in terms of the research intensity index for these departments, with DfID spending more on social science than might be expected, and Transport and Defra spending less.

Figure 6.11 Estimated total expenditure by UK government departments on social science research by UK universities (in £ m)

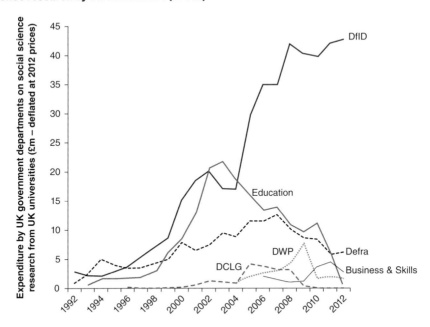

Source: Taken from departmental research databases where publicly available (Defra, DCLG, DfID) and Freedom of Information requests where unavailable (Education, DWP).

Figure 6.12 Estimated expenditure on social science research and research intensity score, by UK central government department

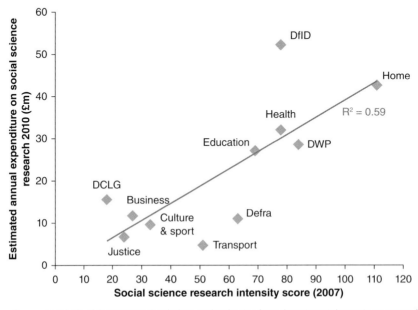

Source: Our own analysis of departmental websites, and estimates from departmental reports on expenditure.

6.3 Social scientists' influence on policy

A habit of basing convictions upon evidence, and of giving to them only that degree or certainty which the evidence warrants, would, if it became general, cure most of the ills from which the world suffers.

Bertrand Russell[7]

The work of an intellectual is not to mould the political will of others; it is, through the analyses that [she or] he does in [their] own field, to re-examine evidence and assumptions, to shake up habitual ways of working and thinking, to dissipate conventional familiarities, to re-evaluate rules and institutions and to participate in the formation of a political will (where he [or she] has [their] role as citizen to play).

Michel Foucault[8]

Like everyone in every career, academics and researchers must constantly balance competing priorities – work/life balance in their personal lives; research, teaching and 'good citizenship' roles within the university; and private-regarding and public-regarding activity in their roles as intellectuals and civic actors. Especially for researchers whose work has strong practice applications, a pattern of 'shifting involvements' between a private-regarding gain orientation and a more public-regarding stance is quite common, on lines that Albert Hirschman (1982) identified at the societal level. Part of this is career-related. Young researchers must complete their PhDs and struggle to acquire the 'slate' of research publications needed for academic appointments (especially in the UK since the RAE or REF). Later on, more senior researchers may be looking to build an academic 'firm' with grant or contract funding, which might include government and public sector sources. And in applied areas of research, established academics often have more of the reputation, organizational experience and time needed to more effectively seek to influence or shape policy. So there is a regular pattern of mid-career researchers becoming more public-affairs orientated. Often too this phase is itself time-limited, with senior staff retiring and scaling down what they do, or by a need to shift back to 'core' academic concerns. Hirschman also argued that people often move out of a public affairs orientation because of 'over-involvement'. They become disillusioned as they realize that public policy change is going to be more complex and time-consuming than they had initially envisaged, especially where policy reversals occur or reforms stall in the 'long grass'.

Many commentators have argued therefore that a key implication for researchers and academics who get involved in advising on or trying to shape public policies is that they need to adopt from the outset a realistic appreciation of the difficulties in getting involved in a politically-shaped domain. At its heart, this is the result of the competing pressures outlined in Figure 6.1 (page 144), which politicians attempt to balance by focusing on multiple policy questions at once and prioritizing quick solutions that can be both understood by a voting public and are possible to

---

[7]Quoted in Simmons (1992).
[8]Quoted in Foucault (1989).

implement. Academics on the other hand, can spend whole careers understanding in depth all aspects of a particular policy question, and some have little experience of having to turn their answers into reality. The cultural differences between these two groups therefore need to be factored in:

> Policy makers and academics are different breeds who speak different languages. Whereas they [politicians] work toward collective goals, we can be isolated loners ... Whereas they focus on the short-term while juggling numerous projects, we can devote years to just one research grant. Whereas they break evidence into small chunks to extract the key messages, we sometimes engage in lofty debates that have no tangible outcome. Simply acknowledging and adapting to this different terrain and culture is difficult but essential. (Goodwin, 2013)

This cultural difference creates specific problems for academics in attempting to develop mutually attractive research ideas, build traction on a particular issue, or to develop long-term links with a government department. Thinking back to the diagram at the start of Part II (Figure II.1; page 108), it seems that the further that academics progress through the six aspects of impact, the more uncertainty and ambiguity prevails in any kind of evaluation about the nature or scale of impact from academic research. Indeed, by the time we reach the higher echelons of government decision-making, it becomes difficult in many ways to predict why certain research has impact, or more likely, why it does not. Ministerial attention, for example, on an individual policy issue is likely to be limited for very sound reasons:

> [M]inisters cannot pay attention to all of the issues for which they are responsible. In fact, they can only pay attention to a tiny proportion ... [Because] policy makers can only pay attention to a small number of the issues for which they are responsible, they ignore most and promote a few to the top of their agenda, often following a major event or a successful media campaign by certain groups. So, for every issue to which ministers (and senior civil servants) pay attention, they must ignore (say) 99 others. (Cairney, 2013)

This can be frustrating for academics who have to accept the likely fact that any given body of research will secure only tiny slices of political attention, most of which will not progress. Two senior researchers recalled in interviews:

> We came in [to 10 Downing Street] on that occasion, and we'd got all these people together, and we huddled around and drank tea. So he [PM Gordon Brown] gave his bit, greeted one person, and went off again. There was no engagement whatsoever. Then nothing from Cameron.

> It is impossible. At the moment, there were amendments passed in the House of Lords that were certainly informed by some of the work we have been doing, but then they get over-turned in the House of Commons because we have a government which is not particularly sympathetic to the [our] perspective. I met [the Secretary of State] to talk about it the other day, and didn't really get anywhere.

Many researchers commented on their feeling that research was often being picked up less because of its merits than because of political opportunism, a search for academic work that was convenient support for whatever ministers or politicians were resolved to do anyway. As one political advisor commented to us:

> [W]e didn't commission lots of evidence. But at the same time, you don't want to look like that. So you will spend time doing things to show that you are meeting with people who are on the leading edge of thinking or doing things, to show you are solid, and that sort of thing. It is quite good to have sessions, to bring in academics, and nod your head, and that sort of thing. ... but I wouldn't say that was really very influential.

Experienced researchers too were often quite cynical about the reasons why their own work had been picked. Three academics commented:

> Research influenced policy in that it fitted the relevant viewpoints of the ministers in charge. That is, it was adding confirmatory evidence to the way that their thinking was going anyway.

> There are pockets of excellence in terms of using evidence in government, but overall it is pretty dire. Overall in [department A] it is driven by political imperatives. Getting the report done for the Minister quickly, identifying all the stakeholders quickly, and then you selectively cite evidence to support what you want to do.

Yet other officials and researchers took a far more benign view, stressing the inevitable need for research and political priorities to be articulated, but denying that this is solely political opportunism. A senior research commissioner said:

> The caricature of 'Here's my policy, now find some evidence' isn't fair. Because what you are actually saying is: 'We're going to have to make a decision about this, so let's find the evidence that will help us do that'. Of course people will have preconceptions. But the biggest difference is that the policy has to be decided in the here and now, and we have to do it on the basis of whatever evidence there is available ... and whatever preconceptions or ideas that people might have.

To counteract some of these ambiguities, relationship building between academics and policy makers is crucial (the fifth aspect in Figure II.1). This often takes the form of informal channels of advice and expertise, rather than via more formally commissioned single research studies. Here conceptual enlightenment processes are more likely to operate when senior officials have time to accumulate links to researchers across their policy area. These are problematic to develop due to the high rate of turnover of research officials in government, particularly at the research director and the relevant policy levels. Relational contracting becomes tricky to do when the personal relationships at the start are continually broken and having to be rebuilt: 'There is no continuity of people. You get them for a couple of years and then they move on'. An academic experienced in doing evaluation studies for government echoed this widely-acknowledged perception:

> It's almost farcical the extent to which the research liaison officers change. The probability that you end the project with the same contact you started with is actually quite low. There is slightly more stability in who the policy customer is. But even that can change. The staff turnover is phenomenal really.

Networking with policy makers emerged time and again in interviews as a critical stage in getting research results taken seriously, and in inducing or persuading policy makers that they could benefit from academic expertise. One academic working in the public health field reflected: 'You need to be out there talking to policy folk. It is really the face-to-face conversations – that is the key'. This academic pointed to the salience of government advisory committees in bridging across to busy officials unable to otherwise evaluate much research: 'It is also about how you perform on those committees. Whether you are sensible. And you've got to be articulate as well. They are only going to invite people who can handle those environments'. Another commented that academic expertise from known senior figures was what really counted with civil servants and politicians:

> It carries real weight because it is trusted advice. So building those relationships of trust with people in government, ministers as much as officials, is really key to having influence.

Government procurement rules often cut across maintaining or developing such relationships through strategic commissioning or consultancy arrangements. In business corporations, research directors can use any academics they choose and are not restricted by requirements to run bidding competitions, so good relationships are easier to maintain. But government research officials need to be relatively equitable in terms of research ensuring that commissioning is allocated across different providers. Even though governments have moved towards more 'relational' models of contracting, at least in the way they have sought to build relationships through such things as strategic partnerships and preferred provider schemes, the difficulties of actually building integrated working partnerships between officials and academics are still latent.

In addition there are much deeper cultural dynamics at work that can act as major barriers to sustained impact. There are, for example, oft-repeated characterisations of academics as unable to respond to the fast-paced, regularly shifting political world. For instance, Goodwin (2013) relayed a senior official's views that he had picked up during a six month Whitehall secondment, who said:

> Academics tend to be long on diagnosis and short on solutions. The question I most often ask myself when sitting in seminars is, "So what should I do about this?" This is closely followed by: "How long is this going on for? I have 15 urgent things to do". We don't expect people to have all of the answers, as that puts me out of a job. But a willingness and ability to help us think through what our response should be will get you invited back.

The need to 'get to the point' is stronger the higher up within the government body that research messages needed to be received. A political advisor bluntly confessed:

> Broadly we didn't have the resources to read academic work. It was way too long. And when they did short pieces, they did short arguments, which wasn't what we wanted either. Usually, we wanted a factsheet that said: "Here are 18 facts" ... that would be more useful. [Or saying] "You are 15 times more likely to have this ... ten times more likely to have this".

Policy makers are often especially impatient of academics' desire to set everything in well-established background:

> One of the guys I worked with had a quote that rang in my ears and I remember a lot ... which is 'Context is death'. Any time you need to explain something, then you've already lost. It should just be obvious from the start. And so that is a big problem for academic research.

Key to the relationship and the development of a mutually attractive quid pro quo is the problem of being able to interpret and translate academic knowledge into the public policy setting. Convincing policy makers and practitioners inevitably requires some degree of 'translation' in order to get clear messages across, and for many observers, this quid pro quo is often not clear from the outset, or becomes dimmer as the research relationship progresses. Two senior government research officials made this point:

> It is really about the translation role. Unless we can distil that evidence down, boil it down into key messages that really have political traction, then we are not going to have much of an impact.

> It may be great research, but unless you can do that translation job ... and often that is the role of my colleagues to say : 'The key thing in this research is X' ... it does take particular skills to do that. And researchers who can do that are going to develop more trust.

One key difference between government and the business sector is a much more developed and systematic infrastructure in government for making links to academic research. Yet some policy officials from central and local government complained about the difficulties of knowing what kind of academic research is out there, and how it can enrich their own policy and practice work. They also complained that academics were too diffident in publicizing their work, and making explicit how their work could be relevant to policy makers. A local government director of research argued:

> One of the key things is actually contacting decision-makers and saying this is relevant. This is why you should be doing this. So I don't think that academia is knocking at a closed door. I think, as head of research at the Council, I can't tell if people are knocking at that door or not.

For many academics though, the concept of 'pitching' their research to policy makers in ways that align with existing or potential messages is a difficult one. Some feel uncomfortable with the idea of becoming an advocate or lobbying for a particular policy position as this runs counter to the independent nature of academic work. To avoid this, some work with intermediate organisations to attempt to influence government policy: 'Do you have to take sides? That is partly why I was providing information for people to lobby. I'm into persuasion at this stage. How compatible is that with objective scientific base?' Working closely with government may also require feeding into processes around policies that are not supported by findings from academic research.

> I'm part of a Department J working group … We are moving into an implementation phase. So you then have the dilemma of how much you maintain the original stance and how much you help the civil servants implement something that you think hasn't got the best structure to begin with.

Where relationships are built, they are particularly valuable at showcasing the cumulative impact of research. For instance, consider the push towards developing outcome-based performance measurement and payment by results (PBR), which bridged across governments of very different political orientations. Government departments and agencies doing this kind of commissioning clearly must be able to establish benchmarks, baselines, and calibrated metrics in order to be able to assess outcomes adequately enough to reward providers and establish performance improvement. Looking at PBR in diverse areas (such as offender management, family interventions, or getting unemployed people back into sustainable work) all of these requirements involve using quite sophisticated social science techniques, quantitative and qualitative, to make the mechanisms work properly. Even in interviews with the private sector firms involved in innovating and delivering these PBR services, they too were attempting to develop metrics to allow them to understand more clearly what the likely outcome effects of particularly interventions might be, and how to cost these interventions given these likely effects. For both government and commissioned service providers, the key is to have access to real-time and reliable data on the effectiveness and cost-efficiency of these services.

This is not the kind of research that lends itself to commissioned academics disappearing for a year or two and coming back with a long report and data that is out of date. What is required, according to policy makers and officials from public services firms involved in running PBR contracts, is a much more disaggregated approach that allows existing academic research to be accessed in more immediate ways, and which encourages academics working in these areas to interact in a more informal style with the providers and with government commissioners. The large scale of many government interventions, and the long tempo of decision implementation in areas like adjusting welfare benefits or pensions policies, also places a huge importance on academic work as part of departments doing horizon scanning:

> We rely on [academics] to get good, sound, expert advice at key stages … That kind of advice based on a range of evidence, the knowledge of the researcher

rather than just a single individual project, can be key in influencing policy thinking.

Especially where Whitehall departments make use of long-term research assets (including those part-funded by UK research councils) to monitor in detail how complex social phenomena are evolving, social science insights are continuously important at a level above that of individual questions answered or solutions tested. A senior official reflected on how some large-scale research at the technocratic edge of the spectrum (see Figure 6.1) was received by professional experts in two departments:

> The research helped to frame the broad narrative and the way in which we thought about the labour market. Rethinking the labour market and how policies should work. At the micro level, the interaction between policy research and analysis at [Department], and people outside working on evaluation of labour market programmes, again that was very influential.

The directors of social science research centres especially highlighted their role to us as independent and trusted custodians of long-term datasets. In another example, social scientists working on homelessness and housing were invited in to brief a joint ministerial working group, an intervention that was acknowledged by the policy makers concerned as having fed directly into the preparation of a government White Paper on these topics. Although this work had grown out of a specific ESRC-funded research 'asset', the researchers themselves argued that it had been the whole body of collective research and expertise in this area over an extended period of time. Similarly, in a further example, policy makers in the field of UK public health talked about the importance of the 'collective' impact on governments over a period of decades from academic work to develop the by-now standard metric of 'quality adjusted life years' (QALY). An experienced policy official warned of the dangers of attributing too much importance to single pieces of research in this broader development.

> It is much broader than that. Really what they have done is to normalize or regularize the notion that they should apply economic techniques to this question. The principles of QALY are used all over the world. They are the principle system by which people do health technology assessment. It is used by the health insurance industry to determine which drugs they will pay for. So its influence has been utterly profound across the system [...] But you wouldn't be able to argue that there is a single paper or piece of work that pushes all of this on. You can argue that there are some influential text books. But it is a movement. An intellectual, scientific, and academic movement, as much as one piece of work.

Of course, most researchers, most of the time, do not serve on committees, do not serially win government research contracts, do not operate out of 'rich tradition' departments, or happen to know ministers or senior officials. So other methods need to be used in an effort to make sure your work is known and considered. Academics and policy makers have frequently highlighted some basic things that can be done to increase the chances of success at each of the six stages in our impact schema above.

Academics can help themselves by increasing the number of opportunities for face-to-face contacts with policy makers. As one high-impact researcher commented:

> If you want policy impact, at the end of the day, you have got to get your ideas in front of the policy makers. If you are opportunistic about it, if you have a chance to have a quick word with them, and you have a pitch to make, there is something really interesting in this … then I think it is actually remarkably easier to build relationships that turn out to be very, very valuable. I'm always amazed that a lot of my colleagues don't seem to do that.

Another professor, for example, described how he and his colleague would make a regular point of inviting prominent journalists writing in their field out for lunch or dinner. And although credible academic blogs are still relatively rare in the social sciences, those already there are regularly followed by policy makers and officials in departments, both for enlightenment purposes and for more strategic reasons in terms of keeping abreast of prevalent issues on which ministers may need briefings. Indeed, officials were frank in stressing that 'Google-based policy making', when ministers ask for information on a policy area with short deadlines, mean that those academics whose work is publicly available are going to be picked up. As discussed, there is usually never time to access more complex materials, especially behind pay walls that even most national government departments and virtually all other public agencies frequently cannot cross. Similarly, 'open data' and the 'big data' movements in government offer a realistic prospect for external researchers to gain much faster and more extended access to administrative databases than at any previous time. One former official speculated:

> It seems to me that the opportunity both for academics and government to leverage what we do is primarily going to come through the use, at least on the empirical side, of some of these much bigger, richer datasets. And there is potential for governments to get things done more cheaply and for academics to proactively approach government and say: 'We could do some stuff that would be really interesting and novel from a research point of view, more cheaply than could have been done five or ten years ago'.

So academics need some strategies to put themselves in those situations that may seem 'serendipitous' or 'right-place-right-time' opportunities. An influential stream of political science research on policy change associated with John Kingdon stresses that 'policy streams' continuously operate in government, as societal behaviours shift in response to many stimuli, as political parties track and change their policy stances, and as other layers of government and actors in the policy community alter their strategies. A key implication is that windows of opportunity for research to be influential in policy making continuously ebb and flow, opening or closing depending on convergence of different factors. Serendipitous moments, as it were, are merely a function of the efforts that academics put in to positioning and publicising within this complex and, in many ways, unpredictable process. A senior official commented:

The question is are we ready as researchers to give good sound advice when it does happen? [an opportunity opens up] Are we good at deploying what we know? Saying, 'Oh minister, you need a five-year research programme before we can answer that' is probably not the most welcome response. It may be the right response, but shouldn't we be able to say something else? Shouldn't we already have some evidence there? Are we ready to give wise advice in those circumstances?

And a professor observed:

The evidence has to be around often for a long time and constantly be reinforced. You need to win hearts and minds of particular pressure groups, particular members of parliament, and then the moment arrives where a particular Secretary of State takes the plunge.

For a wide range of policy makers, in central and local government, the aspiration must be for a much more integrated culture in which research and policy live together in mutually enhancing ways. As one local government official eloquently summed up:

It is about creating that overall mood that is needed to embed research into the decision making process. Because a lot of things we are discussing, it seems like it comes down to this personal meeting, or one piece of research. It has to be more intrinsic, so that all decisions are based on a sort of soaking up of good quality research over a period of time.

Of course, there are distinct emerging factors that provide additional incentives for both groups to alter some of these more chronic patterns. Not least is the pressure of austerity that has forced government into spending considerably less on its own research capacity with public and political opinion also making consultancy research spending somewhat problematic. Instead therefore is a greater emphasis on the value of academic research, funded as it is in part by the taxpayer, to be fully utilized in the effort to rein in public spending and increase growth. And the decrease in ideology-politics has increased the salience of research feeding directly into managerial decision-making by policy makers. Related threats and crises also encourage government to be more open than it might otherwise be:

The idea that the PM would actually talk to academics about economic ideas as opposed to inviting them in for receptions was unprecedented. But during the financial crisis it did actually happen.

At the same time, the new Research Excellence Framework (REF) is providing additional incentives for academics engaging in impact activities, and therefore further reasons for optimism. For those academics who are strongly engaged in applied policy relevant research, these efforts will now be more explicitly rewarded. And with additional resource that will be directed at engagement activities, mainstreaming impact support within universities will become more feasible. Transaction costs for improving communication are also falling with the rise in

Figure 6.13   Trajectory of difficulties in achieving impacts in government and the public sector, compared to private sector and business

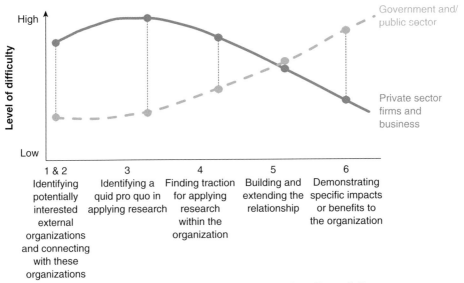

Six aspects of impact in external organizations (see Figure II.1)

academic blogging and social media more generally. The support from both research councils and government for open access will enable more research to be found and therefore used.

Conclusions

Summing up these features of government interactions with social scientists, Figure 6.13 makes clear that barriers and difficulties to be surmounted are different in character from those encountered in Chapter 5 on business. Looking across the six stages set out in Figure II.1, the barriers are end-loaded, not front-loaded. Given the multi-causal processes in policy making, it is very hard for researchers to demonstrate any distinct or individual influence on policy making, still less linked to individual research projects as the research councils and the REF audits undertaken by HEFCE both tend to want. Sustaining any long-term relationships with government agencies is also more fraught than in business, because of regular political changes in policy orientations, procurement rules emphasizing open competition, and prohibiting 'favouritism', and the apparently ceaseless job movement of many civil servants. Yet the early stages of identifying and contacting potential users are relatively straightforward, and government is far more omnivorous than business in at least sucking in and initially considering new research. Finding traction for a one-off piece of research is also not too difficult once a relationship is established – rather it is sustaining it over time or seeing any discernible implementation of research-based conclusions or suggestions that is difficult.

Overall the picture of impacts in government and public policy is significantly different in this chapter compared to the previous one. In the business sector, models of social science impact have been largely absent, and much of the relevant information could only be assembled with difficulty. In the government domain, academics have compiled many case studies and critics have written extensively on the inherent difficulties and complexities of establishing models to predict and explain impacts. In this sense, there has been no lack of analytical coverage. Furthermore, we have seen from our comparative data that social science academics have generally been much more plugged into government and policy making. As a result there are far more normative and administrative structures in place for making the links between researchers and policy making.

However, there are also some important commonalities between the take-up of social science in government and in business. Like business executives (sometimes perhaps in imitation of them) policy makers often complain about the cultural mismatches between the policy sphere and that of research academics – in terms of timeframes, methods of working, professional priorities, and the general standards or quality of work. Many officials and political staff think that academics could do far more to publicise their work and communicate their expertise. Departments and research centres should do more to articulate bottom-line messages of their research, and stream these into a policy making process that is by nature fast-moving, and prone to offering up windows of opportunity that close as quickly as they open. Academics complain of the difficulties of trying to second-guess where policy directions are going, and of keeping track of partisan or ministerial changes of emphasis or direction. They are slowly responding to policy makers' complaints by working more with intermediaries (like think tanks), focusing more on better short-form communication through blogs, and enhancing the public understanding of social sciences. In a world that is inherently unpredictable, the rational response for universities and researchers is to contrive to maximize the potential opportunities for impact – in the hope that this will increase the chances of serendipitous outcomes.

Arguably two of the most potent ways in which social scientists already induce Whitehall departments, reluctant ministers and a huge range of public sector bodies to do more evidence-based policy making is not through direct interactions at all. Instead influence comes through researchers' roles in acting with civil society organizations, and in publicizing and commenting on policy problems with the media and in ways that engage the wider public. No minister, senior department official or public agency leader can afford to lightly ignore a stream of well-informed critique and commentary that social science researchers in their precise policy field may originate. Nor can politicians or top officials risk seeming professionally disreputable or isolated, without academic allies and professional credibility of some kind. Better by far to have some expertise 'inside the tent', and to be able to formulate credible rebuttals to unfavourable evidence and expert commentary from outside. In the next two chapters we explore social scientists' roles with civil society organizations, and their influence (via the media and directly) on public opinion and engagement.

7

Civil society organizations and the third sector

NGOs [non-governmental organizations] like to suggest that they were the products of enthusiastic amateurs, thereby sending out a message that they are just innocent promoters of various non-political good causes. This is disingenuous. Most of the NGOs that have come to have a prominent role in British public life were just as much the product of engineers, scientists, lawyers, and academics as were any of the technocratic solutions proposed by the post-war official planners.

Matthew Hilton et al.[1]

[P]re-existing [drivers for collaboration have been] academics' personal commitment to change, plus a desire to get access to guinea pigs and data for their theories; NGOs' desire to have more impact, solve problems and generally understand what the hell is going on.

Duncan Green[2]

Public policies are shaped by more than governments, politicians and officials. All these insider actors proclaim their deference to external 'stakeholders', whose reactions are followed and studied minutely for auguries that they are or are not shaping 'public opinion'. In practical terms relevant business interests are always key stakeholders in various ways, giving them a 'privileged position' in policy making (Lindblom, 1977; Dryzek and Dunleavy, 2009: Ch. 3). But also involved, and far more organized and publicly voluble and legitimate in many contexts, are a wide collection of civil society organizations and actors. These include professions, trade unions, interest groups, pressure groups, social movements, think tanks, charities, and a huge range of other non-governmental organizations (NGOs). In pluralist theory and British practice these (more or less) autonomously formed and organized bodies exercise a great, if indirect and collective, influence on policy making at the national and local levels. The vigour, independence and critical capacity of civil society organizations are essentially important for the functioning of any liberal

---

[1]Hilton et al. (2013).
[2]Green (2013).

democracy, constituting a key 'third sector' route by which academic (especially social science) ideas are brought to bear on policy making.

In this chapter we first briefly characterize the key British civil society organizations on which we focus attention here, and then look at their role in the 'advocacy coalition framework' view of policy making. The second section explores the quantitative empirical evidence on how extensively third sector organizations use academic research in their campaigns and activities, and how far social scientists participate in supporting civil society activities. Finally, we consider more qualitative factors shaping the interactions of social science researchers with charities and NGOs.

7.1 Civil society organizations and 'advocacy coalitions'

[In public policy making] despite the partisan nature of most analytical debates and the cognitive limits on rationality – actors' desires to realize core values in a world of limited resources provide strong incentives [for them] to learn more about the magnitude of salient problems, the factors affecting them, and the consequences of policy alternatives.

Paul Sabatier[3]

We are conscious that we cannot just say the same thing all the time. We have to keep on building our arguments and our reasoning for why resources might be needed for a particular group, or why things might need to change in how local authorities or police are dealing with the issue.

Charity director in interview

Strictly speaking 'civil society' embraces all the autonomous organizations that exist across the UK, leaving out only hierarchically-organized and profit-orientated businesses on the one hand, and public sector organizations on the other. We have not tried to cover here such a large and disparate canvas, but instead have focused mostly on perhaps the most distinctive 'third sector' organizations, those that:

- are highly dependent on voluntary memberships (hence excluding commercial trade associations and professional organizations);
- draw on significant numbers of people to fund their operations or provide labour for their activities; and
- are often also extensively involved in seeking to shape public policies.

Our focus in this chapter is on charities, trade unions and other mass membership voluntary bodies (including cultural, environmental and faith groups). This means that we cover just over half of the estimated 367,000 civil society organizations across the UK. Yet the mostly less well-funded and smaller bodies that we focus on account for two fifths of the 2.06 million paid staff working in the sector, and a quarter of the £165 billion spending (using 2009–10 numbers) across all civil society organizations,

---

[3]Sabatier (1987: 687).

as measured by the National Centre for Voluntary Organizations (NCVO). The organizations that we have largely excluded in our interviews and data collection for this chapter are typically bodies that operate in closer lock-step with the private sector, such as trade associations, co-operative businesses, mutualized financial firms, and major professions.

There is a close connection between the success of non-governmental organizations and the public policy process, which Hilton et al. (2013: 266–67) stress lies behind their growth and expansion:

> By acting as lobbyists and campaigners they have had a profound impact on the legislative history of the UK Parliament. Most of the major NGOs can add to their portfolios of influence a series of Acts, amendments, white papers, and ministerial directives that originate from or follow their thinking and advice. This means that any view of NGOs as alternatives to the state are deeply misguided. Indeed, they have been at the vanguard of state intervention, in the sense that they have pressured and cajoled government to extend and reform public services in ways that correct the inequities of social service, whether provided by public sector workers or voluntary sector professionals. They have been both drawn into the state apparatus and encouraged its further expansion. The history of governmental and non-governmental institutions has been one of complementary growth and expansion.

NGOs' size, growth, and increased visibility are certainly considerable, as Figure 7.1 demonstrates. By most counts the number of explicit NGOs more than doubled between 1970 and 2010, while the number of NGO members increased sixfold. As charities and NGOs perfected their fundraising (especially for environmental and international development causes), and they also became important agents of the welfare state in social policy sectors, so their staff totals also literally shot up. The professionalization of their approaches and increasingly specialist aspects of their internal organization contributed to a bureaucratization of the largest organizations.

Many charities and NGOs have strong advocacy and campaigning roles that are focused on single or multiple related issues. They work on various fronts to support the interests of their client groups, often in an altruistic mode. For instance, they may seek to protect the interests of social groups who might otherwise get left out of the policy process altogether, or those who will certainly be under-organized relative to the 'big battalions' of business. Many charities and some trade unions also undertake advisory or service provision activities directly to help their target groups. Yet given the salience of contemporary welfare state interventions, much of their work also involves working directly at the interface with national and local policy makers, trying to shape government policies, legislation and implementation so as to benefit their client groups' interests.

It might be feasible still to see the policy process in the way it was portrayed by classical pluralists – as a simple battle of 'interest groups' or 'pressure groups' promoting different sectional interests and causes, albeit within a pervasive (dissimulating) language of concern for the 'public interest'. In this perspective though,

Figure 7.1   The broad growth of non-governmental organizations and charities in the UK since 1950

	Year, or nearest data year available			
	1950	1970	1990	2010
Number of registered charities (in thousands)	57	78	172	180
Number of existing NGOs (as at 1st Jan)	500	760	1,310	1,870
Number of British NGOs registered with the UN	8	25	65	180
Number of staff working in all registered charities (in thousands)	na	17*	410	700
Average number of associations in which people are active members	na	na	0.7	0.61*
Millions of people with membership of environmental pressure groups	na	0.4	1.65	2.6
Average number of staff per registered charity	na	0.2	2.6	3.9*

Source: Hilton et al. (2013). Page references for each row are as follows: row 1. p45; row 2. p45; row 3. p122; row 4. p66; row 5. p42, row 6. p41, row 7. p67.

Note: All data sourced for this table is taken from graphs included in Hilton et al. (2013). We have approximated numbers from reading off graphs, and so they should not be read as exact data. Also, * indicates where we have taken a 'nearest possible' reading rather than exact data for the years included in this table.

what explains the presence of so many apparently altruistic charities and NGOs, advocating for the otherwise under-organized or under-privileged people or issues? The answers given by classic pluralists either appealed to the extended logic of equal electoral competition for votes (every vote counts, so some politician or other will have an interest to mobilize even the most disadvantaged groups); or to the role of a few large or many small 'philanthropists' intervening to redress the societal balance (Walker, 1984). More cynical political economy or rational choice accounts assigned a key role to 'political entrepreneurs' and their ability to better organize otherwise under-represented interests while pursuing their own career advancement.

However, more modern (neo-) pluralist accounts now stress that in advanced liberal democracies at least, the process of shaping public policies has moved past the earlier interest-based patterns of mobilization and organization, crystallizing especially at periodic elections and changes of government. Instead the more complex environment of contemporary governance has produced continuous competition over rival policy solutions. The modern policy process mixes up interest-based activities with a constant, cognitive 'arms race' between two or more 'advocacy coalitions'. Advocacy coalitions bring together eclectic mixes of different interest groups, cause groups and actors, each originating ideas or serving as sources of information – including especially social movements, lobbies for ideas and reforms, think tanks, charities, professional bodies, aligned mass media, and academics and researchers. The central motor of the political battles between advocacy coalitions is:

- the competitive development of ideas and conceptions characterizing issues and problems (sometimes called 'memes', and including here rhetoric, slogans, 'brand names' for ideas);
- working out potential solutions;
- researching the consequences and implications of recent policy implementation and trends; and
- undertaking research and marshalling evidence on recent trends and past policy implementation.

Advocacy coalitions are so mixed, because they link powerful vested interest with aligned media, professions and cause groups on an issue-by-issue basis.

To win political battles rival coalitions primarily seek to analyse trends, using new evidence and information to show that their preferred ideas or solutions are working, and that the other side's solutions are failing. Each coalition also constantly seeks to differentiate, update and modernize its advocacy message in ways that will best persuade non-aligned interests and decision-makers, tending to enlarge support for their approach and persuade erstwhile supporters of the other side to abandon it. What matters all the time, in this perspective, is the ever-changing fortunes and plausibility of each side of the *cognitive plus rhetorical, political debate* across thousands of issues and policy areas.

Yet within each advocacy coalition each organization or actor is pursuing their own distinctive interest in their own particular way, seeking always to maximize their visibility, legitimacy and reputation with all the other actors in the policy community and political system. Some sections of the same coalition may have significant differences or disagreements with others, about tactics, methods and what does or does not advance the coalition's overall purposes. Advocacy coalitions are only very rarely centrally co-ordinated. Each component organization or actor in the network is concerned to safeguard its own corporate image and its distinctive interpretation of the 'public interest'.

The mass media and the growing ensemble of 'niche' media covering specific issues and interests are the chief battleground across which rival advocacy coalitions constantly measure their performance. The actors who monitor the 24 hour progress of issues include well-funded 'government liaison units' inside major corporations, professions and interest groups; key units within the labour or green social movements; press and media offices in lobbies, charities and NGOs; politicians and their communications teams and special advisors; general and specialist media organizations; and now a 'citizens' army' of bloggers, tweeters and Facebookers. Each of them maintains their own logs of which sides of multiple arguments are going up or down, and what issues are trending or declining with 'public opinion'. Sometimes, rather rarely in fact and mostly associated with crises, powerful 'bandwagon' effects can get under way, triggering strong public opinion surges on the necessity for public policy changes or new interventions. Bandwagon effects mostly occur in the 'alarmed discovery' phase of what Anthony Downs (1972) called the 'issue attention cycle', which usually does not last too long as opposition gets mobilized or the issues involved turn out to be more complex than they might appear at first glance.

Far more commonly the balance of arguments is either broadly stable, with debates yo-yoing and policy at best zig-zagging. Or one side is conscious that they are clearly winning the public debate, with public policy trending their way, while a rival coalition is aware of moving backwards in public opinion and policy terms. This last scenario is what advocacy coalitions fear most, for it can trigger a 'spiral of silence' phenomenon that is slower and less dramatic than bandwagon effects, but operates more continuously and insidiously (Noelle-Neumann, 1993). Essentially actors or organizations that start out within coalition A that is losing ground (with no new ammunition of ideas or evidence to offer) respond to the growing hegemony of the rival coalition B by falling silent. As a result, A's prominence in the public sphere declines, so that its viability or legitimacy declines and its least attached members progressively fall even more silent, becoming unwilling to risk supporting what seems a losing cause. As A's advocacy ebbs away, some coalition erstwhile members may 'go neutral' or husband their efforts for other causes or issues in which they are involved. Hence the 'ecology' of advocacy coalitions is an ever-changing landscape of evenly matched conflicts, occasional bandwagons and more common spiral of silence changes, creating the 'policy streams' that Kingdon (2003) stresses constantly open and close windows for achieving viable public policy changes.

This interpretation assigns a considerable potential influence to university faculties and researchers in two roles:

1   More 'aligned' academics or research teams may help one or both sides in a conflict of rival advocacy coalitions to make their case. All scientific and academic professions are committed to objectively and dispassionately assessing evidence, and have clearer standards for evaluating arguments and evidence via peer review, carefully regulated professional debates and the formation of professional consensus. These features can make more committed or aligned researchers and academics attractive as colleagues or allies for aligned NGOs, searching for the best arguments and new ideas to refresh their case.
2   Less aligned and neutral academics often play a key 'arbitrating' or refereeing role, helping media organizations and government decision-makers to assess the balance of plausibility of complex arguments between rival advocacy coalitions. University researchers and academics are also the nearest modern equivalents we have to the independent 'private practice' professions of earlier eras, before so many professionals came under the patronage either of large corporations or of government sector organizations.

We describe role (2) in more detail in Chapter 8, and for the rest of this chapter focus more on role (1).

Intellectuals, academics and university researchers often play key roles inside advocacy coalitions, as aligned actors strongly shaping the ideas, evidence and currents of opinion that they stand for and promote. At first glance, being 'aligned' may seem incompatible with maintaining academic and scientific rigour and objectivity. But a moment's thought shows that there are many cases where in fact academics or researchers are duty bound to be aligned, where there is clear evidence that the public interest lies clearly in one direction. For instance, medical scientists and professions have strongly backed efforts to persuade government to take regulatory action against tobacco, alcohol and most recently sugar-based and fat-based foods that create an 'obesogenic environment'.

Academics also play leading roles in many charities and philanthropic or altruistic NGOs – for instance, by founding them, sitting on their governing boards or trusts, and advizing them on research and strategies for best making their case, usually in an unpaid, pro bono mode. Of course academic or scientific researchers' roles are always circumscribed, since they must constantly act in professionally reputable ways, consistent with their university positions and focused usually on their area of disciplinary expertise – although a small number of public intellectuals may range far more widely. Figure 7.2 shows the main kinds of organizations with close ties to social scientists, either in terms of attracting their personal involvements, or by using and citing their work. Clearly these organizations fit well within the advocacy coalition framework.

One of the most distinctive things that unites such bodies is that they all assign a great deal of emphasis to their voluntary character, as shown by:

- their reliance either upon unpaid labour or freely given donations;
- usually by their being membership bodies, whose internal decision processes are dominated by internally democratic practices (e.g., with members electing boards and voting on key policy stances); and

Figure 7.2   Some major types of UK charities and NGOs with which social scientists (and academics more broadly) are most involved

Campaigning charities	Altruistic groups, seeking to represent or defend multiple or single under-represented social interests through advocacy, lobbying, and watchdog roles. Sometimes they also undertake limited direct service provision to or funding of people in relevant groups.
NGOs or 'third sector' voluntary organizations involved in providing public services	Organizations that primarily act as outsourced providers of services, either wholly or partially on behalf of the government sector departments and agencies.
Policy influencing bodies	Think tanks, accredited charities doing policy work, and other organizations monitoring policies.
Philanthropic bodies	Benevolent foundations or charities funding civic, public-spirited, medical or welfare-assistance projects.
Recreational, cultural interest and environmental charities	Associations representing issues and interests in the cultural sector (e.g. conservation, museums, galleries, arts production and promotion, and running venues), and in the environment sector (countryside, protection of species and habitats, energy conservation and other green strategies).

- a strong 'mission commitment' to doing good in the world. The members and staffs of such organizations are expected to have a positive attachment to advancing the organization's goals and core values, so that its mission forms part of their personal value system and guides what the organization and members do in detail.

Influential work on the economics of 'mission committed' organizations suggests that in undertaking service provision or societal campaigning it can sometimes be highly efficient to select the members of an organization so that they share in common a preference for the core goals or functions that the organization is pursuing (Besley and Ghatak, 2003). People who work full or part time for charities, NGOs or other similar bodies are often motivated by more than just their salaries. Instead their involvement is driven at least in part by a concern to do good in the world as they understand it. As a result two common problems should both be lessened – intra-organizational 'shirking', where employees divert resources to meeting their own private interests; and 'influence costs', where divergences of views about strategies amongst organization members cause delays, lobbying, damaging conflicts or a waste of resources. Salaries for mission-committed employees may also be lower (the 'doing good' effect) and administrative costs may be kept to a minimum. Both these factors are likely to extend the appeal of charities who depend on the public or philanthropists for donations as their main source of finance. In addition, many charities work with more 'mission committed' client groups, those who identify with the organization's own goals, as with cultural bodies assisting new artists or green organizations helping groups with local environmental projects. (However, other charities are very different, working instead with socially alienated, psychologically 'difficult' or otherwise under-organized or little committed clients.)

Sharing a strong mission commitment with an NGO or charity (at least in part) often forms part of what attracts academics and scientists to work closely with them. Sometimes these links stretch over many years and become very close. Here the researcher undertakes a form of 'academic service' or 'good citizenship' with the NGO that is closely analogous to serving on a government advisory committee or service within a professional body (Figure 7.3a). Usually such pro bono associations with social scientists are unpaid beyond expenses, both because the academic is not seeking payment and because 'mission committed' organizations typically minimize their administration costs and have very little money to spend on things outside their primary tasks.

Sometimes a social scientist close to a charity or NGO may undertake research directly for them, but most commonly as a one-off connection and often either carried out free or at a low cost rate in ways that neither the charity nor academics can afford to sustain such links for many years (Figure 7.3b).

Normally the NGOs and charities active in policy sectors relevant to social scientists are relatively small and cash-strapped organizations. They must spend a good part of their time assembling donations and resources, looking for additional funding or government contracts to broaden their work. And in their campaigning behaviours they often move on fairly quickly across current issues and priorities. They can rarely afford to commit their own resources to funding even small pieces of research. So

Figure 7.3 The main types of relationships between civil society charities or NGOs and researchers and social scientists

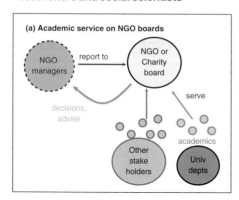

(a) Academic service on NGO boards

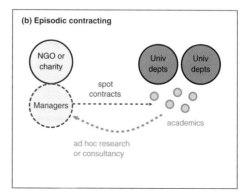

(b) Episodic contracting

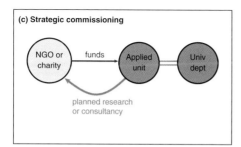

(c) Strategic commissioning

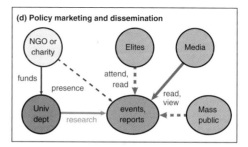

(d) Policy marketing and dissemination

linkages with university researchers tend to be short-term, either one-off associations on a particular matter of common interest, or relatively loose-linkages maintained rather episodically as and when an academic sees an opportunity to be of assistance at low cost to their own university.

This pattern is not true of all third sector organizations, however. Some large medical foundations, for instance, have very large funding budgets and operate a port-folio of science or medical research projects in a continuous R&D programme mode similar to that of governments and big corporations. As shown in Figure 7.3c these continuing links normally run through an applied research unit that has been partly 'hived out' of a mainstream university department, and so look quite similar to this kind of linkage with government or businesses. But charities and NGOs operating with social scientists rarely have the significant resources that this pattern requires.

Finally, charities and NGOs can use a policy marketing approach in much the same way as government departments or agencies do, funding a piece of work that is designed to secure elite and media attention, and may also help the charity involved build its public presence, and thus foster donations also in an indirect way (Figure 7.3d). Charities sometimes get individual donations that are given to help them find and highlight new evidence, and university researchers are always their preferred resource here, because academics are relatively cheap to hire compared to consultan-cies (unless a large consultancy donates staff time as part of its pro bono profile). We turn next to charting the available evidence on the scope of these different forms of linkage.

7.2 The scale of social science research links to civil society

Non-profit activities are the nexus of a modern power elite.

Teresa Odendahl[4]

NGOs have a complicated space in neo-liberal politics. They are supposed to mop up the anger. Even when they are doing good work, they are supposed to maintain the status quo. They are the missionaries of the corporate world.

Arundhati Roy[5]

Despite their limitations, reactive measures again provide a useful starting point in looking at how academics see their links with the civil society sphere. Abreu et al. (2008) included a question in their large-scale survey, asking how many academics reported working with voluntary organizations in the last three years (shown in Figure 7.4). Essentially there are three groups of disciplines. Health science researchers said they had done the most with voluntary organizations, probably reflecting the greater density of large and many local charities in the illness/disease prevention area. Meanwhile, physical scientists on the materials and inorganic side of the STEM group clearly have relatively less contact with voluntary organizations. In the middle, social science, humanities and biological/organic STEM disciplines all showed between 40 and 50 per cent of academics doing things for or with voluntary organizations.

Figure 7.4   Proportion of academics in different discipline groups reporting activities with charitable or voluntary organizations in the last three years, in 2008

	Per cent
Health Sciences	57
Social Sciences	48
Humanities and Arts	47
Biology, Chemistry and Veterinary Science	41
Engineering, Materials Science, Physics, Mathematics	28
All disciplines	**44**

Source: Abreu et al. (2008: 29).

---

[4]Odendahl (1991).

[5]Quoted in an interview for *International Socialist Review* (http://isreview.org/issue/86/india-worlds-largest-democracy).

To get a second perspective on these linkages we looked at 40 prominent charities or NGOs of different sizes and active in a wide range of issues or problem areas, listed in full in Figure 7.5. For each organization we looked through their web profiles collecting all instances that our trained coders could find to social science and university research on their current websites. We collected up to 50 such relevant links, delving into their archived content if we could not find it in current pages. Figure 7.5 shows the most common kind of linkage we found in column (1) – an occasional or one-off reference to academic work included by the charity. Column (2) shows research done by in-house staff at the charity or NGO that more systematically references academic research. The third most common type of linkage (Column (3)) were pieces of work commissioned from academics by the charity or NGO, while the least common kind of linkage we found (Column (4)) was a more corporate or sustained partnership between the organization and a researcher or research team.

The row labels in Figure 7.5 show how we classified charities, beginning with a distinction between 22 charities where we turned up the maximum of 50 links to academic work, versus 18 others where we could not find as many references. In the top row of the Figure, there were 12 bodies that showed a well-balanced use of research across all four columns, where their in-house research was well integrated with external academic research. The second row shows five bodies which are light on internal research, but still link a lot to and commission research from academics. The third row contains bodies which extensively reference academic work but do not undertake their own research or commission work. The penultimate row again shows five organizations making little use of academic research but in a balanced way and finally the bottom row has 13 organizations that rarely use or cite research.

Some of the key differences between charities and NGOs are a factor of size and resources – the bigger organizations tend to be able to employ in-house researchers, who can help them understand and keep abreast of academic research, and so get the maximum advocacy value from it in real time. In short, in-house staff with PhDs or MSc degrees in relevant areas can mediate what academic research is saying to their employing organization, a key concept to which we return below, especially in Chapter 9. Bigger organizations can invest more in extensive societal networks and so keep in touch with more academics. And because they are bigger bodies and understand academic work better, requests from these charities for researchers to assist them will often be more attractive – holding out the prospect of more kudos, publicity (and perhaps REF impact) from the collaboration. We have tried to capture size using the organization's number of Twitter followers in mid 2013 as a convenient metric in Figure 7.6 and it can be seen that generally the two shaded sets of bodies making most use of research are in the top half of the table here, while most of the white-shaded rows for organizations making little use of academic research are in the bottom part of the table. The exceptions here are two big fund-raising organizations – Comic Relief, which is non-political and gets much free publicity from the BBC; and the British Red Cross, which is historically very well established in the UK. There is a potential confounding variable here, since some large but conservative charities have been slow to develop their Twitter followings.

We can get a third type of information about social scientists links' with civil society bodies by looking at the links out to NGOs and charities from the academics in our dataset. We found around a tenth of the total references to our social science academics

Figure 7.5 How third sector organizations link to academics and their research

Cell entries show the average number of linkages found in our website survey

	[1] Other references made to academics	[2] Research done in-house that references academics	[3] Externally commissioned research done by academics	[4] Corporate or sustained links involving academics
Charities for which we found the maximum number of 50 references to social science academics				
Organizations with a strong balance across four areas *(12 organizations)*	16.7	17.2	11.9	2.8
With less emphasis on producing in-house research *(5 organizations)*	21.0	5.8	20.2	3.0
With less emphasis on published research reports *(5 organizations)*	40.8	3.3	1.7	0.7
Charities for which we found less than 50 references to social science academics				
With signs of activity across all four areas *(5 organizations)*	12.7	6.4	1.3	0.1
With lower signs of research-related activity *(13 organizations)*	2.2	0.6	0.5	0.6

Source: PPG survey of 40 UK charity websites.

Note: Cell entries show the average number of linkages found in our website survey

Figure 7.6   The number of Twitter followers for charities and NGOs charted against the kind of use they make of academic research

Organization	Twitter followers	Organization	Twitter followers
Boing Boing	166,700	Crisis [crisis_uk]	12,450
Comic Relief	91,850	Homeless Link	8,950
Unicef UK [UNICEF_uk]	84,650	CAFOD	7,850
Oxfam [oxfamgb]	80,700	Big Issue Foundation [TBIF]	6,450
[AmnestyUK]	78,400	Care International [careintuk]	6,350
British Red Cross	68,450	Muslim Aid	6,250
Open Society	65,600	Citizenship Foundation [citizenship]	5,850
Friends of the Earth [wwwfoecouk]	65,150	World Vision UK	5,650
Save the Children [savechildren]	53,450	Book Aid International [Bookaid]	4,100
Barnardos	52,600	Adoption UK	3,250
Environmental Defence Fund (NY) [EnvDefenseFund]	44,800	Peace Direct	3,200
Christian Aid [Christian_aid]	36,668	International Alert [intalert]	2,550
Water Aid [WaterAiduk]	34,350	Simon on the Streets [simonotstreets]	1,650
Age UK [age_uk]	30,250	Safer World	1,500
NCVO (National Council of Voluntary Organizations)	22,750	ELRHA (Enhancing Learning and Research for Humanitarian Assistance)	850
Islamic Relief Worldwide [IslamicReliefUK]	16,200	Action on Elder Abuse [AEAteam]	800
RNIB	15,950	Gandhi Foundation [GhandiUK]	350
Action Aid	15,550	Child Soldiers International [ChildSoldiersIN]	300
Médecins Sans Frontières [MSF-UK]	14,800	Hope UK [hopeUKuk]	150
Liberty [libertyhq]	12,550	International Justice Mission [IJM]	50

Note: UK Twitter site followers accessed 30 June 2013, rounded to nearest 50. To get Twitter names add @ to organization name (without spaces); or, for non-obvious names, add @ to name in square brackets. Coloured rows are NGOs making greater use of academic research: dark shading and bold font = high and balanced use; medium shading and bold font = medium use; light shading = only one use made of academics. White rows are NGOs that make less use of academic research.

on the websites of civil society organizations or individuals. Civil society organizations were most important as sources of references to our dataset academics in networks or partnerships promoting single issues, followed by campaigning bodies (Figure 7.7). As predicted by the advocacy coalition thesis, more than half of the references to academic research or researchers from charities and NGOs involve the work of issue politics,

Figure 7.7 Where we found references to our academics' work, by type of referencing organization

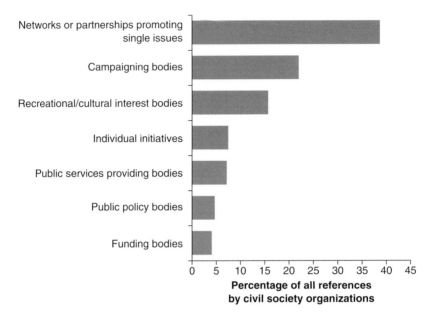

**Percentage of all references
by civil society organizations**

Source: LSE PPG dataset, N = 926 references.

Figure 7.8 Extent to which academics from different disciplines are referenced in civil society domains

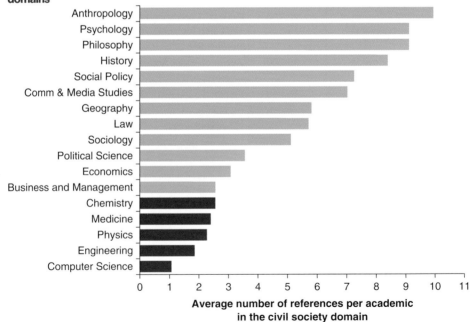

**Average number of references per academic
in the civil society domain**

Source: LSE PPG dataset.

Note: blue denotes science subjects.

lobbying, advocacy, and campaigning. Charities were also important sources of links in cultural and 'recreational interest' areas, where civil society organizations are active in using existing inventories of cultural knowledge. Elsewhere in Figure 7.7 charities and NGOs generated relatively low proportions of links to academics. Perhaps surprisingly in the area of outsourced services (where many charities now play a role given the growth in commissioning), only one in 14 references to academics came from charities.

Overall, 63 per cent of social scientists in our sample were referenced by at least one civil society organization, while 23 per cent were referenced by five or more, confirming that Abreu et al. (2008) were well-founded in suggesting that more than two in every five social scientists have recent links to civil society organizations.

We also find that social scientists have stronger links to civil society organizations than the STEM scientists in our dataset. Figure 7.8 shows that academics from all our STEM disciplines had lower average numbers of references from charities or NGOs than academics in any social science. In common with similar charts from other chapters, the most referenced individual disciplines are anthropology (mostly cited in relation to

Figure 7.9   Review of university department websites for linkages to civil society organizations, by discipline

	Cultural and heritage bodies	Domestic charities	Research bodies	International charities	All links
Social Policy	0.8	6.9	1.6	0.6	**9.8**
Medicine	0	7.2	1.2	0.7	**9.0**
History	4.2	0.5	3.5	0.5	**8.7**
Anthropology	3.6	1.7	1.6	1.4	**8.4**
Law	0.0	2.4	1.6	1.5	**5.5**
Political Science	0.8	1.1	2.7	0.9	**5.5**
Engineering	1.4	0.9	1.9	0.5	**4.6**
Economics	0.1	1.0	2.1	1.1	**4.4**
Psychology	0.2	2.2	1.7	0.2	**4.3**
Business and Management	0.1	2.4	1.0	0.2	**3.7**
Philosophy	0.6	1.1	0.9	0.3	**2.9**
Sociology	0.4	1.1	0.9	0.1	**2.5**
Chemistry	0.2	1.3	0.7	0.2	**2.3**
Geography	0.1	0.8	0.9	0.4	**2.2**
Computer Science	0.2	1.2	0.3	0	**1.7**
Communication and Media	0.6	0.5	0.4	0	**1.5**
Physics	0	0	0	0	**0**

Source: LSE PPG analysis of SQW data. Shaded rows = social sciences. White rows = STEM disciplines.

Figure 7.10 Combined ranking of disciplines on how they are conncted to civil society and charitable organizations

	Rank from our Google search of academics (see Figure 7.9)	Rank from our survey of university departments (see Figure 7.10)	COMBINED TOTAL indicative ranking
Anthropology	1	4	5
Social Policy	5	1	6
History	4	3	7
Psychology	2	9	11
Law	8	5	13
Philosophy	3	11	14
Political Science	10	6	16
Medicine	14	2	16
Economics	11	8	19
Geography	7	14	21
Sociology	9	12	21
Media Studies	6	16	22
Business and Management	12	10	22
Engineering	16	7	23
Chemistry	13	13	26
Physics	15	17	32
Computer Science	17	15	32

Source: LSE PPG analysis of SQW data. Shaded rows = social sciences. White rows = STEM disciplines.

Note: The column on the right-hand side shows the cumulative ranking of each discipline based on two previous charts. It is an indicative overview of how visible each discipline is in the civil society sector. The lower rankings denote higher visibility.

international development) and psychology (often cited in relation to social policy). Yet the cross-over disciplines of philosophy and history (which are less visible in business and amongst government agencies) also show strong levels of references from civil society organizations, perhaps reflecting their greater accessibility to non-expert readers. Other core social science disciplines came lower down, and on closer inspection here the civil society references were again often in relation to development or social policy.

A fourth perspective on academics linking to civil society bodies comes from our web census of university department sites. We coded any references or linkages to third sector organizations in the UK and abroad on the websites of university departments for academics included in our dataset (going wider than just weblinks themselves). In this institution-based view, Figure 7.9 shows that social policy, anthropology and history departments had the most linkages to charities and NGOs,

Figure 7.11 Listing of the topic areas and university departments with linkages from civil society organizations

	No. of references and universities mentioned		Most referenced universities	Examples of social science research areas found in our sample survey of 360 academics
	References	Universities		
Social Policy	352	72	York, Sheffield Hallam, Birmingham	Safeguarding adults, ageing, child welfare, adoption, poverty, social exclusion, violence against women, homelessness, parenting, and substance misuse.
Politics, Public Policy, and Governance	160	51	Bradford, Sussex, Kent	War and conflict studies, disaster response, crisis states, equality, arms trade, political engagement, transparency and accountability, China-Africa relations.
Public Health and Health-related	158	52	Oxford, UCL, York	Primary and secondary care, clinical technology, hip replacements, school food, older people care, diet and nutrition, malaria, health inequality, breastfeeding.
Law and Legal Studies	126	52	Oxford, UCL, Essex	Human rights, labour rights, international law, criminal justice systems, judiciary and judicial systems.
Development Studies (including Anthropology)	93	37	Sussex, Greenwich	Millennium Development Goals, epidemics, African studies, poverty and deprivation, sustainability, water and sanitation, humanitarian aid, fair trade, child welfare.
Environmental Sciences	87	35	East Anglia, Manchester	Climate change, flooding, global warming, green economy, low carbon, coastal and estuarine research, pesticides, sustainable energy, GM technology.
Education and Studies in Education	74	30	Birmingham, Sussex, Institute of Education	Education reform, child rights, lifelong learning, resilience, literacy, citizenship, international education, higher education, curricula, education in deprived areas.
Psychology and Behavioural Sciences	56	23	Brighton, Edinburgh	Child psychology, mental health, dementia and abuse, ageing and mental sharpness, cognitive ageing, happiness and well-being, deviant behaviours, resilience.
Economics and Econometrics	47	23	Sussex, Manchester, Kingston	Innovation, foreign investment, regulation, intellectual property, WTO, TRIPS, free trade agreements, social return on investment, risk and uncertainty, well-being.
Sociology	41	30	Oxford, KCL, Glasgow	Race, gender, criminology and criminal justice, socio-cultural change, grounded theory, society and equality, welfare policy.
Business and Management	19	10	Cranfield, Oxford	Engagement with business, entrepreneurship, leadership, strategy and organizational change, corporate social responsibility, technology and innovation.
Human and Social Geography	12	9	Sussex, Cambridge	Migration and population studies, refugees.

Source: LSE analysis of SQW data.

along with medicine. Medicine departments have the highest numbers of linkages to UK domestic charities. Law and political science are some way behind, and then a cluster of core social sciences along with engineering departments. Anthropology, law, economics and political science have most relations with international NGOs and charities, and history and economics to research-orientated NGOs. The three remaining STEM disciplines cluster in the lower reaches of the figure and the physics departments we covered had no linkages at all to civil society bodies. It is odd that both geography and media studies also fare poorly here.

We can combine the rankings of disciplines in terms of links to civil society. Figure 7.10 shows that on this combined basis the top seven ranked disciplines are all social sciences, beating medicine, while the other four STEM disciplines we covered are at the foot of the listing. Overall this creates a very consistent picture.

We round this section off by listing some of the most common topics that produced references from civil society organizations to the academics (and hence their departments) included in our dataset (Figure 7.11). We have grouped 'development studies' references together across several disciplines and many anthropology links are classed here. In other disciplines the topic listing makes clear the preponderance of internationally orientated subjects, a key area for altruistically-orientated NGOs activity. It should be clear that all of the topics generating repeated or common links are applied ones. We have listed the 'most frequently referred to' universities under one or another topic heading, showing that civil society organizations draw on a wide spread of universities when referring to academic work.

7.3 Growing the impacts of social science in the third sector

Thought is no longer theoretical. As soon as it functions it offends or reconciles, attracts or repels, breaks, dissociates, unites or reunites; it cannot help but liberate or enslave. Even before prescribing, suggesting a future, saying what must be done, even before exhorting or merely sounding an alarm, thought, at the level of its existence, in its very dawning, is in itself an action – a perilous act.

Michel Foucault[6]

'Knowledge' does not suddenly appear, become universally accepted, and suggest unequivocal changes in governmental action programs. Instead, findings that challenge the accepted wisdom concerning the seriousness of a given problem and its principal causes tend to emerge gradually over time.

Paul Sabatier[7]

Many academics interviewing practitioners in any sphere of society are familiar with the disheartening experience of putting theoretically-derived propositions to interviewees or focus groups, only to have them roundly rejected or rebutted. Yet on this occasion we had no such difficulties with Sabatier's advocacy coalition framework. Although charity and NGO staff are robustly practical and in many ways ruthlessly pragmatic people, they had

---

[6]Foucault (1975).
[7]Sabatier (1987: 689).

no difficulty recognizing the mix of interest-based and cognitive competition that lies at the centre of the model, as three senior people made clear:

> I've worked in both policy and campaigning, [and] for us the word is 'credibility'. That's why we use academic research. And I think we use it in lots of different ways.

> Focusing on just us wouldn't be as effective. Focusing on just [names own organization], people would say that we have a vested interest. But if you've got the academics as well to back it up, it really strengthens your case.

> [Research] is key to everything we do. It really informs our policy work, campaigning, 'comms' work, media, so we do a lot. Not many charities invest so much in research in the [Y] sector.

For instance, charities told us that having top-level academics come in and present findings or brief ministers as part of three-way meetings often helps to increase their credibility and reputation, as well as those of the researchers involved. Many charity directors also stressed to us that they operated in fast-moving environments. So research that can be deployed at short notice, and in hard-hitting ways, is immensely valuable, while slow, un-distinctive research is not. As one commented:

> The policy environment moves quickly and there will be windows of opportunity. We do definitely find ourselves in a situation where we want to be able to say something about a particular issue. But we know that we haven't got the evidence ourselves from research we have done.

Contacting relevant academics is an effective way for charities to upgrade or update their knowledge in response to the shifting tapestry of controversy, funding potential and viable opportunities to shape public policies in constructive ways. With no strong repositories of research of their own, charities are particularly reliant on universities to preserve knowledge that has not been immediately relevant, and to cover issues, policy spheres and countries where they may not have had previous experience.

With the increased professionalization of the sector, charities and NGOs have come under more pressure to show that their activities are worthwhile, and are having the positive impacts on society that they claim in fundraising. Charity leaders typically ground their view of what to do in their own inherent expertise of practice in a professional field or of association with client groups over many years. Yet they also recognize that in modern conditions this traditional approach has limits. They pointed to the need for additional sources of expertise in order build the profile and credibility of their organizations in policy making networks. As one put it:

> Just using your 'witnessing' in the field for your advocacy is not enough anymore. You actually need some additional research to figure out what your message should be and to make it credible.

Demonstrating credibility involves being seen to provide 'thought leadership' in a sector, particularly establishing the charity's brand as being a reputed and reliable source of data and insight. As one executive noted: 'That's actually the importance of academics, that independent unbiased research that I get from them'. Another argued that in being able to go to policy makers and present a credible case or argument for change on behalf of the client group, the research base was vital:

> If we're producing things like 'killer facts' and statistics and so on, it's about having the sources. It's about being able to say to policy folk, 'And this is the back-up. This is why we're making these arguments'.

Securing financial support was also seen as an important reason for researching the effectiveness of interventions. One executive commented:

> We are funded by institutional donors. We have a small amount of public funds. So we have to go and look for donor funds. So it is very important that we have a robust evidence base, and that is what this [academic research] has provided.

For many charities, one of the key strategic challenges is to boost their 'nodality', that is their ability to sit at the centre of policy networks or coalitions of interest, to learn of new developments quickly from others, and to be able to reach many other actors in the network with a legitimacy that inspires trust and attention. The more nodal charities can be, the more their status and influence is likely to grow, as governments, civil servants and key media treat them as a trusted source or a 'first port of call' for accessing the voice of particular client groups. Also, the more central organizations are in existing networks, the lower their likely transaction costs of keeping up with policy developments. A large corporate charity such as Oxfam, for example, has elaborate internal structures for handling research, publicity, monitoring or policy change and implementation, and campaigning in different spheres. Successful charities often have a built-in dynamic of seeking to make new connections and forge useful links, which includes links with university departments and academics.

For charities working in narrow or niche areas, there may only be a small group of researchers working in relevant sub-disciplines, and so links or connections can often be made informally and handled at a personal relations level. As the charities grow in scope, this pattern becomes weaker. Nevertheless, the chances that research directors will come across academics in their field are relatively high, if those academics are the kind to be outgoing in the way they publicise or disseminate their work. Two charity leaders remarked:

> [We link] particularly [to] those academics who are more proactive in getting out in the sector and doing more applied research. A lot of it does come down to how much that academic is able to get involved in those policy conversations. Through that avenue we might try to find out more about what they are doing and possibly link up with them.

> We were developing services to support young people who were being exploited. And in parallel to that [University F] were starting to look at that through an academic route. Because it is quite a small niche area, it was almost inevitable that we would come together at some point. The research they do is very much applied.

Despite this 'small world' potential, there is usually 'healthy competition' between leading charities in particular sectors or areas: to attract funding and large donors in a limited pool; to secure the most effective staff; to grab more of policy makers' attention; and to garner more media coverage and elicit more public donations and reputation growth than rival organizations. Critics argue that this can often lead to fragmentation of messages, duplication of efforts, and much higher overall administrative costs than if organizations were more integrated. Charities rebut these claims, arguing that they carefully differentiate their campaigns, research and activities so as to avoid duplication of effort; that their fundraising and media campaigns tap different sub-pools of interested and involved sections of the public; and that a great deal of their work is implicitly co-operative within advocacy coalitions.

However, there is also a recognition that collective action can bring win–win outcomes for all charities concerned, and often academics seek to help with that, increasing coordination and communication amongst bodies in a connected field. The ability for universities to tap research funds can sometimes help to bring charities together, creating an opportunity for joint lobbying or collective action to get funding for priority areas. A senior professor explained how one such initiative by charities triggered subsequent joint research funding, that subsequently led to significant policy impacts:

> What happened was that the homelessness agencies got together and said they wanted some serious and neutral research. They wanted to pool resources, and have a more objective look, and they knew the ESRC [Economic and Social Research Council] was interested in doing that. They got me to write an intellectual case for them and the ESRC programme.

Internally social science research has a good deal to offer charities and NGOs in terms of understanding and improving their operations, especially in the larger organizations and those that provide services commissioned by public sector agencies. Many civil society bodies are under acute pressure from donors or government agencies providing grants or contracts to account for how they spent their funding and what impacts were achieved. Research has become increasingly important in helping charities to account for the impacts of their interventions, particularly in the form of evaluation studies and economic analyses of the impact of their services on client groups. Many directors pointed out that it is important for them to show impact in terms of positive effects for their client groups, but also in terms of providing services in cost-efficient ways, especially where public money is involved. Some reflected how important it had been in recent years to be able to turn up at meetings in Westminster or Whitehall with a strong piece of social science research (usually economics-based) that put the cost-effectiveness of their interventions in explicit terms such as returns gained per pound spent.

In the 2000s, the then Labour government increasingly sought to use commissioning models to integrate third sector organizations more into the provision of public services, providing grant funding to increase their managerial capacity and improve their ability to track expenditure and account for how they spent public monies. From 2010 the Conservative–Liberal coalition government continued similar policies, energized for a few years by the political motif of a 'big society' (and implied smaller state). This stressed that the provision of public services could be given back to society, run in more disaggregated and devolved ways, incorporating new configurations of commissioned services through partnerships, social enterprises, and mutual co-operative structures (Tinkler and Rainford, 2013). This 'big society' rhetoric in fact waned quickly (Macmillan, 2013), and most winners from it proved to be public service contractors. Yet some impetus has continued, generating quite similar pressures for charities to be able to demonstrate performance using payment by results methods, or at least to show an auditing of outputs and wherever feasible outcomes. An executive in a social policy organization commented:

> One thing we are conscious of is that commissioners are getting more switched on to research that has a good evidence base. So, in a way, we have to be switched on to what academic research is saying – because it is becoming more and more a part of the commissioning environment. But we are [also] quite conscious that we want to be using our resources in the best way possible. So we don't want to be doing work in ways that isn't going to achieve good outcomes for children and families. We see that looking at research is one way in which we are most likely to achieve good outcomes.

Where charities are operating overseas, in often very complex government and policy environments, they are often effectively debarred from simple political lobbying or publicly campaigning for policy changes. Here they must rely on research as a legitimate way of raising an issue with a foreign government or public sector agencies in ways that can be helpful and legitimate, and that can also strengthen the hand of local civil society groupings struggling to improve things. For instance, a charity executive discussed collaborative work that they had done in Tanzania for elders in various communities. The resulting research led to a meeting where senior government healthcare officials had to sit down around a table with advocacy groups for older people, and explain why some promised health provisions had not been rolled out across the country, breaking previous pledges. The elder groups managed to get an agreement from the officials concerned that these services would be expanded as promised. This could be seen as a policy impact for the older people of Tanzania, one that would not have happened without the intervention of the charity and presentation of the research findings. Following through on the pledge is also key, for otherwise the putative 'impact' could prove fleeting. Yet keeping consistent focus on issues in overseas or remote locations, requiring interventions by other governments, while also relying on project-based funding, is particularly difficult for development NGOs.

Overall the relations between charities and social scientists are in many ways already reasonably close. Social policy and development practitioners have usually got relevant degrees or Masters qualifications, and they regularly encounter applied academics and research more in their day-to-day work. In this sense, there are strong foundational linkages of the kind highlighted in Figure II.2 (page 110). In addition, in many areas of civil society, and at different levels within large organizations, during interviews, focus groups and documentation research we found individuals with 'various hats', working with one foot in practice-oriented roles but with another foot in an academic environment. As a result, charity and NGO executives tend to understand the dynamics of research and of university organizations far more than business executives or government officials do, and to have more sympathy in explaining the remaining problems of effective collaboration. Of a particular group of academics closely associated with a leading charity, their research director told us:

> I am always impressed with them when I see them speaking at events. They manage to do that translation between very rigorous academic research. But when they are talking about it, in no way is it off-putting to anyone in the sector, or pitched at the wrong level. Quite a few of them come from a practice background as well, which helps. Because they understand how it is on the ground and what research can do to support that ... rather than research sitting in isolation above it all.

An additional foundation for mutual respect is that UK law requires that charitable organizations devote the bulk of funding they raise to doing good, and makes a strong distinction between 'political' bodies that cannot be registered as charities, and altruistic bodies that can. Failing to show a proper concern for research and evidence (for instance, by over-claiming or misrepresenting research findings), or getting too close to being an advocacy supporter of one party, can also be publicly represented by opponents as nakedly political campaigning. Here charities feel an additional imperative to handle evidence accurately, and to diversify their activities to include at least some independent research or evidence-assembly. Periodically individual charities are referred by someone in the opposing advocacy coalition to the Charity Commission, as happened to a Labour-orientated think tank, the Smith Institute in 2007, which had become too identified with simply backing Labour policy positions – it had to make substantial changes in personnel and how it operated to survive. Similarly in summer 2013 an anti-global warming foundation run by Nigel Lawson was referred to the regulator by opponents, who claimed that its treatment of the scientific evidence was so cavalier that it was solely a political body (Ward, 2013).

Most charity directors we interviewed were clear about the value of academics and researchers with whom they had good working relationships. A major part of this appreciation lay in the ability of academics to be involved and to be able to 'speak the language' of practitioners while preserving a sense of independence and authority through high quality research. Civil society staff have a realistic sense of the need for reciprocity and a quid pro quo if practitioner–researcher relations are to be sustained. One research director explained a particular longstanding link with a professor thus:

> It is very much, we support her and she supports us. That is the best relationship we have. It is clear that she really sees it. She is not distant. She gets all the positives of working closely with an organization like us. Not all academics 'get it'. But she does, and that is why it works so well for both parties.

Charity leaders are also far more open than business executives or government officials to doing more to help academics get involved in their work or their field, partly in an 'all hands to the pump' spirit, and because they are mission-committed people. One executive's message to researchers was:

> Give me in one page how your work relates to our work. If you can do that then I will try to put you in the field. And that's very interesting because then you get a completely different view ... And it's really good for us organisations, to sometimes just get a completely different view of certain contacts or situations.

Of course, there are some obvious areas where the interests of both parties might not be aligned. Smaller charities tend to rely most on the goodwill of academics doing pro bono work for them in their spare time, whereas larger NGO organizations are more attuned to joint working or directly commissioning research when it is needed. A leading charity executive commented:

> It's all about you have to get started, you have to get into it [relationships with academics]. But what I noticed from a lot of small organisations is that they think it all comes for free, that academics should do it for free. And that's where we have to get out of that thinking. These people [researchers] have to make money and they also have to have a living.

Leading charity executives also have a more sophisticated understanding of how links between academic research and the 'practical reasoning' that charities advance. As one commented:

> I think that [academics] being in tune is about understanding that NGOs do want robust data. But they want it for a purpose which is beyond the academic research. It is about translating it into practice and policy-influencing, and so on. ...
>
> In terms of the wider lessons of what you are looking at, I think the crucial issue is that both sides understand that there are multiple outputs. There's got to be robust academic research that can stand the test of peers. And obviously universities want to get that research published, and all of that. And I understand that perfectly, that side of dissemination. But from the NGO side, there is both the policy-influencing that we can do using good quality research, because policy makers will take notice. And the interventions we can do on the ground that add even further to the evidence base. So everybody getting something out of it is very important.

In working with universities, charities even recognized some danger that joint working could go too far, that policy networks might become too heavily influenced (or even dominated) by the conventional wisdoms of influential academics, consequently becoming resistant to new kinds of research or original thinking. Many organizations regularly tried to do things to guard against such 'usual suspect' connections. And some research directors lamented that opportunities to connect with young academics and PhDs were limited.

> I think there is the need for more working groups or conferences where academics can meet practitioners. I can only speak of London and the UK in general, but

that is missing. I see, for instance, the Berlin conference I went to: it's one of the few where students and academics and practitioners are actually brought together. It doesn't happen that much.

On the other side of the relationship, leading researchers working closely with charities appreciate their difficulties and pressures, especially the commitment to keeping administrative costs low and the perennial search for funding. They especially valued a sense of working with organizations with a common cause and they are often keen to help them increase the practical resonance of research and can handle the many stages and operations involved in reaching policy makers and shaping advocacy coalition debates. Recognizing that charities can only give part of their attention to the university world, many researchers we interviewed explained how they make a point of keeping in touch with their charity contacts, having coffee every so often, ringing research directors to discuss current trends and opening opportunities, and going to charity conferences and think tank events to maintain and broaden their contacts. As one academic put it:

> Strategic engagement is part of the game. I don't just wait for things to come in. If you haven't seen somebody for a while, you try to find a way of keeping that going. That is obviously for earning the money, as well as doing the impact.

Almost all the researchers that we interviewed who had worked with civil society organizations, in all sorts of areas, also pointed to the value of the links and insights generated for their own academic work – especially the ability to anticipate and look ahead at where policy debates were going, and what new policy-relevant research issues and opportunities were likely to come up.

Academics new to the field are often concerned that the charity they work with might misuse or misrepresent their research, and can be overly concerned to retain minute control of how research findings are re-explained or disseminated. By contrast, however, charity chief executives and research directors feel that the onus should be on them to craft and engineer traction for their campaigns, in response to foundational evidence from the academics. Their view of the division of labour is strictly demarcated, as one NGO executive explained:

> I think more often than not in the cases, it's getting the technical evidence from academia. But then we're the ones who turn it into an advocacy product, because we're the experts in doing that and the academics are not. So we would rarely go to the academics and say: 'Yes, turn this into a campaign or an advocacy product or a media product or a communication product'. We would say: 'Give us the technical evidence and we'll make it look good'.

Another commented:

> With organizations that do lobbying work, like we do, we have a much clearer sense of what is happening on the ground. We know what developments are going on and what affects the research, because things in academia move a bit more

slowly. Not everyone can work with people like us. Things move very quickly. We need things to happen very quickly ... effectively. And we need clear messages that we can push.

As another research director explained:

> Do we want to shape the contents? Yes, of course. But that is because we have a good sense of what will appeal to the public and how key messages need to be drawn out. There is always a tone we like to keep, and to be honest, we do shape all the research we commission, but that is to the benefit of the final product, rather than it being us putting hurdles in front of the people who are commissioned.

Often times these difficulties could be negotiated, serving only to dull the appetite of charity staff for renewing links with researchers. But we also found academics and directors pointing to occasions when research application and findings cut across or ran counter to part of the corporate messages of the commissioning body. For instance, a charity might wish to claim that a problem was worsening or acute, while the research results actually suggested little change. One focus group participant explained:

> There's often that tension in campaigning organisations between the campaigners who have the strong ideologies and so on, that made your organisation what it is. But if you get research that doesn't fit like that, then it can happen that it's actually rejected.

Some problems were seen to be with academic work as a whole in terms of understanding how to undertake the translation or application of their research. Others were more specific to the civil society sector, with some organizations reporting that researchers treated them differently from their business or government clients. One noted: 'Academics did not see us as the clients in the same way ... They were seeing the research as their piece of work'. There were similar perceptions elsewhere – that just because they were charities, the assumption should not be that the research belonged to the academics.

There were some significant points of tension, especially in cases where one or both partners in academic–charity relationships is new to the experience. Many NGO interviewees told stories of being disappointed by the lack of instrumental value from a particular piece of academic research, leading to a general caution amongst the more experienced directors to make sure that they set up research relationships in the right way and with the right people. As one director put it: '[Academic research] can be so disconnected from the real world ... We don't need that. We need very different kinds of things ... We need the other kind of science, that looks at the real world'.

The executives and staff members of civil society organizations also echoed (albeit in mostly milder forms) some of the most forceful criticisms of academic communication practices and preoccupations that we found in other sectors. Common complaints focused on the formats and language in which work is delivered, and interviewees underscored how this does not help to sustain longer-term relationships, beyond isolated and unsuccessful pieces of work in some cases. Charities also expressed the common exasperations with traditional academic time lags in publishing and churning out outputs locked away behind journal pay walls. They felt that academics could be far more proactive in getting their work into the mass media and specialized 'niche' media. This would serve dual purposes. It would add to the weight and quality of debate in their policy community, and it could be a key way of circumventing the problem of charities' severely limited time resources for keeping track of what gets published in the many academics journals. The importance of making 'trigger' connections through intermediaries, clearly written academic blogs and using social media like Twitter was stressed here.

Furthermore, even though charities do tend to employ resources in trawling for relevant literature in areas of interest, very few of our interviewees or focus group participants said that they ever looked at the traditional academic sources for their information. As one focus group participant put it:

> A lot of the research that we do get from academics is second and third-hand, through think tanks or through other blogs or other organisations who are coding those sources. And to the extent that academics are out there themselves, writing on blogs or posting snippets of their research, you can then make those connections and get it known. Because there might be a lot more impactful research out there that we just don't know about, because we don't have those paper subscriptions.

Other forms of 'grey' literature such as research reports played a much more important role for most practitioners. As one told us: 'As far as I can see, within our organisation, we're always on the lookout for research. But it's almost never from academic sources, in the sense of formally an academic publication, or a peer-reviewed article or something like that'. Of grey literature sources, another said: 'Probably in our view these are the things that we come across as the most useful'. Academics who work in fields relevant to charities, but who do not publish their work in forms outside peer-reviewed journals, were hence unlikely to find their work getting picked up in any kind of systematic way by charities keen to broaden their knowledge base.

These difficulties link up with the 'mixed' professional backgrounds of many senior charity and NGO staff, and their emphasis on understanding things 'on the ground' to inhibit their inclination to see 'research' as something that university social scientists can or should do. As one focus group participant put it:

> When we're thinking we need somebody to help us with the thinking about this concept mode or to help us with this evaluation, we're not necessarily thinking 'Let's get an academic' ... we're thinking 'Let's get the best person for the job'. Whether they're someone with their own consultancy who used to be an academic, whether they're part of a consultancy group, whether they're an academic or an academic who does consultancy in their spare time. All of that is less relevant than the fact that they're good. Sometimes the best people are not in academia, and sometimes they are.

There was a general consensus that academics should be more pro-active and forthcoming with their research. Very few directors could name a time when an academic had approached them out of the blue with a research proposal or application. One research director reflected: 'I do wish that more people would get in touch with us with an idea, pitch for things. But that doesn't happen very often, to be honest'. There was one exception. Quite often directors say they are approached at short notice and without consultation by principal investigators who are submitting grant application forms to research councils or foundations for purely academic projects, with the query of whether they would mind giving a letter of support or having their names mentioned as part of the impact section.

But equally in our focus group, we found a general consensus that charities themselves could do more to approach academics with outlines of their research plans or requirements, and discuss in informal environments what each party could do for each other. One participant reflected:

> I [like] this idea of having a clearer idea of what our research agenda is, and then taking that to academia and saying: 'These are the things that we think would be of value where we can help you demonstrate and deliver impact. We think they are areas where impact is waiting to be had'.

And a director of a large and well-known charity reflected:

> It wouldn't take me long to think of dozens of questions or practical situations where organisations could really benefit from someone looking into assumptions and saying what's credible and what's not [...] It could benefit at the level of small NGOs and their planning. It could also benefit at the level of the funder. Because people do all kinds of well-intentioned things, but what are the things that are actually going to make a difference?

Two large areas of potential improvements in how academics might co-operate with charities and NGOs were identified as links with small third sector organizations, and progress in being able to map impacts in widely accepted ways. On the first issue, the large internationally-recognized charities tend to have highly developed in-house research capabilities and budgets, often on a par with small government departments. There is, however, a steep 'drop-off' in terms of resources available for research as charities get smaller and more domestically focused, even amongst the large charities based in the UK. And for many of medium and smaller niche charities, research budgets are relatively small and commissioning is quite rare. So as one focus group participant said:

> The ways that, say, Oxfam or MSF [Medécins sans Frontiers] can engage here or commission research, smaller charities don't really have the resources and the capacity to do that. But we still have a ton of questions we'd love answers to that would genuinely benefit our programmes.

Another commented:

> There are particular types of research that we need or that we're looking for to try
> to establish the causes for certain campaigns that we're working on, and especially
> the impacts of certain interventions. But we just don't see those types of studies
> being done … And we can't afford to necessarily commission them ourselves.

Smaller niche and mid-range charitable sector organizations with limited research resources often feel that they have much to gain by putting in collaborative research bids with academics for research funding from government or benevolent foundations. Some charities opt for a more 'broker-style' model of research funding, where they work collaboratively with academics to get support from third-party funders such as a government research council or a department of government. One director commented:

> It is not easy because we don't have our own funds to finance a piece of research.
> So generally it's like this … We agree the partnership [with an academic] first,
> develop the concept, then go and find the funding.

This way of proceeding is also attractive because the risks of committing institutional resources are predominantly shouldered by third-party research funders with far greater financial capacity. For academics, being included in such ESRC-funded collaborative projects also has advantages, with the research council's involvement providing extra reassurance to protect the independent nature and perception of the research. Many charity directors also acknowledged to us that there is an important role here for research councils in funding and safeguarding collaborative research, particularly involving the small and medium charities sector in order to supplement their incoming revenue and learn more about the services they provide, or the challenges faced by the sectors in which they operate. In this sense, small charities especially use research not merely as a means to achieving strategic and instrumental ends in their activities, but also to build capacity and financial sustainability.

Turning to the second outstanding issue, measuring the impacts of research is an important and problematic area for charities. Well-versed in the multi-causal complexity of different policy areas, their view of 'what works' is continually hedged by caution and uncertainty. Charity executives are deeply sceptical of the single project-focused or single publication-focused strategies pursued by the research councils and HEFCE. Typically third-party funding for charities is for a single project, and even before the project has been completed and the money has run out, the organization has to restart the process of formulating another research and funding partnership in order to revisit and deepen the previous project. Securing follow-on funding is never guaranteed, and in many cases the 'impact capital' that is built up from a previous project potentially dissipates. One charity director explained his frustrations with project-based funding, and how that applied to government funding bodies criteria for academic influence in the REF:

It is frankly chasing the end of the rainbow to try to identify change as the result of one piece of work. You have got to see it as part of a process, and commit to that process. If, for example, a research council sat down with DfID [the Department for International Development] and planned to do a whole process (including research, [and] implementation), and tracked that through during a five year period minimum – then you might reasonably say that you can hold the recipient accountable for change. But to do it in this fragmented way is not efficient. In fact, it is incredibly inefficient.

Practically orientated charities and NGOs often set the bar high for judging their own influence and that of research. For many, particularly campaigner organizations and those seeking to change people's behaviour on the ground, it is not enough to have impact internally within their own narrow policy community. Impact must take place externally, either by influencing public policy and prevailing public opinion, and/or by ameliorating the lives and situations of the specific client groups that they seek to serve. The thinking of senior decision-makers has a built-in assumption that impacts relate to these two priorities, while also recognizing that outcomes in both spheres are always determined by multiple causes, and so often uncertain and unpredictable. Yet they also recognize that the closer you get towards the rarefied atmosphere of high politics, the harder it is to establish clear causal relationships, an idea that without either a particular campaign or a given piece of research the impact would not have happened. For service-providing charities (as for government agencies) there is always at least the potential to count outputs, even if outcomes are too volatile or multiple to measure any counterfactuals on what would have happened without the charity's or NGO's intervention. However, by providing services on the ground such organizations can gather indications that they (sometimes) succeed in making a considerable difference to people's lives.

Conclusions

We can sum up in a diagram (Figure 7.12) the varying difficulties involved in academics and researchers working with charities. As for the business and government sectors we look across the stages of establishing relationships set out in Figure I.1. This shows a double peaked configuration, with most difficulties and barriers occurring at the stages of identifying a quid pro quo to help sustain co-operation between academics and NGOs or charities, and then again at the stage of establishing the impacts of research on activities on the ground or on public policy outcomes. Finding traction to keep linkages sustainable between charities or NGOs and academics is moderately hard, partly because charities' and NGOs' resources are mostly tightly constrained. The possible benefits for NGOs include establishing credibility and independence, sustaining nodality and centrality in networks, being able to demonstrate their own impact and 'value for money', and leveraging their own positions in foreign jurisdictions. The drawbacks revolve around getting research that is sufficiently useable for campaigning and influencing decision-makers. For academics too, choosing to devote time and resources to civil society organizations' priorities is tricky.

Figure 7.12 Trajectory of difficulties in achieving impacts with civil sector organizations, compared to other sectors

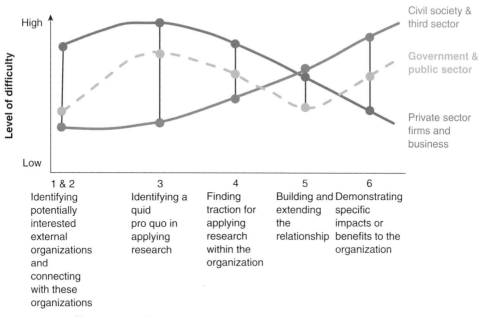

Six aspects of impact in external organizations (see Figure II.1)

Researchers will think through how they might justify their choices in REF terms or explain them to their department head or university. For REF especially, most researchers feel that they must first demonstrate that their research had impacts within the charity, and then also establish the link between the charity's impacts on the policy concerned – both very hard to do. However, it is also important to recognize in Figure 7.12 that the two earliest stages (identifying partners and establishing linkages) are fairly easy to accomplish (bar the problems of academese). And where relationships become established and confer benefits on both parties they are relatively straightforward to maintain.

In some ways the relations between social scientists and civil society organizations shows some characteristics of both the other sectors. The strongly networked world of charities and NGOs, and their non-commercial culture, both mean that it is easier for academics and charity leaders to make contact. In this limited sense, the third sector approximates to the government sector. However, the hard-edged instrumental and mission-committed goals of charities assign a lot of importance to establishing quid pro quos and to translation work, making these factors arguably as important for NGOs and charitable sector organizations as they are for business firms. If academics are able to work on the timelines and expectations of their charity partners then the barriers to forming lasting and valuable working relationships can become less significant than in government.

Overall, the senior staff of civil society organizations showed the strongest, wholly pragmatic approaches to the uses of university social science. Applied work in the charity sector tends to be heavily practice-oriented and geared towards specific instrumental ends. So there are inherent constraints on how elevated or rarefied the potential impacts of the research which they pick up can be. The combination of the limited resources, and the need to maximize 'bangs per buck' in terms of using research to underpin and strengthen messages, means that charities are keenly focused on the net instrumental value for their mission that they get from collaborations with academics. There is no guarantee that academics will be the first port of call if assistance is needed, either for senior managers or for researchers lower down who want to get access to new materials or policy-relevant research. And in many issue areas, small-scale consultants and think tanks compete with academics to provide applied research for charity clients. Futhermore, large consultancies and professional bodies can sometimes undertake pro bono projects that substitute for university research in some respects. In addition, there are the usual quota of potential misunderstandings and tensions, although they are mostly manageable. As one focus group member from a major charity told us:

> There's still quite a huge gap between the perceptions of academics and practitioners and how they see each other. I think a lot of times they have it completely wrong, but on both sides. And that's at least what I noticed. But a lot of the universities here, some of them, think really weird things about the practitioners. Yet I also know from my people, they come with stories about the academics.

None the less serious cases of mismatched organizational cultures, or of incompatible understandings of the role or conduct of research, seemed fairly rare in this sector compared with business or government.

Of the three sectors, civil society seems the most 'naturally' integrated into the world of university social science. Research in the discipline group has tended to be most frequently picked up by civil society organizations, far more so than in business, and perhaps even more than in government. This reflects the comparatively strong latent demand for research and expertise in the sector, as well as the much more integrated and networked worlds of collaboration and knowledge exchange. Charities and applied social science researchers share similar 'mission specific' orientations and they can often play strong entrepreneurial roles in bringing together part of a given advocacy coalition behind an altruistically motivated goal.

Summarizing their major study of NGOs and charities in the UK, Hilton et al. (2013: back cover) concluded:

> NGOs have contributed enormously to a professionalization and a privatization of politics, emerging as a new form of expert knowledge and political participation. They have been led by a new breed of non-party politicians, working in collaboration and in competition with government. Skilful navigators of the modern welfare state, they have brought expertise ... and changed the nature of grassroots activism. As affluent citizens have felt marginalized by the increasingly complex nature of many policy solutions, they have made the rational calculation to support NGOs [whose] professionalism and resources ... make them better able to tackle complex problems.

Yet now there are many indications that the heyday of the NGOs is over. Increasing austerity in UK government public spending has slimmed the scale of budgets, somewhat boosted the political polarization around policy issues, and radically cut the public service funding flowing to many charities and NGOs. Some previously independent think tanks have moved to a place of greater safety within the university sector. And the growth of social media and of network forms of organization has raised the power of many different types of citizen groups and organizations, and their capacity to do their own viral organizing and fundraising. So the rate of growth of formally established NGOs and charities has clearly slowed in recent years (Figure 7.2). If they are to maintain their influence in the public policy process, then renewing the cooperation with academics that became less salient in their boom period may once again be important.

8

The media and public engagement

The principle of this new journalism was 'giving the public what it wants'. To intellectuals this naturally sounded ominous. Intellectuals believe in giving the public what intellectuals want: that, generally speaking, is what they mean by education.

John Carey[1]

When a science subject shifts from its traditional home at [the] science pages to other media beats, new audiences are reached, new interpretations emerge, and new voices gain standing in coverage.

Matthew Nisbet and Dietram Scheufele[2]

Advocacy coalitions continuously contest with each other to set up or engineer coverage of their viewpoints in the media, and to directly inform and shape 'public opinion' and the reactions of citizens at large to the issues they promote. The media battle is the most immediate and visible of these two processes, especially as fought out in conventional 'mass' (one to many) media. The component organizations and networks involved in coalitions (especially business-facing ones) spend millions of pounds a year in seeking to influence journalists and editors. Political parties, unions, NGOs and charities with mass memberships, and companies with large marketing and advertising budgets, are not completely dependent upon shaping media coverage – if need be they can seek to directly communicate with citizens via campaigns and mobilizing voluntary or paid activities by their supporters, staff or contractors. But understandably securing media coverage is always their first port of call, because it is usually far cheaper, more immediate and more effective.

Academics and researchers enter the arenas of media and public engagement with some significant assets and disadvantages. On the plus side there has historically been significant public interest in science and technology especially since the emergence of the popular press in the later nineteenth century, creating strong incentives for the media to cover developments and issues – especially those that can

---

[1] Carey (2012: 7).
[2] Nisbet and Scheufele (2009: 1771).

be fitted into some well-established 'narratives' of scientific discovery, ideally by a lone genius acting against the odds or overturning the scepticism of colleagues. Journalists and editors also depend heavily upon academic expertise when they have to cover stories from both the STEM disciplines and the social sciences. They need help to understand complex issues in the first place, and to then work with them (often in a very short space of time) and fashion an accessible 'story' out of the issue, ideally one that quickly connects with existing public pre-conceptions. Academics and scientists also serve as authoritative sources of comment and arbitration about claims for new research 'breakthroughs' or findings: their expertise, status and neutrality can be taken on trust, saving vital time and simplifying the job of presenting many issues.

On the other hand, academics have many handicaps in dealing with media personnel, still less shaping public opinion. Science and academic research are inherently complex, especially in those STEM and social science areas that are highly mathematicized and involve assessing quantitative data, and in other areas of work that do not lend themselves to intuitive presentation or to conventional narrative, story-telling structures. Conventionally also academic communication has been bulky and long-winded, placing a lot of attention on methods and the detailed presentation of findings, often phrased in esoteric languages and using complex concepts and professional vocabularies that are remote from 'ordinary knowledge'. Journalists and editors searching for people able to succinctly and intuitively summarize ideas in print or on TV and radio have often been sceptical (even scathing) about the communication capabilities of academics – leading to their heavily shaping the terms on which researchers are given coverage or airtime.

Finally, scientists, academics and universities have traditionally lacked much substantial capacity to reach out to citizens or directly shape public opinion. They could not afford heavy advertising, and relied mostly on their professional prestige and networks of alumni and contacts to mobilize public opinion, allied with some basic public relations and limited public lectures or outreach work. These activities worked often very slowly and were only effective on narrow ranges of issues bearing directly upon the operations of the higher education sector itself. Only public campaigns lead by some media-attractive types of science, especially medical doctors defending medical research funding, could previously achieve significant leverage more widely. Cumulatively these have been serious drawbacks that more than offset the advantages that scientists and academics could command.

We consider social scientists' ability to achieve impacts via the media and public engagement under four headings, beginning by looking briefly at how the public see academics in general, and how universities have sought to communicate with lay citizens. The second section focuses down on social science, looking at how the mass media have treated the discipline group's research, in conventional and highly limiting ways, although on a large and increasing scale. Third, we look at the difference made by digital communication developments and the arrival of social media, which can be more directly produced by universities and academics in unmediated ways, giving them more control of the processes and contents involved. Finally we consider high impact social science in the work of public intellectuals and in some large-scale recent experiments involving large numbers of citizens accessing and using social science materials.

8.1 Academic expertise and 'the public'

Whatever universe a professor believes in must at any rate be a universe that lends itself to lengthy discourse. A universe definable in two sentences is something for which the professorial intellect has no use. No faith in anything of that cheap kind!

William James[3]

I've never been an intellectual, but I have this look.

Woody Allen[4]

Most available evidence suggests that 'the public' has a double-stranded, partly contradictory perception of academics and researchers. There is considerable evidence that the public tend to hold academics in fairly high regard, and trust them as an independent and credible source of information. Yet at the same time, people outside universities are often sceptical about the 'real-life value' or practical purpose of academia, maintaining default stereotypical notions of reclusive types beavering away on obscure problems in ivory towers. Similarly, members of the public may perceive that they have relatively little direct contact with universities, academics, or their research. However, they are also likely to consume or benefit from the fruits of university research in all sorts of indirect ways, through the media, through books they read, through the TV programmes they watch, or through the museums or galleries they (occasionally) visit. Even for those with university degrees, 'university' is often a world that graduates 'package up' and leave behind, as they enter into the job market. Clearly they take with them a considerable amount of knowledge, skills and values absorbed from their time at university, which may relate in varying degrees to their subsequent work. But the professional world of university research is a more diffuse and difficult one with which to identify.

A study by Universities Australia (2013) illustrates these complexities. In a survey, a large majority of Australian respondents agreed that research was an 'essential part of what a university does' and believed that 'conducting research to advance knowledge for its own sake is important' (p4). At the same time, however, people's detailed understanding of what academic research entails was low, despite most respondents expressing a general interest in wanting to hear more about it. As the report explained, 'There is little understanding about what universities do in the research space. Most people can relate to teaching at universities, but can't get their head around the research bit' (Universities Australia, 2013: 4). Nearly half of respondents said that they 'had heard about university research over the past twelve months', but mostly in the medical and scientific disciplines. Very few people had heard about research being conducted in other fields, such as psychological and behavioural research, environmental science, or education.

There is no equivalent UK survey evidence, despite some isolated bits of data (such as a 2010 Universities UK study showing that the British public under-estimated the

---

[3] James (1907: 1).

[4] Commonly attributed to Woody Allen.

Figure 8.1a   Levels of public trust in different professions, average from 1983 to 2011

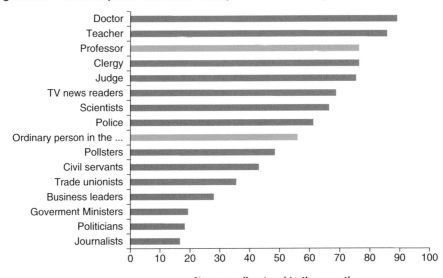

% responding 'yes' to the question:
'For each, would you tell me whether you generally
trust them to tell you the truth or not?'

Figure 8.1b   Levels of public trust in the information provided by different professions, 2013

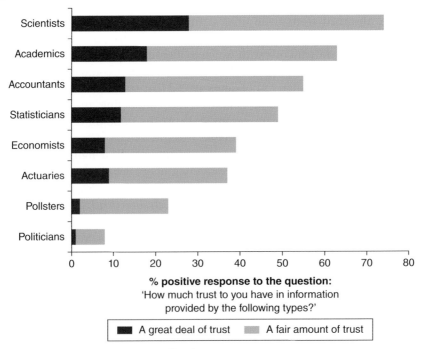

% positive response to the question:
'How much trust to you have in information
provided by the following types?'

◼ A great deal of trust   ▨ A fair amount of trust

Source: Ipsos Mori *Trust in Professions* polling data.

number of UK universities). Yet more general polling suggests that academics are potentially well placed to have influence or impact amongst the general public. Figure 8.1a shows that 'professors' were accorded the third highest level of public trust in a comparative ranking of different professional groups. On average three quarters of respondents have trusted professors over the 28 years of Ipsos MORI polls between 1983 and 2011, with levels not varying a great deal. Two thirds of respondents also trusted 'scientists'. Yet perhaps a more appropriate comparison is the difference between both occupations and the rating for 'the ordinary person in the street' at 56 per cent. The differential for 'professors' was thus +19, and for 'scientists' +10 per cent, but both are somewhat behind the top most trusted professions 'doctors' and 'teachers' – both occupations that far more members of the public have regular contact with. In media terms, however, it is important to note that both types of university personnel are trusted far more than most of the other occupational groups who appear in the press or broadcasting, especially politicians and journalists, rated lowest on this polling. (However, TV news readers do far better, beating scientists. This may reflect the UK's regulated, bi-partisan broadcast media system.)

A slightly contrasting picture is provided by a single 2013 poll, asking a differently worded question about respondents' trusts in the information provided by different university-linked professions (Figure 8.1b). It places 'scientists' top with nearly three quarters trusting them, followed by 'academics' on just under two thirds. However, respondents here were wary of reposing 'a great deal of trust' in either group, with ratings of less than three in ten for 'scientists' and under a fifth for 'academics'. The levels of public trust in four other professional groups (accountants, statisticians, economists and actuaries) are significantly lower, probably reflecting their normal involvement with companies or government, both seen as 'vested interest' sectors by citizens and so less widely trusted.

Turning to how universities themselves seek to influence public opinion, there has been a considerable change in approaches to informing the public, a change that accelerated in the run-up to the REF 2014 exercise, which introduced financial incentives for universities to achieve wider impacts from research. Humanities subjects have traditionally been far easier to explain in intuitive and popularly accessible ways, with flourishing coverage of history, English literature, philosophy and psychology topics in all the 'quality' newspapers, including quite extensive book reviews. Historians, geographers, archaeologists, cultural and literary academics have also always featured prominently in UK broadcasting, including leading TV and radio series, and with an extensive presence on BBC Radios 3 and 4.

Early on in the post-war period some areas of the STEM sciences also developed enviable track records of eliciting public interest and getting across relatively complex information successfully – notably in palaeontology, natural history, zoology, plant biology, parts of geology, and simpler forms of astronomy, medicine and psychology. By contrast, many other STEM disciplines have had to overcome substantial barriers to explaining their complex, often esoteric and mostly mathematized work at all to mass publics. And even in the most accessible STEM areas scientists have wanted to do far better in explaining how research is undertaken; what the scientific criteria and protocols for assessing evidence are; and how methods and critical debates are fundamental to the status of scientific work.

Unlike the humanities and social sciences, STEM sciences funding has been ample. The discipline group also enjoys strong elite support from business and government circles, allowing the substantial development of new professional groups specializing in science communication. A key trigger was an influential Royal Society report *The Public Understanding of Science* (1985), which questioned the extent to which universities and academics were helping to present science and scientific research as a public good in the interest of the population at large (Watermeyer, 2011). The initial framework was a 'deficit model' in which citizens at large were seen as lacking knowledge or awareness of key components of the scientific method and research processes. For almost two decades science communication for lay audience accordingly concentrated on strategies to remedy these 'deficits', finding ways of explaining complex processes more skilfully and intuitively, and seeking to build up more systematically people's knowledge base and abilities to absorb complex scientific information. Presenting science more accessibly so as to expand the appetite for a wider range of subjects and disciplines was an important objective also, and achieved significant successes in the emergence of a 'popular science' genre in books and TV broadcasting, both achieving considerable sales and audiences.

The 'public understanding of science' movement was essentially something of a top-down process, however. Scientists were seen as the bearers of a superior knowledge, which simply needed to be re-presented in greatly improved ways, in order to raise the general level of citizens' 'correct' appreciation of scientific issues. This would grow public trust in science, and hence citizens' acceptance of new technologies and better appreciation of risks and natural processes. Figure 8.2 shows that there was a relatively constant number of references in the media mentions to this approach throughout the 2000s. (To compile this chart we electronically searched all items in UK news publications included in the electronic media database Nexis, and coded any article we found that talked specifically about 'public understanding' and 'science').

However, from the middle of the decade a new, somewhat more democratizing or two-way concept emerged, that of 'public engagement' with science. Again Figure 8.2 includes the results of a comprehensive Nexis search for all mentions of 'public engagement' and 'science' within the same articles. From 2005 the chart shows that this approach grew rapidly in terms of media mentions, and by 2012 even slightly overtook public understanding of science mentions.

Key elements in the public engagement approach are that citizens are no longer seen as simply deficient in knowledge, but rather as having working models of their own for handling information, models that scientists need to take far more seriously and connect with more effectively. Engagement also stresses involving citizens in science research far more actively, potentially even as co-producers of knowledge, as in some 'citizen science' projects that enlist lay people to record observations. An example is the annual UK bird survey by the Royal Society for the Protection of Birds, or the 'networked science' project which successfully asked amateur astronomers to help scientists classify millions of different stellar objects. The twin movements to create 'open access' to all scientific and academic work on the web, and towards making research information systematically available in 'open data' mode, have both received massive government and business elite backing, at least in relation to work

Figure 8.2   References to 'public understanding' and 'public engagement' relating to science research in UK media publications

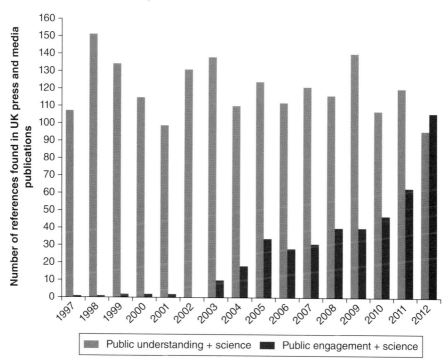

Source: Our own analysis of Nexis UK press database.

that has been funded by taxpayers or foundations. A key 'open' rationale is that we cannot predict what research or what data will be useful to which scientists or organizations or citizens. So we can best foster the maximum possible exploitation of both by removing pay barriers to reading scientific and academic publications, and licensing and permissions barriers to reusing scientific data (Neylon, 2013). The wider concept of public engagement (including the 'open' agenda) essentially seeks to create far more of a two-way process of communication, instead of the one-way, top-down 'public understanding' model.

Looking in more detail, Figure 8.3a distinguishes between references to 'public engagement' that were specifically institutional, for example, referring to a particular Chair of Public Engagement or a Centre for Public Engagement. During the last ten years, new and well-funded STEM centres have been set up in Aberdeen, Bristol, and Surrey universities, as well as individual chairs elsewhere. These new academic posts were generally filled by professors of engineering, biological and physical sciences, and the chart shows that this strong form of institutional support accounts for nearly two-fifths of all the news items mentioning public engagement.

How deeply has the change of orientation towards a two-way concept of engagement penetrated in the media system? In the early days of the movement Figure 8.3b shows that there were years when one specialist publication in the Nexis database (the *Times Higher Education*) accounted for a substantial share of mentions. But in recent years

Figure 8.3a   References to 'public engagement' in UK media publications

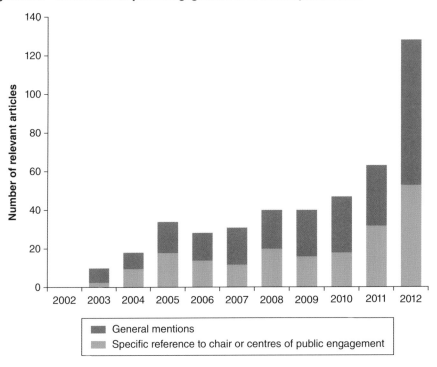

Figure 8.3b   References to 'public engagement' in different types of media publication

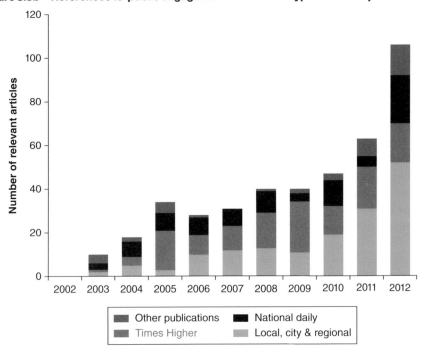

Source: Our own analysis of Nexis UK press database.

much of the growing mentions come at the level of city, local or regional newspapers, with a reasonable number of national newspaper stories also. These patterns suggest that the change of tack by universities has reached quite far down.

A large literature on science communication, public understanding of science and public engagement research has grown up covering overwhelmingly the STEM sciences. Especially recently, much of this work stresses that the audience or 'public' for science research pieces in different media outlets mostly seek to link new knowledge to their existing concepts and ideas, although responding to cues about the salience of new findings ('priming') from the media. For instance, Nisbet and Scheufele (2009: 1769) argue that lay publics are likely to apply the following criteria in reaching judgments:

- Does scientific knowledge work? Do public predictions by scientists fail or prove to be true?
- Do scientists pay attention to other available knowledge when making claims?
- Are scientists open to criticism? Are they willing to admit errors and oversights?
- What are the social and institutional affiliations of scientists?

In other words, do they have a historical track record of trustworthiness?

Similarly, do they have perceived conflicts of interest relative to their associations with industry, government, universities, or advocacy groups?

- What other issues overlap or connect to a publics' immediate perception of the scientific issue? [For example] in the case of genetically modified food, both Chernobyl and mad cow disease ... undermined public trust in [UK] government claims about risk.
- Specific to risks, have potential long-term and irreversible consequences of science been seriously evaluated and by whom? And do regulatory authorities have sufficient powers to effectively regulate organizations and companies who wish to develop the science? Who will be held responsible in cases of unforeseen harm?

This may well seem a fairly demanding list of criteria. But it is one that most STEM disciplines have recently been able to address, using increasingly well-designed and sophisticated science-communication approaches. We turn next to the situation for social scientists in securing media attention for their research, looking first at conventional ('mass') media.

8.2 Social scientists and conventional news media

Journalists repeatedly stressed that social science had associative rather than intrinsic news value, that it only became worthy of their attention if it achieved newsworthiness by association.

Natalie Fenton and colleagues[5]

---

[5]Fenton et al. (1998: 96).

In a proletarianized intelligentsia with a mass audience, anonymity is the stigma of powerlessness, and powerlessness the punishment for anonymity.

Régis Debray[6]

For most of the post-war period the key features of modern communications media were taken to be their massing of readers, listeners or viewers into huge audiences, receiving from their chosen outlet a centralized and highly shaped stream of news, commentary and more extended information, set by the media organization's staff in a 'one to many' mode. This was the heyday of the corporate power of media corporations spanning TV, newspapers and publishing empires, fuelling the views of Marxisant commentators who argued that here (as elsewhere) concentration of control over the means of production (and dissemination) was critical (Debray, 1981). Subsequently, though, press outlets shrank, and the numbers of TV channels and radio stations increased with competition and decreasing production costs. From the late 1990s key innovations created 24-hour 'rolling news' channels, and 'niche' TV channels with specialist orientations have multiplied. So over time the 'massness' of conventional media has tended to fall quite rapidly, especially after the advent of the web and digital multiplication of media types. Audiences per channel have become smaller overall, apparent 'choice' has increased, and audiences also give far more conditional loyalty to key media sources than in the past. None the less, the conventional media (especially press, radio and 'network' TV) are still strongly distinguished by concentrated ownership, their large scale of operations, and their adherence to a very strong and constantly moving news agenda.

For social scientists (and academics more generally) dealing with the media can essentially only take one of two forms. The overwhelmingly most common form is a one-off or opportunistic relationship, shown in Figure 8.4a. Examples here would be the citation of social science research in a press story, or the appearance of an academic on a TV or radio news show or channel. The terms of these exchanges are dominated by the media professionals. The newspaper, radio station or TV channel is dominant, because the organization is producing a heavily branded and carefully calculated product, usually one that commands the long-run loyalty of a large audience. Next in salience is the sub-branding of the particular broadcast programme or section of the programme, and then perhaps the brand identity and often powerfully known image of the journalist writing the piece or conducting the interview. Battling to be noticed against these strong messages, with which readers or viewers are usually fully familiar, the ability of an academic researcher to project their own personal 'brand', or the institutional brand of their centre or university, is extremely restricted. In a few lines or even paragraphs of a press item, or in the few seconds or perhaps minutes allotted to a broadcast interview, not much of the research or the researcher can usually be got across.

Academics who have agreed to be 'talking heads' on TV, or comment on the radio, especially told us of their vivid sense of dispensability, with the news programme sweeping on to another topic seconds after their item ceased airing, with no visible follow on or residue. For many years conventional broadcast slots were largely irrecoverable once transmitted, unless cumbersomely recorded on video or tape, and

---

[6]Debray (1981: 145).

Figure 8.4   Patterns of linkages between social scientists and conventional media organizations

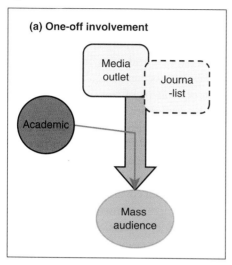

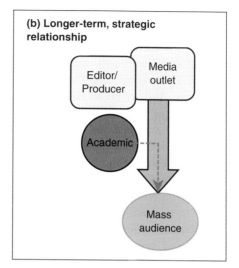

even then they were not subject to any practicable further dissemination. So, unless picked up by the press, most one-off broadcast contributions essentially vanished into unfindability, in a highly transient manner. However, progress in the e-storage of news outputs, plus web searching, have both begun to give a greater ability to re-find broadcast contributions in the last five years. By contrast, press items have always had a more enduring quality, for the text remains after reading, and can be searched for and permanently accessed and cited thereafter, initially in print or for the last two decades in database forms.

The only other mode of social scientists interacting with conventional media shown in Figure 8.4b was a more sustained or strategic relationship, where the academic more extensively defines the shape of their own contribution. For example, an academic might write a full article or an 'op ed' piece for a newspaper, perhaps even becoming a regular columnist or commentator for the outlet. Alternatively an academic might initiate and substantively lead the production of a whole radio broadcast or a whole TV programme, or even a whole radio or TV series. Perhaps the researcher might even appear in person to guide listeners or viewers through the argument in 'telly don' mode, as happens extensively with scientific, cultural and historical programmes. Here the academic's own distinctive approach and the details of the research process and evidence involved may all emerge much more when set against the channel's brand. However, inherently in mass media systems, and still in today's conventional media, the number of such opportunities is strictly limited – and historically few of them seem to have come to social scientists.

Seen in these terms, social scientists have far more commonly been involved in one-off relationships with the media than sustained ones. This is not well-covered terrain and the existing literature is sparse: 'Even within social science, studies of how scholars work with mass media to secure the public impact of their research seem rare' (Flyvberg, 2012: 171). A lot of media links were reported by our interviewees, and documented in our dataset of academics, but the vast majority are one-off and not strategic ones. A few top professors did cultivate media contacts in a systematic way, especially where they were also working with charities and NGOs in an advocacy coalition. However, even they did not point to anything more than isolated cases of coverage linked to a particular piece of research or NGO campaign. There are many cases of social scientists writing pieces for newspapers, and even inspiring whole radio or TV programmes. But very few social scientists become regular media commentators. And we could find no social science equivalent of the common history, STEM science or medical series led and fronted by academics.

The best evidence assembled by UK media scholars covering social science communication is also now rather dated, defined by Fenton et al. (1998) in a pre-internet period at the end of the 1990s. Yet in default of better materials it is worth considering the patterns that they carefully constructed by analysing a large dataset of social science news coverage. Figure 8.5a shows firstly that much coverage of social science relates to research done outside universities – by companies, media organizations, consultancies, think tanks, government and charities or NGOs. Strictly speaking, Fenton et al. traced less than one news item in every six back to universities. This proportion more than doubles if we include what they call 'independent research institutes', however. Most social science coverage resulted from either the completion or dissemination of research by the bodies set out in Figure 8.5b, with around ten per cent generated by societal developments without this stimuli, and a scattering of items from new research initiatives and academic conferences.

Fenton et al. found social scientists appearing overwhelmingly in two media roles, either as the research protagonists themselves explaining their findings or the relation between their work and societal developments (the preponderant role); or as an expert commentator, arbitrating in a controversy or discussing societal developments. In terms of topics (Figure 8.5c), two-fifths of social science coverage dealt with social integration and control (a baggy category covering crime, children and education, gender and sexual behaviours), followed by economics issues, public policy questions, health and lifestyle/relationships coverage (Figure 8.5c). The researchers excluded opinion polls from their definition of social science items, and so showed less political coverage than might be expected.

We can update this analysis a little using a systematic analysis of the online UK national press database, Nexis. In May 2007 we combed six groups of UK national newspapers for all references to 'professor' paired with 'academic research' in the same article, and all instance of 'doctor' or 'Dr' paired with 'new findings', and then analysed their content further in detail. Figure 8.6 shows the main types of reference found, amounting to 600 relevant items. The breakdown varies considerably depending on the precise combination of search terms employed, but the largest category on both counts consisted of quotes or comments from academic sources, suggestive of a one-off type of relationship. Coverage of research with a more systematic quality, and articles by academics themselves, were less than half as common. A surprising feature for us was the prevalence of letters from academics, who relatively often seem to comment on press items where they have specialist expertise.

In recent years there have been a considerable number of changes in conventional media that are likely to have changed the media prominence of social scientists. The

Figure 8.5a   The origins of social science media coverage, 1997

Source of news item	Per cent
Research by others (companies, media, etc.)	32
Think tanks, independent research institutes	17
University research	15
Response to public concern	10
Government research	7
NGO or Charity research	6
Another source	6
New research initiated	3
Conference	3
All sources	*100%*

Figure 8.5b   The characteristics of two kinds of social science coverage, 1997

Focus of news coverage of research	Research is focus of coverage (%)	Social scientist as arbiter or pundit (%)	All coverage (%)
Publicizing or disseminating research	41	6	39
Advising, informing, commenting	21	48	31
Highlighting issues	22	20	21
Criticizing or supporting others' policies or work	13	23	15
Other	4	4	4
Total	*100%*	*100%*	*100%*
N of items	*1072*	*370*	*1442*

Figure 8.5c   The topic focus of social science coverage, 1997

Topic	Per cent of coverage
Social integration and control	41
Economy and private sector	17
Health	12
Government and policies	10
Lifestyle and relationships	9
General and other	7
Demographics	4
Total	100
N of items	*1464*

Source: Computed from Fenton et al. (1998): a = Table 2.3, p 28; b = Table 2.4, p 28; c = Table 2.5, p 34.

Figure 8.6   Types of references to academic research found in a 2007 review of UK national newspapers

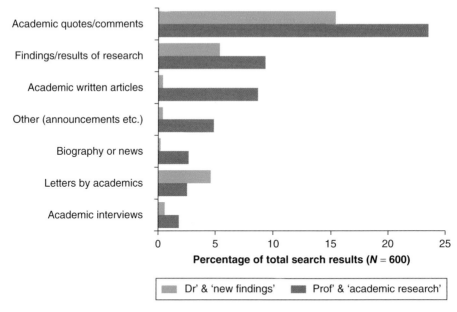

Note: Using the Nexus publications database, we searched six groups of UK national newspapers (*Financial Times, Times and Sunday Times, Guardian, Independent and Independent on Sunday, Daily Telegraph and Sunday Telegraph, Daily Mail and Mail on Sunday*) for all references to the two sets of search terms during May 2007 (*N* = 600 for both searches). For each group of newspapers we looked at the top 100 results and for each result we coded the type of reference.

advent of 24-hour rolling news TV (in the UK from the BBC, Sky and overseas channels) has extended the range of issues given coverage. It has clearly created a far larger media appetite and need for commentators, especially on world political news and economic matters. These changes have also greatly extended the broadcast time available for one-off commentators in some circumstances, from the seconds common on national news programmes to slots lasting 3 to 5 minutes in many cases on rolling news channels.

Print newspapers have greatly expanded their digital presence in partial response, and also differentiated themselves from rolling news TV somewhat by extending their features coverage in online editions. The 'quality' papers have looked more energetically for academics as in depth commentators on non-time sensitive issues for their large and mushrooming websites. As a result the economics, social policy, education and political/polling sections now commonly include social scientists, including as semi-regular commentators. Partly because of these changes, more national newspapers now have sector correspondents with 'beats' relevant for social science. But equivalents of science correspondents are still rare. By contrast to both press and TV, radio channels have seen relatively less change in recent times.

University press offices and their expertise in communications have also both expanded greatly in the last decade, with more sophisticated and more frequent press releases, better connections with broadcast media, and with more professional media training being provided for academics. Press offices are no longer just 'nudging the more recalcitrant' academics into making their work known (as Fenton et al. found), but increasingly orchestrating relatively sophisticated campaigns and launches, especially in the STEM disciplines. This is much less common in the social sciences. However, all actors in advocacy coalitions, and all the 'stakeholders' trying to influence media outlets, have done much the same kinds of things to improve their communications capabilities. So it is not clear if the universities' heightened activities do more than maintain their place within the conventional media flow, rather than increasing the prominence of academic work.

Other aspects of how journalists and editors in conventional media treat social scientists have scarcely altered in the last decade. Media staff still often make clear to academics that social science research is rarely important to cover on its own merits, and acquires news worthiness or topicality chiefly from some link to or association with events happening elsewhere in society (Fenton et al., 1998: 96). The generally collective nature of social science research, particularly the absence of the 'discovery' research breakthroughs that form the staple diet of STEM science journalism, are also unhelpful. Sometimes they mean that media attention often fastens on 'rogue' studies (such as poor opinion polls or eccentric research), or fastens on authors producing surprising (or because mostly wrong?) results. Journalists still generally evince distrust or lack of understanding of qualitative methods work, and place greater trust in quantitative methods, especially hunting for key factoids that sound authoritative. Social science research regularly also encounters more pushback from journalists, editors and, when published, from the public – perhaps because it deals with more intuitively accessible or experienced phenomena on which a huge amount of 'ordinary knowledge' exists, albeit of varying quality.

Journalists and editors need social science academics' expertise and neutrality to make many items feasible within the limits of time, space and bi-partisanship that they must operate in. Yet still they characteristically 'hedge their bets' in how they present social science relative to STEM subjects – in a way that is well analysed by Evans (1995: 173) for the US:

> By routinely referring to physical and medical scientists as 'scientists' and 'researchers' journalists bestow a special status on [them]; these scientists' specialized training and expertise are implicitly invoked, and they are thereby demarcated from laypersons. In social science news, however, the phrase 'social science' is seldom used. Even the seemingly unproblematic designation of 'researcher' is uncommon when referring to social scientists. By stressing only the act of writing in identifying social scientists (e.g., 'the authors of this study') journalists fail to demarcate social scientists from others who may write, argue, or otherwise enter the fray of the broader, interest-laden socio-political arena. In public conceptions, *writing* is a more subjective and less exclusive activity than *researching*. To refer to someone's research findings as being *written* rather than *reported* (or *discovered*) is to call attention to the role of human interests in the production of knowledge, to make the finding seem less fact-like.

Even the most media-prestigious social sciences, still economics and social psychology, do not escape this kind of treatment.

The more subtle and pervasive influence of conventional media on the representation of intellectual work arises from the elaborate organizational operating processes of media companies, and their competitive struggle to define or follow a common 'news agenda':

> [L]ike all modes of communication, television, radio, and newspapers observe certain rules and conventions to get things across intelligibly, and it is these, often more than the reality being conveyed, that shape the material delivered by the media. (Said, 1997: 48)

Social scientists who dip into media activities episodically must face up each time to the importance of:

- media priming, which determines how mass publics appreciate the salience and orientation of issues and problems;
- mediation through accepted vocabularies, and resistance to academic ones; and
- gatekeeping effects, setting the boundaries of what will be asked and what can or cannot be said.

In seeking to roughly estimate the scale of such effects for researchers' external impacts we were hampered in our dataset work with individual academics (discussed in Chapters 2 and 3 above) by the difficulty of retracing or re-capturing broadcast appearances by social scientists in our study period (2004–09). However, we were able to examine the rate at which our dataset academics were mentioned in the press. Again we used the comprehensive Nexis UK databases to search individually for all our 370 academics, and to record the location and the type of reference. Figure 8.7 compares 12 social science and our five STEM disciplines in terms of the average number of press mentions per year per academic, shown on the vertical axis. Four of the social science disciplines (political science, geography, media and sociology) compared well with medicine in achieving average coverage of more than 1.5 items per year. Four more social science subjects were clearly ahead of the remaining STEM disciplines, with an average of more than one media item per academic per year. We also looked to see what the association might be between levels of coverage and the average citation rates in disciplines (shown on the horizontal axis). The relationship here is not close, but insofar as there is one it is negative – so that greater academic citation clearly does not explain why some kinds of social scientists get more media coverage than others.

Looking beyond discipline averages is important, for in each subject there tends to be a long tail of researchers with no or only a single press mention for our study period (2004–09). Excluding the no-scores, Figure 8.8 shows that there is a considerable variation in media scores across individual academics. The vertical axis uses a log scale here and so excludes 120 people amongst our academics (32 per cent) who were not mentioned by the UK press at all in this period. Some 265 out of our 370 academics (70 per cent) gained only one or fewer press mentions per year over a

Figure 8.7   Average press mentions per year per academic, by discipline 2004–09

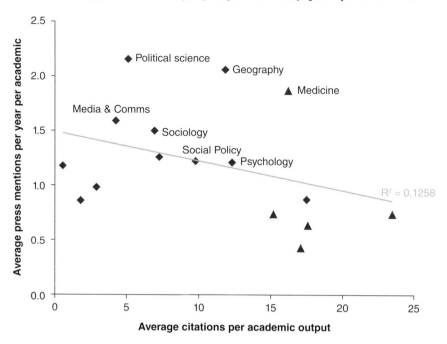

Figure 8.8   Total press mentions per individual academic, 2005–09

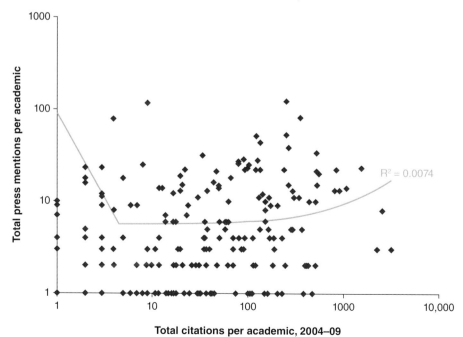

Source: LSE PPG dataset

five year period – shown as all those in Figure 8.8 with less than 5 references in total. Meanwhile, at the other end of the scale around 6 per cent of the researchers in our dataset gained more than five press mentions per year across five years, and the top ten in Figure 8.8 achieved considerably more.

The horizontal axis of Figure 8.8 again seeks to ascertain whether media coverage of academics is inversely related to their academic citation, as implied by the discipline averages and claimed in other work on public intellectuals by Richard Posner (2001). The regression line is shown here in blue and suggests a three way pattern. At low levels of individual citations there is a negative association between citations and coverage, with a sprinkling of scarcely cited but well covered academics. However, there is a break around the level where researchers are being cited just over once a year. Thereafter there is pretty well no relation between coverage and citations level for the large mass of academics in our dataset. Finally, beyond around 20 cites a year, a 'premier league' if you like, it seems clear that a smaller group of highly cited academics shows an increasingly positive relationship between press coverage and academic reputation.

Figure 8.9 Frequency with which LSE academics were interviewed for broadcast and press media during the calendar year 2012

	Not at all	1–5 times	6–10 times	10+ times	Total %
For print press media	62	28	3	7	100
For broadcast media (TV or radio)	56	32	6	6	100

Source: LSE PPG survey of LSE academics (*N* = 122).

The data considered in these last two Figures has some key limitations. Looking only at press mentions ignores broadcast coverage. And explicit press mentions will considerably under-play the extent to which social scientists help conventional media journalists via background briefings or informal commentary. Many experienced or well-known researchers answer far more queries from journalists than they get press mentions, across a very wide range of issues. And of course they do this for both the press and for broadcasters. An internal survey conducted at the London School of Economics in spring 2013 gives insights here, as Figure 8.9 shows. Around a quarter of the academic staff responded, but probably with something of a selection bias towards more media-active members. Around half had interacted with broadcasters and slightly fewer (two fifths) with print media journalists. About one in ten were contacted multiple times. The LSE is an unusual and more globally known institution than many other UK universities, with an academic staff that is older, better paid and more published than some institutions. So these data do not give us a generalizable picture. Yet these numbers at least suggest that broadcasting activities are considerable when set against press contacting; and that each overt press mention may reflect a greater level of underlying contacts between researchers and journalists.

The dynamics of social scientists interacting with the media are still something that are defined individually. Although UK universities now provide media training and more press office support than in the past, academic job roles rarely include any requirement for staff to help journalists with queries or undertake explicit dissemination work. So one of our more media-savvy interviewees told us:

> You build your own relationships. Those who care about changing things. You can spot who they are. Do they talk to the press? Do they put the phone down when journalists call? Do they present to industry meetings? Or purely academic conferences?

Where academics are engaged with businesses, and can be a good ambassador for a message with wider resonance, their industry collaborators often value media outgoingness highly. One major corporate figure described a relationship with a leading business school academic:

> [Academic K] partners very effectively with us and is media-hungry. A number of the others that we have worked with at his business school and elsewhere are more interested in getting things published in academic journals than they are in going into a television studio or the front of the FT [*Financial Times*]. So he has built relationships with the journos.

Before leaving the subject of conventional media, it is worth noting that two of the key drivers of conventional press items are still books and events (such as lectures or elite seminars). These are some of the most traditional kinds of university activities, yet ones with considerable consequences for media coverage. Looking at the academic and popular science book market, Figure 8.10 shows that the financial value of all academic and 'popular science' books was more than £1.1 billion over five years. More than four-fifths of this market was accounted for by physical paper books, while the remainder was the growing digital e-book market. Fully three-quarters of the academic books market fell within social science and humanities combined, again with a rapidly growing sixth of revenue accounted for by digital publishing. The average price of social science and humanities books was considerably lower than for STEM disciplines, which might be taken as an indication of greater average sales, or of these books' smaller size or lesser complexity. Some accessible academic books generate reviews in newspapers, especially true in the period since 2008 which has seen a strong growth in 'popular social science' books, notably in psychology, economics and philosophy. The publication of other more scholarly books by noted researchers can also form the basis for longer articles about or by the person themselves. Similarly, serious columnists in the quality press often like to link to a prestigious academic's newest article or recent book to provide some intellectual 'cover' for their argument. Normally such cited material must be either brand new, or have become enough of a classic piece that their readers may be interested to learn about it.

Finally, some press and radio coverage is driven by a range of things that academics and universities do to transfer knowledge directly to an interested general public. Social scientists have tended to be perhaps the most conventional and limited of the subject groups here, focusing almost completely on public lectures and seminars, with few of the science fairs, open-days and even pub talks that have been adopted in recent years by science engagement specialists. Equally the discipline

Figure 8.10   The financial value of social science academic books sales, 2008 to 2012

Academic book sales	Physical books	Digital ebooks	All
Value in £m of all academic book sales	893	175	**1068**
Percentage change since 2008	*+5%*	*+51%*	***+15%***
Of which:			
£m on Social sciences & humanities books	636	139	**775**
Percentage change since 2008	*+8%*	*+85%*	***+16%***
£m on Science, technology & medical books	257	36	**293**
Percentage change since 2008	*–0.1%*	*260%*	***+10%***
Average book price			
Social sciences & humanities			**14.10**
Percentage change since 2008			***+27%***
Science, technology & medical			**19.93**
Percentage change since 2008			***+15%***

Source: The Publishers Association (2012).

Figure 8.11   Events put on by universities designed for the external community, during 2010 and 2011

2009–10	Free events		Charged events	
	Attendees (000s)	**Academic staff days (000s)**	**Attendees (000s)**	**Academic staff days (000s)**
General and other	334,490	19	3,945	6
Public lectures	985	15	127	3
Performance arts	577	8	1,705	14
2010–11				
General and other	262,063	25	13,653	7
Public lectures	1,364	18	163	3
Performance arts	645	9	1,703	18

Source: HEFCE HE-BCI Survey Part B tables 2010 and 2011.

Note: performance arts include music, dance and drama etc. Figures rounded to the nearest 1,000 and are shown in 000s.

group has eschewed the exhibitions, films, plays, concerts and cultural events frequently mounted by humanities and creative arts faculties. Figure 8.11 shows that (according to data from HEFCE) UK universities have provided free access to events attended by more than 1.8 million people in each of two recent years, and provided charged events attended by somewhat lower numbers. Perhaps the activities most reliably linked to research are the free public lectures, where the number of public attendees varied between 985,000 and 1,364,000 across the two years, consuming 15,000 to 18,000 academic staff days to organize. If we pro rata on the basis established in Chapter 1, which established that around a third of UK university activity takes place in the social sciences, then this is a substantial effort.

8.3 Social science and social media

For those in my profession, being readable is a dangerous goal. You have never heard true condescension until you have heard academics pronounce the word 'popularizer'.

James Boyle[7]

Persuasion, as Matthew Arnold once said, is the only true intellectual process.

Sir Arthur Quiller-Couch[8]

The digital age has generated a highly effective answer to the problems of mediation in a communication chain, namely 'disintermediation' – which essentially means cutting out the middle man. Digital change has generally functioned to remove some key transmitters, brokers and intermediate providers across many different kinds of service market. Figure 8.10 already shows that in academic publishing nearly a fifth of sales by value now come from ebooks, which will rarely go via bookshop chains, but either directly from publishers' own websites or via huge central retailers such as iTunes or Amazon. More broadly, the open access movement represents a major challenge to the dominance that an oligopoly of large academic publishers (such as Elsevier, Wiley and Prentice Hall) have exercised over journal publishing, where corporate profit margins on journal subscriptions have historically been very high – up to 35–40 per cent in recent years (McKechin, 2013). Some universities are already extensive publishers via their university presses, and with the rise of e-presses focusing on digital-only books, reports and even journals, there is little doubt that this activity will increase greatly in future.

Similarly Figure 8.11 shows that universities have been major providers of public content in the form of freely available or charged-for lectures, seminars and conferences. The development of digital technologies has had huge implications here also. It has opened up public access to research-driven events to much larger audiences remote from the university's geographic location, and no longer confined to the discipline-specific area of the occasion. For example, a 2011 LSE Public Policy Group conference tackled the subject of 'Moving Social Security Systems Online'. Held at a prestigious central London venue, it attracted a relatively elite audience of 85 people, solely from the UK and drawn from public policy makers, professional staff from NGOs, some industry representatives and entrepreneurs, and a sprinkling of academics. Yet when we posted the podcasts of the discussion online for free at the London School of Economics' podcast site and on iTunes U, within three months these

---

[7]Boyle (2008: xv).
[8]Quiller-Couch (1916: 21).

outputs were downloaded and listened to by over 16,000 people. Obviously the LSE is not typical here: its events programme is well-known and it already has a reputation for making its lectures accessible online in this way. Yet it is significant that in 2012 this university's podcasts were downloaded over 16 million times by a worldwide audience.

In short, UK and international universities are already extensive broadcasters. In the US Ivy League universities such as Harvard and Stanford also disseminate much of their research materials online in innovative and high quality broadcast productions. A particular Stanford innovation is the Massive Open Online Course (or MOOC), which puts the mainstream curriculum teaching of the university online in accessible forms to an open audience, without the pre-screening and costly fees that are such integral and heavily filtering effects of conventional higher education. The future of MOOCs is still fiercely debated between:

- those who see it as disintermediating costly 'bricks and mortar' higher education as a whole, in a liberating way;
- those who think it will accentuate the 'proletarianization' of academic staff and commodify the learning experiences of students outside elite universities, in the process degrading standards and creating 'another brick in the wall' of bureaucratized or privatized provision;
- those who forecast that MOOCs will either be a flash in the pan (replicating the dispiriting history of previous much-touted 'teaching technologies'); and
- those who believe it will have effects chiefly in terms of 'blended learning', with e-technologies mostly being incorporated into innovative forms of campus learning, rather than displacing campus and in-person provision.

What none of the MOOC camp deny is that there is likely to be a huge expansion of the scale of universities publishing video and TV content, and a step change in the efficacy with which it can be easily searched and accessed, and made effectively available to very large audiences for universities to interact with. In the US there are already three or four major private sector MOOC providers and one major company in Britain. Universities in the UK already employ many video and podcast technicians and are likely to expand their studio facilities and in-house expertise considerably.

We can get some idea of the potential scale of transformation that may lie ahead for universities in the publishing and broadcasting domains – and understand a good deal of the lure of escaping from restrictive controls by mediators on the priming, framing and gate-keeping of content – by looking at the effects of the recent rise of blogs and social media in UK higher education. From the late 2000s onwards, blogs, Facebook, the micro-blogging site Twitter, and other social media (such as Pinterest for images), gave academics a greatly expanded opportunity to undertake their own dissemination activities directly and personally – without submitting to the restrictive and polarized demands of conventional news media or academic journals. A minority of academics and researchers took up these opportunities with alacrity, especially in the STEM sciences where there was already a long tradition of using pre-publication online newsfeeds to circulate interim research results and professional information.

Most blog activity here took place on sites run by a single academic, an individualist pattern that has proved quite resilient (Figure 8.12a). The problem here is that running a solo blog is very demanding for any researcher, or even a single research group. Either the academic gets overloaded trying to maintain a regular sequence of posts; or new posts become intermittent or unpredictable and the blog hence reaches only small audiences. Larger multi-author blogs (MABs) developed after a time lag, at first around the science specialist press, but later run by universities or groups of authors (Figure 8.12b). Here authoring burdens are spread across many academics, who need only write new posts a few times a year, and when they have useful material. In each MAB blog a central team provides effective social media support, ensuring a constant flow of new posts and content accompanied by tweets and Facebook activity that helps generate a larger audience-community – one that pools attention across the many authors.

Figure 8.12   Patterns of solo and multi-author blogs

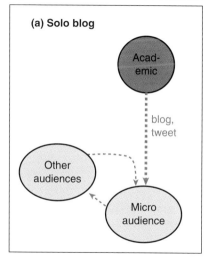

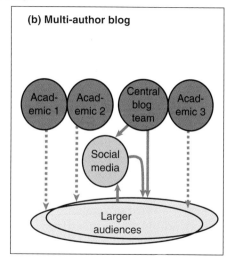

In general social scientists were initially much more conservative about online academic communication than STEM scientists – although there were a few exceptions, including the philosophers and linguists who early on created sites whose scale of operation and global reach remains impressive.[9] In particular most UK social scientists were slower to adopt blogs and Twitter as dissemination mechanisms for research, but since 2010 these have been systematically embraced by a number of high-profile UK universities and academics thereby changing the UK's previously lagging status. Similarly in the humanities a very wide-ranging digital humanities movement spread rapidly from the US, finding many UK academic supporters. Yet the ferment of these forefront activities should not disguise the generally slow picture of change across the academic disciplines as a whole.

---

[9]For philosophy see the unrivalled *Note Dame Philosophical Review* (http://ndpr.nd.edu/recent-reviews/) and for linguistics the equally impressive *Linguist List* (www. http://linguistlist.org/).

Figure 8.13   How academics in our dataset actively used digital-era tools

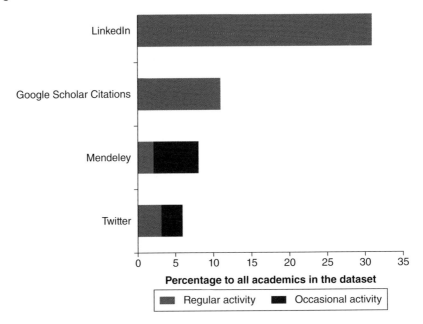

We can get some picture of the adoption patterns for social media by looking at our dataset of social science (and some STEM) academics in late 2012. Figure 8.13 above shows that at that time:

- nearly a third of academics were active on the major professional networking site, LinkedIn;
- one in eight had a publications profile up on the Google Scholar Citations site, a key resource showing how often each academic's publications have been cited, and by whom;
- one in eight was using the social media aspect of the online referencing system Mendeley by creating a public profile page; and
- one in six was using Twitter in more than just a personal capacity.

We can get another perspective on the growing importance of blogs in the armoury of academic communication in the social sciences by looking at Figure 8.14, which covers the growth in visitor numbers for four of the LSE's multi-author blogs. These are professionally run, carefully edited academic blogs that host posts from hundreds of different authors each year. The objective for them to be knowledge exchange platforms means that the blogs draw only around 40 per cent of their posts from in-house LSE authors, with around 35–40 per cent coming from other universities and 20–25 per cent from people working in NGOs, think tanks, political life and professional occupations outside academia. In 2012–13 the four multi-disciplinary blogs (covering British and European politics and policy, BPP and EUROPP; the impacts of the social sciences; *Impacts* and large-scale reviews of social science books,

Figure 8.14   Growth of monthly visits to four of LSE Public Policy Group's academic blogs[10]

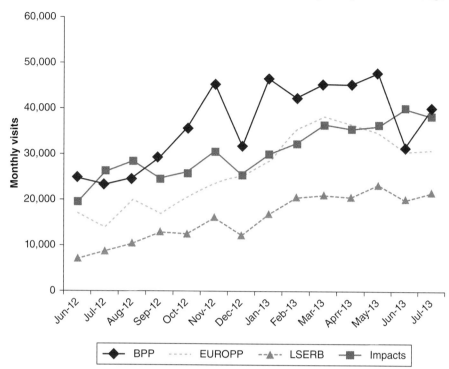

Source: Google Analytic data for four LSE PPG blogs.

LSERB)[10] achieved one million downloads of blog posts, attracted posts from more than 400 authors, and each built up many thousands of Twitter followers (over 50,000 in mid-2013 when taken together).

Multi-authored blogs feed into the creation of an academic blogosphere where academic research is also being extensively referenced by many other authors and sites, with a pattern that varies a good deal across disciplines. Figure 8.15 shows that in media studies and philosophy more than one in eight of the citations we uncovered to academics in our dataset came from blogs, with psychology, history and law not too far behind. Yet most social sciences lagged behind this pace, especially in economics, international relations and (surprisingly) business.

For academics a key benefit of blogging is that it allows them to escape from complete reliance on conventional news mediators, meaning their work can speak directly to much wider audiences if it is written appropriately for lay readers. Authors and researchers are able to control their own content in a manner that is professionally and methodologically responsible. And these new, low cost means of publishing research can significantly enlarge the academic and lay audiences for new work. Blogs, for instance, are not hidden behind journal paywalls and they are normally

---

[10] The blogs covered are: *British Politics and Policy* (http://blogs.lse.ac.uk/politicsandpolicy/); *Europp – European Politics and Policy* (www.Europp.eu); *LSE Review of Books* (www.LSEReviewofBooks.com); and the *LSE Impact of Social Sciences* blog (http://blogs.lse.ac.uk/impactofsocialsciences/).

Figure 8.15 Percentage of total references to our dataset academics that were found on blogs

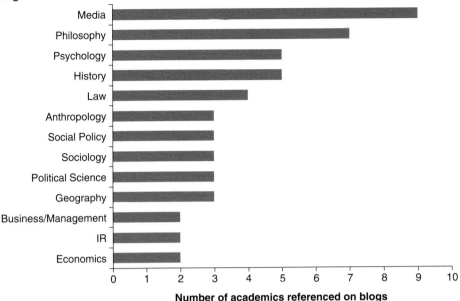

Source: LSE PPG dataset of social science academics.

written in more accessible and 'get to the bottom line' ways than full academic papers. Yet once more readers know that work is there, they may easily progress from reading about a paper to downloading the whole treatment, as Figure 8.16 demonstrates. This is one case highlighted in a World Bank study of blogs in economics which concluded that they radically improve audience sizes and reach. In this case, a paper that was being downloaded from an economics journal about once a month or less was written up on the *Freakonomics* blog, an accessible spin off from a popular social science bestseller about economics. The reference led to a startling (but in the event one-off) surge of interest in reading the paper, with 150-or-so extra downloads – some proportion of which will have led to knock-on links and perhaps citations.

A more sustained effect can be achieved by academics who both blog their outputs, and place open access versions in their university e-repository (where they can be downloaded free, without paywall restrictions), and where the researcher also tweets about their work or 'advertizes' it themselves on Facebook. The effect is initially confined to a highly selective group, those professionals or members of the public whom an academic has attracted (and accepted) as 'friends' or 'followers'. Yet if these contacts pick up and retweet or pass on news of an author's work, then multiplier effects may occur in a wider network, and especially interesting news may 'go viral' (Priem and Costello, 2010; Priem et al., 2011; Bar-Ilan et al., 2012). For example, Eysenbach (2011) shows that highly-tweeted articles were also eleven times more likely to be highly-cited articles in a traditional academic sense.

Figure 8.17 also illustrates how regular tweeting and subsequent re-tweeting can increase the download rate of an academic article (Puustinen and Edwards, 2012).

Figure 8.16   Impact of blogging about an article on average article downloads

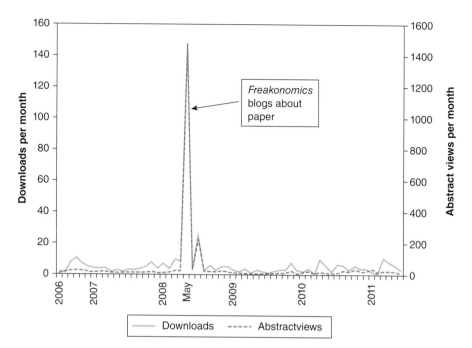

Source: McKenzie and Özler (2011).

Here a paper was made available online in late March 2012, and tweeted on the following day to the Twitter followers of the National Centre for Research Methods (NCRM). During the next day it was re-tweeted ten times to over 5,000 additional followers. This resulted in over 860 downloads within 24 hours. As the paper was not publicized anywhere else, this effect was solely explained by the Twitter publicity. In total, the paper was downloaded nearly 4,000 times, and subsequently became one of the NCRM's most popular papers.

We tested broader Twitter effects for one week's activity in May 2013 for three of the LSE PPG blogs featured in Figure 8.14 above: *British Politics and Policy* (BPP), *European Politics and Policy* (EUROPP), and *Impact of the Social Sciences* (Impact). We published 14 posts on these blogs during that week, and sent out 102 tweets to publicise them, each time to between 8,000 and 22,000 followers. We recorded 297 re-tweets of the tweets that we originally sent out. From this activity, we generated around 2,000 clicks onto our posted blogs, out of the 7,000 unique visits to our blogs that week. Hence, we estimated that a minimum of 30 per cent of our weekly traffic came directly from Twitter activity.

So far these new behaviours are confined to a minority of academics. A 2012 study estimated that only around 4 per cent of academics worldwide were on Twitter. And in an internal LSE survey run in March 2013 we found that only one in five academic staff had written a blogpost in 2012 for LSE's blogs or other blogs. Yet these behaviours are growing rapidly at the time of writing. These are clearly encouraging

Figure 8.17   Impact of tweeting on downloads of an academic paper in 2012

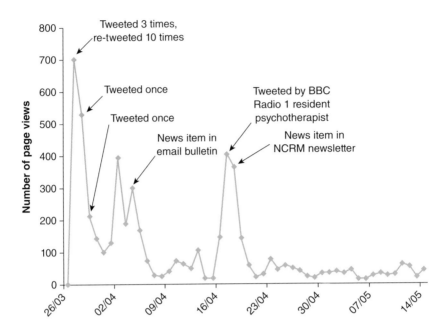

Source: Puustinen & Edwards (2012).

times for academia as a whole. But despite the strong relevance of social media for public policy making and the charity/NGO world it is hard to escape the feeling that the social sciences are a lagging area in digital scholarship still, behind most STEM disciplines in their take-up of new methods of scientific communication and lagging even behind the digital humanities sub-field at least.

To some extent the reasons here are not hard to fathom. The social sciences do not have the generous financial support for research and dissemination that STEM disciplines do. Nor do they have the immediately engaging cultural materials, imaginative artefacts and literary attractiveness that are often feasible in digital humanities. Perhaps the one area where UK social scientists have made their most distinctive (and large-scale) impact on social media remains multi-author blogging, where key academic blogs are pioneering new models of large-scale social science engagement with both policy elites and mass publics.

Social media also gets round continuing problems with academic communication like the very long time-lags between publication and first citation dates, even for sources that later go on to be very well cited. This is particularly an issue for the most hidebound disciplines like political science, where the publication of whole journal issues is still the main trigger for researchers to notice articles, citations of 'early online' articles not yet in issues is very rare (even though the queues for being bundled into an issue now takes over two years in some political science journals), and there are no accepted forums for pre-circulating working papers (also rarely cited). Here too it is rare to find blogs being referenced.

In some subjects, like history, there has been an active debate with some academics refusing to cite blogs (or even multi-author blogs), on the grounds that they have not been peer reviewed, and even suggesting that blogging is a contra-indicator for academic commitment (Brabazon, 2010; Tribble, 2005). More progressive researchers strenuously insist that blogs are a perfectly valid form of academic communication, especially those multi-authors blogs with proper editing and vigorous post-publication commentary from expert audiences (Maitzen, 2013; Zwaan, 2013), and that there can be no question of citing high quality blogs as valid sources, any more than citing magazine or press articles.

8.4 Innovating with social science in the media

Some social scientists have already clearly reached out to large audiences with considerable success. This final section looks at two different kinds of high impact social science: the work of public intellectuals; and the development of some large projects that have achieved mass engagement with social science questions, in collaboration with major media outlets.

There is a large literature on *public intellectuals* and pointing to one or two clear-cut social scientist examples is not too difficult on an international basis. For instance, Paul Krugman, the Nobel prize-winning economist (who is extensively involved in *New York Times* journalism), had 1.1 million Twitter followers in July 2013. We cannot point to any similarly well-followed UK academic – the nearest equivalent might be the British TV celebrity and polymath, Stephen Fry, a self-styled public intellectual who at the same point had amassed over 6 million Twitter followers. Some critics have argued that UK academia is poor at generating strong public intellectuals who engage with big issues, with researchers modestly preferring to hug their niche rather than venture out more creatively with solutions to the big issues of the day (Blond, 2013). In response, defensive posts have generally pointed to 'broad-front incrementalism' as a more effective strategy, but without really denying a general shortage of 'guru' intellectuals in Britain (Ford and Goodwin, 2013).

There is an ambiguity central to debates about public intellectuals. For the general public (and others), it may be difficult at times to know what is academic knowledge, and what is not. There have been many critics of the REF process, and of the research councils' rather desperate scraping around to find highly linked 'impact' from individual research projects (which cannot be done). A key objection here is that neither citizens nor policy makers can realistically separate out what they learn from academic research and what they learn from mediated-academic or completely non-academic sources. The concept of a public intellectual claims that the personalities involved are able to rise above the narrow specialisms and constraints associated specifically with academic research (Jacoby, 1989; Posner, 2001; Etzioni and Bowditch, 2006). Instead they are able to write for and engage with the public at large, acquiring a 'voice' that is critical, innovative and high-profile – one that is accepted across a range of issues and subjects. Public intellectuals may be specialists in a whole range of areas, but it is in the nature of their enhanced or 'guru' profile, that they speak as generalists who can apply their knowledge and reason across the board. For many citizens or sub-elite groups, well-known public intellectuals are one key mediating channel through which academia filters into the realm of consciousness of the everyday. They are the kind of academic personalities, even celebrities, that appear regularly on TV, or in magazines and the broadsheet press. Usually they are known as much for the ideological or critical slant of their viewpoints as for the distinctiveness of their academic or research contributions to their specific 'home' discipline.

Richard Posner's (2001) study of public intellectuals provides one of the few attempts to compare necessary and sufficient conditions for reaching this higher status, and how these relate to being an academic. He selected 500 people meeting his criteria for public intellectuals, including many well-known names from culture, politics, academia, and current affairs in the US, UK, and continental Europe (living and deceased). His research team then collected data on their biographical backgrounds, academic credibility, and public visibility in the media and on the internet (a study somewhat similar in design to our Chapters 2 and 3). Posner was perhaps ahead of his time in terms of using the internet to assess public visibility. He found that 322 public intellectuals in his set were academics or had strong academic backgrounds. The academics tended to have less public visibility than other public intellectuals who had established their public credibility through other professions. Posner used this as a basis to argue that, for a public intellectual, having a stronger academic focus and credibility, or a university base, is to be associated with weaker public visibility, both in the press and on the web. A key implication was that being an academic is neither a necessary nor sufficient condition for being a 'public intellectual'.

Furthermore, Posner implied that the relationship between academic credibility and public visibility is a negative one. He argued that the professionalization of academia since the 1950s in the US and Europe has done much to undermine the culture of the public intellectual, and instead to push academics towards more inwardly-focused specialization rather than making publicly-focused generalizations. However, despite this generally pessimistic line, Posner actually found that more than three-fifths of his total set of 500 people can be labelled 'academic public intellectuals'. So the prognosis for the university world is not that bad.

A mood of pessimism is pervasive in much of the literature on public intellectualism. Russell Jacoby's (1989) *The Last Intellectuals* and Posner's work in subsequent years, did much to set this tone, charting a 'decline' in the importance and the impact of 'great' public intellectuals, and linking this to an increasing specialization, professionalization and an inward-looking, risk-averse academic culture – all of which could potentially narrow the scope for research to be influential or strong in public engagement. An element of sentimental hankering for a lost golden age seems to hang around such 'declinist' interpretations.

Other critics have argued that such pessimism is unwarranted and only partially evidenced. Etzioni and Bowditch (2006) point out that Posner's own detailed study of the alleged decline of public intellectualism is in fact packed with pages of colourful examples of academics as public intellectuals.

[I]t seems safe to suggest, on the basis of the[se] limited observations, that

- [Public intellectuals] have far from disappeared,
- their contact with governing elites has increased and so, it seems, has their influence, and

- while such contact may have weakened criticism from public intellectuals who work or want to work closely with the powers that be, there is no shortage of outsiders who strongly challenge those in power. (Etzioni and Bowditch, 2006: 21) [*Slightly re-edited*]

Clearly, the expansion and diversification of conventional, digital, and now social media, have increased the sources of expertise and knowledge available to the public, and in some views have produced quantum increases in the numbers of people reading information, and the sum total of all the materials they are reading. For 'celebrity academics', or those that enjoy a high profile through regular appearances in the media or through large book-sales, using Twitter or Facebook to communicate with their audience offers important new opportunities to develop their public visibility, and to flesh out their 'brand', with the usual multiplier effects for further TV or media appearances. So one possibility is that the conventionally perceived decline in the prominence of public intellectuals – either as authors, or as elite commentators or arbiters on 'mass' media – may be just a reflection of a greater diversity of views and channels. Rather than reducing in any absolute terms, the emergence of social media and digital scholarship may mean that public intellectualism is in the process of evolving into a new, more distributed and more accessible pattern – one that is less captured by the cultural, social, and academic elites or media staffs, and lies more in the hands of regular academics and their direct relationships with audiences. To Régis Debray's three eras of French public intellectualism – identified in *Teachers, Writers and Celebrities* (1981) – we may yet add a fourth age, whose character reflects the (relative) decline of conventional media and the rise of digital and social media. Since most social media are orientated to contemporary phenomena, and lend themselves to practitioner-academic dialogues in specialized communities, the prospects for improving the visibility of leading social scientists should be good, if current trends continue.

Two recent high-profile examples already point a way to *realizing large-scale public engagement* with social science research by collaborating with large media organizations. These projects were both run by prominent but by no means 'guru'-level academics. Our first case is the 'Reading the Riots' project led by Professor Tim Newburn from the LSE. This was a response to the wave of riots that swept London and other English cities in the five days following the police shooting of an unarmed black man in Tottenham on 4 August 2011. The public protests that ensued were not well handled by police and from an initial north London base, rioting spread widely around the capital on the two following nights, and then to five other major cities around England. The riots followed a common pattern with bands of rioters looting properties, setting cars and some property on fire, and moving quickly to new locations in ways that caught the police by surprise. The rioters were apparently co-ordinated using social media messaging systems. With the PM, Home Secretary and London Mayor all away on holiday, and police initially unable to match officers on the ground to the scale of rioting, this was an important crisis for the UK state which revealed profound fragilities in its ability to maintain public order (Dunleavy, 2011).

When order was at last restored, through blanket policing of the capital, the political reaction was swift, condemnatory and emotive, construing the unanticipated events in terms that justified an apparently blankly repressive response. The PM David Cameron declared that: 'This is criminality, pure and simple, and it has to be confronted and defeated'. The Home Secretary (Theresa May) blamed 'a violent gun culture in our cities' and the Justice Minister (Ken Clarke) declared that 'the hardcore of rioters came from a feral underclass'. Police raided hundreds of homes and rounded up anyone who could be identified as a rioter and summary courts met in all night sessions to hand out exemplary punishments – for instance, an 18 month sentence for accepting a stolen pair of shorts. The Conservative and Liberal Democrat government refused to hold a public inquiry into the riots or their origins, or what they might say about British cities and policing, although this had been the course of action followed with previous serious riots. Instead there were some sessions by parliamentary committees, hearing almost solely from official witnesses.

The liberal *Guardian* newspaper became very unhappy with the overwhelmingly repressive slant of the official response, and the seeming failure to learn any deeper lessons about the riots. They saw this as the government pushing the roots of this sudden explosion of discontent under the carpet. The editors sought a senior social policy and criminology academic to lead a joint academic-media inquiry to fill this gap, and reached Tim Newburn at LSE, who agreed to help lead the research. *The Guardian* and Newburn assembled £120,000 of funding in record time, publicly launched the project a month after the riots, and recruited fieldworkers and analysts to begin the research within two months. Fieldwork took six weeks, with over 30 part-time interviewers, five research analysts and a roster of writers, including journalists and academics. The preliminary results were generated in time for a BBC *Newsnight* TV programme special in the first week of December 2011, to coincide with the first of six days of lengthy *Guardian* coverage (23 pages) and then a conference at LSE in mid-December. This part of the research dealt with the evidence from police, rioters, victims of disturbances, and looked at the sequence of events and the role of social media (considerable) and gangs (small). The lead researchers gave 50 media interviews on the launch day, and the *Guardian* coverage was downloaded millions of times.

So successful was the initiative that the follow-on conference attracted attendance from many elite figures and the *Guardian* and Newburn were able to raise additional funding for a second phase of the research exploring more policing issues, the response of the criminal justice system, and the experiences of victims and vigilantes (who emerged in some areas to protect property). This phase was conducted over the next six months and secured three days of *Guardian* coverage in July 2012, with another BBC *Newsnight* special to again coincide with the first day of publication. There was also a BBC verbatim drama shown in August 2012 that used interview material from phase one of the project. Both phases won 'Innovation of the Year' at the British Journalism awards. Newburn gave evidence to the main Parliamentary inquiry, the only source of non-official evidence, and to the 'Victims and Communities Panel', the government's only concession to the need to learn lessons. It is safe to say that the LSE/ *Guardian* effort created the definitive contemporary history account of the 2011 riots, and received far more coverage and endorsements than the official accounts, despite some media hiccups along the way. The researchers and journalists also saw off considerable attempts by Conservative MPs to malign the project's social science methods and the reliability of its evidence. As a direct response to the riots, and perhaps to the LSE/*Guardian* project, the Economic and Social Research Council have now instituted a new type of fund, the Urgency Grant Mechanism, which allows researchers to bid for resources to respond to fast-moving or unfolding situations.

Our second case is the 'Great British Class Survey' (GBCS), a joint venture set up and sponsored by the BBC but led by sociologists from LSE, Manchester University, City University and York University. Its aim was to map out a new class structure for British society, one that would work better than the conventional indices in use since the 1950s. It began in January 2011 with the largest web survey undertaken in Britain involving 161,000 volunteers recruited via a BBC TV programme compiling returns to a large-scale and detailed survey. At the same time because early analyses of the web survey showed it was highly skewed, the academic team persuaded the BBC to commission a smaller nationally representative survey, using quota sampling methods. The team analysed both sets of data and produced a final seven-class categorization and a simplified survey test for people to self-evaluate their class position. The analysis stressed the widening gap between elite groups and a 'precariat', where a fifth of the population subsist either on benefits or in low income work and with fragile means of surviving.

The results and new class schema were launched in spring 2013 in a co-ordinated way between the research team, the BBC and the British Sociological Association (BSA). Firstly on BBC Breakfast TV and then simultaneously released as a refereed journal article (Savage et al., 2013) and explained at the British Sociological Association conference. The publicity massively enhanced readership of the academic paper, with 20,000 downloads in April 2013 (easily the most ever achieved from the journal *Sociology*). The new class categories created a huge stir, far more than the BBC had anticipated and 200,000 people went online to complete the simplified Great British Class Survey afresh. Social media and journalistic coverage was extensive and 7 million people used the Class Calculator hosted on the BBC Labs website. This interest was not just in the UK but internationally, making the *New York Times*'s story on GBCS the most read international piece of 2013 to that date. The academic collaboration stimulated the archiving of the BBC web data in the UK Data Archive.

Both these projects succeeded in engaging very many members of the public and the attention of dozens of journalists and newspapers, securing massive coverage not only for the media companies that sponsored them, but from the media at large, including thousands of social media commentators. Each showed that dialogues with the public that are either topical or less time-sensitive but fundamental, could arouse huge levels of interest. Both worked on the principle that evidence, especially high quality and well-controlled information or 'big data', should trump intuitive or political characterizations of society and how it works. Both connected strongly to public values, the riots study attracting great support from the portion of UK public opinion that rejected the government's instant, snap, political judgements. Both studies aimed and succeeded in attracting the participation of large numbers of ordinary people, 'going deep' to grass roots sources in unprecedented and innovative ways and 'going broad', appealing widely beyond elite audiences. Neither of them was strictly a 'citizen social science' project analogous to, say, amateur astronomers helping professional researchers to classify star pictures. Yet both moved a long step towards the co-production of social science with mass publics, assisted by strong media organization involvements in both cases.

Conclusions

Writing in 1997, just as the internet, the web and digital changes were beginning to transform modern media systems out of all recognition, Fenton et al. concluded their survey of *Mediating Social Science* with a rather downbeat assessment:

> Essentially the role of social science tends to be a confirmatory and legitimatory one, tweaking at the edges of the referential structures of the news media, rather than helping to develop alternative visions and approaches ... Patterns of partiality and exclusion in media representation [of social science] are rooted in the pressures and residual value system of the mediators [journalists and editors], as well as in the abdication of social scientists. (1998: 168–69)

Their work continued a stream of analysis first inaugurated much earlier in studies of science journalism and the 'public understanding of science' literatures, which stressed the unavoidable role of non-expert journalists and editors as intermediaries with a gatekeeping power that could not be evaded. Social scientists had struck a quasi-Faustian (not too bad) bargain with the media, Fenton et al. argued. In return for journalists' unquestioning public deference to their professional expertise (especially on broadcast media), social scientists accepted the media, framing of issues, only fitting within established narratives and implicitly consenting to a non-coverage of issues around methodologies, uncertainty and intra-disciplinary disputes. As a result, an artificially simplified and largely unexplained image of what social scientists do was maintained, so that the chances of ordinary citizens understanding or engaging more effectively with what social science research does were constantly stunted.

There remains a good deal of truth in this traditional picture. But it now describes only a part of the overall media landscape. And via open access research publications, the internet, blogs, Twitter and social media, social scientists in universities and research labs are able to increasingly provide their own information for informing citizens directly. Elite universities at least, in the UK perhaps as much as or more than in America, are now in transition to becoming increasingly important and direct centres of expert news-like production, and extensive publishing and quasi-broadcasting of social science research. The future of massive open online courses (MOOCs) remains in play, especially on exactly how 'massive' they may turn out to be. But whether or not they succeed as their exponents hope, universities' existing 'broadcasting' roles via podcasts and videocasts seem certain to expand.

The less mediated, more direct communication that digital changes have already made possible may not in the end lead to academics and universities fully 'disintermediating' the roles of journalists and editors in major media, since they arguably add value in broadening audiences and may improve communication to lay audiences. Yet more media roles are likely to move within universities, as has already clearly been the case for science communication in STEM subjects. And social scientists' dependence on the media has clearly reduced. In blogs and social media, researchers already can and do discuss methods intelligently and have begun 'upgrading' the knowledge of 'lay' citizens outside academia in ways that journalists, editors and conventional media outlets have already had to respond to and even imitate. With public engagement in the UK increasingly recognized financially via the REF impacts process (especially in the humanities and social sciences), the incentives and resources for academics to improve the communication of social science have also grown strongly.

PART III

Patterns of Knowledge and Impacts

> To find out what happens to a system when you interfere with it you have to interfere with it (not just passively observe it).
>
> *George Box*[1]

> Do what you can where you are with what you have.
>
> *Theodore Roosevelt*[2]

Leading intellectuals shape our lives and civilization in profound ways, but when they talk or write about impacts they can often seem oddly pessimistic in their evaluations. 'Laughter rather than hostility is the natural reaction of the many to the philosopher's preoccupations and the apparent uselessness of his [or her] concerns', wrote Hannah Arendt (1978: 82). An explanation for this relates to the sheer complexity of societies, the multiplicity of actors, organizations, institutions, markets, interventions and causal factors at work simultaneously, and the difficulty of tracing out influences that are multi-causal, multi-level, multiply lagged and, as yet, little understood. Even if we could establish a linkage from academic work to a social effect, the likelihood is that it would not long endure in its original form, since human beings often react to new knowledge by changing their behaviours to 'aim off' for it. And since human society and not nature is the domain of the social sciences, these considerations weigh especially heavily here.

Yet we have shown in Part I that the patterning of social scientists' individual influence on the world outside higher education can be traced out using a range of methods, indices and tools. We cannot yet do this as well as we can map intra-academic influence processes, but still we can gain valuable insights. And since the study of social scientists' impacts is a brand new field we may realistically expect it to make advances in leaps and bounds over the next decade or so.

We also demonstrated in Part II that the social sciences have huge influence in government and public policy making, and a considerable role in the operations of civil society organizations and contemporary media and cultural systems. Even in business, where social science influence has been least well developed, the growth of a services economy in advanced industrial states, and the interpenetration of social, business and technological changes that mark the modern age, have made social science insights increasingly valuable. With the new data sources and methods surrounding 'big data' and the immediacy of digital information becoming available, there are grounds for optimism that a new methods revolution in social sciences is already under way.

Yet we need now to step back a little, and to refocus on some of the macro-themes with which we started this inquiry in Chapter 1. Seeing clearly through the fog to establish the overall societal role of social sciences research is a first task, tackled in Chapter 9. It begins by looking at how knowledge production contributes to societal development at the strategic level, and then scales the economic

---

[1]Box (1966: 629).
[2]Quoted in Mason (1996).

importance of UK social science in terms of the immediate professional audience closely involved in using and mediating social science research.

Chapter 10 then rounds out the book in slightly more speculative fashion, considering the ways in which the social sciences may or should change in response to digital transformations in many sectors of society and in research. Three areas of change are likely to prove critically important:

- moving the social sciences towards a rapid advance/lower dissensus mode of operating, while also fostering cross-disciplinary integration within the subject group on a broad-front;
- converging the human-centred disciplines far more, with a greatly expanded STEM to social science interface, especially in human-dominated disciplines; and
- progressively developing a more global (less national) social science.

This is a large agenda by any standards. And focusing on improving the external impacts of the social sciences may not fit wholly consistently with some parts of it. But as the Roosevelt epigraph above reminds us, the effort to secure applied change is generally a constructive impulse.

9

The dynamic knowledge inventory and research mediation

The theory of our modern technic shows that nothing is as practical as theory.
Robert Oppenheimer

If you suddenly need expertise you haven't got, the fastest solution and way of building internal capacity is reaching out and collaborating with someone who is doing it anyway. And that's what universities do. They do stuff that has no immediate interest out there, until suddenly it does.
Corporate executive in interview

In 2008 we were presenting a very early version of some ideas in this book to an advisory committee of a top UK learned society, amongst whose members were several leading business people. One aspect of our presentation argued that work in the social sciences and humanities contributed to a 'knowledge inventory'. This was enough to trigger an impassioned lecture from one member, a former corporate executive, on the undesirability of inventories as unsold goods, the stuff nobody wants, that sits in your warehouse for years going out of date while racking up costs. From his perspective, stock inventories should ideally be eliminated, and in all circumstances they must at least be minimized. In response we added the word 'dynamic' to our central concept, in order to underline in future that knowledge is not like physical goods. In many circumstances having more knowledge inventory than you are currently using (or think you need) can be a very good thing, especially for an advanced industrial society and a services economy.

Applied knowledge that is up to date and responds directly to contemporary issues and problems is highly desirable. But so too is an understanding of how to generate knowledge afresh; analyse new issues and problems on first principles; give an integrated, theoretical explanation of a problem or process; stay abreast of multiple detailed ways of doing something that are not currently being applied; and retain knowledge of what was previously attempted and failed, or what might be attempted but was never yet tried. Aiming only to make our knowledge fit immediate needs, with minimal wastage, no safety margins, and no imaginative or 'just in case' investment for potential future needs, will not work well, certainly not for long, not even for companies.

At a societal level achieving the right mix and balance to keep a knowledge inventory dynamic and responsive to current conditions and future needs is not straightforward. Especially in relation to the social sciences, with their 'collective knowledge' character and the strong interaction of published knowledge with the subjects and behaviours being analysed, citizens and elites often have a high degree of uncertainty about how to ascertain impacts. Social science always deals with an inherently multi-causal environment, and it is tricky to get anything like experimental conditions, even with randomized control trials. So governments and their agents fret about determining the efficacy of academic investments in better understanding social processes and problems. Reductive criteria tend to be deployed by even better-informed commentators, with journalists and politicians looking for STEM-like stories of discovery research and 'lone genius' breakthroughs that cannot be provided (and are anyway atypical even of physical sciences research).

We seek to set in place a better framework for judging the contemporary role of the social sciences by first fleshing out the concept of a dynamic knowledge inventory (or DKI) in more detail, showing how it works and develops, and the range of actors that contribute to its constant evolution. The second section of the chapter focuses on arguably the central dynamic in the DKI, the way that research knowledge is 'mediated' by university and societal actors, a process that in turn churns and feeds knowledge back into the DKI where it can once again be accessed, re-used and 'mashed' in new combinations. We examine synoptically the extent to which other sectors outside higher education itself employ staff specifically to translate or mediate social science research into their work and operations.

9.1 The dynamic knowledge inventory

> Basic research is what I am doing when I don't know what I am doing.
>
> *Werner Von Braun*[3]

> The trouble is that social scientists, whether they see themselves as contributors to the development of discipline-based theories, or as policy analysts committed to the alleviation of practical problems, are governed by a wrong-headed but robust notion: The stock of knowledge created by economics, political science, sociology, and other disciplines must be present before we can engage in effective social problem solving. On the contrary, reasons Lindblom: Social problem solving is not a process of applying knowledge so much as a process of probing what to do in the presence of ignorance.
>
> *William Dunn*[4]

One of the hallmarks of an advanced industrial society is the existence amongst its members of a large dynamic knowledge inventory that contains multiple possible

---

[3]Quoted in an interview in the *New York Times*, 16 December 1957.
[4]Dunn (1997:277).

solutions for myriads of actual or possible civilizational problems. Only a proportion of this knowledge is normally drawn down and used at any given time, but advanced industrial societies have a capacity to rapidly re-access (or develop afresh) many appropriate solutions, even for radically new, highly intermittent or rarely encountered problems. Academic work that influences other academics or external organizations forms part of this societal-wide stock of knowledge and expertise, and plays key roles in keeping it constantly developing, looking over the horizons of what is currently feasible or 'relevant' to other possibilities.

Universities (and their libraries, repositories and databases) are important guardians of the DKI. But they are far from being its sole contributors or custodians, and may not necessarily be even its most important ones. The philosopher Michael Oakeshott (1962: 194) once assigned the role of 'caring for and attending to the whole intellectual capital which composes a civilization' exclusively to universities. This was always deeply implausible and now it should be crystal clear that this core role is in fact widely shared. The DKI is constantly looked after, activated and recombined by many different institutions and actors – professions, companies, industrial laboratories, trade unions and 'guilds' of all kinds, government agencies and departments, consultancy and think tank organizations, civil society bodies, international institutions, individual writers, inventors and entrepreneurs, and so on. For instance, almost brand new organizations like Google or Wikipedia are probably more salient now in structuring and organizing the DKI than any individual university.

As we noted above, conventional thinking in the business world sees the concept of any kind of inventory – construed as 'unsold goods' or things unused, gathering dust on storage shelves – exclusively as a bad thing. Contemporary businesses have invested a lot of time, money and energy in minimizing their inventories, paring down stocks and bringing in 'just in time' delivery so as to transfer storage and inventory costs to other firms further up the supply chain. In this view a DKI may seem to be an 'odds and sods' store of both useful and bric-a-brac knowledge, some of it without conceivable applications, expensively produced initially (often at taxpayers' expense), and now kept going in ways that must equally be costing someone to store, curate and maintain.

Yet there are fundamental differences between the static inventories of physical goods that are fixed-in-form (once created) and the DKI. Multiple factors are at work that strongly *reduce* over time the costs of storing knowledge ready to deploy. Knowledge that is employed or applied is always routinized and simplified in use and over time. Partly this is because 'practice makes perfect' at an individual level, and experience counts, especially for the most esoteric or unformalized forms of tacit knowledge and skill, such as craftsmanship (Sennett, 2008). In intellectual life also, devoting a critical mass of time (perhaps 10,000 hours) to perfecting capabilities is associated with exceptional individuals achieving radical innovations or breakthroughs in perception of how to tackle problems (Gladwell, 2008).

The same processes, of re-simplifying the initially complex, or routinizing the initially *sui generis*, or converting an initially unique solution into a more generic one, is also implemented far more powerfully at the collective level, across groups, occupations, professions, industries and communities of interest. We discussed above (in Chapter 2) the importance of 'integration' forms of scholarship within academic disciplines. The initial work here involves isolated and hard-to-fathom discoveries being recognized as related, re-conceptualized and then synergized into more complete yet parsimonious theoretical explanations. At a more macro-level, many initially distinct-looking phenomena in the STEM disciplines may be recombined and re-understood through a new scientific 'paradigm' that unifies understanding of them in an intellectually coherent and logically consistent way (Kuhn, 1962). Later on, much of the detail of initial research advances becomes less relevant and is screened out by improved understandings and synthesized in progressively more formalized expressions. 'Every science must start with metaphor and end with algebra', claimed Max Black (1962: 249). The final stage of integration scholarship is that new ideas or discoveries are filtered through many layers of the research literature and into authoritative core textbooks and the professional practices and teaching of academic disciplines. Through all these stages, and in all these ways, knowledge often becomes 'easier' to understand over time, *less* costly to curate, store and maintain, as the fragmentary or disorganized discovery knowledge moves further and further behind the research frontier and is re-processed and re-understood.

In the social sciences the full concept of a scientific paradigm is rarely applicable. Although the term has been widely bandied about, it is important to note that Kuhn (1962) stressed that science paradigms are exceptional, because they are far more rigorously evidence-based, must meet very strong criteria for credibility, and only one can be dominant in a discipline (or conventionally accepted) at a given time. These conditions do not apply in most social sciences, nor across all the humanities. Here the criteria for preferring one interpretation over another are more disputed, less clear cut, and the operational sifting of results is less comprehensive, less logic-based and less rigorously empirical. At best the social science disciplines have 'quasi-paradigms', with only certain limited resemblances to the full Kuhnian scientific paradigm:

1   Quasi-paradigms have two intellectual levels, the first being an overall macro-theory that orientates, justifies and pulls together a wide range of contributions at a second, more detailed level: 'Kuhn was often careful to say that a paradigm involves not only theoretical ideas but a swarm of other implicit and explicit notions and practices, all of which contribute to the application of these ideas to nature' (Buchanan, 2000: 233–34); and

2   Quasi-paradigms too are marked by rapid transitions from one dominant macro-theory to its successor, when a substantial accumulation of problems occurs with the previous view. However, the motor of change here is often only a marked shift in theoretical or philosophical plausibility rather than a logical refutation or decisive empirical discrediting that marks real Kuhnian paradigm transitions. Unsurprisingly the transitions from one conventional paradigm to another in social science are less complete and always more contested than in STEM sciences. For philosophy, Collins (2001) argues that a 'law of small numbers' operates limiting the number of salient positions extant at any time to a minimum of two (because you cannot debate with yourself) and six (the practical maximum 'carrying capacity' of intellectual debate).

In the qualitative social sciences, in earlier periods, many individual-level propositions were influential for customary, purely rhetorical or 'political' reasons only (Hood and Jackson, 1991). However, in our view, macro-level quasi-paradigms have now largely replaced earlier propositional-level arguments as key vehicles of social science thought. Some causal influences here have been the growth of evidence-based social science, faster and wider comparative market-learning and policy-learning, the development of 'best practice research', and the growth of think tanks and other NGO and charitable organizations at the interface between academia and public policy. These developments have boosted and speeded up the institutional processes for sifting, piloting, 'pivoting' and selecting what works in social science, albeit in a rough way still. These changes especially focus on shifts of quasi-paradigms in response to empirical crises or acute theory problems accumulating with existing approaches, or new social problems emerging in unanticipated ways.

Once knowledge is produced, via science, scholarship or technological application, we typically embody it in multiple cultural artefacts that function to make far easier the next round of knowledge acquisition and re-use. At root we embody knowledge in new languages and concepts, new intellectual equipment that redeploys old knowledge or the development of many new knowledge products (such as dictionaries, encyclopaedias, textbooks, review articles and journals, databases and online networks) that make information accessing more comprehensive, quicker and better-validated. Equally knowledge is embodied in physical tools and equipment, from laboratory equipment, through machine tools and process manufacture capabilities, through to statistical and data representations and first analogue and now digitized information storage and retrieval tools and machines.

The modern period is of critical significance in this respect because of the divergence between what Anderson (2009) terms:

- the 'world of atoms', where storage and retrieval are still expensive, inventories must be limited or minimized, and because everything costs, so everything has a price; and
- the 'world of bits', where storage and retrieval are effectively free in marginal cost terms (although substantial still when aggregated at scale), so adding new users of existing knowledge or information goods cost nothing, and information and inventories can expand (almost) without limit. Hence companies like Google can build a business on 'a radical price', offering many services for free.

Digitization has already transformed private sector commerce and business, and has made feasible the 'long tail' in retailing, perhaps most notably for books (Anderson, 2006). The digitization of the DKI is the most important post–1945 step in human culture and development. And despite multiple premature sceptical voices, its implications have only just begun to track through academia, university research and cultural processes, and the ways that they influence wider society.

It may help to summarize some of these themes diagrammatically, as in Figure 9.1. The top picture (a) shows the dynamic knowledge inventory as a flat-topped iceberg shape, but one marked internally by a relatively long frontier between

Figure 9.1   The dynamic knowledge inventory

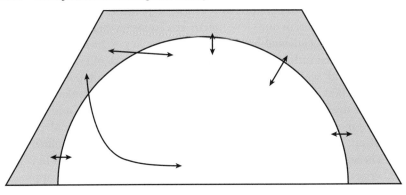

(a) Varied pathways by which knowledge comes into or falls out of use

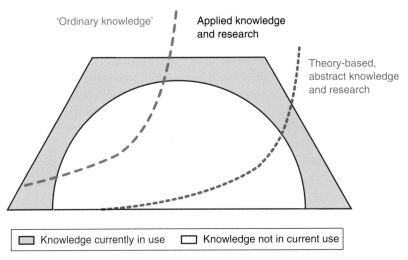

(b) The roles of 'ordinary knowledge', applied professional knowledge and theory-based knowledge in the DKI

knowledge in current use and not in use (or possibly latent) knowledge. Most transfers into or out of use take place at the margins of the two areas, and perhaps in directions that are varied but predictable if you know where you are on this boundary. But some connections bringing ideas and knowledge into use are longer and less predictable. Note too the relatively fragile nature of knowledge-in-use, which rests everywhere upon the stock of currently unused knowledge. Take away this support by allowing gaps or lacunae to accumulate in the base and the upper layers of knowledge in use may fracture and change in unpredictable ways – much as the collapses of parts of icebergs often shift their centre of gravity, producing dramatic changes in their orientation and appearance.

Figure 9.1b additionally shows that the DKI includes a great deal of 'ordinary knowledge' (perhaps with a relatively high current utilization rate); as well as applied knowledge and research (perhaps in the middle on utilization rates); and theory-based knowledge (where the current utilization rate might be relatively lower). These are admittedly only rudimentary propositions, and in practice of course there are likely to be many involutions and inter-wrappings of these different types of knowledge. Certainly, a large research agenda remains to be addressed in this area.

How does the DKI involving social science function? In some ways it is almost easier to answer the inverse question. The DKI does not operate here in the simplistic ways that most governments and hierarchs within the university sector believe it works, or should work, or could work. In the first place, there is no simple or direct relationship between any organization adding to the DKI and economic, industrial, societal or even more widespread intellectual changes. Our interviewees from all sectors, as well as from academia, stressed to us the complexity of the processes in their experience, as these three quotes (from a corporate executive and two professors) testify:

> I think [the models of impact for social and natural sciences] are qualitatively different because the output from social sciences is conceptual, whereas so much of engineering and science is directly tangible – it's a thing or a body of data. Social science can create bodies of data too, but where it is policy advice or understanding it is much, much harder to quantify. If I build a left-handed widget and some company licences the technology and sells two billion dollars' worth, that's a very, very easy number for someone to crunch when doing an impact statement. If I say I've done a piece of work that changes someone's view about how computing is taught in schools, I would have to wait twenty years before I could tell you whether it was a good thing or bad thing.

> Because we're not an engineering school, we don't turn out widgets. That 'tech transfer' model of commercialisation is something we can't do. And actually we've realised it's not for us, not possible because of our subject area.

> I wish it was that direct ... Create innovation. Disseminate. And then impact. But because it's more ad-hoc and [about] opportunities, the best we can do is to have those relationships in place with external stakeholders – banks paying for expertise, government bodies, professional bodies – to engage with what you are creating.

In addition, academics are famously diffident, or alternatively punctilious, about claiming impacts, as we noted in all the Part II chapters. Indeed, as two more interview quotes make clear, they often set themselves high (almost disabling) criteria for recognizing impact:

> What I've been mainly talking to you about is dissemination. Impact is: "Does anybody do anything different in relation to contact with [client group Y]?" I think that is a much, much harder question to answer. There are times when I feel like I have wasted 16 years.

> My personal links are very extensive. But is it actual impact? It is very difficult to say that I have changed policy in this place and that place. I can't say. And it would be very arrogant to do so. And anyway, I wouldn't give it much credence. Just because you've asked somebody to say so?

In the second place, the DKI sums complex processes by which professions, institutions and knowledge-communities accumulate, store, re-package, and re-deliver knowledge, often over long time periods. Many worthwhile innovations or discoveries made by academics, corporate or state scientists, or professionals get institutionally marginalized or forgotten, either for long periods or sometimes all but completely (Douglas, 1986). Many concepts and experiments, tests or implementations get ignored at first, but re-emerge later (Gillies, 2008). Much knowledge is extended or finds application in unexpected ways, or metamorphoses from 'pure research' to applied knowledge in unpredicted conjunctures, or is uninfluential in its original, isolated form yet suddenly becomes important and contributory when 'mashed' with other contributions or in specific conjunctures. Meanwhile what does get quickly picked up may not last long, or may prove to be a dead end trajectory.

As we have seen, the knowledge flowing into the DKI is not only of the instrumental 'impactful' kind, where those creating it had its function and use accurately in mind at the start of the process. All types of knowledge exist within the DKI – basic, applied, tacit, explicit, experiential – it is this very variability that allows the wider social science community, both within and outside universities, to utilise and operationalize aspects of it for their own ends. And it is the collective and constantly changing nature of social science research that assessment exercises such as the REF process so signally fail to grip.

There are significant differences amongst theorists and sociologists of science about the speed and efficacy of the scientific consensus process. We noted earlier Randall Collins' (1994) characterization of STEM science as 'high consensus, rapid advance' disciplines where most academic prestige focuses on making new discoveries, and few scientists want to pull up the roots of current knowledge in order to query fundamentals – by contrast with the social sciences. Yet this interpretation is by no means generally accepted. For instance, in their discussion of tacit and explicit knowledge Harry Collins and Robert Evans (2008) formulate two propositions (amongst others) about the amount of tightly focused scientific disagreement at the research forefront concerning applicable knowledge:

> *The fifty year rule*: Scientific disputes take a long time to reach consensus and thus there is not much scientific consensus about.
>
> *The velocity rule*: Because of the fifty year rule, the speed of political decision-making is usually faster than the speed of scientific consensus formation, and thus science can play only a limited part in technological decision-making in the public domain.

However we characterize STEM disciplines, the social sciences clearly remain considerably less consensual.

Third, as all of Part II demonstrates, the DKI is a collective process, operating at least at three levels – the intra-organizational level, the level of an individual society, and the wider international-or-global level. It is not something easily owned or controlled by any actor or coherent set of actors. Indeed, there is often competition. For example, companies make efforts to restrict knowledge outflows, as some executives explained:

There is a value in trying to bring existing knowledge and research together. But there are also barriers, in terms of the competitive environment. And the question 'Why should we?' If we have found something that works, why would we tell anyone else?

Yet even here the DKI can only be partially dammed, and usually for quite a short period – enough to give comparative advantage, but not for long, unless the initial innovative edge is continuously supplemented, enlarged and built upon. Perhaps in all disciplines, just especially noticeably in the social sciences, the accumulation of professional, scientific or scholarly knowledge is necessarily inter-personal and normally inter-organizational. As one professor observed:

The thing is that it is a pathway to impact. It's not a one-off impact. You do something, somebody else picks it. So you can't say that it is a direct impact, but an indirect impact, yes.

Key elements of the core DKI processes most relevant to social science and wider academic research work include:

1   Direct influences from specific university researchers on an individual societal organization (a firm, a government body, a profession, a social movement or a civil society organization). These are one-to-one linkages, limited to only some (maybe relatively few) organizations.
2   The cumulative but diffuse impact of academic research distributed across a complete set of organizations (an industry, a tier of government, a professional sector). These are collective-to-many linkages, spreading more widely.
3   The influence of an academic profession on a whole 'community of practice', with effects condensed in industrial, professional or social movement organizations and networks; their events and socialization processes (such as conferences, seminars, meetings); specialized professional media; and now social media. These are many-to-many linkages.
4   The mediated influences of academic work operating within the community of practice itself, operating at two levels:

    o   collectively mediated via the community's 'condensing' institutions defining 'good practice' with some academic-influenced component, at a national or general level; and
    o   individual mediation via professional staff members working in non-academic organizations within the community of practice, whose work wholly or partly involves 'translating' and applying research in organizationally relevant ways, meshing with the specific logic of operating for their firm, agency or civil society body.

Drawing on a long tradition of work on firms (but also some other types of bodies) we can envisage the DKI as operating somewhat like a large-scale and networked (inter-institutional) version of the knowledge development process within individual organizations. Ikujiro Nonaka et al. provocatively claim that 'The *raison d'etre* of a firm is to continuously create knowledge' (2000: 6). They go on to outline a vision of collective cognitive evolution in firms, where 'the organisation is not merely an information processing machine, but an entity that creates knowledge through action and interaction'. A first key dimension concerns transforming or perpetuating tacit and explicit knowledge. *Externalization* involves actors taking steps to condense out and formalize tacit knowledge held by organization members into explicit knowledge that can be embodied in durable and transmittable artefacts (e.g., organization structures, handbooks, IT systems). Also important is the inter-personal transmission of tacit knowledge from one person or group to another, and over time within 'the same' groups or units, typically via *socialization*, induction and other norm-defining and group-building processes. *Internalization* involves organization members converting explicit knowledge into individual values, mental models and habitual behaviours. Explicit knowledge too has to be renewed, reactivated and perpetuated, with corrective actions against institutional forgetting, and new *combinations* of ideas and knowledge linkages sustaining organizational learning.

Second, firms develop 'knowledge assets', resources that are distinctive and key for creating values (Nonaka et al., 2000; Nonaka and Takeuchi, 1995). These include tacit and experiential knowledge, and related phenomena like trust, loyalty; conceptual knowledge embodied in symbols, brands and common language; routines, standard operating procedures, and methods for acting; and systematic capacities for analysing problems and identifying opportunities or potential advances. The circulation, connection and deployment of knowledge assets are not easily accomplished, especially within hierarchical organizations.

In particular, Nonaka et al. espouse a dialectical 'vision' in which degrees of tension or contradiction are integral to creating a progressive (upward) spiral of knowledge growth. Against the hierarchist and 'leaderist' tendencies of conventional organizational and managerialist thought, they stress five elements vital for achieving rapid advances:

- *Autonomy* is key if work teams are to define, grip and re-understand their own work tasks.
- *'Creative chaos'* involves disruptions deliberately introduced by leaders, not to disorder the organization, but to create a (manageable) degree of pressure for change and advance.
- *Redundancy* is 'the intentional overlapping of information about business activities, management responsibilities and the company as a whole' (Nonaka et al., 2000: 27). Redundancy or duplication of information is important for growing tacit knowledge, and in allowing organization members to orientate themselves individually towards key tasks and missions.
- *Requisite variety* is needed internally, to allow organizations to adapt to environmental pressures, but in a constrained way so as to also maintain organizational integration. Internal information processes that are fast and (relatively) equally accessible by organization members sustain more complex structures.

- *High trust* within an organization is normally key to individuals having the confidence to offer up information, rather than being locked into defensive stances where they hold back knowledge as a private resource to secure their position or protect their existing role (and see Miller, 1992).

These elements fit well with the processes we have explored in earlier chapters. At a societal level the DKI operates in a far less controlled (or controllable) way than any single organization. It has looser internal networking and cross-connections. But the 'small world' literature shows that this need not prevent powerful linkage processes from arising. With many small-scale local links in place, often only a few and random long-scale linkages are needed in order to evenly distribute information across large populations (Watts, 1999). A degree of chaos is built into the DKI, since it is not centrally controllable. Yet with no real capacity for central leadership, lapses into either unproductive disorder or stagnation are always feasible. Governments and business elites may exert some influence in edging disordered processes more towards potentially creative zones.

The operations of the DKI at a societal level seem likely to have strong dialectical characteristics. Nonaka et al. (2000: 6) suggest that within firms, important lines of (partial) contradiction are likely to be between action and cognition; body and mind; emotion and logic; tacit and explicit knowledge (Collins, 2010); micro and macro processes; and chaos and order. It seems plausible that turbulence structured around similar polarities will also feature in inter-organizational networks, within policy communities and communities of practice, and between universities and other knowledge-producing and knowledge-using sectors, and we have charted some closely related aspects in Part II.

In advanced industrial societies, a hidden iceberg mass of knowledge (of what might have been, or could yet be) stabilizes and supports the far smaller field of knowledge-in-implementation. In many ways universities (and their associated libraries, databases and research centres) have become key custodians of this hidden mass – so here 'universities' means all the component parts of the 'traditional academic' block in Figure 2.14 (page 56), and large parts of the remainder as well. Yet information and knowledge barriers are also strong in networks, and only sections of the knowledge landscape where academic, professional and industrial logics most overlap fit Nonaka's sense of 'redundancy' – that is, the deliberate 'over-provision' of information to all actors in the network. These areas co-exist with others where knowledge is confined within one sector, and areas where existing knowledge is weakly developed in all sectors – with universities and other knowledge institutions failing to study that which has no immediate practical take-up. Sector autonomy in the DKI is typically strong, with each specialist sector tending to develop in 'autopoetic' fashion, obeying its own logic of development and differentiation, and so only opening up to other university research or other sectors at the margin. Finally, trust within DKI networks is often low and knowledge-pooling consequently restricted (Luhman, 1982; Bachmann and Zaheer, 2008). The lengthy delays in academics accessing 'big data' stores held by governments or companies, or the decades-long locking of academic knowledge away behind journal paywalls, both testify to this effect. But as we have seen in Chapter 8, university researchers still maintain positions that are more trusted than other actors.

One key end product of the DKI is a form of societal learning that Flyvberg (2012: 4) terms 'phronesis', which is

> a resource – a stock of experiential knowledge. As a quality of persons, it is what enables acquisition and appropriate use of that knowledge – a capacity. And as action, phronesis involves doing something – a practice in which experiential knowledge is both used and gained.

Yet the DKI encompasses much more than just this, ranging from 'pure' academic knowledge (without application and pursued for curiosity or aesthetic reasons) through to weakly based 'ordinary knowledge' or common sense. It seems likely that many forms of knowledge are important for societal guidance, and that the neglect of any form can potentially have deleterious consequences. For instance, Scott (1998) makes an important case that social reformers' ignoring 'métis', or detailed practical-knowledge-in-use, has been a key reason for 'seeing like a state' problems and policy fiascos. Radical attempts to reshape social or economic practices have often failed through taking an inherently top-down and too coarse-grained view of social practices. (In a similar vein, Hayek (1988: 76) once remarked that: 'The curious task of economics is to demonstrate to men [or women] how little they really know about what they imagine they can design'.) Lindblom and Cohen (1979) argue that 'ordinary knowledge' (much of which can be well-founded and good quality) will necessarily remain the indispensable organizing frame within which must sit all the insights and information that 'professional social inquiry' can produce.

At any point in time, much of the value of the DKI must be latent. Estimating what a well-functioning DKI brings to a society is exceptionally tricky. The differences are visible enough to anyone contemplating the key factors that separate advanced industrial states from those that are still developing and industrializing – in terms of social capital, educational and professional competences, industrial or governance capacities for getting things done well and speedily. Yet valuation of things not necessarily directly used, nor clearly paid for, remains very difficult. Some useful analytic techniques have been developed in environmental economics for imputing values to things not paid for, or assigning values to the continued existence of things even when they are not currently being directly used – for instance, the value of wilderness areas that are visited by few people. These techniques could potentially be extended to other areas, such as valuing cultural institutions (O'Brien, 2010), or valuing university education and research efforts, or the overall efficacy of DKI operations.

To the extent that professionals working to translate, break down or mediate academic work also form part of the social science research community, they make up an immediate audience participating in different ways and levels in the definition of professional good practice and the collective use of research. And so in the next section we attempt to provide a partial value for the DKI in terms of the scale of the sector that utilises, refreshes and mediates the social science knowledge contained within it.

9.2 The mediation of social science research

What seems to happen is that generalizations and ideas from numbers of studies come into currency indirectly – through articles in academic journals and journals of opinion, stories in the media, the advice of consultants, lobbying by special interests, conversation of colleagues, attendance at conferences or training programmes, and other un-catalogued sources. Ideas from research are picked up in diverse ways and percolate through to office-holders in many offices who deal with the issues.

Carol Weiss[5]

I think it's taken some time to shake off that linear technology transfer conceptualisation of impact, of getting innovations to market. It's far more nebulous than that.

Business school professor in interview

The value of accurate and well-based knowledge can sometimes be many times what was paid to produce it, as two recent UK public policy examples illustrate in different ways. The first concerns the sale of radio spectrum for 3G phones undertaken by the government in 2000 (LSE Public Policy Group, 2008: 19). A sale using a conventional auction with one-off sealed bids was estimated by City of London banks as likely to generate revenues of £4.5 billion. Instead the Treasury chose to undertake the sale using an 'open auction' process with no limits on the number of bid rounds, so that each firm bidding knew what all its competitors had bid and could adjust its next bid to ensure that it gained one of the four available spectrum slots. The theory for such a bid process had been developed by a UCL economist and game theorist, Ken Binmore, over many years, and subsequently simplified and made more applicable by an Oxford economist, Paul Klemperer. This was the first time this kind of open auction process had been employed, and it eventually generated bids worth over £22 billion for the government. In the regular 'arms race' of ideas and strategists between the government and the phone companies, the innovative approach at first won a huge bonus for taxpayers. Subsequently other national governments followed the same path, but the returns gained slimmed very fast, partly because industry players better understood the game and so improved their strategies; and partly because of contextual changes in the business environment, especially the 2002 fading of the original dot.com boom in technology stocks.

Our second example concerns negotiations between another UK government department, for Transport, and a range of bidders for the franchise to run the West Coast train line. In autumn 2011 (after an eight month delay over uncertain policy goals) the department issued a very complex contract document. Several major companies bid for the franchise, and the Department awarded it to one bidder, taking it away from its incumbent, Virgin Trains. Virgin first complained publicly that the bid process was flawed, and then launched a legal challenge to it. The Department initially intended to defend its processes, but subsequent investigation by civil servants revealed that an economically and statistically flawed method had been used to assess

---

[5]Weiss (1982: 290).

the bids by the small official team responsible. The contract process had to be scrapped in October 2012, and the bidders all reimbursed their tendering costs. The franchise was temporarily re-awarded to the incumbents Virgin for two more years while a new franchising procurement operation was mounted all over again (Public Accounts Committee, 2013). NAO estimates the costs to taxpayers were at least £50 million.

Both examples show that using the best available social science methods can be intensely valuable to government, firms and other organizations. In the 3G phones case the government gained a huge receipts bonus, but the companies may have suffered economic damage through over-bidding in the innovative decision process. In the West Coast train line case the government suffered a comparatively large loss from the malfunctioning of a small block of work, involving the statistical methods used by a handful of officials. In both cases the sums involved dwarfed the amounts being paid by the government and companies to the staff members, consultants and advisors involved in the decisions. Of course, most routine implementations of social science knowledge will involve smaller stakes. But the important point is that the social value of accessing and correctly applying expertise can be far greater than the costs involved.

Research applications to concrete situations such as these typically require the 'translation' or the intervention of experienced, research-trained staff. These qualified personnel – perhaps civil servants, consultants, or other well-qualified practitioners – can read research, statistics and updates generated in the research community. They then:

- break down, specify and re-present the information involved using expert judgement, so as to pick out its salient features;
- simplify key aspects and select those more immediately relevant for their employing organization;
- combine the external research within internally generated data and knowledge; and then
- motivate decision-makers in their organization to take account of the trends and changes involved.

We have seen in Part II how all sorts of different users of research have done this processing and repackaging work in one way or another. Thus, qualified in-house staffs 'mediate' between the constantly evolving body of social science research and the rest of the people in their organization. Their synthesizing intervention is key to the successful incorporation and application of the knowledge involved. Directly contracted research from consultants or academics is more likely to be tailored to the needs of the user organization than is general university research. So it contributes more directly to public policy and business performance. But even here the research typically has to be commissioned and managed by an in-house specialist, or entrusted to another consultancy with the required expertise. Of course this way of working is not confined to social science, and accounts for a large proportion also of the social value of the STEM sciences.

To address questions about the wider value of social science research we commissioned Cambridge Econometrics to undertake an economic analysis. One part of this work involved estimating the economic value of UK university social science departments, and we have already presented these results in Chapter 1. The second part of this work is more directly relevant here for thinking about the wide-ranging value of social science research, seen in terms of the value derived by a wide range of societal organizations – firms, government, and charities – from accessing and mediating social science knowledge. In short, what is social science research worth in economic terms to the country? As a proxy for assessing economic value, Cambridge Econometrics made the assumption that the value of research outputs to external organizations can be seen as equivalent to the money spent by these organizations either in employing staff who play a role (not necessarily a full-time role) in mediating social science research, or in purchasing commissioned research directly.

In the rest of this chapter we work through the Cambridge Econometrics analysis step-by-step, and show how we are able to get to a preliminary estimate on the economic value of the social sciences to the UK economy.[6] We begin by looking at the UK workforce and estimate the level of underlying social science experience by examining university-level qualifications held. In 2011, the most recent year for which Labour Force Survey data was available, 1.7 million workers (6.4 per cent of the total) across the economy as a whole had a degree in a social science subject (narrowly construed), a third of which were postgraduate degrees. As a means of narrowing down the workforce into roles or categories of people that would most likely use or mediate social science research, we fixed upon a particular professional or associate professional cadre made up of the following:

- all staff with a social science degree or postgraduate degree working in higher-level occupations whose job title includes the word 'professional'; and
- some staff in the category of 'associate professional', which denotes less advanced or more semi-professional work. We only include here people who also have a postgraduate social science degree.

These six groups are marked with an asterisk and written in bold in Figure 9.2. Teaching and research professionals were excluded from the analysis since these staff mainly focus on adding to the human and knowledge capital stock inside higher education (or the schools system), rather than on translating or mediating research to final users in other sectors.

Having narrowed down the analysis to the six roles outlined in Figure 9.2, the next step is to look at the industry sectors in which the UK workforce is employed.

---

[6]It is important to mention at this point that the definition of the social sciences used by Cambridge Econometrics is not exactly the same as our own definition used in Chapter 1, but instead more restricted because of data limitations. Only rather limited information on educational backgrounds is available in the main disaggregated UK employment datasets used here, meaning that we cannot distinguish the overlap area inside cross-over social science and other disciplines. Hence the Cambridge Econometrics 'social sciences' category is largely confined to the core, wholly social science disciplines. (The one exception is psychology, which is included here as a social science. It can be appropriately thought of as almost wholly a social science discipline when being used in the economy outside the university sector.)

Figure 9.2   UK workers aged 16–64 by occupation and degree subject and level, 2011

In thousands	Social sciences		Other subjects		No degree
	Postgraduate degree	Degree	Postgraduate degree	Degree	
Business and public service professionals*	**105.5**	**202.1**	**188.3**	**609.6**	**305.0**
Corporate managers	101.6	183.1	118.0	567.2	874.8
Teaching and research professionals	95.5	58.1	582.6	523.4	95.7
Business and public service associate professionals*	**79.0**	**217.5**	**103.9**	**597.5**	**903.1**
Administrative occupations	29.1	139.4	46.2	462.4	1639.5
Science and technology professionals*	**26.2**	**49.6**	**262.5**	**672.7**	**360.2**
Managers/proprietors in services/agriculture	19.8	47.9	33.9	205.7	499.2
Health professionals*	**15.3**	**23.0**	**203.7**	**798.3**	**87.0**
Sales occupations	11.1	32.7	15.5	228.7	1409.0
Health and social welfare associate professionals	**10.3**	**29.0**	**23.0**	**157.9**	**183.9**
Elementary administration and service occupations	6.4	26.6	15.0	250.5	2216.0
Secretarial and related occupations	5.4	21.9	8.8	108.8	537.7
Culture, media and sports occupations	5.2	17.3	62.4	244.3	211.7
Caring personal service occupations	4.8	39.4	23.1	403.2	1425.9
Customer service occupations	4.3	28.8	8.1	96.0	373.1
Protective service occupations	4.3	23.1	5.9	89.4	242.9
Science and technology associate professionals*	**3.5**	**12.5**	**33.5**	**187.0**	**259.8**
Skilled agricultural trades	2.5	2.1	6.5	45.3	230.5
Textiles, printing and other skilled trades	2.0	7.4	6.8	68.3	489.3
Leisure and other personal service occupations	1.5	10.4	4.7	82.6	469.4
Skilled construction and building trades	1.5	5.5	2.9	80.7	912.3
Skilled metal and electronic trades	0.4	3.2	11.5	145.3	912.7
Process, plant and machines operatives	0.5	4.1	3.2	58.2	668.5
Elementary trades, plant and storage related	0.5	2.1	1.6	36.8	419.1
Not applicable/no answer	0.3	1.3	1.8	10.8	76.7
Transport and mobile machine drivers/operatives	0.0	6.3	5.8	73.7	901.9
Total	536.4	1194.2	1779.2	6804.2	16704.8

Source: Cambridge Econometrics (2014), Table 11, p 19. Data from Labour Force Survey 2011.

Note: Shaded cells indicate over-representation of the qualification (column) for the given occupation (row) compared with the average across all occupations (the shares of each qualification in the 'Total' row).

Figure 9.3   UK workers aged 16–64 by industry and degree subject and level, 2011

Cell entries are in thousands of staff (000s)	Social sciences		Other subjects		
	Postgraduate degree	Degree	Postgraduate degree	Degree	No degree
Public administration, education and health*	252.6	389.5	1042.4	2746.8	3748.8
Banking and finance*	131.7	363.2	300.4	1254.6	2286.3
Transport and communication	35.1	103.0	117.0	600.4	1468.9
Distribution, hotels and restaurants	33.0	136.6	81.2	755.0	4048.0
Other services (including consultancy)*	32.4	74.6	76.2	346.2	968.8
Manufacturing	27.0	66.9	84.5	579.0	1896.2
Construction	14.6	33.6	37.2	330.7	1615.1
Energy and water	6.4	17.0	27.6	113.7	319.4
Not applicable/no answer	1.9	5.7	7.4	31.8	124.0
Agriculture, forestry and fishing	1.8	4.1	5.1	45.9	229.3
Total	536.4	1194.2	1779.2	6804.2	16704.8

Source: Cambridge Econometrics (2014), Table 13, p 21. Data from Labour Force Survey 2011.

Note: As Figure 9.2.

Again, this is based on 2011 Labour Force Survey data. Figure 9.3 breaks down the same labour force by type of industry and whether they have a social science or non-social science degree. We find here that public sector administration, health and education account for just under half of those with postgraduate social science degrees. This is followed by banking and finance, and then a long way behind by other service industries. Interestingly there is not a great mismatch with other degrees here, and relatively few STEM postgraduates work in manufacturing compared with say public services.

Again, we are interested in narrowing down the workforce to focus on particular sectors that are most likely to use or mediate social science research. Three sectors in particular that make heavy use of social science expertise and knowledge are:

- Public administration, education and health;
- Banking and finance;
- Other services (including consultancy).

Figure 9.4   Occupations and sectors identified as engaged in translating or mediating social science research

Cell entries are in thousands of staff (000s)	Occupational group	Social science post-graduate degree	Social science degree	Total
Banking and finance	Business and public service professionals	41.9	83.4	125.3
	Business and public service associate professionals	32.3		32.3
	Science and technology professionals	6.4	10.8	17.2
	Science and technology associate professionals	0.7		0.7
	Health and social welfare associate professionals	0.5		0.5
	Health professionals	0.0	0.7	0.7
	Total	*81.8*	*94.8*	*176.6*
Public administration, health, education	Business and public service professionals	33.0	55.4	88.3
	Business and public service associate professionals	21.7		21.7
	Health professionals	14.2	22.3	36.6
	Science and technology professionals	8.4	8.3	16.7
	Health and social welfare associate professionals	3.8		3.8
	Science and technology associate professionals	1.6		1.6
	Total	*82.7*	*86.0*	*168.7*
Other services	Business and public service professionals	10.6	20.8	31.4
	Business and public service associate professionals	4.9		4.9
	Science and technology professionals	0.5	1.4	1.9
	Total	*15.9*	*22.3*	*38.2*
Overall total				**383.5**

Source: Cambridge Econometrics (2014), analysis of Labour Force Survey data 2011.

Of course, other sectors will also have analysts that carry out important social science mediation roles. In fact these roles will also be undertaken by social science-educated professionals in all the other sectors here (for instance, in the retail sector, energy or construction). But we cannot easily identify the personnel involved from the Labour Force Survey data. Finally, it is important to recognize that the Labour Force Survey data do not take us very far in analysing the roles of substantial numbers of people working in the charities and NGO sector. Again we know that here people in professional roles and with social science degrees or postgraduate qualifications undertake translation/mediation roles in relation to large-scale 'evidence in practice' knowledge stores that exist in this sector (Ravenscroft, 2013). Some staff may be included in the government/health/education category used here, but many others are not. So narrowing down to the three key sectors above gives us only a minimal or conservative estimate of the human resources involved in mediating social science research.

The next step therefore is to combine both 'cuts' of the Labour Force Survey data into one integrated picture that gives an impression of total human resources involved in social science mediation. Figure 9.4 does this for the 380,000 staff who meet the criteria set out above. For each of the three sectors, we are able to get a breakdown of the six different types of professional or associate professional staff, and attach some overall figures to each of the sub-types. The much higher concentration of post-graduate qualified staff compared to graduate-only staff in these sectors is noticeable. For those with social science backgrounds in the banking and finance sector, for example, there are almost as many postgraduates (81,800) as degree-only staff (94,800). The pattern is replicated in the field of public administration (82,700 postgraduates to 86,000 degree-only staff).

The next step of the analysis computes the likely costs of these mediation activities by these 380,000 or so professionals. The key proxy here is the salary level of staff members with social science degrees. We obtained 2011 wage data at a disaggregated level, and then multiplied these numbers by the size of the labour force involved to generate an estimated wage bill. Figure 9.5 shows the results. The largest estimated wage bill was for banking and finance, closely followed by government and the public sector services, and then after a large gap by the much smaller 'other services' sector (including consultancy).

Cambridge Econometrics also refined their consultancy sector estimate from retail sales data, suggesting that large firms typically do many other direct production and services tasks, and relatively little mediation/translation work (perhaps as low as 5 per cent). By contrast, the smaller organizations in the consulting industry are far more focused on mediation (which perhaps accounts for as much as 75 per cent of their work). Around half of the consultancy work undertaken is for government sector services, and the remainder is chiefly for private sector industries where firms do not have the large in-house social science staffs found in banking and finance.

Overall, the Cambridge Econometrics estimate is that in 2011 around £14.2 billion a year was being spent by leading UK employment sectors outside higher education on hiring staff whose work is likely to centre on translating or mediating social science research to their organizations. This spending is especially concentrated in banks and other financial institutions on the one hand, and in the large government sector services on the other. This total spend was more than four times the scale of the wage bill associated with the social sciences in higher education itself in 2011. In addition, for both the banking and finance sector and for the government sector in-house staffs, looking at the wage bill needs to be supplemented by reference to 'on-costs' – the other costs of hiring, such as national insurance tax, property costs, IT

Figure 9.5   The wages and wage bills for occupations and sectors identified as engaged in translating or mediating social science research

Sector	Occupational group	Average annual wage for staff member with social science degree (in £000s)	Estimated wage bill (full-time and part-time) in £m
Banking and finance	Business and public service professionals	52	5,053
	Business and public service associate professionals	44	1,203
	Science and technology professionals	49	685
	Science and technology associate professionals	36	28
	Health and social welfare associate professionals	35	0
	Health professionals	53	22
	Total	*47*	*6,991*
Public administration, health, education	Business and public service professionals	37	3,419
	Health professionals	32	1,118
	Business and public service associate professionals	36	946
	Science and technology professionals	37	446
	Health and social welfare associate professionals	27	253
	Science and technology associate professionals	33	35
	Total	*35*	*6,218*
Other services	Business and public service professionals	31	866
	Business and public service associate professionals	36	136
	Science and technology professionals	39	83
	Total	*33*	*1,084*
Overall total			14,293

Source: Cambridge Econometrics (2014), Table 17, p. 25.

Note: As per Figure 9.2. Data for associate professional occupations look at those with post-graduate degrees only.

Figure 9.6 Summary of estimated salary and overhead costs in main sectors translating/ mediating social science research

	Direct salary costs (£m)	Overhead costs @ 40% (£m)	Total estimated costs (£m)
Banking and finance	7,000	2,800	**9,800**
Public administration, education and health	6,200	2,500	**8,700**
Other services (including consultancy)	1,000		**1,000**
Total salary and overhead costs	**14,200**	**5,300**	**19,500**

Source: Cambridge Econometrics (2014).

costs and so on. In the UK the conventional add-on for such costs is 40 per cent and this is applied in Figure 9.6 (but not to the consultancy wages bill where clients bear all costs). The total in this Figure estimates overall spending of £19.5 billion being spent on the translation and mediation of social science research by sectors outside universities.

These estimates are necessarily somewhat 'rough and ready' for three reasons:

- they operate with a restrictive definition of social science;
- they adopt a 'precautionary' stance in conservatively identifying occupations and sectors where research mediation of social science is likely to be taking place; and
- they focus down on just three of the clearest-cut sectors, leaving aside the smaller industrial sectors in Figure 9.2 where relevant occupational clusters exist but could not be identified here.

Equally, however, there are some other available information sources, apart from the Labour Force Survey, which allows some triangulation. For the other services/ consultancy sector looking at the turnover data for firms is pretty convergent with the estimates made here. These data suggest a roughly half-and-half split between government agencies hiring consultants and non-banking private industry. Looking at some other civil service data – narrowly focused on government professions drawn from core social science disciplines, like economics and social research – it produces much lower estimates for staff doing social science translation or mediation in core Whitehall departments. But this apparent gap reduces greatly if we take account of the full social sciences scope discussed in Chapter 1 (which includes law and media fully as social sciences for instance); look at overlap areas like IT where some 50,000 staff work across 19 occupations in government; and recognize that Whitehall is a relatively small part of overall public sector services. This still perhaps leaves room for more debate about whether more or fewer government and public service officials have jobs where they mediate social science research. But overall, the results presented here are broadly consistent with the rest of our research across this book.

They unambiguously indicate a very substantial external engagement and impact from social science research.

The analysis above also potentially provides only a partial picture because of its focus predominantly on the UK social science economy. Professionals mediating social science in sectors outside universities can also read directly and draw on the work of other social scientists working overseas, not just those active in the UK, especially American, Canadian and Australasian scholars, and European social scientists writing in English. Some overseas work is mediated via the mass media and by NGOs, especially think tanks. But most international inputs are sifted and evaluated by UK social scientists before they reach 'end users'. Because social science models are not Valery's 'recipes that always work', the question of how to adapt something developed or successful in other business or policy contexts to match British conditions is usually salient. Hence domestic scholars add value in showing the potential application or limitations of international work. Admittedly the level of this domestic 're-mediation' is probably lower in the UK than in countries operating in smaller language communities – where domestic social scientists and consultants normally play a key intermediating role simply by translating relevant overseas work into the home language for decision-makers.

There are other limitations of this analysis too. One possible basis for scepticism put to us is that we cannot be entirely sure that professionals in banking or government really are directly using what they learnt at university in their mediating work. The image apparently conjured up by critics here is of hard-working and often mature professional staffs somehow directly consulting their university textbooks or lecture notes, if not for their undergraduate degree at least for their Masters or some recent 'refresher' course. The claim seems to be that only if these linkages are clear and direct in this simple-minded way are the people involved still linked effectively with their educating institutions. This argument is not just heard used against the social sciences, but also sometimes about the continuing influence of STEM disciplines. However, this 'naïve' view is typically expressed with far more force here than it is for STEM disciplines, and it may well colour some survey responses amongst professional staff themselves.

Actually, in any subject, it is a serious misconception to imagine that there can or should be any very close fit between the knowledge deployed in highly specific occupational or professional practices, and that taught (or conceivably teachable) in a three or four year general degree. In an influential essay on 'The Aims of Education' A. N. Whitehead (1962: 42, 57) wrote frankly but realistically to students about the likely residue of their studies, across all disciplines:

> Your learning is useless to you till you have lost your text-books, burnt your lecture notes, and forgotten the minutiae which you learnt by heart for the examination. What in the way of detail you continually require will stick in your memory as obvious facts like the sun and moon; and what you casually require can be looked up in any work of reference. The function of a University is to enable you to shed detail in favour of principles ... A principle [is] ... the way the mind reacts to the appropriate stimulus in the form of illustrative circumstances. ... Get your knowledge quickly and then use it. If you can use it, you will retain it.

University learning typically leads to the internalization of particular academic values, intellectual frameworks and ways of thinking and doing that are then adaptable to the usually far more specific and far more commonly repeated demands of working in any given job. So it is not in any way important to the notion of large numbers of professionals translating and mediating disciplinary and broader social research insights to their organizations that they should be operating with the same textbooks or resources that they once used at an earlier stage of their professional learning, but only that this learning is present in a significant way in situating their work and defining their current capabilities.

Conclusions

Research is inherently likely to be a 'portfolio investment' where many projects succeed and others do not. Not all research pays off or generates results that in some sense offset its costs. Yet much research pays off handsomely, and much of the rest regularly covers its costs. Not undertaking or ignoring research can also lead to disastrous consequences, so that the opportunity costs of 'unresearch' are substantial. As with most share portfolios, successes and failures in research mostly cannot be accurately predicted in advance, not least because societal needs and priorities constantly change. As one of our interviewees commented: 'Occasionally the timing is quite unpredictable, and some ideas might catch on. But the unpredictability of it is the most impressive feature'. The dynamic knowledge inventory concept seeks to capture some of this complexity (shown in Part II) in a reasonably well-structured but also realistic characterization of what sets advanced industrial societies apart from still developing countries.

The social sciences play a central role here in monitoring, analysing, and condensing information on societal development, the operations of the economy, new social and cultural trends, and the causal influences driving changes. Human societies never stand still, and nor do they evolve solely in ways that 'ordinary knowledge' or 'common sense' can analyse – as recent controversies about the effect of austerity policies in recessions illustrate. The social sciences' role in the knowledge inventory is inherently dynamic, responding to past patterns and seeking to understand current evolution in better theorized, more precisely tested propositions. It also tries to devise integrative frameworks that could assist in and predict future trends and developments.

These functions have huge significance for many influential actors in sectors beyond higher education. We have shown that a small fraction of the workforce, around one worker in every 200, has a job in business, government or civil society where they follow, translate, break down and mediate social science research in ways that make it applicable and valuable for their organization. This proportion is not large, around half of one per cent. But at this professional level neither is it cheap. The fact that businesses, governments and civil society bodies (each with their own powerful incentives and priorities) bear substantial costs in mediating social science research provides strong prima facie support for its social value. 'In a world so charged and sparkling with power', as Emerson (1862) put it, can we not legitimately assume that these social actors (in the aggregate) know what they are doing?

10

Social science for a digital era

Measure what is measurable, and make measurable what is not so.

Gallileo Gallilei[1]

I don't think writers are sacred, but words are. They deserve respect. If you get the right ones in the right order, you might nudge the world a little.

Tom Stoppard[2]

In one of his essays (on 'Old Age') the nineteenth century author Ralph Waldo Emerson (1862) wrote: 'Skill to do comes of doing; knowledge comes by eyes always open, and working hands; and *there is no knowledge that is not power*'. In one of the ironic quirks of the internet age, the italicized words were taken up as a dictum by the online game 'Mortal Kombat', achieving global dissemination. Emerson himself clearly meant his connection of knowledge and power in a more prosaic and less mystical sense than the youthful gamers, as espousing the value of applied experience and the life-long development of capacities (powers). If only we too could take as self-evident 'There is no knowledge that is not power', then much of this book would not have needed to be written. Yet in the case of academic knowledge, and perhaps especially for the social sciences, there have been plenty of critics ready to declare that a great deal of research does not add to our capabilities, because in their view it lacks any immediate or obviously cost-commensurate pay off. In addition, social scientists themselves have not come to a unitary or securely settled view of the 'laws' of social change, which for many critics damns any claim to scientific status. '"Science" means simply the aggregate of all the recipes that are always successful', said the novelist Paul Valery (1970: 372). 'All the rest is literature'.

However, the issues involved in understanding social, economic, technological or cultural issues and choices are often momentous ones. They are neither resolvable by common sense, nor capable of being fixed in any determinate way that 'stands outside time', as STEM laws do. There are few social science 'recipes that are always successful'. The best that can normally be done is to narrow down or fine-tune the

---

[1]Raskinski and Griffith (2008: 64).
[2]Quoted in *The Real Thing* (Stoppard, 1982: Act II, Scene V).

general probability of a given outcome, adjusted to the particular times and conditions applying in a unique period of economic and social development.

Take the issue of whether governments should pursue austerity policies after the onset of a severe recession. For an individual household or firm, retrenching in the face of reduced income, cutting back net outflowings and paying off debts, makes sense. But if government also responds to its fiscal stress by joining households and firms in drastically reducing spending in a recession, the effects can be a disastrous downwards spiral according to neo-Keynesians, a proposition denied by neo-liberals. Here (as elsewhere in science) resorting to 'common sense' reasoning in order to decide what to do may lead to catastrophically sub-optimal actions. The social science approach is to assess the balance of arguments and reach a conditional probability, taking full account of all available information and theory; take actions that respond to the balance of arguments and evidence for a particular economy and time; and then rigorously and continuously monitor how the economy responds after policy action is taken, being open-minded about adjusting the mix of policies.

However, as the economist Paul Krugman has often remarked, public policies in this area continue to be determined in a political atmosphere clouded by analogies drawn from 'common sense' and a political rhetoric of complete certainty. Many decision-makers, policy-advisors or lobbyists are apparently content to casually cast aside the weight of economic theory and evidence in defence of their own convictions. The psychological roots of such widespread reactions were well captured by Friedrich Nietzsche, who wrote:

> To trace something unknown back to something known is alleviating, soothing, gratifying and gives moreover a feeling of power. Danger, disquiet, anxiety attend the unknown – the first instinct is to eliminate these distressing states. First principle: any explanation is better than none. ... The cause-creating drive is thus conditional and excited by the feeling of fear (1990: 62).

Undoubtedly then, the wider environment in which the social sciences operate creates recurring difficulties. But in a liberal democracy, scientists have realized that they cannot just whinge on about the limited public understanding of their disciplines, nor operate as if a Platonic rule by educated 'guardians' ever could or should exist in liberal democracies. The effort put into public engagement, and into a collective push to explain what (STEM) science is and how it creates distinctive knowledge has paid off over many decades. Most references to 'public engagement' and 'public understanding' in our press and media search in Chapter 8 related specifically to STEM scientists playing a public role. By contrast, the social sciences have only recently begun to betray the signs of the collective consciousness as a discipline group that is likely to prove crucial for their future. In the rest of this chapter we sum up some of the key lessons of the book and consider the future trajectories that hold out most prospect of improving the status of the social sciences under two headings. First, joining up the social sciences more effectively will continue to be critically important for their intellectual development as well as their external impacts on business, government or civil society. Second, a lot will depend on how we re-frame the ways in which all human-centred disciplines operate – so as to span the social science and physical science divide, and to find ways of integrating both that help us to shed light upon the largest social, cultural, and technological challenges ahead. This leads us to ask how the social sciences, particularly those based in the UK, can better scale their efforts towards the gradual emergence of a single, global civilization.

10.1 Joining up 'broad-front' social science

> The purpose of models is not to fit the data, but to sharpen the questions.
>
> *Samuel Karlin*[3]

> My engagement with academics tends to be about larger theoretical questions: How do we develop new conceptual models? How do we create the possibility of new conversation, that allow new sorts of thinking inside the company and outside the company?
>
> *Technology firm executive in interview*

The social sciences predominantly achieve external impacts by influencing people to think about things in a different, more precisely reasoned and better informed way, one that will (hopefully) produce better decisions and societal outcomes than would have been achieved without the presence of these disciplines. In many of the quotes and insights from interviewees in this book, we have seen how social science frameworks and methods have provided exactly this kind of foundation for thinking and reasoning inside organizations, across private firms, government, civil society and media sectors. In business, social science contributes mostly to what NESTA (2007) has called 'hidden innovations' that are rarely productized but instead need to be implemented by skilled staff trained in relevant disciplines. And the complex process of what Weiss (1977; 1982) calls 'enlightenment' by which public policy evolves to respond to changing problems and priorities, and analogous processes throughout civil society organizations, reflect the impact of social science research primarily through the influence of ideas. Much of this thinking and reasoning has been shaped by direct interaction with social science academics and their research (charted in Chapters 5 to 8). But far more has been the product of staff in these organizations drawing on their own social science skillsets, most often (although not necessarily) underpinned by university social science degrees or training. They use this knowledge to access, interpret, and adapt existing materials, information and models that are 'out there' in the world. In discussing the dynamic knowledge inventory (DKI) and the 'mediating' role of all staff in many different types of organizations, we have charted an ever-renewing 'broad-front' of foundational knowledge – that is continually churned, utilized and added to by a wide variety of societal actors.

Yet there is still a relative dearth of accurate information on the scale and the resources making up the dynamic knowledge inventory. We found almost no established picture of this in the existing literature. And our analysis in the opening

---

[3] Taken from 11th R A Fisher Memorial Lecture, Royal Society, 20 April 1983.

Figure 10.1   The size of the 'research community' in social science

In 2010–11	000s
Academic and research staff in social science departments, engaged in research	30.5
Estimated number of professional staff with social science qualifications working on translating or mediating social science research	
Government and public services	177
Finance institutions and banking sectors	169
Consultancy	38
Total estimated staff in translation/mediation work	384
Total population of social science 'research community'	*410*

chapters of the book offers only a ball-park impression (although a detailed and reasoned one) of the overall size of the social sciences in the UK. Chapter 2 showed that we can scale the social sciences in terms of how many people are directly employed in university research roles, and how large is the immediate professional audience receiving and mediating their research. Around 30,500 academics are research-active in the social sciences in UK universities (Figure 10.1). And over 380,000 people form the most engaged part of the wider social science 'user' community – on average, 12 first-order users to every one social science researcher. Chapter 9 showed that these people mostly work in the finance sector, and in the public services and Whitehall, with smaller numbers in consulting and technology sectors. As a cautious low-end estimate we can say that the social science research front in the UK consists of at least 410,000 individuals, all involved in accessing, mediating, adding to, and churning the DKI in a variety of ways.

Undertaking an equivalent exercise to estimate the economic value to the UK of the social sciences, the university core of the social sciences is worth around £5 billion annually (at 2011 prices), over half of which is accounted for by the value added by university social science departments (shown in Figure 10.2). In addition, we have calculated a low-end estimate for the economic value generated by first-order users in organizations outside higher education itself who mediate social science research. The estimated salary and overhead costs for the 380,000 or so mediating individuals form the major component here, plus other additional estimated revenues generated by bought-in consultancy in the business and government sectors. In total, this spending on translating or mediating social science research amounts to around £20 billion per year, and it is worth re-emphasizing here that this is a low-end or minimal estimate. These headline numbers give the first outline of the overall size and the scale of the social science enterprise in the UK.

We have encountered a range of sceptical reactions to the 'critical mass' picture of the social science 'broad front' drawn here. Some critics argue that this aggregate concept has little meaning. 'Social science' is only a reification of a set of disciplinary practices that are in actuality much more fragmented than our account suggests: researchers involved in the core practices in universities are resolutely siloed into

Figure 10.2   Summary overview of total estimated economic impacts of UK social science departments, 2010–11

Economic impacts of the spending of UK social science departments, 2010/11		£ billions
Value added in social science departments		2.7
Value added elsewhere in the economy ('indirect')		0.5
Value added stimulated by spending from wages ('induced')		1.6
Total UK value added for university social science		*4.8*
Estimates of spending on research translation/mediation (as a measure of the benefits of social science research)		
Government (including education and health)	In-house staff	6.2
	Overheads (40%)	2.5
	Bought-in consultancy	0.5
Finance	In-house staff	7.0
	Overheads (40%)	2.8
Sectors outside of government	Bought-in consultancy	0.5
Total spending on translating/mediating social science		*19.4*

Source: Cambridge Econometrics (2014).

Note: For further details on the breakdown of total UK value added, see Chapter 1 and Figures 1.7, 1.8 and 1.9, and for detail on the research mediation/translation spending estimates see Section 9.2.

multiple different disciplinary approaches. And in external sectors, the professional staffs enumerated in Chapter 9 may see themselves as alumni of this or that specific department and discipline, but not as linked to a wider social science community. Yet are such perceptions an effect or a cause of the previously weak institutional identity of the social sciences? Without prior attempts to account for the size and value of social science, could things seem otherwise at some level? What is not explicitly defined or measured in aggregate terms is unlikely to feature highly in the perceptions of actors involved. So there does not seem to be any inherent reason why the social sciences would not have a stronger and more explicit broad-front identity to match their evident importance in terms of human resources and economic value.

Part of the overall identity problem for the discipline group has been the perception amongst many social scientists that they have been poorly served by their learned societies, while a clear lead body for the discipline group as a whole has also been lacking. The professional bodies for disciplines in the social science/STEM crossover areas (such as geography and psychology) have generally been the strongest. Here too 'supplementary' bodies like the Royal Geographical Society or more developed specialist media (like the magazine *Psychology Today*) also play important roles in encouraging elite and public engagement with the disciplines involved. By contrast, learned societies in the core social sciences have been widely seen as comparatively weak and silo-orientated. Their organizations tend to be relatively younger, and have not had time to build up anything like the assets and prestige of the best-established STEM learned sciences. The social science associations typically depend for between a third and two-thirds of their income on closed-access subscription journals. This market stood them in good stead from the 1950s until the end of the 2000s, but since then clouds have gathered over it with the transition towards open access publications and the digital distribution of science and scholarship.

Another hallmark of weak learned societies in social science has been partial membership, with many academics conspicuously refusing to join the professional body for their disciplines. Sometimes this is for personal or ideological conflict reasons, e.g., the association is seen as clique-run, too provincial or too elitist. Sometimes it is because UK researchers' focus lies elsewhere, often with far larger American or European associations for staff in elite universities. And sometimes it is just because the academics have been unwilling to bear modest subscription costs, even when offset with an income tax break. Finally, the failure to mobilize all potential members interacts with the smaller size of the individual social science disciplines and the associations' scant assets to create only slender or even 'shoestring' administrative capacities at their associations' headquarters.

There is also generally poor and at best episodic co-operation amongst different disciplines' associations. They appear to operate most of the time in splendid isolation, repetitively addressing common problems in fragmented and mostly ineffective ways. In the UK there is no social science equivalent to the prestigious top-level STEM science body, the Royal Society – with its more than 350 year history, substantial assets, prestige in facilitating cross-disciplinary exchanges and consensus, and an extensive role as a conduit of significant government funding. The British Academy (BA) claims the same mantle, and has a small government funding stream and a headquarters building situated on the same central London street as the Royal Society (Carlton House Terrace). But it is a mixed body covering both the social sciences and the humanities, who have historically been dominant within the ranks of its Fellows. The BA's membership is also relatively elderly, resolutely un-technological, and hampered by a public reputation for promoting elite exclusivism and a lack of openness or wide consultation. As a result the BA's attempts to represent its component social science disciplines have been undistinguished.

Years of discontent with this situation, especially the continuous under-playing of the importance of the social sciences and failure to represent most subjects in the discipline group fairly (except perhaps philosophers and economists), led to the setting up of the organization that became the Academy of Social Sciences (AcSS) in 1989. The AcSS has its own somewhat larger set of academicians and a more open reputation. It seeks mainly to play a *formateur* role in building coalitions that attempt to co-ordinate the 44 learned societies (some quite small) which exist across its area. However, it has in turn been regarded with some scepticism and suspicion by the British Academy and some other learned societies, and by some discipline groups, especially economists.

Figure 10.3   Percentage of total references to our academics that make up the 'mediating middle'

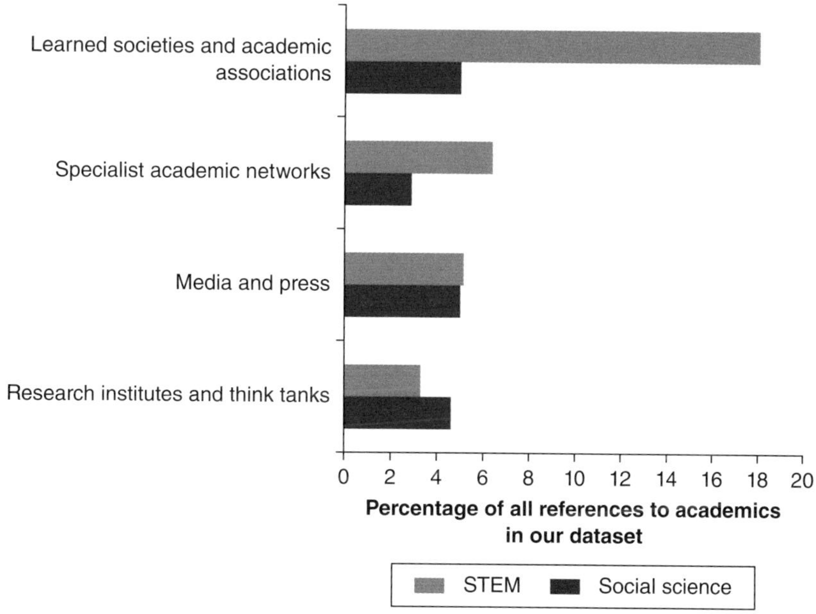

Percentage of all references to academics in our dataset

STEM   Social science

Source: LSE PPG dataset.

The division of top-level focus between two top bodies (the AcSS and BA) has not helped the public representation of the social sciences in the media or to public policy makers. In media terms both have proved unremittingly conservative in their public engagement efforts, doing too little too late in fostering cross-social science academic communications, apparently preoccupied with status anxieties, and (like many single-discipline learned societies) content to reach out only to diminutive audiences, even on digital media.

The comparative weakness of learned societies has serious consequences in relation to government. One Chief Scientific Officer for a Whitehall department told us that: 'Learned societies have an important part to play in all of this. They can give a route in by brokering policy engagement. Organizing forums, working with government departments, and so on'. When seeking 'stakeholder' views civil servants like to feel that they have tapped into a professional consensus. They are used to dealing with well-organized STEM science learned societies, co-ordinated effectively via the Royal Society and government research councils. The smoothly operating scientific elite routinely covers all related government consultations and can mobilize impressively around diverse opportunities for influence – for instance, commanding the engagement of many legislators in both Houses of Parliament.

Our analysis above provides some index of the comparatively weak prevalence of learned societies as mediators between social science research and potential research users. Figure 2.14 showed that the visibility of learned societies as mediators of research is nearly four times greater in the STEM sciences than in the social sciences (see also Figure 10.3). Specialist academic networks were also more important in

Figure 10.4 Twelve most frequently referenced professional and learned societies in our dataset of academics

# of refs	Name	Host country (originated)
77	Royal Society of Chemistry	UK *(1841)*
49	American Chemical Society	US *(1876)*
46	Association of Computing Machinery	US *(1947)*
46	Institute of Electrical and Electronic Engineers	US *(1884)*
27	Institute of Physics	UK *(1874)*
22	British Sociological Association	UK *(1951)*
19	National Academy of Sciences	US *(1863)*
18	European Communication Research and Education Association	EU *(2005)*
18	International Society for Optics and Photonics SPIE	US *(1955)*
17	British Medical Association	UK *(1832)*
16	American Institute of Physics	US *(1931)*
15	American Association for the Advancement of Science	US *(1848)*

Source: LSE PPG dataset.

STEM subjects, and there was virtually no compensation for this effect coming from the links between think tanks and social scientists. Figure 10.4 shows some further evidence of the comparative influence of STEM societies. Yet amongst the top 12 learned societies referencing our academics' research, we found only two social science societies, with the remainder composed of large STEM associations. An important implication of this comparative weakness in the 'mediating middle' for social sciences is to put more pressure on the strength of the bilateral relationships between academics (or university departments) and potential research users. Yet Chapters 5 to 8 show there are many signs that these are still quite precarious relationships: they are not systematically strong or widespread enough to do without the mediating role played by the learned societies and professional associations.

The main UK research council for the discipline group is the Economic and Social Research Council (ESRC), and it clearly could have an important mediating role in fostering joining up across the social sciences. The social sciences account for only a twelfth of total government research council funding (see Figure 1.6, page 11), small beer against the funding of much more capital intensive STEM sciences. Although comparatively small in this sense, many social science academics and practitioners acknowledged to us the value of ESRC funding in stimulating cross-disciplinary co-operation – for instance via broader research programmes, issue-specific joint research centres and now broader doctoral training centres (DTCs). Yet much else in ESRC's activity set still operates on single-discipline silo lines – for example, with no equivalent to the digital humanities effort at developing digital scholarship across the social sciences.

These institutional barriers and difficulties are not decisive for the integration of the social sciences, however. As Stephen Poole (2011) once remarked: 'There's only so slow you can drive along a freeway'. The broad avenue of digital change in modern scholarship has already formed one main area where integration across social science disciplines has been able to flourish autonomously – in the rise of new and common methods; the development of social media and new ('shorter, better, faster, free') perspectives on digital and open scholarship. Some of these innovations have spread in from the STEM sciences and we focus on them in the next section, in the context of a wider integration across the full range of 'human-centred' disciplines. But others have been distinctively developed in social science and cognate areas, especially the growth of multi-author blogging sites as a key form of knowledge exchange. We see academic blogging as very important in Chapter 8 above, and elsewhere (Dunleavy and Gilson, 2012; Dunleavy and Tinkler, 2014), and so we do not replay these arguments in detail here. In a nutshell though, any well-written blog-post makes academic research instantly more accessible to lay audiences, and also creates integrative potential for academics to learn about intellectual developments and methods in disciplines other than their own. As one leading economist said in our interview:

This is something where I think blogs do have a role to play. As far as I can tell, my blog in trying to translate some of the work into understandable English and send it to policy makers, my blog has had somewhat more impact than some of the more academic papers that we [at institute N] produce. Worthy as they have been in research terms.

Similarly an NGO executive commented in a focus group: 'To the extent that academics are out there themselves writing on blogs or posting snippets of their research, you can then make those connections and get it known'.

However, with solo blogs written by a single author, the academic part of the audience is still quite likely to come mainly from that researcher's particular discipline. People in other social science subjects will often confront substantial difficulties in finding out about potentially relevant or interesting solo blogs, given their huge numbers, weak branding or signposting, and often variable quality and frequency. Multi-author blogs (MABs), on the other hand, attract contributors from dozens or even hundreds of different authors, often spanning across many disciplines (Marsh, 2013). Under direct academic control MABs greatly boost the opportunities for multi-disciplinary learning that were previously limited to a few specialist media (like the *Economist*, *Nature* or *Scientific American*). This effect is especially strong because each MAB is integrally linked to terse social media like Twitter which allow content search to be greatly extended; to full texts on open access; and now to creating open access databases and supplementary resources accompanying published research. There are huge potential gains for the post-publication replicability of research, and for scholars in other subjects being able to fully access and re-create what has been done.

Thus, many different barriers to the cross-disciplinary circulation of ideas have reduced simultaneously. The transmission time for salient innovations to cross between social science disciplines has shortened from around five years in the recent past to a matter of months now. This is especially the case for those researchers and disciplines most keyed in to digital scholarship innovations (Weller, 2011). Key techniques now include sophisticated search; electronic tagging and note-taking from diverse materials (Johnson, 2013); large online book review databases, operating in weeks since publication rather than many months or even years; automatic alerting from large machine databases, like Google Scholar; and participation in academic interaction networks, like Research Gate or open source software networks.

An interesting way of characterizing these recent changes across the social sciences (and other disciplines too of course) is as a radical improvement in the accessibility (and universal applicability) of academic knowledge, methods, texts and 'tools'. In *Tools for Conviviality* (1973: 101) the theorist Ivan Illich wrote:

> Crucial to how much anyone can learn on his [or her] own is the structure of [their] tools: the less they are convivial, the more they foster teaching... Tools are convivial to the extent to which they can be easily used, by anybody, as often or as seldom as desired, for the accomplishment of a purpose chosen by the user.

Although Illich's focus was on extending ordinary knowledge outside formal education systems, some similar factors condition the success of researchers acquiring new knowledge outside their previous area of specialization. The speedier, fuller and more reliable transmission of ideas at this stage is likely to be especially important in stimulating the creative framing of initial research questions, a key stage in the overall process:

> Most of the knowledge and much of the genius of the research worker lie behind his [or her] selection of what is worth observing. It is a crucial choice, often determining the success or failure of months of work, often differentiating the brilliant discoverer from an otherwise admirable but entirely unproductive plodder. (Gregg, 1941: 8)

The recent history of the social sciences also testifies to a quickening pace of intellectual, theoretical, methodological and empirical pooling. Waves of new theory have transformed the previous isolation of separated disciplines. Rational choice and game theories swept across many social sciences from economics by the 1990s (Poundstone, 1993; Hindmoor, 2006). More recently behavioural psychology and economics (including ideas about framing effects and 'nudge' approaches in public policy) have also spread quickly (Thaler and Sunstein, 2008; Kahneman, 2012). Post modernist theory influenced many qualitative social sciences and ended up having effects even in apparently distant fields, such as marketing and branding.

And the pooling of methods across the social sciences has similarly progressed a lot further in recent years with:

- the mathematization of parts of many disciplines;
- the spread of experimental methods focusing on randomized control trials (RCTs) (for example, Kittel et al., 2012);

- the development of quantitative and systematic textual analysis capabilities;
- qualitative comparative analysis (QCA) or 'fuzzy set' methods for systematizing case research (Ragin, 2000);
- the importing of 'systematic review' concepts from health sciences and medicine;
- the growth of digital and online research methods prioritizing non-reactive or unobtrusive data instead of relying on reactive survey measures (Dunleavy, 2010);
- the development of 'big data' research methods for acquiring and making available large digital databases such as administrative data; and most recently
- the importing of software engineering and programming methods into the social sciences (Hoyt, 2013).

Taken together there are grounds for arguing that the next five to ten years will see the biggest change of social science methods since mass surveys were perfected as the key research tool of the early post-war period.

Finally, the adoption of the 'open' agenda from the STEM disciplines is fast gathering momentum in UK social science, thanks to the particular backing of the UK research councils and of philanthropic donors, such as the Wellcome Trust. The main government body distributing research support funding to universities in England (HEFCE) is also likely to require that if the REF exercise is repeated in 2020 the books and articles submitted should be available on an open access basis, free to read for any user. There is a strong democratizing strand in the 'open' movement, an affirmation that the sources of new and creative innovations, new uses and re-uses of ideas and data cannot be pre-planned or predicted (Neylon, 2013). The development of open source software and most recently of 'networked science' systems for improving the potential for inter-personal problem-solving and ideas generation (Nielsen, 2011) are two concrete manifestations of this approach, so far with few social science counterparts. A shift towards more co-producing of knowledge with the involvement of amateur scientists has also underlain the development of 'citizen science' initiatives (Royal Society, 2011). There have been some recent innovative efforts to enlarge public engagement with the social sciences that go only some way down this road (discussed in Section 8.1 above). The 'Mappiness' project uses a widely distributed web app to let thousands of citizen-participants update their state of mind and happiness levels at different times and places (MacKerron and Mourato, 2010). It is one example of the potential scope for innovative 'citizen social science' projects to bring about major improvements in the quantity and quality of available relevant data.

All of these developments are cross-disciplinary, helping to push and pull the social sciences together in almost unprecedented ways. Achieving the critical mass of developments needed could never have worked in the previous frame of single-silo disciplines. The re-prioritizing of applied knowledge, better social science communication and public engagement implied in the impacts agenda, digital scholarship and the shift to 'open', all push in the same direction.

10.2 Re-framing human-centred disciplines and integrating STEM and social sciences

A science is any discipline in which a fool of this generation can go beyond the point reached by the genius of the last generation.

Max Gluckmann[4]

Science would be ruined if (like sports) it were to put competition above everything else, and if it were to clarify the rules of competition by withdrawing entirely into narrowly defined specialties. The rare scholars who are nomads-by-choice are essential to the intellectual welfare of the settled disciplines.

Benoit Mandelbrot[5]

In the Egyptian gallery of the British Museum the statue of Ramesses II is a huge, single carved bloc of granite, fashioned into a stunningly beautiful likeness of the pharaoh. Up close the figure is strikingly smooth, the craftsmanship and execution flawless. Yet this apparently perfect artefact is around 3,250 years old. Amongst figurative sculptures it is hard to see how it could be improved. Of course, the work is static, monumental and almost abstract in conception. So there were innumerable ways in which later sculptors no doubt found their own work superior, for instance, in conveying movement, or achieving realistic individual characterization. None the less, the Ramesses statue stands as eloquent testimony to the 'timelessness' of great works of art, the difficulty of 'improving' what has been achieved by human creativity in an earlier age. And for hundreds of years even physical science scholarship in western and other civilizations also harked back to a previous 'golden age' of knowledge once held by 'the ancients' and deemed incapable of improvement. Scholars chiefly sought to recapture fragments of this unifying classical vision long lost.

In the contemporary world we now expect instead that scientific knowledge will constantly change, improve and update, with new models and evidence eclipsing the old. New theories and ways of seeing develop the accuracy of predictions, our ability to control natural phenomena and the depth and aesthetic unity of our understanding. As the epigraph from Max Gluckman above suggests, in some ways this incessant progress and achievement is as definitive of modern science as other key characteristics. STEM science is also general and international. Once a physical process has been correctly identified and understood, or a mathematical problem or model has been fully analysed, the result becomes a 'recipe that always works' and can be adopted and applied by other (well-qualified) scientists. We consider how the social sciences might be (or already are being) re-framed, so that these desirable features (insistent knowledge progress and generality) apply to them also. We start in this section with the idea of insistent knowledge progress and its relevance in the social sciences realm.

In the modern social sciences there is a strong and pervasive sense of constant advance in how they operate and conduct research. The methods, criteria of proof, and extent of the evidence base in all disciplines have transformed every decade for as

---

[4] Gluckman (1965: 32).

[5] Quoted in his entry in Who's Who in Mackay (1991: 163).

long as anyone now living can look back. The relatively static and in some ways only incrementally changing social science disciplines of the 1940s and '50s have been replaced since the late 1960s by a progressive expansion of data, the computer-based and later digital transformation of quantitative research, more recently the extension of digital changes to qualitative research, and the spread of (competing) social science understandings to almost all features of social and economic life. The mathematization and formalization of parts of subjects across the discipline group has been a major change. But so too have successive waves of contesting intellectual agendas and methodological advances that maintain every social science at a distance from simply conforming to a Kuhnian 'normal science' uniformity of view.

The rapid knowledge dynamism of the social sciences clearly aligns them alongside the STEM disciplines. It also orientates them away from the sense of timeless success and potentially un-improvable human achievement (perhaps embodied in the concept of a 'canon') that is still powerful in some parts of the creative arts and humanities. Social scientists' generally incremental and collective modes of accomplishing 'discovery' research, and their scholarly deference to major theoretical texts from their early history, are sometimes seen as radically differentiating the discipline group from STEM science with its rapid advance changes. Yet even here there are few 'across the board' changes, and the history of science has shown convincingly that path dependencies and historical legacies abound. As the mathematician Henri Poincaré (1905: 14) observed more than a century ago:

> The advance of science is not comparable to the changes of a city, where old edifices are pitilessly torn down to give place to new, but to the continuous evolution of zoologic types which develop ceaselessly and end by becoming unrecognizable to the common sight, but where an expert eye finds always traces of the prior work of the centuries past. One must not think then that the old-fashioned theories have been sterile and vain.

Similarly, commenting at the peak of one of the fastest periods of post-war STEM discipline changes, Robert Oppenheimer (1954: 53–4) also stressed that:

> A new theory, even when it appears most unitary and all-embracing, deals with some immediate element of novelty or paradox within the framework of far vaster, unanalysed, unarticulated reserves of knowledge, experience, faith and presupposition… We neither can, nor need, rebuild the house of the mind very rapidly.

So a theory legacy that is continuously reactivated and drawn-on does not preclude the social sciences from rapid advance.

However, it is true that the allocation of academic prestige remains none the less distinct across the social and physical sciences. In the STEM sciences the ideological stress is on achieving primacy in 'discovery' research, creating new, secure knowledge that is timeless. This is a test that social science research can rarely meet (despite the apparatus of proofs and lemmas in more mathematicized work). Discovery research is also more collective across the social science disciplines, and establishing 'primacy' is harder to do. Add in the customary deference to established thinkers, and sometimes top prestige in at least some social sciences may still seem to be allocated to theorists or writers who are remote from new forefront research. The scholarship of 'integration' remains continuously important and difficult in these subjects. We constantly need to adapt existing understandings to encompass not just new scientific results, but new social phenomena and technologies, and new conjunctures in social and historical development. But this is not inconsistent with the social sciences progressively assigning more prestige to rapid knowledge advance, necessarily in theory-plus-empirics mode, even as 'discovery' research remains inherently more collective or incremental. The pace and scope of application research in social science are also likely to improve as 'impact' attracts more funding (and with it scholarly appreciation), and as social media radically cut the costs and time in research and dissemination, and improve the efficacy of social science communications.

Traditional mechanisms and stimuli for inter-disciplinary learning (see previous section) have been important in enhancing a stronger social science identity. Bridging across disciplines has previously been most associated with major public intellectuals, distinctive in their ability to overcome single subject silos and make broader connections. A degree of local integration (usually across closely cognate disciplines) has been regularly achieved by universities grouping departments into faculties, but almost never with a single inclusive social sciences unit. Sometimes local integration has fed through to applied research strongly in particular places and times – as with Stanford University (and to a degree Harvard) and the Silicon Valley IT industry. Academic service has also been the third historic pillar of cross-disciplinary influences. Senior academics moving up to managerial positions inside universities or out into government or professional advisory roles often added impetus to a drive for more connected university solutions to joined-up 'real world' problems.

There are strong signs that a regrouping of academic subjects in terms of human-centred fields has already begun. We noted in Chapter 5 the strong push by executives and research directors in critically important and well-resourced IT corporations towards integrating social science insights with engineering working methods and IT algorithms, moving towards 'big data' analyses. Early signs of this kind of joining-up of disciplines into new hybrid forms of 'computational social science' are already visible in large mainly-US technology firms and closely linked universities. The need for university social science to move with these changes has not been lost on perceptive authors. In 2007, for instance, Savage and Burrows foresaw a 'coming crisis of empirical sociology' because corporate resources (analysed with non-social science techniques and algorithms) were threatening to outstrip the kinds of data sources assembled (using dated and smallish scale survey methods for the most part) by social science professionals. An American executive in the technology sector remarked to us:

There was a sociologist from Cornell once in the audience of one of my lectures. After the talk, he said to me 'Sociology has moved to Palo Alto'. Now I don't pretend to be a sociologist but the fact we can do large social studies by monitoring behaviour online means that we can do things. We can study economic systems by looking at how money gets transacted on the internet. So I don't think that data collection needs to have the famous two to three years. You can do most of these things very quickly now because of the technology.

Beyond a certain level, though, big data may only expand the kind of financially consequential but actually rather banal knowledge important for business control processes, but un-illuminating on fundamental causes (Cukier and Mayer-Schonberger, 2013; Gitelman, 2013). Similarly, uniting big data with randomized control methods allows a forcing of the pace for testing incremental changes and 'nudge' techniques, but it may shed little light on more imaginative , dynamic or 'whole system' changes. Oftentimes mass prototyping combined with 'democratizing innovation' in a user-orientated way (von Hippel, 2006) may yield a temporary comparative advantage for firms. But after 'easy wins' have been harvested, developing more fundamental innovations and insights will probably rely on more dialectical (apparently contradictory) interactions of forms of knowledge.

None the less, in the next few years some capabilities in big data analysis, electronic piloting and online RCT trials, previously reserved only for Google, Amazon, Facebook or Walmart, will get broken down and applied within social science disciplines. This change will enhance the scope for the discipline group to work more closely with STEM sciences. And it is likely to generate a major methods shift – towards more software engineering and IT methods, and more 'pure' maths analysis adapted to big data plenty.

To better foster such processes and linkages, universities might reorganize their faculty structures or strengthen their 'local integration' processes so as to converge together more all the human-dominated disciplines. Essentially this means bringing the social sciences closer together with IT and computer science, and with medicine and the health sciences, as a means of tackling looming scientific and policy challenges. Two critically significant challenges for advanced industrial societies first, and perhaps for modern civilization as a whole, are coping with digital change on the one hand; and on the other, adjusting to a stable (non-growing) population with a high proportion of elderly people and apparently insatiable demands for healthcare. In a broader way the 'socialization' of engineering and the improvement of large-scale planning and risk-management systems to better handle human and social risks raise similar challenges (Flyvberg et al., 2003). So too does the worrying potential for past over-use of drugs to push up human resistance to previously effective antibiotics, or for a global pandemic or more regional disease problems to catch out medical science and public health services. In both fields the long-run improvement of how public policy systems interact with STEM sciences, social sciences and social behaviour is likely to be of major significance.

Yet despite the widely recognized salience of such topics, and a growing realization amongst some social scientists of the need for adaptation, the current, deeply-entrenched patterns of university governance and professional siloing have been very slow to change. Fostering greater convergence across the full range of human-dominated disciplines will not be easy. Most progress has been achieved in the US where corporate research donations are greater and respond more flexibly and quickly to changing priorities. In the UK some grand-scale aspirational statements from larger Russell Group universities about the need to address inherently joined-up challenges, and integrate STEM with social science and humanities have promised change along these lines. But looking closer at many US and UK initiatives suggests that actual integrative change in the structures, cultures, and outputs of key departments towards inter-disciplinary research has been relatively surface-level. One danger is that such integrative efforts (especially when backed by one-off external donations) only end up creating new overlaying centres, initiatives or courses, rather than fostering more base-level integration of research perspectives and programmes.

In more 'statist' higher education economies, such as those in Europe, changing the set up of research funding at a governmental level to converge human-dominated science would also mean tearing up powerful institutions that embody an earlier 'STEM versus social science' divide. Equivalent territorial barriers to change exist in the UK context too. For example, the structure of research councils in the UK locates funding responsibility for IT in the EPSRC (covering engineering and the physical sciences), and for health sciences in the Medical Research Council (MRC). Within both bodies there are academically and politically dominant 'big science' lobbies, who many see as having chronically starved funds from the far cheaper fields covering the social application of IT and of medicine/healthcare, in order to maintain professionally more important and costly infrastructures.

One might expect that social sciences co-operation with physical scientific fields that are only 'human-influenced' would be less than for human-dominated disciplines. Yet that is not apparently true. A great deal of closer working with STEM subjects takes place in these areas and there have been some encouraging signs of progress. For instance, in the fields of global warming and climate change, a lot of funding has gone into scientific research on mitigation. Most STEM researchers here acknowledge the critical importance of social, cultural, political and economic understandings in promoting any worthwhile or sustainable mitigation efforts. And in our conversations with social scientists over three years we found numerous interesting examples of climate scientists working with social scientists to integrate cutting-edge climate change science into social and cultural practices in environmental management, farming and agriculture, particularly in developing countries. Some joined-up centres for research around all human-centred aspects of climate change provides an institutional underpinning. Similarly the history of resistance to genetically modified food and the importance of legal, social and cultural sensitivities across wide fields of bio-genetics and pharmacology research, have also tended to underscore the social and political dimensions of their practice more to STEM scientists.

If the sciences of human-dominated systems, and of human-influenced systems, are to pull together more, then it may be that the 'least social' parts of the physical sciences (those dealing with purely natural systems) also need to be grouped more together – and perhaps allowed to float off on a different path from the human-centred components of their disciplines. Yet, on current trends this kind of cross-disciplinary regrouping seems unlikely to happen, and would cut across some currently powerful mindsets in 'physical science' thinking about the missions and unity of particular STEM disciplines. However, some observers have pointed to a considerable fluidity in department structures within STEM subjects in American universities where change within disciplines has been relatively larger than in most other subjects:

Departments of anatomy, histology, biochemistry and physiology have disappeared, replaced by innovative departments of stem-cell biology, systems biology, neurobiology and molecular biophysics. Taking a page from Darwin, the natural sciences are evolving with the times. The perfection of cloning techniques gave rise to stem-cell biology; advances in computer science contributed to systems biology. Whole new fields of inquiry, as well as university departments and majors, owe their existence to fresh discoveries and novel tools. (Christakis, 2013)

There are several different possible ways forward to improve the co-operation of social science departments with still-specializing STEM subjects. But not all of these futures seem benign ones. For instance, Christakis (2013) argues that:

In contrast [to STEM disciplines], the social sciences have stagnated. They offer essentially the same set of academic departments and disciplines that they have for nearly 100 years: sociology, economics, anthropology, psychology and political science... It is time to create new social science departments that reflect the breadth and complexity of the problems we face as well as the novelty of 21st-century science.

So far so good. Yet Christakis' advice then is to leave only a small 'palace guard' to monitor the largely unchanging 'core topics' of old-style social sciences, recognizing that core social problems (like the linkage of poor health to social inequality) are essentially irresolvable. Instead he suggests putting all the real effort into a fragmented spread of mini-departments on the social science frontier with STEM:

These would include departments of biosocial science, network science, neuroeconomics, behavioral genetics and computational social science. Eventually, these departments would themselves be dismantled or transmuted as science continues to advance.

This kind of methods-privileging approach is a reductionist retreat into micro-specialisms, and is exactly what we do not argue for in the contemporary social sciences.

Certainly, research priorities need to change and modernize, and we need to build up a 'rapid advance' research culture with (somewhat) more scientific consensus, far greater interaction with the closest STEM subjects, and far better 'big data' methods. However, rather than micro-co-operations occurring in niche sub-fields, we have argued here for a broad front advance, strengthening the peak-level identity of the social sciences, using digital scholarship. The current US trends pointed to by Christakis represent a retreat into a kind of intellectual hyper-siloing that would only remove social science further and further from constructive application.

There are grounds for believing that the changes we envisage are feasible and sustainable. In a 2008 online survey for the British Academy, both social scientists and humanities scholars expressed strong views that their subject's relevance for the physical sciences was important but under-developed (LSE Public Policy Group, 2008). Three main incentives currently work in favour of greater (broad-front) joining up across the discipline groups:

- STEM disciplines are far better funded than social science, especially in the US and UK, two countries with the greatest concentration of research funding on physical science. As social scientists work more with STEM researchers in overlapping ways, funding and grants should improve. For example, an increment of 2 or 3 per cent points in the share of total government research funding going to social sciences may be small in overall terms, but would be equivalent to around £50 million per year.
- Citation rates are systematically higher in STEM subjects, reflecting their greater sizes and better citation and review practices. Social scientists whose research moves more towards joint working can expect to see their citation rates increase, shifting the balance of academic power within their disciplines towards fostering co-operation.
- The impacts agenda will give cross-discipline group co-operation more impetus, because the largest scale potential lies in understanding and improving the handling of social, political and economic problems in human-dominated systems. Rapid and consequential changes are most likely to occur in the areas discussed above. Environmental, ecological and climate change aspects of human-centred systems are also very large-scale and multi-causal.

10.3 Towards a more global social science

[W]e are increasingly made aware that while we live on one planet, we belong to worlds apart. And if the social sciences are not even on the same map, what should be done? Does a more integrated world require a more integrated social science?

   Gudmund Hernes[6]

Social scientists should consider identifying not with the harder sciences or the humanities but with engineering... [Engineers] don't seek 'the truth', a unique and universal explanation of a phenomenon or solution to a problem... They seek merely answers to specific, localized, temporary problems... In spite of its weaknesses, social science – when applied wisely – can do even more than the hard sciences to make the world a better place. Comte was right about that.

   John Horgan[7]

In the 2000s many 'globalists' in academia made energetic predictions that political power was migrating away from nation states (Held, 2003). The major recession which struck western countries in 2008, and the fiscal crises of many states which followed, demonstrated (yet again) that in fact the tax-raising powers of individual nation states remained absolutely critical to contemporary capitalism (Dryzek and Dunleavy, 2009). Compared to the fundamental importance of this

---

[6]Gudman Hernes (2010: viii).
[7]Horgan (2013).

function, international institutions proved weak and completely ineffective. States with solid precautionary economic policies survived relatively untouched, and those that had veered most towards 'casino capitalism' triggering bank collapses suffered greatly.

Research and development programmes across the world are still set up on national lines, operated by single-country institutions, funded from state or corporate budgets, predominantly within a rhetoric of fostering greater domestic economic growth. (There is a one major exception – the European Union's large scientific programmes, which amounted to €17.9 billion in 2002–06 and €50.5 billion in 2007–13. However, the social science *plus* humanities share of this largesse was a shockingly low 1.5 per cent in the first period, falling to 1.2 per cent in the second – effectively tokenistic (International Social Science Council, 2010: 84)). Hence country-specific strategies dominate decisions about how governments devote money to fostering science innovations and scholarship. Figure 10.5 shows that for 27 countries for which we have data, the median share of country-level research and development funds flowing to the social sciences *plus* humanities was just under 8 per cent, with many large countries spending below 6 per cent. Some of the larger amounts here also reflect strong humanities spending to support national language communities. Hence the vast bulk of funding worldwide goes to STEM disciplines. The UK is not included in this figure, but we estimate R&D funds channelling into the social sciences at around 12 per cent.

This set-up opens the door to what David Edgerton (2008: 1031) has called 'techno-nationalism', with individual states looking for focused economic benefits, and yet in a way that cannot work:

> Only in techno-nationalist fantasies... does national invention drive national economic growth, and national investment in science, technology or R&D correlate positively with national economic growth. In the real world, global innovation leads to national growth, and national innovation leads to global growth.

The spatial leakage involved in supporting research is always likely to be substantial. This is not an industry (like, say, tourism) where the benefits of spending can be easily circumscribed to a local area. So Edgerton argues that: 'science policies based on techno-nationalist thinking and fantasies about the past technological revolutions will get us nowhere fast' (2008: 1030).

One of the potential drawbacks of re-prioritizing impacts and applied research is that it might add a further impetus to such domestically-focused tendencies, especially in the social sciences. Achieving policy impacts on a smaller local and regional scale might easily seem more determinate and concretely measurable or auditable than only contributing one small element to the resolution of larger national, European or international policy problems. To its credit, the body running the UK's Research Excellence Framework audit (HEFCE) was quick to stress that impact could be claimed not just within the UK, but anywhere in the world and at any spatial level. The grounds for assessing impact were also specified as 'significance', perhaps more demonstrable at a local level, but also likely to be greater at wider

Figure 10.5 The proportion of research and development funding in 2005 flowing to the social sciences and humanities, across 27 countries

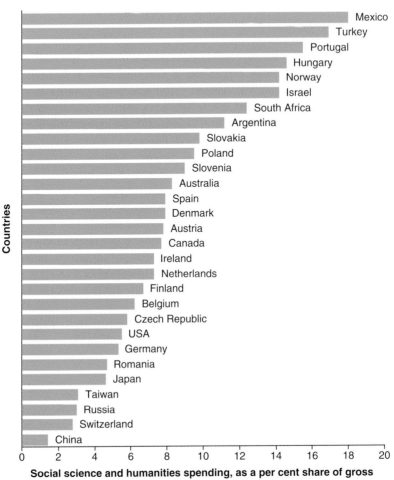

Source: International Social Science Council (2010: 370–1).

spatial scales; and 'reach', which seems unambiguously tipped towards rewarding impacts that are general or wider scale.

Even so the research publications element of the REF remains resolutely orientated to publication in highly cited international journals, mostly American or European. So some academics are sceptical that after decades of UK policy fostering only purist academic research, the balance can now be easily redressed. One geographer commented in interview:

It needs a change in values. That's not going to happen easily. It would be nice to see more value placed on things that actually happen on the ground. In the old days, geographers used to work with local geographical societies and talk about local issues. These days the pressure is that you've got to be international.

Despite these tensions there are grounds for optimism that UK social science is well placed to continue succeeding internationally, while yet reorienting somewhat more towards a scholarship of application. The UK remains the number two country in the world after the US. It benefits both from strong trans-Atlantic and linguistic community connections with America, and spatial proximity and increasingly a common professional language with European scholars. Indeed, in our own dataset around two-thirds of references to the (370) UK-based academics were found on non-UK or international websites, the large proportion of which were in North America, Europe and Australasia. In this sense, UK social scientists 'export' two-thirds of their knowledge abroad. After a patchy post-war record, European social science outside the UK was flourishing and catching up well, before the onset of the 2008 recession. In the next two decades, developing a more effective social science of India, China and Asia generally will prove a huge challenge to both American and European (including British) social science disciplines.

The UK economy, society and polity also provide a still-important (if diminishing) basis for British social science to be internationally influential (UK National Commission for UNESCO Secretariat, 2013). The British economy is still the seventh largest in the world, and its make-up (78 per cent services sector) is typical for advanced industrial societies. In social terms Britain has also been remarkably socially stable and yet adaptive, over many decades, and it is now a more multi-cultural society. And although the UK welfare state now offers only a low level of benefits income to pensioners, the sick and (especially) the unemployed, its comprehensive ambitions remain and healthcare remains strong. Politically and constitutionally the UK's set up has proved remarkably stable over time, despite relying mainly on elite consensus and politicians' self-restraint for much of its 'democratic' kudos. The UK's centralized public administrative system has been one of the most dynamic in the world, with a ceaseless push towards trialling new public management and public policy solutions by politicians and a powerful civil service. As Chapter 6 noted, innovations with mixed economies of public services provision and payment-by-results more than ever require sophisticated methods and tools for assessing performance and standards. Other countries have continually kept a close eye on potentially importable public management developments from the UK. Finally, the country's former role as an imperial power remains influential in sustaining London as an important centre of financial and corporate power, and a continuing (if second-tier) focal point in international policy making. UK overseas aid has remained extensive and a strong record in the social science of international development (reflecting the strong budget position of the Department for International Development, itself one of the world's major aid agencies). There are well-developed cultural links with Commonwealth developing countries especially.

So British social science remains a strong interlocutor, historically most with American disciplines, but increasingly also with the major European countries. Probably no single country (even the US) can now sustain a global social science capability. Certainly no single university can do so, despite the increasingly bizarre efforts of some Ivy League institutions, and in the UK, Oxford and Cambridge, to sustain such a claim. Considered together, UK universities at least retain some significant research capacity across most other areas of the world. This is an important basis if

British researchers are to help foster the emergence of a more spatially balanced global social science community, one that might scale-match better and culture-match far more effectively with the emergence of a single planet-wide mode of production and form of human civilization. This level of ambition may seem demanding, but in global social sciences rankings many British universities score highly across different disciplines. The UK academic publishing industry provides additional strong support, as does the growth of digital scholarship and development of social media for academic purposes. So it is not being unrealistic to believe that a small island off the north-west shores of Europe can make a significant contribution, in coalition with similar movements and efforts in European and perhaps American social science also.

How large is the global social science research community and audience? We have no statistics of proven provenance, but it is feasible to make some reasonable estimates. The academic referencing company Mendeley, which accumulated 2.5 million users between its founding in 2009 and take-over by Elsevier in 2013, estimated in 2012 that there were 60 million people working in universities worldwide (including professors, teaching and research staff, and students at all levels). Beyond the university sector, Mendeley analysed their cross-national data to argue that there were twice as many people again (120 million) working in business, industrial, government, media or civil society jobs that involved them in using academic work regularly – thus needing to store books and papers, and catalogue and reference them in documents and bibliographies.

Estimating the social science share of such global numbers is tricky. Mendeley attracted users first in medical and bio-sciences, and then became popular in other STEM subjects. Yet despite a later start, by 2012 around one-fifth of its users were in the social sciences and humanities. This skewed distribution at least places a bottom limit on the scale of the global population of university and associated staffs working in social science, while the UK social science share (30 per cent of university staffs) indicates a maximum. We estimate that around a third of university staff and students globally (that is, around 20 million people) are in social science departments, in the broad definition adopted in Chapter 1. Worldwide we suggest that perhaps another 20 million people who work in the government, business, media and civil society sectors make regular use of or mediate social science research. Taken together these numbers suggest a ball-park social science audience of around 40 million people. This number may sound a lot, but it represents just 0.6 of one per cent of the world's 2011 population, or 0.9 per cent of those of working age. The essential mission for UK social science has long been to reach out to and engage with as large a proportion as possible of this potential global audience, inside and outside universities.

Conclusions

Looking ahead is often risky. Perhaps intellectuals more than most tend to embrace science-tinged versions of prophecy, 'the kind of thinking that told us in the 1940s with supreme confidence that the future would be one of rockets, atomic power and automation' (Edgerton, 2008: 1031). The next stage in the evolution of the social sciences is the focus of many different efforts and struggles, between powerful academic interests, mostly determined to keep things broadly as they are, and various alternative scenarios. We recognize that the courses foreseen and advocated here – a broad-front joining-up of the discipline group; a rapid adoption of digital scholarship and 'big data' research; and far better integration with STEM subjects studying human-dominated or human-influenced systems – form a particular, optimistic scenario. Yet we hope to have shown in the most extensive manner to date that UK social science is a substantial and successful industry in its own right, with a large research audience. Upon the choices that the social science community make collectively will depend whether the discipline group will move forward into a globalised era in good shape.

Glossary

aculturation The process of cultural and psychological change that results from the meeting or merging of two cultures.

altmetrics (or 'alternative' metrics) A diverse set of new measures that seek to identify the impact of academic journal articles beyond simple citation analysis.

autopoeisis Originally used to define and explain the logic and development of living and adaptive systems, but the concept has now been applied to sociology and business contexts.

bibliometrics A set of techniques used to quantifiably analyse books or articles, examples include citation and content analysis.

bibliometric databases Databases such as ISI Web of Science or Scopus that provide information on citations to outputs held within them.

blogosphere The connected community or social network of all those contributing to blogs.

British Academy (Fellows of) The national organisation of humanities and social sciences in the UK. The Fellows of the British Academy are distinguished academics and researchers within their disciplines. The society works to enrich and promote the humanities and social sciences.

CAD disciplines The creative arts and design academic disciplines.

citations A reference included in an academic work to another published or unpublished piece. It is used to uphold intellectual honesty by acknowledging a piece of work's debt to an earlier piece, to support an argument and to enable a reader to independently check academic sources.

constructivist A philosophy of science which holds that science is a series of mental constructs designed to explain measurements taken of the natural world. There is thus no single method of science, but rather a collection of competing approaches.

core social science Those social sciences that have little to no cross-over with the humanities or natural sciences.

crossover social science Those social sciences that straddle the divide between the social sciences and the humanities or natural sciences.

dependent variable The outcome variable in any potential causal relationship that is being examined. As opposed to the *independent variable* (see below).

dummy variable A variable in a statistical regression which is either 1 or 0 thus representing a binary yes or no, for example whether an academic has a PhD or not.

Excellent Research in Australia Australia's national research assessment process, broadly equivalent to the *REF* in the UK (see below).

grey literature   Non-traditional academic literature such as working papers, research reports, blogs and practitioner-focused presentations.

gross value added (GVA)   An economic measure of the total value added to the economy by activity in a particular sector.

human-dominated systems   Physical systems on Earth that remain mostly or essentially autonomous in their modes of operation but where there are none the less significant human interventions or efforts at control.

human-influenced systems   All the numerous artefacts of human civilisation, all aspects of social and economic organization and issues created, and the human physiology and medical/health sciences interventions.

humanities   Academic disciplines primarily focused on examining human culture, including such fields as philosophy, languages and theology.

impact   An auditable or otherwise recordable occasion of influence.

independent variable   A term used to refer to those variables in a potentially causal relationship which are believed to have either a causal effect or some degree of correlation with the outcome in question (i.e., the dependent variable(s)).

intellectual property (IP)   An idea, design or concept for which exclusive rights have been granted to a single individual or company, generally its creator. Common forms include copyrights, patents and trademarks.

Ivy League Universities   A group of eight prestigious universities in the United States generally thought to represent the best in teaching and research.

knowledge exchange   A two-way process in which researchers and civil society, business or government actors share data, information, experiences or methodologies.

mediating middle   The set of organisations who play intermediary roles in translating and cumulating new work produced by social science researchers in forms useable by potential end users elsewhere in society.

mixed HSS disciplines   Disciplines which straddle both the social sciences and humanities: for example history, law and media.

Moore's Law   The observation made by Gordon E. Moore that the number of transistors on integrated circuits tends to double every year. The law is currently used by the software industry to plan technological development.

multivariate regression analysis   A statistical technique that is used to identify patterns of relationship between a dependent variable (e.g., number of citations) and a number of independent variables (e.g., academics age, institution).

natural sciences   The disciplines concerned with understanding the rules of the natural world through empirical investigation: biology, chemistry, physics, earth sciences and astronomy.

new public management   A concept summarizing broad public management reforms throughout the 1980s and 1990s, introducing market orientated or business-inspired approaches into the public sector.

patents   An exclusive set of rights granted to an inventor for a number of years in exchange for the inventor publicly disclosing their invention.

peer-review The evaluation of academic work by peers within the same field so as to maintain or enhance the quality of the research and communication in that field.

physical sciences A sub-type of the natural sciences encapsulating Physics and the Chemistry of Nature.

positivist A philosophy of science which holds that truth can only be derived from mathematical and logical treatments and from empirical observation.

proxy variable A variable that is used as a substitute for another variable which cannot be obtained.

public engagement A two way process that attempts to share the activity and benefits of higher education and research with the public in order to generate mutual benefit.

public intellectual Someone who is able to relate knowledge on one topic or discipline and take it to the wider social, cultural, and political world in a way that opens up the discussion for a general audience.

public understanding of science A catch-all term summarizing the attitudes, behaviours, opinions and activities that comprise the relations between the general public to scientific knowledge and organization.

QR Funding Quality related funding, the primary means by which the Higher Education Funding Council of England distributes research funding. It is based on a national audit assessment, the volume of research, relative research costs and government research priorities.

qualitative A type of information which deals with qualities or characteristics, it is thus subjective as opposed to objective quantifiable data.

quantitative A type of information based in quantities and thus referring to objective data.

randomised control trials (RCT) A statistical technique used to evaluate the impact of an intervention by comparing the outcomes of those treated with a control group. The two groups are randomly composed, preventing any factors other than the intervention from affecting the outcome.

Research Assessment Exercise (RAE) The UK's research assessment process that ran from 1986 to 2008, now replaced by the Research Excellence Framework.

Research Excellence Framework (REF) The UK's research assessment process that was announced in 2008 as replacing the Research Assessment Exercise. It will first be used in 2013 and includes an impact element for the first time.

Russell Group University A group of 24 prestigious universities in the United Kingdom generally thought to represent the best in teaching and research.

scientometric The application of bibliometric to study the development and spread of scientific ideas.

social sciences The academic disciplines aimed at understanding human society: economics, sociology, anthropology and political science.

socialization The process by which humans gain the necessary skills to be able to function in a society.

statistical significance A term from multi-variate regressions indicating that a correlation is not just randomly occurring and in turn that a relationship between two variables is valid.

STEM disciplines A catch-all term for the academic fields of science, technology, engineering and mathematics.

systematic review A literature review that aims to synthesize all the high quality research conducted on a research question. Systematic reviews tend to focus on very high quality research, such as Randomised Control Trials.

trademarks A recognisable sign or design that is used to identify a product or brand. Trademarks can be owned by companies and individuals and prevent any other actor from making use of the design in question.

value added (direct) Amount of value added to the economy by direct activity in a particular sector such as salaries and consumption costs.

value added (indirect) Amount of value added to the economy by indirect activity in a particular sector.

Bibliography

Note: A living bibliography for this book including links to all electronically available references is hosted on the *Impact of Social Sciences* blog at http://blogs.lse.ac.uk/impactofsocialsciences/ book. URLs are therefore not provided here.

Abramo, Giovanni and D'Angelo, Ciriaco A (2010) 'Evaluating research: from informed peer review to bibliometrics', *Scientometrics,* 87: 499–514.

Abreu, Maria, Grinevitch, Vadim, Hughes, Alan and Kitson, Michael (2008) 'Knowledge Exchange between Academics and the Business, Public, and Third Sectors. A report by the UK Innovation Research Centre'. Cambridge: Centre for Business Research, Cambridge University.

Adler, Nancy J and Harzing, Anne-Wil (2009) 'When knowledge wins: transcending the sense and nonsense of academic rankings', *Academy of Management & Education,* 8(1): 72–95.

Anderson, Chris (2006) *The Long Tail: Why the Future of Business Is Selling Less of More.* New York: Hyperion.

—— (2009) *Free: The Future of a Radical Price.* New York: Hyperion.

Ansoff, H Igor (1986) 'The pathology of applied research in social science', in Heller, F (ed.) *The Use and Abuse of Social Science.* London: Sage. pp. 19–23.

Archambault, Eric and Vignola-Gagne, Etienne (2004) 'The use of bibliometrics in the social sciences and humanities'. Report prepared by Science Metrix for the Social Sciences and Humanities Research Council of Canada (SSHRCC). Quebec: Science Metrix.

Arendt, Hannah (1978) *The Life of the Mind.* London: Secker & Warburg.

Auden, WH (1946) *Another Time: The Poems of W.H. Auden.* New York: Random House.

Bachmann, Reinhard and Zaheer, Ackbar (2008) *Handbook of Trust Research.* Cheltenham: Edward Elgar.

Bar-Ilan, Judit, Haustein, Stefanie, Peters, Isabella, Priem, Jason, Shema, Hadas and Terliesner, Jens (2012) 'Beyond citations: scholars' visibility on the social Web'. Paper presented to the *17th International Conference on Science and Technology Indicators.* Montreal, Canada. 5–8th September.

Bastow, Simon, Dunleavy, Patrick and Tinkler, Jane (2014) '*The impact of the social sciences: research design and methods report*'. London: LSE Public Policy Group.

Bate, Walter Jackson and Strauss, Albrecht B (eds) (1968) *The Rambler. By Samuel Johnson.* New Haven and London: Yale University Press.

Baumgartner, F.R. and B.D. Jones 2009. *Agendas and Instability in American Politics*, 2nd edn. Chicago: The University of Chicago Press.

Becker, Gary (1983) 'A theory of competition among pressure groups for political influence', *Quarterly Journal of Economics,* 98: 371–400.

Besley, Tim and Ghatak, Maitreesh (2003) 'Incentives, choices, and accountability in the provision of public services', *Oxford Review of Economic Policy,* 19(2): 235–49.

BIS (2011), 'International Comparative Performance of the UK Research Base 2011'. A report prepared for the Department of Business, Innovation and Skills. London: UK Department of Business, Innovation and Skills.

Bishop, Dorothy (2012) 'How to bury your academic writing', *Impact of Social Sciences* blog, 29 August 2012.

Black, M. (1962) *Models and Metaphors: Studies in Language and Philosophy*. Ithaca: Cornell University Press.

Blake, William (1908) *The Poetical Works of William Blake*, edited by John Sampson. London, New York: Oxford University Press; Bartleby.com, 2011.

Blond, Philip (2013) 'Britain needs to think bigger: looking at structural problems that can blinker academic innovation', *The World Today*, 69(5).

Boulding, Kenneth E (1966) *The Impact of the Social Sciences*. New Brunswick, NJ: Rutgers University Press.

Bower, D Jane (1992) *Company and Campus Partnership: Supporting Technology Transfer*. London & New York: Routledge.

Box, Gregory (1966) 'Use and abuse of regression', *Technometrics*, 8: 625–29.

Boyer, Ernest L (1997) *Scholarship Reconsidered: Priorities of the Professoriate*. London: John Wiley & Sons.

Boyle, James (2008) *The Public Domain: Enclosing the Commons of the Mind*. New Haven CT: Yale University Press.

Brabazon, Tara (2010) 'How not to write a PhD thesis', *Times Higher Education*, 28 January. Accessed at: http://www.timeshighereducation.co.uk/news/how-not-to-write-a-phd-thesis/410208. article

Brembs, Björn (2011) 'High impact factors are meant to represent strong citation rates, but these journal impact factors are more effective at predicting a paper's retraction rate', *LSE Impact of Social Sciences* blog, 19 December 2011.

Brembs, Björn, Button, Katherine and Munafo, Marcus (2013), 'Deep impact: unintended consequences of journal rank', *Frontiers in Human Neuroscience*, 7(291): 1–12.

British Academy (BA) (2007) *Peer Review: The Challenges for the Humanities and Social Sciences*. London: The British Academy.

Buchanan, M. (2000) *Ubiquity*. London: Weidenfeld and Nicholson.

Burrows, Roger (2011) 'Living with the H-index? Metrics, markets, and affect in the contemporary academy'. Working paper.

Butler, Linda and McAllister, Ian (2007) 'Metrics of peer review? Evaluating the 2001 UK Research Assessment Exercise in Political Science', *Political Studies Review*, 7(1): 3–17.

—— (2011), 'Evaluating university research performance using metrics', *European Political Science*, 10: 44–58.

Cairney, Paul (2013) 'Making sense of policymaking: why it's always someone else's fault and nothing ever changes', Paul Cairney blog, 4 June.

Calhoun, Craig (2008) 'Social science for public knowledge', In Eliaeson, Sven and Kalleberg, Ragnvald (eds) *Academics as Public Intellectuals*. Newcastle: Cambridge Scholars Publishing.

Cambridge Econometrics (2014) 'Assessing the impacts of academic social science research: modelling the economic impact on the UK economy of UK-based academic social science research'. A report by Cambridge Econometrics on behalf of the LSE Public Policy Group. Cambridge: Cambridge Econometrics.

Caplan, Nathan, Morrison, Andrea and Stambaugh, Russell (1975) *The Use of Social Science Knowledge in Policy Decisions at National Level*. Ann Arbor MI: University of Michigan.

Carey, John (2012) *The Intellectuals and the Masses: Pride and Prejudice Among the Literary Intelligentsia 1880–1939*. London: Faber and Faber.

Carley, Michael (1980) *Rational Techniques in Policy Analysis*. London: Heinemann Educational Books.

Chesterton, GK (1915) 'The Fallacy of Success', *All Things Considered*. London: Methuen.

—— (1917) *A Short History of England*. London : Chatto & Windus.

Christakis, Nicholas (2013) 'Let's shake up the social sciences', *New York Times Sunday Review*, 19 July.

Collins, HM (2001) 'Tacit nowledge, trust, and the Q of Sapphire', *Social Studies of Science*, 31: 71–85.

Collins, Harry (2010) *Tacit and Explicit Knowledge*. Chicago IL: University of Chicago Press.

Collins, Harry and Evans, Robert (2008) *Rethinking Expertise*. Chicago IL: University of Chicago Press.

Collins, Randall (1994) 'Why the social sciences won't become high-consensus, rapid-discovery science', *Sociological Forum*, 9, 155–177.

Corley, Elizabeth A and Sabharwal, Meghna (2010) 'Scholarly collaboration and productivity patterns in public administration: analysing recent trends', *Public Administration* 88(3): 627–48.

CSTS (2007) 'Scoping Study on the Use of Bibliometric Analysis to Measure the Quality of Research in UK Higher Education Institutions'. Report to HEFCE by the Centre for Science and Technology Studies, Leiden: Leiden University.

—— (2008) 'Development of Bibliometic Indicators of Research Quality'. A report to HEFCE by the Centre for Science and Technology Studies, Leiden: Leiden University.

Cukier, Kenneth and Mayer–Schonberger, Viktor (2013) *Big Data: A Revolution That Will Transform How We Live, Work and Think*. London: Hodder and Stoughton.

Cusumano, Michael A (2010) *Staying Power: Six Enduring Principles for Managing Strategy and Innovation in an Uncertain World*. Oxford: Oxford University Press.

Debray, Régis (1981) *Teachers, Writers, Celebrities: The intellectuals of Modern France*. London: New Left Books.

DORA (2012) 'San Francisco Declaration on Research Assessment'. San Francisco CA: American Society for Cell Biology.

Douglas, Mary (1986) *How Institutions Think?*. Syracuse, NY: Syracuse University Press.

Downs, Anthony (1972) 'Up and down with ecology: the "issue–attention" cycle', *The Public Interest*, 28: 38–50.

Dryzek, John S and Dunleavy, Patrick (2009) *Theories of the Democratic State*. Basingstoke: Palgrave Macmillan.

Dunleavy, Patrick (2010) 'New worlds of political science', *Political Studies*, 58(1): 239–65.

——(2011) 'The vulnerability of the British state – deeper lessons from the urban riots', *LSE Impact of Social Sciences* blog, 10 August 2012.

—— (2012), 'E-books herald the second coming of books in university social science', *LSE Review of Books* blog, 6 May 2012.

Dunleavy, Patrick and Carrera, Leandro (2013) *Growing the Productivity of Government Services*. Cheltenham: Edward Elgar.

Dunleavy, Patrick and Gilson, Chris (2012) 'Five minutes with Patrick Dunleavy and Chris Gilson: "Blogging is quite simply one of the most important things that an academic should be doing right now"', *LSE Impact of Social Sciences* blog, 24 February 2012.

Dunleavy, Patrick and Margetts, Helen (2013) 'The second wave of digital-era governance: a quasi-paradigm for government on the Web', *Philosophical Transactions of the Royal Society A: Mathematical, Physical and Engineering Sciences*, 371 (1987).

Dunleavy, Patrick, Margetts, Helen, Bastow, Simon and Tinkler, Jane (2006a) 'New public management is dead – long live digital-era governance', *Journal of Public Administration Research and Theory*, 16(3): 467–94.

—— (2006b), *Digital Era Governance: IT Corporations, the State, and e-Government*. Oxford: Oxford University Press.

Dunleavy, Patrick and Tinkler, Jane (2014) *Improving the Impact of University Research: How to Grow the Influence, Take-up and Understanding of Academic Work*. London: Palgrave Macmillan.

Dunn, William (1997) 'Probing the boundaries of ignorance in policy analysis', *American Behavioral Scientist*, 40(3): 277–98.

Edgerton, David (2008) 'The charge of technology', *Nature*, 455: 1030–31.

Emerson, RW (1862) 'Old age', *The Atlantic Monthly*, 9(51).

ESRC (2006) *Demographic Review of the UK Social Sciences*. Swindon: Economic and Social Research Council.

Etzioni, Amitai and Bowditch, Alyssa (2006) *Public Intellectuals: An Endangered Species*. Lanham, MD: Rowman & Littlefield Publishers.

Etzkowitz, Henry (2008) *The Triple Helix: University–Industry–Government Innovation in Action*. New York: Routledge.

Evans, William (1995), 'The mundane and the arcane: prestige media coverage of social and natural science', *Journalism & Mass Communication Quarterly*, 72(1): 168–77.

Eysenbach, Gunther (2011) 'Can tweets predict citations? Metrics of social impact based on Twitter and correlation with traditional metrics of scientific impact', *Journal of Medical Internet Research*, 13(4): e123.

Feldman, Martha S (1989) *Order Without Design: Information Production and Policy Making*. Stanford, CA: Stanford University Press.

Fenton, Natalie, Bryman, Alan and Deacon, David (1998) *Mediating Social Science*. London: Sage.

Flyvbjerg, Bent (2012) 'Why mass media matter to planning research: the case of megaprojects', *Journal of Planning Education and Research*, 32(2): 169–81.

Flyvbjerg, Bent, Bruzelius, Nils and Rothengatter, Werner (2003) *Megaprojects and Risk: An Anatomy of Ambition*. Cambridge: Cambridge University Press.

Ford, Rob and Goodwin, Matthew (2013) 'Academics may not be celebrities, but their careful research is improving public policy', *LSE Impact of Social Sciences* blog, 18 June 2013.

Foucault, Michel (1975) *Discipline and Punish: The Birth of the Prison*. New York: Random House.

—— (1984) 'Nietzsche, genealogy, history', in *The Foucault Reader*. New York: Pantheon.

—— (1989) 'Interview: the concern for truth', *Foucault Live*. New York: Semiotext. pp. 455–64.

Gerring, John (2011), *Social Science Methodology: A Unified Framework*. Cambridge: Cambridge University Press.

Gillies, Donald (2008) *How Should Research be Organized?* London: College Publications.

Gitelman, Lisa (2013) *Raw Data is an Oxymoron*. Cambridge MA: The MIT Press.

Gladwell, Malcolm (2009) *Outliers: The Story of Success*. London: Allen Lane.

Gleick, James (2012) *The Information: A History, A Theory, A Flood*. New York: Fourth Estate.

Gluckman, Max (1965) *Politics, Law and Ritual in Tribal Society*. Oxford: Basil Blackwell.

Goodwin, Matthew (ed.) (2013) *Making an Impact: How to Engage with Policymakers*. Nottingham: Ballots and Bullets blog, University of Nottingham.

Gouldner, Alvin (1973) *For Sociology: Renewal and Critique in Sociology Today*. London: Allen Lane.

Green, Duncan (2013), 'Why are NGOs and academics collaborating more?' *LSE Impact of Social Sciences blog*, 18 September 2013.

Gregg, Alan (1941) *The Furtherance of Medical Research*. New Haven CT: Yale University Press.

Griffiths, Dave (2010) 'Academic influence amongst the UK public elite', *Sociology*, 44(4): 734–50.

Harnad, Stevan (2007) 'Open access scientometrics and the UK Research Assessment Exercise'. Keynote address to 11th Annual Meeting of the International Society for Scientometrics and Informetrics, Madrid, Spain. 25–27 June 2007.

—— (2008) 'Validating research performance metrics against peer rankings', *Ethics in Science and Environmental Politics,* 8: 103–07.

Harzing, Anne-Wil (2010) *The Publish or Perish Book: Your Guide to Effective and Responsible Citation Analysis.* Melbourne: Tarma Software Research Pty Ltd.

Hayek, Frederich A (1988) *The Fatal Conceit: The Errors of Socialism.* London: Routledge.

HEFCE (2009) *Report on the Pilot Exercise to Develop Bibliometric Indicators for the Research Excellence Framework.* Bristol: Higher Education Funding Council for England.

—— (2010) *Higher Education – Business and Community Interaction Survey 2008/09.* Bristol: Higher Education Funding Council of England.

Hegel, Georg F (1892) *Lectures on the Philosophy of History.* London: Kegan Paul, Trench, Trübner.

Held, D. and A. McGrew (eds) (2003) *The Global Transformations Reader: An Introduction to the Globalization Debate,* 2nd edn. Cambridge: Polity Press.

Hilton, Matthew, McKay, James, Crowson, Nicholas and Mouhot, Jean-Francois (2013) *The Politics of Expertise: How NGOs Shaped Modern Britain.* Oxford: Oxford University Press.

Hindmoor, Andrew (2006) *Rational Choice.* Basingstoke: Palgrave Macmillan.

Hirschman, Albert (1982) *Shifting Involvements: Private Interest and Public Action.* Princeton, NJ: Princeton University Press.

HM Government (2013) *What Works: Evidence Centres for Social Policy.* London: Cabinet Office.

Hood, Christopher (1998) *The Art of the State: Culture, Rhetoric and Public Management.* Oxford: Oxford University Press.

Hood, Christopher and Dixon, Ruth (2013) 'A model of cost-cutting in Government? The great management revolution in UK central government reconsidered', *Public Administration,* 91(1): 114–34.

Hood, Christopher and Jackson, Michael (1991) *Administrative Argument.* Aldershot: Dartmouth.

Horgan, John (2013) 'Is "social science" an oxymoron? Will that ever change?', *Scientific American Blogs,* 4 April 2013.

Horn, Murray J (1995) *The Political Economy of Public Administration: Institutional choice in the Public Sector.* Cambridge: Cambridge University Press.

Hoyt, Jason (2013) 'By cross-pollinating career skills with the ideologies of "hacking", academics can seed creative avenues of research', *Impact of Social Sciences* blog, 26 June 2013.

Huang, Li-Shih (2012) 'There's a disconnect between "scholarly value" and how we reach audiences who need research', *LSE Impact of Social Science* blog, 2 October 2012.

Illich, Ivan (1973) *Tools for Conviviality.* London: Calder and Boyars.

International Social Science Council (2010) *World Social Science Report 2010: Knowledge Divides.* Paris: UNESCO United Nations Educational, Scientific and Cultural Organization.

Jacoby, Russell (1989) *The Last Intellectuals: American Culture in the Age of Academe.* New York: Basic Books.

James, Williams (1907) 'The present dilemma in philosophy', *Lecture I in Pragmatism: A new name for some old ways of thinking.* New York: Longman Green. pp 1–16.

—— (1909) *The Meaning of Truth.* New York: Longman Green.

Johnson, Allan (2013) 'Best practice for tagging academic notes', *LSE Impact of the Social Sciences* blog, 5 July 2013.

Johnson, Terence (1972) *Professions and Social Power.* London: Macmillan.

Kahneman, Daniel (2012) *Thinking, Fast and Slow.* New York: Penguin.

Kaufmann, Walter (1954) *The Portable Nietzsche.* New York: The Viking Press.

Kaufman, Herbert (1976) *Are Government Organizations Immortal?* Washington DC: Brookings Institution Press.

King, Gary (2013) 'Restructuring the social sciences: reflections from Harvard's Institute for Quantitative Social Science', Working Paper. Boston, MA: Harvard University.

Kingdon, John (2003) *Agendas, Alternatives and Public Policies.* Second edition. Upper Saddle River NJ: Pearson.

Kinsley, Michael (2009) 'A Cuba policy that's stuck on Plan A', *Washington Post Online,* 17 April 2009.

Kittel, B, Luhan, WJ and Morton RB (eds) (2012) *Experimental Political Science: Principles and Practices.* London: Palgrave Macmillan.

Klingstrom, Allan (ed.) (1986) *Cooperation between Higher Education and Industry.* Proceedings from the Seminar in Uppsala, 24–25 April 1986. Uppsala: Almqvist & Wiksell International.

Kuhn, Thomas S (1962) *The Structure of Scientific Revolutions.* Chicago IL: University of Chicago Press.

Lariviere, Vincent, Archambault, Érich, Gingras, Yves and Vignola-Gagné, Étienne (2006) 'The place of serials in referencing practices: comparing natural sciences and engineering with social sciences and humanities', *Journal of the American Society for Information Science and Technology,* 57(8): 997–1004.

Leavis, FR (1962) *Two Cultures? The Significance of CP Snow.* London: Chatto & Windus.

Lee, Sooho and Bozeman, Barry (2005) 'The impact of research collaboration on scientific productivity ', *Social Studies of Science,* 35(5): 673–702.

Leeds, Ruth and Smith, Thomasina (1963) *Using Social Science Knowledge in Business and Industry: Report of a Seminar.* Homewood, IL: Richard D Irwin, Inc.

Lindblom, Charles (1977) *Politics and Markets: The World's Political and Economic Systems.* New York: Basic Books.

Lindblom, Charles and Cohen, David (1979) *Usable Knowledge: Social Sciences and Social Problem Solving.* New Haven CT: Yale University.

LSE Public Policy Group (2008) 'Maximizing the social, policy, and economics impacts of research in the humanities and social sciences. A report to the British Academy'. July 2008. LSE Public Policy Group: London.

LSE Public Policy Group (PPG) (2011) *Maximising the Impacts of your Research: A Handbook for Social Scientists.* A report from the LSE Public Policy Group. London: London School of Economics.

Luhmann, Niklas (1982) *Trust and Power.* Chichester: Wiley.

Luhmann, Niklas (1986) 'The autopoiesis of social systems', in Geyer, F and van der Zouwen, J (eds) *Sociocybernetic Paradoxes.* London: Sage. pp. 172–92.

Mackay, Alan L (1991) *A Dictionary of Scientific Quotations.* London: Taylor Francis.

MacKerron, George and Mourato, Susana (2010) 'LSE's mappiness project may help us track the national mood: but how much should we consider happiness in deciding public policy? ', *LSE British Politics and Policy* blog, 28 October 2010.

Macmillan, Rob (2013), 'Making sense of the Big Society: perspectives of the third sector', Working Paper 90. Birmingham: Third Sector Research Centre.

Maitzen, Rohan (2013) 'Accept no substitutes: blogging is a valuable supplement to scholarship and rightfully challenges the status quo', *LSE Impact of Social Sciences* blog, 25 June. Available at: http://blogs.lse.ac.uk/impactofsocialsciences/2013/06/25/blogging-accept-no-substitutes/

Marsh, Alex (2013) 'Going solo or joining someone else's show: multi-author blogs as a way to maximise your time and exposure', *LSE Impact of Social Sciences* blog, 18 February 2013.

Mason, John L (1996), *Conquering an Enemy Called Average.* Tulsa OA: Insight International.

McKechin, Ann (2013) 'Academics and universities must continue to develop open access alternatives to break the monopoly of large publishers', *LSE Impact of Social Sciences* blog, 22 April 2013.

McKenzie, David and Özler, Berk (2011) 'Academic blogs are proven to increase dissemination of economic research and improve impact', *LSE Impact of the Social Sciences* blog, 15 November 2011.

McNeely, Ian and Wolverton, Lisa (2009) *Reinventing Knowledge: From Alexandria to the Internet.* New York: W.W. Norton.

Miller, Gary J (1992) *Managerial Dilemmas*. Cambridge and New York: Cambridge University Press.

Milligan, Spike (2003) *The Essential Spike Milligan*. London: Fourth Estate.

Mintzberg, Henry (1983) *Structure in Fives: Designing Effective Organizations*. Englewood Cliffs NJ: Prentice Hall.

National Audit Office (NAO) (2010) *Reorganising Central Government*. HC452, Session 2009–10. London: The Stationery Office.

NESTA (2007) *Hidden Innovation: How Innovation happens in Six "Low Innovation" Sectors'*. London: National Endowment for Science, Technology and the Arts.

Neylon, Cameron (2013) 'Open is a state of mind that actively encourages the opportunity for unexpected contributions to scholarly work', *LSE Impact of Social Sciences* blog, 11 July 2013.

Nielsen, Michael (2011) *Reinventing Discovery: The New Era of Networked Science*. Princeton NJ: Princeton University Press.

Nietzsche, Friedrich (1990) *Twilight of the Idols*. London: Penguin.

Nisbet, Matthew C and Scheufele, Dietram A (2009) 'What's next for science communication? Promising directions and lingering distractions', *American Journal of Botany*, 96(10): 1767–78.

Noelle-Neumann, Elizabeth (1993) *The Spiral of Silence: Public Opinion – Our Social Skin*. Chicago IL: University of Chicago Press.

Nonaka, Ikujiro and Takeuchi, Hirotaka (1995) *The Knowledge Creating Company: How Japanese Companies Create the Dynamics of Innovation*. New York: Oxford University Press.

Nonaka, Ikujiro, von Krogh, Georg and Ichijo, Kazuo (2000) *Enabling Knowledge Creation*. New York: Oxford University Press.

Norris, Michael and Oppenheim, Charles (2007) 'Comparing alternatives to the Web of Science for coverage of the social sciences' literature', *Journal of Informetrics*, 1: 161–69.

Oakeshott, Michael (1962) *Rationalism in Politics and Other Essays*. London: Methuen.

O'Brien, David (2010) 'Measuring the value of culture'. A report to the Department for Culture Media and Sport. London: Department for Culture Media and Sport.

Odendahl, Teresa (1991) *Charity Begins at Home: Generosity and Self-Interest Among the Philanthropic Elite*. New York: Basic Books.

Oppenheimer, J Robert (1954) *Science and the Common Understanding*. New York: Simon and Schuster.

O'Reilly, Dermot and Reed, Mike (2010) '"Leaderism": An evolution of managerialism in UK public service reform', *Public Administration*, 88(4): 960–78.

Pascal, Blaise (1958) *Pascal's Pensées*. New York: E. P. Dutton & CO., Inc.

Pawson, Ray (2006) *Evidence Based Policy Making: A Realist Perspective*. London: Sage.

Political and Constitutional Reform Committee (2013) *The Impact and Effectiveness of Ministerial Reshuffles*. Second Report. London: House of Commons.

Poincaré, Henri ([1905] 1946) 'The value of science ', in *The Foundations of Science: Science and Hypothesis, The Value of Science, Science and Method*. New York: The Science Press.

Poole, Steven (2011) 'Etcetera: Steven Poole's non-fiction reviews', *The Guardian*, 9 December 2011.

Posner, Richard A (2001) *Public Intellectuals*. Cambridge, MA: Harvard University Press.

Poundstone, William (1993) *Prisoner's Dilemma: John Von Neumann, Game Theory, and the Puzzle of the Bomb*. New York: Anchor Books, Random House Inc.

Poundstone, William (2010) *Priceless: The Myth of Fair Value (And How to Take Advantage of It)*. New York: Hill and Wang.

Priem, Jason and Costello, Kaitlin (2010) 'How and why scholars cite on Twitter'. Paper for 73rd Annual Meeting of the American Society for Information Science and Technology, 22–27 October, Pittsburgh US.

Priem, Jason, Costello, Kaitlin and Dzuba, Tyler (2011) 'First-year graduate students just wasting time? Prevalence and use of Twitter among scholars'. Paper for Metrics 2011: Symposium on Informetric and Scientometric Research conference, 12 October, New Orleans, US.

Public Accounts Committee (PAC) (2013) *Department for Transport: Lessons from Cancelling the Inter City West Coast Franchise Competition*. HC 813 Session 2012–13. London: Stationery Office.

Publishers Association (2012) *The Publishers Association Statistics Yearbook 2012*. London: The Publishers Association.

Puustinen, Kaisa and Edwards, Rosalind (2012) 'Who gives a tweet? After 24 hours and 860 downloads, we think quite a few actually do', *LSE Impact of Social Sciences* blog, 18 May 2012.

Quiller-Couch, Arthur (1916) *On the Art of Writing*. Cambridge: Cambridge University Press.

—— (1992) '"Casing" and the process of social inquiry', in CC Ragin and HS Becker (eds) *What is a Case? Exploring the Foundations of Social Inquiry*. Cambridge: Cambridge University Press.

Ragin, Charles (2000) *Fuzzy Set Social Science*. Chicago IL: University of Chicago Press.

Rasinski, Timothy and Griffith, Lorraine (2008) *Building Fluency Through Practice and Performance*. London: Shell Education.

Ravenscroft, Charlotte (2013) *The Secrets of Success? How Charitable Funders Use and Share Evidence in Practice*. London: Alliance for Useful Evidence.

Redner, Sidney (1998) 'How popular is your paper? An empirical study of the citation distribution', *European Physics Journal B*, 4: 131.

—— (2005) 'Citation statistics from 110 years of *Physical Review*', *Physical Review*, 58(6): 49.

Reul, Sabine (2003) 'What genius once was: reflections on the public intellectual', *Critical Review of International Social and Political Philosophy*, 6(4): 24–32.

Richards, Keith, Batty, Mike, Edwards, Kevin, Findlay, Allan, Foody, Giles, Frostick, Lynne, Jones, Kelvyn, Lee, Roger, Livingstone, David, Marsden, Terry, Petts, Judith, Philo, Chris, Simon, David, Smith, Susan and Thomas, David (2009) 'The nature of publishing and assessment in Geography and Environment Studies: evidence from the Research Assessment Exercise 2008', *Area (The Royal Geographical Society)*, 41(3): 231–43.

RIN (Research Information Network) (2009) *The UK's Share of World Research Output: An Investigation of Different Data Sources and Time Trends*. London: Research Information Network.

Royal Society (1985) *The Public Understanding of Science*. London: The Royal Society.

—— (2011) *Science as a Public Enterprise*. The Royal Society Science Policy Centre report 02/12. London: The Royal Society.

Sabatier, Paul (1987) 'Knowledge, policy-oriented learning, and policy change: an advocacy coalition framework', *Knowledge: Creation, Diffusion, Innovation*. 8 (June): 649–92.

Said, Edward (1997) *Covering Islam*. London: Vintage.

Savage, Mike and Burrows, Roger (2007) 'The coming crisis of empirical sociology', *Sociology*, 41(5): 885–99.

Savage, Mike, Devine, Fiona, Cunningham, Niall, Taylor, Mark, Li, Yaojun, Hjellbrekke, Johs, Le Roux, Brigitte, Friedman, Sam and Miles, Andrew (2013) 'A new model of social class? Findings from the BBC's Great British Class Survey experiment', *Sociology*, 47(2): 219–50.

Schumpeter, Joseph (1949) 'Science and ideology – Presidential address to the American Economic Association', *American Economic Review*, March 1949. pp 345–59.

Scott, James C (1998) *Seeing Like a State: How Certain Schemes to Improve the Human Condition Have Failed*. New Haven CT: Yale University Press.

Sennett, Richard (2008) *The Craftsman*. New Haven CT: Yale University Press.

Shelley, Percy B (1904) *A Defence of Poetry*. Indianapolis IN: Bobbs-Merrill.

Silberman, Bernard S (1993) *Cages of Reason: The Rise of the Rational State in France, Japan, the United States, and Great Britain*. Chicago IL: University of Chicago Press.

Simmons, George (1992) *Calculus Gems*. Mathematical Association of America: New York.

Stephenson, Neal (2008) *Anathem*. New York: William Morrow.

Stoppard, Tom (1982) *The Real Thing*. London: Faber and Faber.

Stokes, Donald E (1997) *Pasteur's Quadrant: Basic Science and Technological Innovation*. Washington DC: The Brookings Institution.

STSC (2012) 'Higher Education in Science, Technology, Engineering and Mathematics (STEM) subjects'. A report by the Science and Technology Select Committee of the House of Lords. HL Paper 37, 24 July 2012. London: The Stationery Office.

Thaler, Richard H and Sunstein, Cas R (2008) *Nudge: Improving Decisions About Health, Wealth, and Happiness*. New Haven CT: Yale University Press.

Tinkler, Jane (2012) 'The REF doesn't capture what government wants from academics or how academic impact on policymaking takes place', LSE *Impact of Social Sciences* blog, 27 March 2012.

Tinkler, Jane and Rainford, Paul (2013) 'Championing and governing UK public service mutuals'. In Valkama, P, Bailey, SJ and Anttiroiko, A-V (eds) *Organizational Innovation in Public Services: Forms and Governance. Governance and Public Management*. London: Palgrave Macmillan.

Tribble, Ivan [pseudonym] (2005) 'Bloggers need not apply', *Chronicle of Higher Education*, 8 July. Accessed at: http://chronicle.com/article/Bloggers-Need-Not-Apply/45022

UK National Commission for UNESCO Secretariat (2013) *What Could Be the Contribution of the UNESCO Social and Human Sciences Sector?* London: UK National Commission for UNESCO Secretariat.

Universities Australia (2013) *Public Perceptions of Australia's Universities*. Canberra: Universities Australia.

Valery, Paul (1970) 'Analects'. In Matthews, J (ed.) *Collected Works of Paul Valery*, Volume 14. Princeton NJ: Princeton University Press.

von Hippel, Eric (2006) *Democratizing Innovation*. Cambridge MA: The MIT Press.

Wagenaar, Hendrik C (1982) 'A cloud of unknowing: social science research in a political context', in Kallen, DBP, Kosse, GB, Wagenaar, HC, Kloprogge, JJJ and Vorbeck, M (eds.) *Social Science Research and Public Policy-Making: A Reappraisal*. Windsor: NFER-Nelson Publishing Company Ltd. pp. 21–31.

Walker, Robert H (1984) *Reform in America*. Lexington: University Press of Kentucky.

Ward, Bob (2013) 'Is the Global Warming Policy Foundation complying with Charity Commission rules?', *LSE British Politics and Policy* blog, 2 July 2013.

Watermeyer, Richard (2011) 'Challenges for university engagement in the UK: Towards a public academe?' *Higher Education Quarterly*, 65(4): 386–410.

Watts, Duncan J (1999) *Small Worlds: The Dynamics of Networks Between Order and Randomness*. Princeton NJ: Princeton University Press.

Webb, Eugene J, Campbell, Donald T, Schwartz, Richard D and Sechrest, Lee (1999) *Unobtrusive Measures*. London: Sage.

Weber, Max (1904/1949) *The Methodology of Social Sciences*. Shils, E and Finch, H (trans. and eds) Glencoe IL: Free Press. pp. 49–112.

Weiss, Carol H (ed.) (1977) *Using Social Research in Public Policy-Making*. Lexington, MA: Lexington Books.

—— (1982) 'Policy research in the context of diffuse decision making', in Kallen, DBP, Kosse, GB, Wagenaar, HC, Kloprogge, JJJ and Vorbeck, M (eds) *Social Science Research and Public Policy-Making: A Reappraisal*. Windsor, Berks: NFER-Nelson Publishing Company Ltd. pp. 288–305.

Weiss, Carol H and Bucuvalas, Michael J (1980) *Social Science Research and Decision-making*. New York: Columbia University Press.

Weller, Martin (2011) *The Digital Scholar: How Technology Is Transforming Scholarly Practice.* London: Bloomsbury.

White, Anne and Dunleavy, Patrick (2010) 'Making and breaking Whitehall departments: a guide to machinery of government changes'. A report by the LSE Public Policy Group and Institute for Government. London: Institute for Government and London School of Economics.

Whitehead, Alfred N (1962) *The Aims of Education and Other Essays.* London: Ernest Benn Ltd.

Wittrock, Björn (2010) 'Shifting involvements: rethinking the social, the human and the natural', in International Social Science Council *World Social Science Report 2010: Knowledge Divides.* Paris: UNESCO United Nations Educational, Scientific and Cultural Organization. pp. 205–8.

Wilson, Edward O (1995) *Naturalist.* New York: Warner Books.

Wuchty, Stefan, Jones, Benjamin F and Uzzi, Brian (2007) 'The increasing dominance of teams in production of knowledge', *Science,* 316: 1036–39.

Zwaan, Rolf (2013) Pre-publication posting and post-publication review will facilitate the correction of errors and will ultimately strengthen published submissions', *LSE Impact of Social Sciences* blog, 19 April. Available at: http://blogs.lse.ac.uk/impactofsocialsciences/2013/04/19/pre-publication-posting-and-post-publication-review/

Index

New and bestselling titles across the social sciences

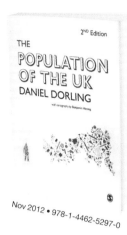

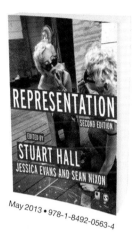

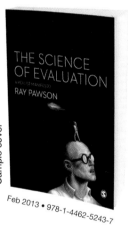